TEMPLES OF DEMOCRACY

OTHER BOOKS BY
HENRY-RUSSELL HITCHCOCK
AND
WILLIAM SEALE

HENRY-RUSSELL HITCHCOCK

The Architecture of H. H. Richardson and His Times
Modern Architecture, Romanticism and Reintegration
Early Victorian Architecture in Great Britain
Rhode Island Architecture
Architecture: Nineteenth and Twentieth Centuries
In the Nature of Materials: The Buildings of Frank Lloyd Wright
The International Style (with Philip Johnson)
Latin American Architecture Since 1945

WILLIAM SEALE

Texas Riverman: The Life and Times of Captain Andrew Smyth
Sam Houston's Wife: A Biography of Margaret Lea Houston
Texas in Our Time: The Lone Star State in the Twentieth Century
The Tasteful Interlude:
American Interiors Through the Camera's Eye, 1860–1917

TEMPLES OF DEMOCRACY

THE STATE CAPITOLS
OF THE USA

HENRY-RUSSELL HITCHCOCK
AND WILLIAM SEALE

HARCOURT BRACE JOVANOVICH

NEW YORK AND LONDON

Printed in the United States of America

Library of Congress Cataloging in Publication Data

Hitchcock, Henry-Russell, 1903-
    Temples of democracy.

    Bibliography: p.
    Includes index.
    1. Capitols—United States—History.
2. Architecture—United States—History.
I. Seale, William, joint author. II. Title.
NA4411.H57   973   75-35973
ISBN 0-15-188536-2

First edition

B C D E

To William J. Murtagh, for the idea

CONTENTS

ACKNOWLEDGMENTS

Beginning in 1971 the Victorian Society in America sponsored a two-year research project on the history of state capitols. This entire effort was funded by the National Endowment for the Humanities, and conducted in the fifty states of the Union by the authors of this book. We are grateful to both organizations for making such an extensive program possible.

It would be impractical to list again every state archive, historical society, and private collection which we used. The institutions are mentioned in the notes and bibliography. Their archivists, and in some cases their owners, have been more than generous in permitting unrestricted use of materials and in answering the many letters which inevitably followed.

We owe special thanks to the following people: Dr. Antoinette J. Lee, Mae O'Neill, Brendan Gill, Margaret N. Keyes, Chuck Wilson, Jean Ann Stewart, Maricca Lutz, John L. Sanders, Arthur Scully, Jr., Walter E. Langsam, William B. Osgood, Zara Cohan, Marjorie Maurer, Jared I. Edwards, E. Blaine Cliver, John Maass, Peter Goss, Stephen Dennis, the Reverend Maurice Hopson, Mrs. David Gracy, Jeffery Aronin, Bruce Brooks Pfeiffer, Alan Fox, William Barrow Floyd, Joan Waggener, Russell W. Fridley, Frederick H. Porter, Michael Warner, Jane B. Davies, Pat Spicer, Anne T. Zaroff, Ernest Allen Connally, and Laurie Orseck.

LIST OF ILLUSTRATIONS

The dates given here are those of the illustrations

TEMPLES OF DEMOCRACY

I
THE SYMBOLS
ARE BORN

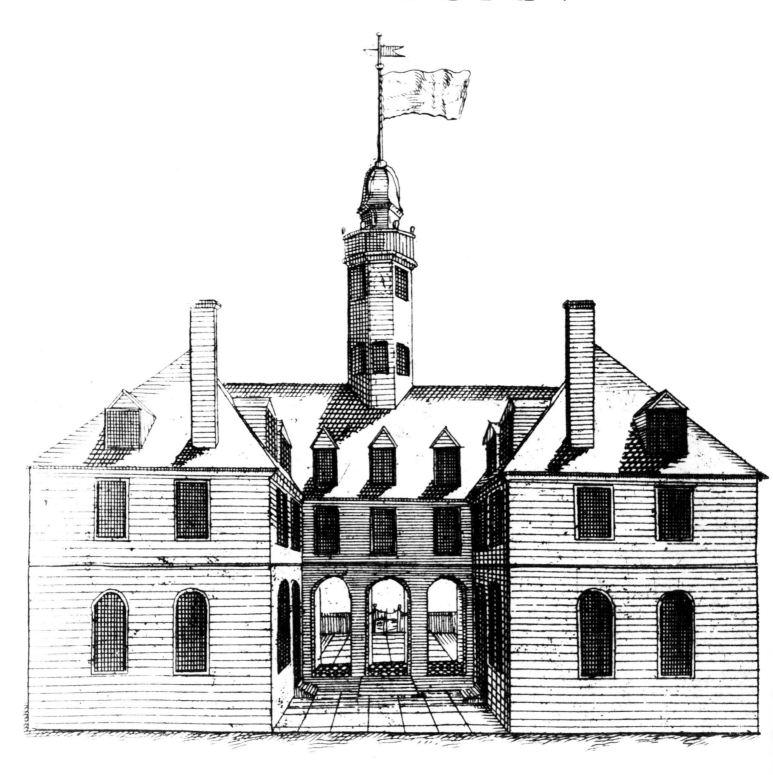

The storm of democracy that swept British America in the eighteenth century gave birth to a new sort of symbolism in monumental architecture. Skyscrapers and state capitols are America's unique contributions to monumental architecture. The skyscraper is a product of function and structure; the state capitol owes its special character to symbolism. To most Americans today architectural symbolism means church design—the steeple and the pointed Gothic arch. Yet far more significant to the United States are earlier, Classically inspired architectural features, first built by colonial legislatures long before the opening guns of the Revolution. Their creators were legislators who saw in the dramatic possibilities of architecture a means of expressing the spirit of liberty. The vision was an accurate one: Those architectural features developed into symbols for the young nation, eventually taking on an abstract authority in the architecture of state capitols. Since the second decade of the nineteenth century the symbols have dominated every legislative building erected in the United States. Their story through two centuries of American building is a chronicle more continuous than any other, even that of church and private house.

Like the colonies themselves, the symbols were born separately, then united as a stable young nation emerged. The acceptance of the symbols was the first major event in American architecture. The men who adopted them were not architects; their work was clumsy and crude, but their language was clear and readily understood. Through two hundred years of American history the authority of the symbols can be seen in every capitol. Yet in the beginning they seemed quite as incidental an element in American architecture as the colonial assemblies then seemed to the future of government in the world.

Before the democratic symbols appeared, the English government's request for monumental colonial buildings paved the way for them. At Jamestown, Virginia, the charred remains of the old statehouse scarcely had cooled seven months when, on May 18, 1699, the House of Burgesses stopped quarreling over the relocation of the seat of government to read a dispatch from Francis Nicholson, Royal Governor of Virginia: "I do now cordially recommend you the placing You Publick Building (which God willing you are designed to have) somewhere at Middle Plantation nigh his Majesties Royall Colledge of William and Mary which I think will tend God's glory, his Majestie Service, and the welfare and Prosperity of your Country in Generall."[1] The House responded immediately with a bill honoring Governor Nicholson's request, providing for the town of Williamsburg and an elegant new house of government which would "for ever hereafter be caled and knowne by the name of the Capitoll."[2]

So the name "capitol" was fixed by law. This new legislative building was not to be called a statehouse like its predecessor and counterparts in most of the other colonies; nor was it to be known as a colony house or a courthouse, even if it was to be used as both. The Virginia Capitol at Williamsburg was the first building in the New World to take its name from the Capitolium, the ancient Temple of Jupiter overlooking the Roman Forum. A derivative term designated the principal structure of a Roman colony, whether temple or, later, the main governmental building. More important than its name, however, the wilderness Capitol of Virginia was the first monumental structure built to house an American legislature.

The question of moving the government from Jamestown was of long standing in the Virginia Assembly. Almost certainly the burning of the old statehouse helped weight the final decision, but even more influential was Francis Nicholson's timely return to the colony for a second term as Governor.

In his long and ambitious American career, Nicholson was Crown Governor of four different colonies, and while he never seems to have left many friends when he moved on, his service was always marked by accomplishments. The world has remembered nothing much about the man except that he built towns. His reputation in America as a town-builder impressed the party of Virginia politicians who wanted to move the seat of government away from Jamestown and who themselves had failed to found a great commercial center amid the plantations of Virginia. Yet in neighboring Maryland, Governor Nicholson had been able to build the port town of Annapolis on the site of an existing village where every circumstance favored the rise of a rich city. With little fanfare he then extracted the government from Catholic-controlled St. Mary's and reestablished it at Annapolis. The plan of the new town reflected current English ideas in its mazelike layout. To a bird's eye, it looked like a handful of knitting needles spilled around two balls of yarn, the main streets diagonal spokes from a great Statehouse Circle; a smaller circle was set aside for the edifice of the Church of England. The Governor's meaning was clear.

Williamsburg likewise bore his imprint, and it bespoke a proud amateur with grand ideas. Through old fields and stands of pine, oak, and cedar, Nicholson cut wide streets. The principal one was Duke of Gloucester Street, a broad thoroughfare running nearly a full mile between the existing College of William and Mary and the site of the new Capitol. A pattern of smaller streets interrupted the sweep of the main axis and formed in plan the Royal cypher, *W* and *M*. At the termination of a cross-vista, acreage was reserved for a mansion the Virginians would dub the Governor's Palace.

The prospect of having a handsome capitol appealed to the majority of the Virginia Burgesses, who hurriedly levied taxes upon liquors and upon imported servants and slaves for extra revenue. Even with enough money to begin, however, work went slowly because of the chronic labor shortage common to all the American colonies. Nicholson issued a proclamation to the whole dominion inviting interested workmen to Jamestown to be interviewed by the building committee, but there were more promising alternatives open to craftsmen in America than commitment to single building projects. When carpenters and laborers *were* available, they usually stayed only long enough to make a little money and then drifted away.

The project overseer Henry Cary, built two houses on the Capitol site to accommodate the carpenters and brickmasons. Food had to be cooked and eaten there, for the Capitol crew was not permitted to leave the premises and local tavern keepers were prohibited by law from entertaining or selling liquor to them. The labor shortage became so acute by August of 1700 that the House of Burgesses sent to England for three bricklayers and three carpenters; four Negro slaves and the indentures of eight laborers were purchased in Jamestown. From then on work progressed steadily until the project was completed in the fall of 1703.

Nicholson was in Virginia long enough to see his Capitol finished. He lovingly watched its assembly from the bricks in the brickyard to the shingling for the roof.

4

The finished Capitol turned away from the main axis of the town—like Rome's Capitolium, it was approached from the side. It faced the Jamestown-Yorktown road, a direct highway to Jamestown much older than Williamsburg itself. The general aspect of the building was that of a great city gate, a pinkish brick mass, formidable in perspective but shallow-looking when seen head on. Both feet of the H-plan were semicircular, and from the main front they resembled cylindrical towers with pointed roofs, joined on the sides by a thin gallery, glazed on the upper level, with open arcades below. The view extended through the arcades to the landscape beyond: With the Capitol's open-armed architectural welcome went an invitation to venture deeper into the Virginia wilderness.

In plan, the building consisted of a pair of parallel wings each about the size of the former statehouse at Jamestown. On the first floor of the right-hand wing was the chamber of the House of Burgesses, with a series of committee rooms. The left wing, toward town, housed a decorative chamber on the second level for the Governor's Council, a body considerably smaller than the lower house and not requiring so much space. Between the two balanced wings the glazed gallery above the arcade served as a conference room for joint sessions. In more than two hundred years of subsequent capitol building, various sorts of central spaces between equal wings would seem perfect locations for large meetings, but the idea never worked again.

On the ridge of the connecting link's steep roof rode a tall hexagonal lantern rising in several stages, with balustrades, windows, and clock faces. Governor Nicholson ordered the symbols of the sun, moon, stars, and the planet Jupiter cut into the brick. Beneath these was written a tribute to his gracious sovereign: HER MAJESTY QUEEN ANNE HER ROYAL CAPITOLL.[3] He then had the several bare faces of the lantern emblazoned in color with the Nicholson arms. Before he departed for another colonial governorship, late in the summer of 1705, Nicholson spent eleven pounds thirteen shillings of his own money in London to acquire a portrait of Queen Anne for the Capitol. It was a debt the Governor's attorneys had trouble collecting from the Treasurer of Virginia after Her Majesty's loyal servant had gone.

Monumental government architecture was thus introduced to English America. The Virginia Capitol was Nicholson's Capitol; left to its own devices the Assembly would probably have been less ambitious. Governor Nicholson understood the value of "permanent" public architecture in symbolizing the authority and stability of the Crown to people an ocean away from London. His love for architecture and building found an outlet in fulfilling that need, for because of his position, all that he did was motivated by politics.

In all the colonies the job of a governor representing the English Crown, as outlined by the Board of Trade and Plantations in London, was a difficult one. His mission was to bring the King's colonies into full economic participation in support of the kingdom's burgeoning world position. Part of the program was successful in the 1690's, when it was new and had full support in the English government. But in 1701, the outbreak of the War of the Spanish Succession turned English attention to that most formidable enemy, the France of Louis XIV. When colonial support was demanded, the American assemblies balked, and resentment of Royal authority took the form of universal opposition to the improvement programs of the governors.

American unrest in the early eighteenth century sprang from sources deeper than statehouse

5

conflicts with individual governors or the fickle attentions of the English Board of Trade. At the root of the Crown's colonial troubles was the constant vigilance of the popular legislatures. They were not only ready to point out the shortcomings of official administration, but greedy to fill any gaps. By the beginning of that century, there were democratically elected assemblies in all of England's American colonies. Parliament was not the real historical source of those bodies, though the claim seemed so obvious at the time that it was freely made. However, neither Crown nor Parliament had initiated the representative institutions of colonial America; they were originally created by private interests. Therefore, the organs of American government were never a mirror of the English combination of King, House of Lords, and House of Commons. England's triad had the primary purpose of preserving the English Constitution. No such duty fell on the American assemblies. America's supposed parallel—Governor, Council, and Assembly—had the responsibility of legislating local government. In the course of accomplishing this, a very peculiar distribution of authority had developed between the assemblies and the English officials. Crown governors, nearly always arriving in America as strangers, faced colonial assemblies which were far more potent forces than the mother country had ever intended them to be.

Over the years, the assemblies collected more and more power from a succession of governors. The important privileges of appointment to public offices, which gave the governors some means of purchasing support among the individual assemblymen, gradually ebbed until the governors were forced to deal with the assemblies largely on a political basis. Observers back in the days of Queen Anne considered the elected assemblies of America harmless enough. As the eighteenth century progressed, however, there were increasing clashes between the representatives of the home country and the colonial institutions. The Crown governor was at a disadvantage in American politics. Officials in London seldom understood the strong cliques within colonial government; American "parties" might be regional, familial, social, religious, urban, rural, or economic. Small and fleeting—sometimes born or dying over one minor issue—these groupings were not really similar to anything in the English system. Differences between the governments in the various colonies further muddied England's understanding.

The Board of Trade and Plantations petitioned Parliament on three major occasions to royalize all the colonies, removing the several surviving charters and proprietorships so that one all-embracing colonial system could be established to wipe out the tiny power pockets and to make the overall operation more efficient. But Parliament's ambition in eighteenth-century England was to take power from the Crown, not to give it, and the requests of the Board were refused.

Under what amounted to parliamentary protection, the colonial assemblies burst into a strange sort of democratic bloom as the century passed its midpoint—a time, in fact, when the assemblymen in session were then the freest men anywhere. But men are seldom able to make such judgments in their own times. It did not occur to the assemblymen to realize their status or be grateful for privilege. They took for granted their freedom of speech, total jurisdiction over their own elections, and immunity from arrest while in public service and away from their farms or shops. By and by, they denounced any infringement of those remarkable colonial privileges as an affront to their rights as Englishmen—according to their special interpretation of those rights.

The statehouses in which these powerful colonial bodies met were very plain. They usually looked like private houses outside, except for their prominent locations on central squares or at the terminus of main streets. Council and Assembly chambers were usually balanced on each side of a central hall. Assemblymen debated the financial affairs of the colonies in the simplest of whitewashed rooms, usually heated by iron stoves or open fireplaces, and sometimes not warmed at all for fear of fire. In the summer, the meeting rooms were the domain of wasps and spiders and traveling preachers until autumn, when the elected officials were greeted by chambers scrubbed and patched, smelling of new candles and musty record volumes.

Lacking architectural precedent, most colonial builders recalled the town halls and county buildings of England and Ireland in their American statehouses. In Boston, for example, the statehouse served as a combination town hall, market, and seat of the sometimes turbulent Massachusetts government. A structure bearing some similarity to the arcaded section of the Virginia Capitol, the Boston structure of 1712, as rebuilt in 1748, was, according to the diary of a visitor, "a very Grand Brick Building, arch'd all Round, and Two Storie High, Sash'd above; its Lower Part is always Open, design'd as a Change. . . . In the upper Story are the Council and Assembly Chambers & C."[4] The sellers of vegetables, fowl, and country produce rented stalls from the city, and on sunny days moved onto the open street that ran down to the Port of Boston.

Lifting governmental offices above ground level had been found practical in hot climates. In the West Indies open windows behind closed blinds admitted the trade wind; guards could be stationed at the external stairs to ensure privacy for the Assembly above, while marketing and the daily drudgery of public life could be carried on in brick-floored spaces below. A particularly handsome example of this sort of architecture was the House of Assembly in Spanish Town, Jamaica, with its central portico and flanking decks open to the sky, all atop a brick arcade. Begun in the middle 1760's, this was the handsomest government house in the islands, and the Assembly was, as usual, housed on the second level from the ground. The chamber was a long rectangle with walls of whitewashed plaster and a ceiling of wood. Tall glass windows in orderly rows lit the large room and overlooked the square and beyond, to King's House, the Governor's residence. But the assemblymen of that jewel of the Indies soon became annoyed with the intense heat and glare of the sun and the rotting of the deck's floors. They engaged a carpenter who built crude roofs over the balustraded promenades, with homely little supporting columns that dulled the effect of the portico.

A wider variety of public buildings ornamented the colonies of Spain and, to a lesser extent —if only because there were fewer of them—those of France. Some of the provincial Baroque forms of Latin America even reached missions on colonial Spain's own remote northern frontiers. Government on that rim of Christendom was housed more simply. The governor and offices of Spain in New Mexico occupied a row of plain rooms on one side of the plaza of the Villa de Santa Fe. Single-storied and flat-roofed, the Palacio was built of native sunburnt adobe; its dirt floors were moistened with ox blood and packed so hard that they were loosened neither by the feet of dancers nor the rain that sometimes leaked through the earth roof. By the standards of the city of Mexico, capital of the Viceroyalty of New Spain, it was a hovel. But in its setting of

7

open land, hotly colored at dusk and daybreak, its whitewashed walls blazing in full sun or shimmering in the rain, the Governor's Palace conveyed an aura of authority that has never diminished in all its 350-year history.

After about 1775, the French and the Spanish in New Orleans used a former customhouse, the Contrôle de la Marine, for their government house. Its upper gallery gave a fine view of the Mississippi River, through the masts of boats in the port. There were no halls on the ground floor; from the lower gallery, one walked directly through French doors into rooms with plaster walls where soldiers loitered. The smells of the kitchen pervaded that whole part of the waterfront and were overridden only by the downwind stench of the fish market or gallows. Out back, adjacent to the brick-floored lower gallery with its thick-plastered piers, were parterres of vegetables tended by the black slaves of the officials. An outside stair connected the lower and upper galleries; in the breezy apartments above, the Governor of Louisiana conducted his official affairs.

Francis Nicholson, who also served as Governor of the colony of New York, was responsible for another monumental structure in America: In 1704 an H-shaped official building was erected in Manhattan, bearing a vague resemblance to the Williamsburg Capitol. But a far more prophetic step in the American story was taken at Newport, Rhode Island, in 1739, when the local tavern keeper and carpenter, Richard Munday, built the superb little Colony House of red brick and theatrically trimmed it in brownstone. Only in its setting among the low buildings of Newport was Munday's Colony House really monumental, but it had a certain clarity of concept not present in those earlier and grander buildings. Rhode Island was one of four colonies that had successfully evaded being royalized. Like Connecticut, it had the distinction of keeping its original charter and of having two separate seats of government (a tradition stemming from its origin as two settlements). Because the Newport Colony House would be used as a courthouse all the time but only in alternate years for the sessions of the Council and Assembly, Munday split the building's functions horizontally, instead of vertically into wings. He omitted the usual center hall. Downstairs was one big courtroom, in the right-hand corner of which a staircase of some pretension led to the second floor, where Council and Assembly chambers were balanced on each side of the so-called Middle Room. Over the main door outside, from the Middle Room, extended a richly carved balcony of painted wood. Easily accessible from the two legislative halls, this balcony drew attention upstairs to the democratic function of the Colony House and provided a lofty stage for ceremonial activities. Through architecture, Munday thus gave visual definition to the governing bodies. Eventually the Middle Room was incorporated into the Assembly chamber and with it the only means of reaching the balcony. It was from that elevated spot that the Declaration of Independence was read to the citizens of Newport.

In contrast to the Newport carpenter's design was the Governor's house in North Carolina. Governor William Tryon commissioned the erection of a palatial mansion at New Bern by English architect John Hawks. The big red brick house, with its wings and semicircular connecting colonnades, was completed in 1772, soon after the Bostonians, far up the eastern seaboard, began their rioting against Royal officials. Tryon had allowed space in his mansion for certain select colonial functions only: There was a chamber for the Governor's Council, but none for the lower house, the House of Commons. North Carolinians contemptuously called the building Tryon's Palace and cursed it both for the drain it made on public funds and for the exclusiveness of its uses.

But the Palace at New Bern and the Colony House overlooking Newport—both monumental, both political statements of sorts—were not major influences in eighteenth-century American architecture. Like the works of Nicholson before them, they were the creations of individuals, not governments. Only three great statehouses to be used exclusively as such were built by colonial assemblies in the six decades preceding the adoption of the United States Constitution. Not one of those was particularly monumental as originally conceived or, for that matter, as first completed. Politicians left the jobs to builders who put up what one might expect: enlarged versions of colonial house-types. Not one of the three profited from the ambitious ideas of a Nicholson, a Tryon, or a Munday. But the assemblymen quickly recognized this and were displeased enough to intervene. They approved, and in some cases even specifically ordered, certain showy additions—major architectural postscripts to proclaim their own political importance. At that point, the architectural symbols of American democracy began to appear.

More than a full quarter of the eighteenth century passed before the strength of the American assemblies began to show in public architecture. What finally happened could be better described as a series of coincidences than as a movement among the colonies, since there were few geographical crosscurrents. Except for economic connections between port cities on the Atlantic, American colonies were separate entities related less to one another than directly to the mother country. The English contributed little or nothing toward the building of statehouses— unlike the Spanish and French, who nearly always absorbed most, if not all, of the cost of official colonial construction. By the 1720's, building was not an entirely new endeavor for politicians in the English colonies. The midcentury saw their appetites move beyond the idea of practical shelter and sharpen for an architecture that would speak for them.

I.

At Philadelphia in 1729, funds were appropriated to build the first Pennsylvania statehouse. The bill was managed by the well-known trial attorney Andrew Hamilton, in that same year elected Speaker of Pennsylvania's young and boisterous Assembly. Since Hamilton found it "dishonourable" that the lower house met in borrowed rooms, he was an obvious choice as a member of the building committee. So was Dr. John Kearsley, an assertive physician and amateur architect who was already receiving wide acclaim in the city for his dramatic design of Christ Church, then under construction. On the topic of the new statehouse, Kearsley and Hamilton disagreed at once. The third committee member, Thomas Lawrence, a rich merchant and attorney from an old Philadelphia family, represented Governor Penn's Council on the committee. He seems not to have been especially interested in the project to begin with, and the bitter quarrel between Hamilton and Kearsley finally drove him away from active participation in the issue.

The first point in their disagreement was location. Hamilton, a rural representative, felt the statehouse was safer on the outskirts of Philadelphia. Dr. Kearsley, a city dweller, demanded a location on one of the five public squares in town. Hamilton wanted the building to be a state-

9

house exclusively, the property of the entire colony; Kearsley wanted it to share some city functions as well, such as that of a ground-floor market. Time increased what seemed to be irreconcilable differences until the autumn of 1730, when Hamilton, with no authority at all, approved the purchase of land on the south side of Chestnut Street between Fifth and Sixth, a good distance from the center of the city. Two years later, he obtained a plan from a carpenter named Edmund Woolley.

Kearsley coldly ignored these activities, but when excavation began and materials arrived at the site, he no longer contained his rage. He appeared before the Assembly and drew Hamilton into open debate. Hamilton, stepping down from the Speaker's seat, responded to his accuser with his celebrated courtroom technique. Kearsley was a popular lecturer with dramatic abilities of his own, but he could not stand up against Hamilton's overpowering political influence. The Speaker was given full control over the statehouse project. Kearsley and Lawrence were reduced to the positions of advisers; united against the entire effort, they damned the work in every possible way until the last windowpane was in place.

Woolley had drawn the plan in close counsel with Hamilton, using several English architectural design books popular during the period. The carpenter was given the title of Undertaker in Charge of Carpentry, and he seems also to have served as mechanic and engineer for Hamilton, who remained in personal control of the work. By 1735, the building's mighty mass was recognizable. It presented a long façade, its large central portion more than one hundred feet wide and linked by low arcades to a pair of flanking office structures, each half the width of the central block and quite as large as most statehouses in the smaller colonies. These balanced wings were ordered by a special act of legislature after the main building was formally presented on paper. But money ran out and work stopped in 1736, before the central pile was finished inside. Even so, observers in the narrow street delighted in the red brick structure—a statehouse grand in scale, yet softened by a cascade of marble steps and marble trim and panels. The low arcades, at first unroofed, tied the finished offices into a five-part composition, of the sort more commonly associated with mansion architecture in eighteenth-century America.

Hamilton, sixty-one and ailing, pushed the project forward. Paying some of the bills from his own pocket, he had the office buildings made usable for the assemblymen by 1736, then haunted their halls politicking for more money. He withdrew from politics in order to devote more time to the project. But the next year Woolley, apparently weary of being ordered around, abandoned him; and the politicians, tired of him now that he was no longer one of them, ordered an investigation into the causes of alleged construction delays. Hamilton convinced the committee that his craftsmen had disappointed him with poor work, that he had to personally supervise construction, and was anxious as anyone to finish the job. Bringing workmen from England would initially require more money, he argued, but considering the insolence and high rates of Philadelphia craftsmen, it would be cheaper in the long run. The committee was impressed enough to recommend that the Assembly give Hamilton full financial support to complete the building and further enrich it with ornamental plasterwork.

Soon after the 1741 session of the Assembly, Hamilton died in his sleep. "He steadily maintained the cause of Liberty . . . took pains to unmask the Hypocrite, and boldly censured the

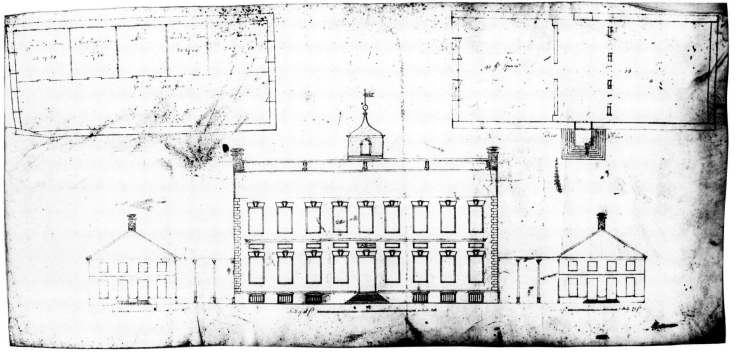

Historical Society of Pennsylvania
Pennsylvania Statehouse, Philadelphia, plan and elevation, c.1739, found
among the family papers of Andrew Hamilton

Knave," wrote Benjamin Franklin in the *Gazette*.[5] A new committee of supervisors was appointed two weeks after Hamilton's death. The committeemen approached the assignment in a sober, businesslike manner, dividing the responsibility three ways. To Thomas Leech, the distinguished Philadelphia politician and assessor, went complete control of finances; to Isaac Norris, a rich and cultivated Quaker, went the duty of making any decisions which required a gentleman's taste; and Edward Warner, self-made contractor and merchant, was given matters requiring a practical knowledge of construction.

There were quick results. In the summer of 1744, the Supreme Court chamber was opened for a grand council with the Delaware Indians. The Assembly met in its chamber for the first time in the winter of 1746, and in the following year the provincial council met in theirs. By 1748 the statehouse was completed, probably in much the same form Andrew Hamilton had intended. The official public rooms were in the middle building, entered through a door in the center of the principal façade. On the first floor was a broad corridor with a staircase and a paved floor. On the left of the hall was the Assembly chamber, accessible through doors; on the other side, the Supreme Court was separated from the hall by an open arcade. The second floor housed the Long Gallery, a banqueting hall that ran the full width of the central block and had great windows overlooking Chestnut Street; this was the grandest and most aristocratic interior space in colonial America, and even today the sudden height and sweep of the rectangular enclosure

Pennsylvania Statehouse, with the Assembly's great steeple, from a map of Philadelphia published in 1750, the year the steeple was begun

is breathtaking. The rear portion of the second floor was divided into a Council chamber and a Records Room, with the stair rising between them.

After 1739, the Library Company of Philadelphia established headquarters on the second floor of the west wing. The Assembly's doorkeeper and his family lived on the level below, and must have enjoyed little privacy. Official guests, particularly Indian chiefs, frequently occupied the east wing. The general public roamed through the central building, and the more adventurous begged to be permitted to climb to the balustraded roof to view the city. It was a magnificent statehouse, and its vastness was the wonder of Philadelphia.

Still, many members of the dominant Quaker party of the Assembly did not share the electorate's fascination with the building. The party, then in its political flowering, was one of the most potent legislative bodies in the colonies. Its new statehouse was admittedly very large, but otherwise no more noteworthy than any other colonial courthouse or town hall. So significant a public structure should have risen above the mundane world of Philadelphia, but here was a building only a little taller than the tallest of the some 2,000 houses along the streets. It was quickly forgotten in the horizontal flow of the cityscape, and by no means did it announce loudly enough the importance of the Pennsylvania Assembly.

In 1750, the Assembly passed an act to correct the situation. The statehouse committee was ordered to build onto the rear of the statehouse an architectural feature that would make Pennsylvania's government house the most monumental edifice in English America. This addition was to contain a spectacular open stairhall with a grand staircase, and above that a tall bell tower and steeple. The act authorizing the new tower was probably written by the building committee, for its expert in artistic matters, Isaac Norris, became Speaker at the time the act was passed. In any case, it gained the support of the whole Assembly. There would now be a new dimension of magnificence to the statehouse and to Philadelphia: a vertical thrust rising high above that horizontal city of houses, making the seat of government the crown of the largest city in the colonies and second largest in all the British dominions.

A contract signed with Edmund Woolley brought the carpenter back to the building he had left a full decade before. The work took six years, not so much because of what was originally planned, but because the committee kept elaborating—always with the Assembly's blessing. The brickwork was level with the eaves of the statehouse after three years. A huge bell ordered from England developed a crack. The Assembly, too impatient to wait for another, had it hung in the tower anyway, in the echoing open reaches above the new stair. Using the tower as a foundation, Woolley and his carpenters began framing the wooden steeple. While other parts of the statehouse were also expanded and enriched, the main work from then on was to make the steeple as magnificent as imagination and skilled hands would allow. The woodcarver's bill belies the Quaker majority's regard for simplicity.[6]

Jan[y]	29th 1753. Carved Work Done for the State House by Samuel Harding for the out Side of the Stepel	£	s	d
	to 8 bases for the balconey hurns at 10[s] p[r] blase	4	0	0
	the outside of the back door to 5 flowers at 4[s] p[r] peice	1	0	0
	to all flowers for ditto door at 2[s]- 6[d] p[r] peice	1	7	6
	to 6 flowers & 6 fishes for the pillars of ditto door	0	6	0
	to 4 Compositta Capittals 2 pilasters & 2 quarter plasters in them five fronts at 1 15[s] 0[d] p[r] front these Capittals for the green room	10	10	0
	to 21 brackits for the uper Stairs at 5[s] p[r] peice	5	5	0
	to 53 Mundulyouns within the Stepel at 8[s] p[r] peice	21	4	0

The finished steeple soared over Philadelphia. It dominated the land for miles away; seen from boats in the river or carts on the road, from horseback or on foot, it was an arresting sight—in the sun with gulls floating around it, in the snow, or as a dim image behind a veil of rain. Again and again, it reminded the observer of the presence of the Pennsylvania government. To a building designed to be a handsome and functional complement to Philadelphia, the Assembly added a tangible statement of its own identity in the only idiom of architectural grandeur eighteenth-century America knew: the church tower.

Had the painter Gustavus Hesselius, from his perspective high on the steeple, brushing lead paint over the wooden fishes and urns, looked down into Chestnut Street below, he might from time to time have seen the stooped figure of Dr. Kearsley, muttering before the monument of his old enemy Hamilton. Ironically, the doctor himself was building a taller steeple a short walk away, the last stroke in the completion of his own masterpiece, Christ Church. Even the unsmiling Kearsley must have been amused.

II.

On January 30, 1747, clerks discovered fire in the attic of the Williamsburg Capitol. Soon flames raced over the shingles of the roof. Citizens and clerks hurriedly carried armloads of books and papers from the offices upstairs. Portraits of the Royal Family were rescued. Within the mass of flames that obliterated the lantern, the bells and the clock crashed down into the roaring inferno. The upper floors collapsed, then those beneath, until at last the fire weakened and died, leaving naked brick walls standing stark against the bleak sky. Someone observed that it was "the fatal and ever Memorable" anniversary "of the Martyrdom of King Charles the First."[7]

There were rumors that the House of Burgesses would not rebuild the Capitol, but might move the seat of government elsewhere. Williamsburg's businessmen, completely dependent upon trade engendered by the college and the colony's government, were understandably alarmed. A fortune, they argued, was already invested in the Governor's Palace and in the dozens of shops, stores, and taverns that stood shoulder to shoulder along Gloucester Street. Committees soon called on Governor Gooch.

In the spring, the aged Governor summoned the House of Burgesses to meet with him in council. That fire, he said, was the "horrid Machinations of desperate Villains . . . God forbid I should accuse or excuse unjustly; Yet I may Venture to assert, such superlative Wickedness could never get Admittance into the Heart of a Virginian . . . as Fathers of your Country . . . apply the most effectual Means for restoring that Royal Fabric to its former Beauty and Magnificence. . . . I hope nothing will intervene to retard the Execution of that most necessary and important work."[8] A few weeks later, the House roundly defeated a bill calling for the reconstruction. Governor Gooch's speech traveled through newspapers across the English colonies. A New Yorker wrote a scurrilous parody that traveled perhaps even farther. Back in Williamsburg, the ruins stood solitary at the end of Gloucester Street, disturbed only by the smiths who were salvaging the iron.

In the fall of 1748, the Burgesses returned to their temporary chamber in the college. The Governor met with them in Council and once more implored them to rebuild the Capitol. Crowds of townspeople collected anxiously in the hallways outside. Gooch said that many considerations made him "an Advocate for building upon the old Foundation." He urged the Burgesses to hear the opinions of "the People without Doors, which from the natural Desire of all Men to Self preservation" were concerned about the future of Williamsburg.[9] Some weeks afterward, a member of the Carter family defiantly proposed the establishment of a new town on the Pamunkey River, but according to the vote taken, the delegates were not interested in moving. Doubtless the persuasive powers of everyone from tavern keepers to tradesmen led to the

Calloway Jones for the Victorian Society in America
Conjectural elevation of the Capitol at Williamsburg as rebuilt in 1751–54

passage in November of An Act for Rebuilding the Capitol in the City of Williamsburg.

The title of the bill was ultimately a misnomer. Although small portions of the brick walls seem to have been used and the shape was partially retained, Nicholson's Capitol—which might be called Late Stuart or Queen Anne—was not exactly rebuilt. James Skelton got the job of Undertaker on the Capitol project, which he began in 1750 by removing the wreckage. He found the walls not so safe as everyone had imagined; the iron balconies over the side doors had to be removed immediately, and most of the surviving walls soon followed. By the spring of 1751 construction was started on the foundation. The first windows were installed in June; staircases were under way in the fall. On a "fine day" in December 1751, Councillor John Blair walked home from the Capitol and wrote in his diary: "This afternoon I laid the last top brick on the capitol wall, and so it is now ready to receive the roof, and some of the wall plates were raisᵈ and laid on this day. I had laid a foundation brick at the first buildᵍ of the capitol above 50 years ago, and another foundation brick in April last, the first in mortar towards the rebuilding and now the last. . . ."[10]

With some modifications, the interior repeated the Nicholson plan. In the new Georgian structure the H-shape was kept, but the apsidal ends were squared. The main changes were made outside. To build a steeple like Philadelphia's would have been meaningless, for forest trees would have blocked any distant view of it, and anyone walking the five or so sandy streets of the small town would be too close to it to enjoy the effect of dramatic height.

Practical governors and the habits of life since Nicholson's day had altered the original town plan until Williamsburg was essentially a grid spotted by several ample greens and cut in half by Gloucester Street, that mile-long avenue between the Capitol and the College of William and Mary. Treeless and deep in white sand, the grand axis of Williamsburg was split midway by a gulley. Most of the several hundred houses of the town crowded along this wide thoroughfare, and between sessions loose animals nibbled the weeds that grew in the street. At public times there was no more crowded place in Virginia.

The Capitol Directors, as they were called, decided that the new building should be revised to face Duke of Gloucester Street. Something would now have to be done to give importance to what had been only a side entrance, and one always quite out of line with the main street. The solution was to add a portico, a Classical theme hitherto not used in America.

Those Burgesses who went to session in Williamsburg in 1754 found the rebuilt Capitol strikingly different from the old. The building that had always seemed remote was suddenly the visual climax of the town. To the center third of the west side had been appended a heavy, two-story portico with four Doric columns below and four smaller Ionic ones above. Over them, projecting from the roof, the steep pediment framed the Royal arms in gilded wood. Like the colonial legislature that built it, the portico was a rough collection of parts that had never been put together quite that way before. Here was a tall stack of wooden elements resembling the rolling stage of a medieval passion play more than a proper Classical portico. Yet for all its provincial vulgarity, it accomplished a monumental purpose. In effect, it drew the Capitol from the quiet pasture east of town into the heart of Williamsburg, to challenge in architecture the authority of England's governor, college, and church.[11]

III.

More than twenty years later a custom official at Annapolis, the colony of Maryland, wrote to a friend: "In our little metropolis the public buildings do not impress the mind with any idea of magnificence, having been chiefly erected during the infancy of the colony, when convenience was the directing principle, without attention to the embellishment of art." Nevertheless, he continued, the "spirit of improvement is predominant."[12]

That spirit had seemed universal in the American colonies in the four years following the Stamp Act crisis of 1765. In that year of tax protests, the American colonies had first realized that the problems of one colony were sometimes the problems of all. There was now some communication among the colonies along the Atlantic coast. The Sons of Liberty had already expanded. They maintained an intercolonial correspondence scorned by some as revolutionary, but openly permitted to exist. Everyone talked politics. The deliberations of the assemblies attracted great notice, filling the newspapers as never before; people began reading papers from cities other than their own.

In November of 1769, the Maryland Assembly passed an act to replace its tiny brick statehouse with a new one. The act read in part: "That one good and Commodious House to be called the Stadt House shall be built as soon as conveniently may be in the City of Annapolis on the Hill whereon the present Stadt House stands to be well and securely covered with good Slate Tile or Lead . . . with good and convenient Rooms for the use of Jurors attenting the Provincial Court and four convenient Rooms for the use of Committees of the Lower House of Assembly And also good convenient safe and secure Rooms for Offices and Repositories of the Records. . . . And be it further Enacted that the said Parade shall be Laid with Flag or other Stone or Gravel and shall be inclosed with Iron Pallisades to be set up and fixed upon a good Stone or Brick Wall."[13]

Through the *Maryland Gazette,* the superintendents advertised for plans and estimates. Joseph Horatio Anderson, apparently a temporary resident of Annapolis, entered the chosen drawings. He seems to have been a man of some experience in architecture, judging from his solution to the problems posed by the site. Francis Nicholson's city plan for Annapolis had generally been maintained, with its two public circles and narrow diagonal streets; the old statehouse, though small, carried an open lantern on its rooftop observation deck. Narrow secondary streets gave fleeting views of the statehouse, but the circle seemed to be little more than a shapeless clearing.

The brick structure Anderson designed extended to eleven bays, with three-bay central projections repeated on three of the façades and a single-story octagonal bay on the fourth. The intended character of these projections is unclear, since the surviving plans and elevations do not match. Surmounting the statehouse was to be a lantern-like cupola with painted roof, topping the building's unique feature—a tall saloon rising uninterrupted through all three floors.

Anderson relieved the constricted feeling of the public circle by visually reducing the structure's bulk. Shallow arcades framing the windows on the lower level were inspired by St. Anne's Church on the other circle, and recalled familiar town halls and public markets in America and the British Isles. On the second story, the surfaces were plain but capped by a modillioned cornice and wooden parapet which concealed the low roof. At the main door was a small porch with two correctly detailed columns, framed in quoins which were perhaps meant to be made of pale marble. According to the design scheme, Anderson, like Munday in Newport, meant to split the impression made by the statehouse, relating only the first story to the circle, and all the rest to the diagonal vistas along the streets and from the bay and the rivers.

Charles Wallace, a local merchant and member of the Committee of Superintendents, signed a contract for building the Maryland Statehouse in the summer of 1771. The old statehouse was razed and the new work began where it had stood. At noon on March 28, 1772, the governor and a party of the "principal Gentlemen" of Annapolis marched to the building site and laid the first stone of the foundation, "on which occasion a cold collation was provided for the Company, and after a few loyal and constitutional Toasts had circulated, the Gentlemen retired, the workmen giving Three Cheers on their Departure."[14]

The walls reached the top of the second level in fifteen months, but changes in the original design became necessary when skilled labor proved scarce and funds ran low. The arches were omitted and the windows were enlarged. In altering the dimensions, though only slightly, the superintendents lost the scale which would have made the structure a rival to the central block of the Pennsylvania Statehouse. Wallace framed the roof, only to later realize that its pitch was too slight to make the use of slate practicable. In June 1773, he petitioned the colonial Assembly for permission to substitute copper. But it was not a good time to petition for anything: Parliament's recent Tea Act threatened ports such as Annapolis; even the most conservative merchants were deeply worried, and noisy radicals sought opportunities for official protests on every issue that arose. Wallace's roof bill started a debate which really had little to do with the roof.

The dispute ran on through the autumn, when word came that the first shipment of East India Company tea was on the high seas. Wallace was finally granted his permission in December, and plates of copper roofing were ordered at once from England. But that same month, 150 Sons of Liberty in Indian costume dumped £15,000 worth of East India Company tea into Boston harbor. Maryland's legislators had already gone home when the news reached America in May 1774 that Parliament was responding by closing the Port of Boston in June. Immediately, New York proposed a general meeting of delegates from the major port towns, and made proposals for broader colonial conclaves. The Virginia Assembly, dissolved by the Crown Governor for its treasonous outbursts, drew up in private a resolution for a grand congress of all the American colonies.

Charles Wallace's workmen were fixing the squares of copper on the rafters of the Maryland Statehouse that summer when all of colonial America was discussing the autumn congress in Philadelphia—a congress called by the Assembly of Massachusetts, which had been forced to meet secretly in Boston. Annapolis sent money to strangled Boston that autumn; some of it was collected door to door. The day the congress was called to order in Philadelphia, the workmen, by then on the second floor, could look over the rooftops to a now very quiet Port of Annapolis.

The Continental Congress was an initial step of rebellion on a united colonial front. By the winter of 1774 provincial congresses—larger and more democratic than the assemblies—effec-

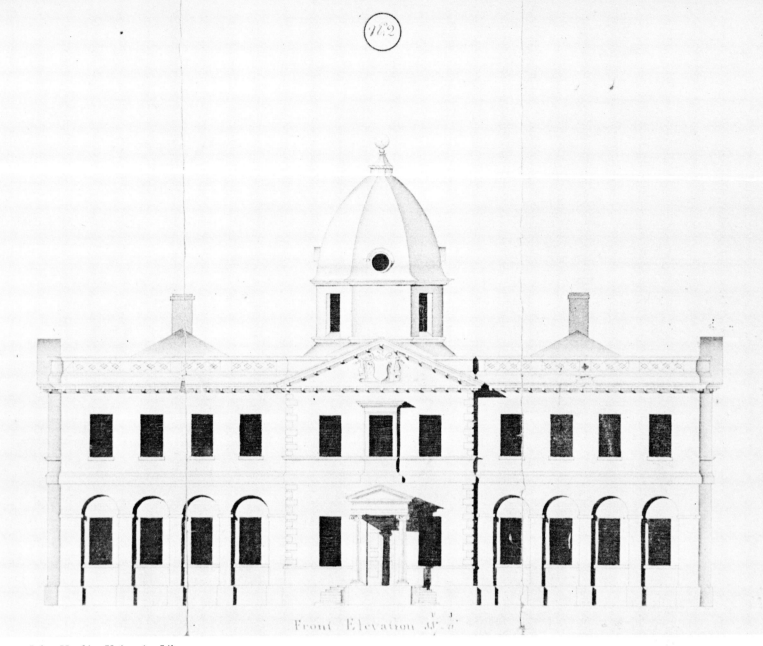

Johns Hopkins University Library
Maryland Statehouse, elevation of project, probably
by Joseph Horatio Anderson, c. 1772

tively controlled every colony. Maryland had formed one of the first. The Royal Governor promptly fled, leaving this congress to rule the colony through its executive committee until the next Assembly met three years later.

Work on the Annapolis Statehouse continued all the same. In September 1775, a hurricane nearly ruined the building, skimming copper from the roof so that rain soaked the fresh plaster. Even though Wallace knew that the destiny of the colony was uncertain and that he might never be repaid, he invested his own funds in rescuing the damaged statehouse. He covered the existing roof structure with a duplicate of steeper pitch so that wooden shingles could be used. Repair continued through the entire rainy fall and into the winter, until the building was weathertight once more.

For practical reasons, Wallace would have been better off had he abandoned the roof design. Its shortcomings should have become evident long before the storm. In his original effort to sink the whole roof behind a parapet, Anderson had contrived a pair of hip roofs, side by side, with the domed cupola rising from the crotch. Consequently, all the watershed of the cupola and most of that from the two other roofs drained into the central valleys; from there the water was expected to flow peacefully to gutters inside the parapet wall and through leaderheads to down-spouts at the corners of the statehouse. But there was too much water all at once. Even when rain only sprinkled Annapolis, the statehouse roof soon reached flood tide. Water backed up in the valleys and along the parapet wall. Sometimes, in the long winters of the Revolutionary War, pools of trapped water froze behind the clots of leaves that built up in the gutters.

Despite the war, Wallace was able to keep the statehouse crew at its task. When the war-time shortage of cash made it difficult for him to pay his men, Wallace granted them credit at his store in town. In the year the Declaration of Independence was signed in the Assembly chamber at Philadelphia, Wallace began the decoration of the first floor of the Maryland Statehouse, as though all trouble would soon end and the Assembly would be able to glory in its rich new quarters. The structure must have inspired him, for an investigator from the Assembly later sneered that he had recklessly exceeded his original charge by finishing the rooms with "more elegance than was required by the contract."[15] But in August 1777 the sails of the British fleet were sighted beyond the bay, and Wallace's workmen dropped their tools and fled inland. Some of them may have joined the militia, but all were anxious to escape impressment by the British. Their departure ended work on the statehouse for two years.

The completed statehouse differed markedly from Anderson's original plan. Maryland politicians were responsible for a democratic change—spectators' galleries for both houses, an innovation of the Revolutionary era. The doors to the new galleries opened on the intermediate landings. And Wallace himself must have made major alterations, for the documents at least hint that the staircases, as Wallace located them, were not according to the original layout. It is likely that Anderson envisioned a full T-shaped hall leading to the three matching projections of the front and side façades. If that was indeed the case, Wallace split each side arm of the hall in 1777, thus creating anterooms with windows and inner stair alcoves opening from the saloon. Anderson's plan was also modified in many other ways, particularly by the addition of north and south windows in the chambers and the partitioning of more offices.

The first legislature to meet in the Maryland Statehouse was called to order in the fall of 1779. Only a few of the fireplaces had their decorative mantels, and the wooden interior shutters lay in stacks in the halls. Odd places still needed plastering; some openings had no doors and some rooms were, in their finish, "indifferent." For the most part, however, the statehouse was complete. In executing the front entrance, Wallace corrected the earlier mistake of omitting the quoins Anderson had designed to border the central projection. He substituted pilasters, which stood only as high as the porch columns. Some country legislators found the doorway too elaborate, and for the same reason denounced the "great hall" and the semioctagonal courtroom—a war, after all, was in progress.

But Maryland's Statehouse was built for great ceremonies, and most of the politicians liked it. The entrance to the building was several steps up from the ground, through a porch that opened into a huge cubical vestibule. To the right of the vestibule was the upper-house chamber, successor to the Governor's Council. An ornate Speaker's "throne" was raised on a dais and meant to be curtained. On the other side of the vestibule was the lower-house chamber, also with its throne and steep little gallery supported by carved columns. Elsewhere on the main floor and upstairs were offices, committee rooms, and rooms for records, all plainly finished in white-washed plaster, with painted chairboards and washboards.

What was exciting about the building was the central space that lay beyond the vestibule. Through a screen of tall columns, the saloon offered a spellbinding view up into the cupola; a second screen of columns divided the saloon from the rear courtroom, with bench and bar on axis in the octagonal bay. Flanking the saloon were the alcoves for the twin staircases. These rose behind more columns to unfinished balconies set somewhat higher than those of a church, but giving the illusion of being even higher up because of the narrow space they encircled. This saloon was not merely a tall square chamber like the one containing the stair in Philadelphia. The alcoves and balconies were dark, while daylight from windows in the cupola above bathed the walls and floor, producing through light and shade a dramatic effect.

Maryland's Statehouse proved too much of a burden for Charles Wallace. He suffered the harsh criticism of the legislature and was sued by one of his partners in the store for the unpaid bills his wartime laborers left behind. He submitted his resignation to the ungrateful Assembly in December 1779. Charles Wallace's love affair with the statehouse must have left him bitter memories, for someone else (not identified in existing records) was soon hired to finish his work.

Annapolis became the capital of the United States in the fall of 1783. The guns of York-town had been silent for twenty-four months; it was recognized, at least for the present, that England had lost her mainland colonies on the Atlantic. But there were those, even in the former colonies, who were not so confident that independence would last for long. Trouble was brewing within, as well as across the sea. Maryland had only reluctantly ratified the suspect Articles of Confederation, and had been the last state to sign at that. The term "nation" was universally abhorred. In the sudden calm after so long a storm, the implications of peace were hard to foresee. The previous June at the Pennsylvania Statehouse, a mob of 500 mutinous soldiers had rioted and kept the delegates imprisoned in the building for four hours. Terrified and indignant, the delegates hurried to Princeton, New Jersey, a placid spot but lacking adequate accommodations.

Annapolis was one of many cities with economic reasons for presenting itself as a capital. Besides the obvious convenience of its location and its fine port, the little city offered great pleasures to the delegates. There was a fine race track, a theater, and excellent taverns. The local merchants had suffered such financial distress during the war that they promised lavish hospitality to the Congress, hoping that the presence of the government would preserve the town from ruin. Late in November, the offices of the Confederation moved into the Maryland Statehouse, but business was delayed until mid-December because of the usual malady of the Congress: no quorum.

Congress met in the Maryland Council chamber, the lofty room to the left of the vestibule. The chamber was finely proportioned, and the light from its six exceptionally large windows varied the illumination of the room according to the day's particular mood. Furniture for the Congress was a haphazard collection of chairs and tables borrowed from private houses in Annapolis. The fireplace in the west wall was stacked with four-foot logs. A door next to it led to the adjacent committee room. The chamber was not quite complete; only the east windows were equipped with shutters. Just how much effort the eager townsmen had expended in pre-

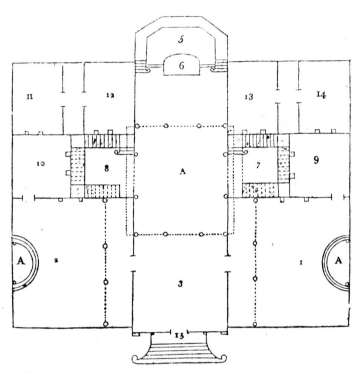

Columbian Magazine, *1789*
Maryland Statehouse, plan of ground floor, as completed during the Confederation

paring the statehouse is questionable. It is supposed that they whitewashed the chambers anew and had chintz cushions made for the deep window seats. The iron fireback may have been procured by them. Local penury in that area since the war would suggest that the most they provided were basic comforts.

The United States government was housed in Annapolis for ten months. As they had pledged, the merchants staged frequent balls and banquets. Tavern owners strained for the best their kitchens could produce. Time and time again, the statehouse was illuminated, its windows filled with candles from the dome to the basement and the surrounding circle lit with torches. It became a familiar setting for ceremonies. General Washington resigned his commission there at noon on December 23, 1783. The galleries were crowded that morning, and official guests lined the walls, although only twenty of the delegates presented themselves. Several weeks later Alexander Hamilton rose in the same room to defend his former Commander in chief, whose haughty conduct and free spending had been criticized by a number of the representatives. The Treaty of Paris was read to the Congress in that chamber during the winter that followed, and it was there that the Congress approved it, officially ending the War of American Independence.

Work of one kind or another was always being done on the Annapolis Statehouse after the Revolution. Meanwhile the politicians listened with increasing interest to appealing offers of capitol sites in other cities. By August 1784, the Congress had moved to Trenton on its way to New York. Maryland officials found their empty statehouse a bit disheveled after its brief brush

Maryland Statehouse with its new dome, as it was in 1810

with immortality; repairs had not been made in the crowded Capitol for nearly a year. The curious public—particularly foreign seamen—had wandered in and out and had taken souvenirs. The low roof, crouched behind the parapet wall, leaked water into the plaster walls of every upstairs room. Water even stood on some of the floors. The windows in the cupola, and some of the attic framing, were rotting away.

An investigation made in November 1784 revealed that it would be unwise to rebuild the roof according to the old plan and that the cupola had also been built "contrary to all rules of architecture." The dome should have had an inner and outer shell, with access between the two.[16] A contract for repairs was let in the winter; by summer it was clear that the committee had decided upon extensive additions as well. One of the carpenters wrote this letter to a friend in Baltimore:[17]

Annapolis, June 3rd, 1785

Dear Sir

Imbrace the Opportunity of Writing these few Lines to let you [know] that I and My Father has Gone Down to Anapolis to Work for with [work] Being Very Scarce in Baltimore and Indeed for what You Do there You cant get Your Money. . . . We Git one Dollar a Day each of us & Gits our Money Every Saturday Night. . . . we are a Going to take the roof [off] the state house and . . . a Going to Raise it one story higher and the Doom is to be Sixty foot higher than the old one. . . . it will be a Constant Jobb all the Summer and Winter If you Chose to Come You May Get Imply. . . . No More at Preasant But I Remain Your Humble Servent

Joshua Botts

After the Governor and Council had moved temporarily from the second floor into a rented house, all structural work above the brick walls was torn away. The builder was Joseph Clark, a sometime merchant and architect whose fortunes surged and dropped with the years. A wealthy man at the time of the project, he was well-known in Annapolis and could enlist co-operation in a moment; even Charles Wallace readily lent assistance in finding materials during the remodelling period.

The elaborated exterior stood in its finished form when the money ran out in 1787. Whether what now burdened the roof was a dome or merely a fancy steeple is academic; it could only have been an object of wonder. One might even say that the gardenlike plan of Annapolis had at last received its visual climax: a gigantic architectural folly in the Baroque taste of Nicholson's time. Relating less to its own public circle than the diagonal streets and the landscape beyond the city, the wooden structure seems only accidentally associated with the statehouse beneath it. A building which in colonial times had seemed so large in scale was within a decade dwarfed by a new crowning feature.

Clark covered the entire statehouse with a single hipped roof that terminated in a large platform. On this lofty stage stood an octagonal tower, the first in a telescopic series of three, with long, roundheaded windows on the eight surfaces. Above the tower, a concave pent roof,

Maryland Statehouse today
Historic American Buildings Survey

capped by a bold torus, formed the base for a second, smaller stage, this time with an elliptical window in each face. With almost no defined break, the eight faces bent inward to form an octagonal dome. Surmounting the dome, a balcony with balustrade entirely surrounded still a third and smaller octagonal section of tower pierced by doors and small square windows. A shallow, concave pent roof curved upward above the dome to the feet of the fourth and final stage, the tower's tall, straight, octagonal conclusion, arched with small windows in its faces and terminated by a hemispherical domelet.

No one passing through the region would consider anything less than a thorough inspection of the Maryland Statehouse. It was featured in the diary of every visitor who experienced its splendor. To a people newly free and hungry for the original and flamboyant, it gave pageantry to liberty's name. Nothing about it was genteel in the current Georgian manner. After climbing on rough wooden ladders through the space between the inner and outer dome, a tourist would suddenly find himself on the octagonal balcony, feeling the wind and the enchantment of such an elevation. A visitor wrote from there in 1787, "the city appears on an Island surrounded by the river & creeks that almost meet each other, exhibiting a most delightful rich extensive prospect."[18]

Maryland's monumental dome and the delicately redecorated upper stages of the saloon were carried out at a time when the future of the American Confederation was uncertain. There was already threat of a counterrevolution in New England and in the settlements beyond the Alleghenies. Even in Annapolis, the town's dream of the Congress as its economic savior had come to nothing. The new dome was not a manifestation of prosperity. It was an expression of faith.

With Clark's completion of the work at Annapolis, the architectural symbols of American democracy had all made their appearance. They were principally exterior ornamental features, fragments waiting to be united. Balanced legislative chambers were in one form or another common to nearly every colonial statehouse; their symbolic importance was established early. The tower steeple and portico signaled the rise of the colonial assemblies. A state legislature had authorized the addition of the even more ambitious domed variant of Philadelphia's vertical tower element. Unencumbered by a model—for Philadelphia's steeple had already rotted and been torn away—Maryland replaced its original cupola with a huge steeplelike dome. Rather than building this on a tower attached to the main block, the new dome was mounted on the center of the roof, where the earlier lanterns had stood on colonial statehouses. To relate the newly dramatized exterior to the interior, the central open space was expanded to monumental scale and embellished, wholly integrating the new dome with what lay below.

The democratic symbols were in evidence well before the adoption of the United States Constitution. But their rise to real domination was slow. While a scattering of gentlemen and carpenters built their own versions of proper statehouses, a series of events on land and sea drew the infant nation into closer union. Soon after, the symbols were also united, in one building, to begin their reign in the architecture of state capitols.

II
THE CLUSTERING

Virginia State Library
Virginia Capitol, Richmond, soon after its completion in 1798, showing
the side entrance and the separate bell tower

"There is nothing old in America," wrote Chateaubriand in 1791, "save the forests, children of the earth, and liberty." In distant parts of the new nation, that aristocratic young émigré sought traces of the ages. "The cities . . . are lacking in monuments, especially old monuments. Protestantism, which sacrifices nothing to imagination and which is itself new, has not raised those towers and domes with which the ancient Catholic religion has crowned Europe. Almost nothing at Philadelphia, New York, Boston rises above the mass of walls and roofs. The eye is saddened by this level appearance. The United States gives rather the idea of a colony than of a nation; there one finds customs, not mores. One has the feeling that the inhabitants do not have their roots in the ground. This society, so fine in the present, has no past; the cities are new, the tombs date from yesterday.'"[1] Except for the addition of the steeple on the statehouse in Philadelphia and the dome at Annapolis, there had been no effort in governmental architecture to break that monotony.

The few Americans intellectually interested in architecture were stimulated by the newness of the nation. In the colonial structures of brick and wood, these men of the 1790's and early 1800's saw only gloomy reflections of the British colonial past. To their way of thinking, the barricades of provincialism had been cast aside by the new Constitution of the United States. This small, scattered number of artistic Americans innocently saw themselves as citizens of the world, with the happy challenge of influencing the future architecture of a dawning nation unlike any that had gone before. They no longer sought precedents in England alone, but in the common history of mankind; paradoxically, they did not aspire to create something completely new. From the first, America had been the place to re-create and improve on historical models, in politics and in everything else. When choosing and adapting from all architecture, Americans were delighted by their own ability to pick the best.

Two gentlemen architects, Thomas Jefferson and Charles Bulfinch, saw their fondness for foreign architectural models materialize in American state capitols. One, a modern building, grew to symbolize the coming of age of a great commercial region; and the other, patterned on an ancient temple, came to be recognized as a landmark in the architecture of the western world.

I.

As author of the bill which moved the Virginia capital from Williamsburg, Thomas Jefferson was acting somewhat in the interest of friends who owned land in Richmond. But he could not have avoided sentimental thoughts that Christmas Eve of 1779 when the legislature adjourned for the last time in the old columned Capitol. It had been eighty years since the move from Jamestown, and only twenty years since Jefferson himself had arrived in Williamsburg to enter the College of William and Mary. He had neither experience nor good looks to recommend him; but his wit and curiosity quickly took him amazingly far in Williamsburg's tiny intellectual community. In the company of men much older than he, Jefferson's passion for learning developed rapidly. Later, as a legislator in the Capitol, he became one of the radicals of prewar days, known for his practicality and clear thinking.

While he gave the Capitol credit for being the only handsome building in Virginia, he expressed, in writing at least, little feeling for it; he had begun drafting a capital removal bill for Virginia only a few months after the Declaration of Independence was signed. The bill was defeated by the Assembly, just as it had been in colonial times, and for the same economic reasons. Most of the legislators—tobacco planters still—could see no purpose in abandoning a town which already had sufficient public buildings. There were influential people with profitable investments in Williamsburg, and everyone knew that without the government the town would die. The situation was not much different from what it had been when the first Capitol went up in flames. Commerce by now had climbed inland following the upper reaches of the James River, and tobacco plantations now thrived where there had been only wilderness.

The proposed new capital, Richmond, was at the highest point of navigation on the James. Equal accessibility to all Virginians would be assured by its central location, or so the argument ran. The fury of war tilted the scale in the Assembly, rushing to victory a bill that varied little from the one Jefferson had taken along with his papers to Philadelphia. In spite of the war, Jefferson, now Governor of Virginia, had made specific demands that remained unchanged: "six whole squares of ground, surrounded each of them by four streets . . . and on an open and airy part . . . one house for the use of the general assembly, to be called the capitol, which said capitol shall contain two apartments for the use of the senate and their clerk, two others for the use of the house of delegates and their clerk." On other squares were to be built a hall of justice and jail, a house for the executive boards and offices, a governor's house, and a public market. "The said houses shall be built in a handsome manner with walls of brick or stone, and porticoes where the same may be convenient or ornamental, and with pillars and pavements of stone."[2]

Broad authority was given to the board of "Directors of the publick buildings" to administer the new bill. Certain parts of the government were still to be housed in different buildings, as they had always been in Williamsburg. The long-standing plea of lawyers and judges was answered in the creation of a separate courthouse, though actually the court and Assembly wings at Williamsburg had always been more or less divided. The familiar Capitol portico now became, by law, the architectural emblem of Virginia government. Nothing about the bill could have disturbed the most practical delegate; it was flexible enough to permit the radically new, but read as though it were merely an improvement on the old. Such was Jefferson's political cunning. It is unlikely, however, that even the most visionary delegate would have guessed that Thomas Jefferson was proposing a Roman Forum—or, perhaps more accurately, a Capitoline—on a hill overlooking the James River of Virginia.

That spring, few legislators would admit they had voted to move to such an uncomfortable place as Richmond. Along the water a shabby row of warehouses crowded against a road on the land side. The main street of Richmond was always deep in water, mud, or dust. A number of taverns had opened since Christmas, but not enough to provide even half the beds Williamsburg had to offer. Though there were some presentable private houses higher up, among the seven hills just beyond the waterfront streets, Governor Jefferson, his children and ailing wife, and ten slaves occupied a plain wooden house rented from his cousin. Every three days the militia marched up the hill from its camp on Bacon Quarter Branch to fire salutes and give huzzahs to His Excellency. There was hardly more ceremony in the pine hills of Richmond.

Jefferson's interest in architecture was well-known. He could lose himself for hours with his pencils, meticulously plotting designs on large sheets of scored English drawing paper. He had already developed a personal taste in domestic architecture, and on a far simpler plane some of his work was not dissimilar to that of the leading younger French architects of the day.

He had never traveled abroad. Only through books had he come to know the great monuments of ancient and modern times. The treatises of Andrea Palladio and Robert Morris gave him not only models, but clear mathematical rules to ensure correctness in his designs. An inveterate amateur in love with Classical forms, he never wearied of devising ways to build those timeless qualities of beauty into his surroundings. Where a trained architect could satisfy Classical taste subtly by introducing only certain historical elements in a modern structure, Jefferson, in isolation, took the plates in his books at full face value. At a time when the only truly Classical things being built in Europe were garden structures, Jefferson was sketching plans for a pair of Roman temples to crown Virginia's Capitoline.

In May of 1780, Jefferson was one of nine men appointed to serve as Directors of the Public Buildings. The site he favored for the Capitol was a high eminence called Shockoe Hill. In his plans he retained the peak of the hill for the public squares and partially designed a series of Classical structures, beginning with a hall of justice and a capitol. These were apparently to be twin buildings, rectangular with Ionic porticoes on the ends. Ten columns on each portico outlined the three open sides of the porch and were reflected by pilasters on the side walls.

The plans of the two "temples" were similar, if not identical. Only a sketch for the hall of justice survives. It shows a long, narrow corridor which extended from one portico between two large rooms and terminated in a square stairhall flanked by small rooms. In this hall, double staircases made a dramatic ascent to the second floor which in the companion building housed the Senate chamber. Jefferson changed his mind on the Capitol plan, tucking the stair away in an obscure closet to the side and cutting out the ceiling of the former stairhall to create a monumental saloon like the one he had undoubtedly already seen at Annapolis. The windows of the House of Delegates were matched along the opposite wall by niches, indicating that the chamber was probably intended to be more ornamental than either the Senate chamber or the various committee rooms. Sketches for the other public buildings have been lost, although a fragment of a plan for the Governor's house survives, indicating that it was to be patterned after Palladio's Villa Rotonda.

All work on Virginia's public buildings was suspended in the winter of 1781, when the British arrived at Richmond and the officials scattered to safety. Four years later, when the project was again taken up, Jefferson was in Paris as American minister to France, and the Directors seem to have been unaware of any plans he had drawn. The Richmond business community became alarmed when some of the legislators wished to return to Williamsburg, although one bill to move the government had already been defeated. Suddenly it seemed advisable to get the new buildings under way, and to that end the Directors finally agreed upon a plan. Due to a lack of time and money, they obtained permission from the Assembly to build only one statehouse, instead of the various structures called for in the original act. The plan the Directors drew was a rectangle, its four façades somewhat similar to the porticoed one of the old Capitol at Williamsburg. A friend of Jefferson commented on the laymen's scheme: "I do not think the Directors believe it is possible to build a more magnificent House than the Wmsburg Capitol— It seems impossible to extend their Ideas of architecture beyond it."[3]

By the spring of 1785, the Directors themselves agreed that they needed help, and contacted Jefferson. Enclosing a draft of their plan, they explained, "Altho it contains many particulars, it is not intended to confine the Architect except as to the number and area of the rooms." Jefferson was asked to "consult an able Architect on a plan fit for a Capitol, and to assist him with the information of which you are possessed . . . we wish to unite economy with elegance and dignity." A brick mason named Edward Voss, "skilful in plain and rubbed work alone," was engaged. The Directors determined to begin construction in August, maintaining that "the foundation of the Capitol will silence the enemies of Richmond in the next October session."[4]

Building problems at the Virginia Capitol point up the shortage of skilled labor in America —a problem even greater after the war than it had been in colonial times. The lure of cheap land beyond the mountains, together with the need for fast construction, had changed the construction business. Standards of joinery dropped. The many new avenues to easy wealth in America made it harder to interest youths in being apprentice craftsmen; in colonial times their inexpensive labor made possible the tedious processes of fine woodwork and bricklaying. To a family moving west, however, a strong boy was another pair of hands to clear land and work the fields. On the frontier a son was legally considered to be under his father's control until he was twenty-one.

A skilled mason like Edward Voss found fewer requests for his rubbed work as its cost climbed. Dying fast was the practice of rubbing bricks until their edges were sharp and their surfaces smooth and even, to provide crisp corners and tight borders for openings. Stucco and paint now covered up sloppy work done in haste.

Jefferson proposed sending an expert stonecutter from Europe to finish the columns and the exterior architraves of the doors and windows, and providing him slaves for the rough labor because, "under his direction, negroes who never saw a tool, will be able to prepare the work for him to finish." The carpenter should be English, because "nothing can be worse than the house-joinery of Paris."[5] Brought to Paris en route to Virginia, the English joiner and plasterer would be instructed to make their working drawings under the supervision of Jefferson and the French architect he employed.

Jefferson selected Charles Clérisseau as the architect, and so informed the Directors by letter. He was a famous man, a frequent visitor at court, and associate of the celebrated brothers Adam. Clérisseau's book on ancient architecture, *Monuments de Nismes*, was known to Jefferson. It consisted largely of magnificently detailed engravings of the beautiful Maison Carrée, the ancient Roman temple at Nîmes which Louis XIV had restored in the seventeenth century. This temple, which had earlier been published by Andrea Palladio in Book IV of his *Quattro libri*, might very well have been already the original inspiration for both of the twin buildings Jefferson designed for Richmond. There is every reason to believe that Clérisseau's main role was merely to advise Jefferson and allow him the use of his facilities for making drawings. Indeed, Jefferson's search for more accurate information on the Maison Carrée, which he had not yet seen, had led him to Clérisseau in Paris in the first place.

The specific Classical model was not mentioned until Jefferson received the alarming news in the fall of 1785 that the Directors, true to their words, had already laid the foundations for the Capitol. They informed Jefferson that they had retained the dimensions of 148 feet by 118 feet of the scheme sent him earlier, and had also made provision for the four projecting porticoes. The plan they drew up was a bizarre series of square rooms around a central atrium-like Delegates chamber illuminated only by a skylight. Thus it was the lower house of legislature that dominated architecturally. Offices and other rooms specified in the bill were in the cubicles surrounding the chamber. "We hope," they now wrote to Jefferson, "we shall be able to avail ourselves of your assistance without incurring much expense."[6]

Pressed by the urgent need to start construction and thereby save Richmond, the Directors had necessarily made many decisions on their own. Their pride in their unusual plan was what Jefferson feared most. In replying to their first request, he had obviously waited too long. He now wrote a carefully accommodating reply, pointing out that when they initially asked for his help, he had considered two solutions: one, to go to an architect for a plan "in which experience shows that about once in a thousand times a pleasing form is hit upon"; or secondly, instead of engaging an architect, to go out and find an existing building, proven by time, and use it as a model. "I had no hesitation in deciding that the latter was best," wrote Jefferson, "nor . . . was there any doubt what model to take. there is at Nismes in the South of France a building, called the Maison quarrée, erected at the time of the Caesars, and which is allowed without contradiction to be the most perfect and precious remain of antiquity in existence." He admitted that he had not seen the building firsthand, but that M. Clérisseau was the greatest authority on it. Jefferson had taken the specifications of the Directors and his own sketches to Clérisseau because the architect "was too well acquainted with the merit of that building to find him restrained by my injunctions not to depart from his model. in one instance only he persuaded me to admit this. that was to make the Portico two columns deep only, instead of three as the original is. his reason was that this latter depth would too much darken the apartments. oeconomy might be added as a second reason. I consented to it to satisfy him and the plans are so drawn."

Jefferson argued that the Directors were not being asked to change to his or Clérisseau's plan, but to a design that "has pleased universally for near 2000 years."[7] It was not the reasoning of art, but that of the marketplace—the best and safest buy. He quickly ordered a plaster model made of his modified Maison Carrée. The substitution of the Ionic order where the original columns were Corinthian was a practical measure adopted from the start. Pilasters along the sides were retained until the last sketches, then abandoned, probably because the Capitol would necessarily have windows where the temple did not. Jefferson knew the Directors would resent anything they did not understand; the purpose of the model was to explain diplomatically the mysteries of the plans.

Lists of cost estimates made in 1785 make one wonder just what the Directors would have built if left to their own devices. Venetian windows, pilasters, "Dorick entablature round the house," were called for, together with considerable ornament, including "5 Triumphal Arches to the passages."[8] Whatever its nature, the Directors' new plan was abandoned after "some difficulty" in the summer of 1786.

Samuel Dobie, the superintendent, was ordered to adapt Jefferson's plan to the foundation already built. "By this doctrine," one of the Directors explained, "we were saved from a great embarrassment. For the lowland interest and a strong party of the upland, in the Assembly, are laboring to stop the progress of the building. To pull up all that had been done would have been to strengthen the opposition."[9] By removing several minor foundation walls, and slightly altering the front of the building, work could continue virtually uninterrupted. The walls were built

Virginia State Capitol, Richmond, Jefferson's saloon as reconstructed in 1909, with
Houdon's Statue of Washington

to the top of the principal story by October. Ambassador Jefferson was thanked by the Directors
for the "Interest you have taken in procuring proper Plans and a model for the Ornamenting of
the Capitol of your native Country."[10]

Because of financial troubles and politics, the Virginia Capitol was not finished for thirteen
years. The bankers of Richmond kept the project in motion. Every imaginable source was tapped
for money, but the most lucrative was the sale of confiscated Loyalist property. People crowded
in the government's riverside shanty to study the pretty stucco model made in Paris, but few
could see how the huge brick mass rising on Shockoe Hill would ever bear any resemblance to
it. To rush the building operation to a usable stage, the Directors built a flat roof of brick in 1787
—ironically, just when the new dome at Annapolis was rising—and on October 25, 1788, the
Governor was informed that the chambers for the two houses were completed.

The Capitol as first occupied was merely a rectangular block of naked brick with a high
parapet around the flat roof. A dirt road twisted from the Richmond waterfront very indirectly
to the Capitol through stands of pine. A raft could be hired on one of the creeks for transportation to a point near the foot of the hill. A path led from there up to the seat of government.

For a whole year the delegates refused to appropriate additional funds for improvements, and sat instead in unplastered rooms beneath a leaky roof. Finally, in 1789, they appropriated £4,000, to be raised from a tobacco duty, "for the purpose of building a pediment roof on the capitol, to be covered with lead,"[11] as well as some other improvements. In the following year, Voss contracted with the Directors to begin his work on the portico, and by June had completed the brick base, the columns, and the timber framing for the pediment. Samuel Dobie drew many of the working plans. His roof was pitched more steeply than Jefferson's. The pilasters reintroduced along the sides were doubtless his idea, for he had some familiarity with Classical architecture. In the summer of 1791, the Directors accepted the proposal of a twenty-eight-year-old Richmond storekeeper named Moses Austin; he sold them on the wild notion he could cover the roof with Virginia lead from the mine he was attempting to develop in the southwestern part of the state.

The final years of the Capitol's construction were filled with changes proposed and changes made. Many were Dobie's, but every man's idea had its moment. Some of the delegates were convinced that the roof needed a spire to serve as a belfry; it was finally built, as a separate structure of wood some distance in front of the great portico, and in later years was rebuilt to the side in brick.

Miraculously, the Capitol, as completed in 1798, did bear some resemblance to Jefferson's scheme—due in part to the model, which visually trained the delegates and Directors to be watchdogs over the work. It must have been a stunning sight on its hill, surveying the wooded landscape surrounding Richmond. The whitewashed stucco was dazzling amid the green countryside. Distance obscured the coarseness of the clumsy finish, the rough compromise roof of shingles, and even made impressive the substantial increase in dimensions from the original design. Steps leading to the portico had been omitted, since they would have darkened the offices beneath and have allowed the politicians' grazing horses to stray up to the high platform. The entrance to the Capitol was on one side, which was not unacceptable since people had always entered the old Williamsburg Capitol that way to avoid passing through the courtroom behind the portico.

The saloon beyond the vestibule at Virginia's new Capitol did not have the colonnaded basilican treatment of the Jefferson project. When the Senate was moved to the main floor adjacent to the portico, additional space was taken from the saloon, precluding its intended use for large official gatherings. The saloon as executed was not at all antique, but distinctly Anglo-Palladian. Its square balcony rested upon large scrolled brackets, in place of the proposed colonnades popular in England. Over the saloon was a shallow dome rising out of the flat ceiling to the base of a small skylit cylinder that cut through the roof.

The saloon, reduced in size, became a shrine to a living hero. In its center, like Jupiter in his Roman temple, stood the pale marble statue of George Washington in his Continental Army uniform—an arrangement reminiscent of the marble memorial statue of the Royal Governor Lord Botetourt in the arcade at Williamsburg. The French sculptor Jean Antoine Houdon, commissioned for the Washington statue, had journeyed to Mount Vernon to take precise measurements of the hero!

There was nothing else extraordinary about the Capitol. Parts of the interior were ornamented with pilasters, friezes, and pediments, as one might have expected in any pretentious American house of the day. Jefferson, home again, studied his creation. Even after the European travel which had refined but circumscribed his taste—the villas, the chateaux, the ruins, and the Maison Carrée itself—he was proud of the structure on Shockoe Hill. He wrote to a friend who had earlier been discouraged about the project: "Our new Capitol when the corrections are made . . . will be an edifice of first rate dignity. Whenever it shall be finished with its proper ornaments belonging to it (which will not be in this age), it will be worthy of being exhibited alongside the most celebrated remains of antiquity."[12]

The Virginia Capitol was the world's first adaptation of an ancient Roman temple model to a complex modern purpose. In the new American nation it was one leading intellectual's answer to the special problem of governmental architecture in a democratic society.

II.

Jefferson's Virginia temple was under construction when Charles Bulfinch addressed the Massachusetts Committee to Consider the Propriety of Building a New Statehouse. That was on November 5, 1787, about ten months after the impressionable young man had returned to Boston from a trip to Europe. "I take the liberty," he wrote, "to offer for your consideration a plan for a new State-house. —It is in the stile of a building celebrated all over Europe; I have endeavored to accommodate it to the convenience and necessities of the country, and have attempted to give it an air of magnificence, without departing from Oconomy."[13]

We can only suppose that this plan somewhat resembled the statehouse built eight years later. If that was the case, the model was London's new Somerset House, designed by Sir William Chambers and one of the most monumental governmental buildings of the Georgian Age. Bulfinch took his cue from the completed central section of the river front, of what would eventually become an enormous complex housing a variety of fiscal, military, and cultural agencies. Somerset House has two main stories over a heavy, rusticated basement which contains a single great entrance room with Doric colonnades and big arched windows at the front and rear. On the upper stories the brick walls are pierced by a loggia of unfluted Corinthian columns *in antis*. On the fourth level a pedimented attic recedes beneath a dome.

Bulfinch's proposed statehouse for Boston probably had all these characteristics, but his plan was turned down by the Massachusetts committeemen. They were courteous, to be sure, to one with such good family connections, but the statehouse question was postponed. Bulfinch's drawing was undoubtedly rough, for he was inexperienced; but it may have more closely resembled Somerset House than the statehouse he eventually designed: At that early date with no site decided upon, there was no building program to restrict or limit him.

Although he later changed his first plan, he must have been very disappointed over his defeat at the time. He may well have felt that the legislative committee was too unsophisticated to appreciate what he wanted to do. For over a decade, Massachusetts politics had been controlled by what he considered country folk. Boston had not completely settled down since the turmoil about their takeover, when most of the old ruling class of the city fled with the colonial officials

35

to escape the riots. The new people who moved in during the Revolution were associated with a political machine called the Essex Junto. How the Essex County men took over Boston nobody quite knew, but the city's climate quickly changed. Street demonstrations stopped; the patriots of a few months before were silenced as though they were rabble. The city of the Tea Party, the Stamp Act protest, and the Sons of Liberty fell under the grip of reaction. Nor was this hold relaxed even under the new Federal Constitution. All Massachusetts was transformed by the new postcolonial government. The old concept of political representation based on all towns was altered to that of popular majority rule—which of course threw authority almost entirely to the urban seacoast. Communities in the west of the Commonwealth protested their loss of power as the strong and rich of the New England coast swarmed into the city in increasing numbers.

Yet Bulfinch was what was called "old Boston," with a family background deep in the city's past. By 1787, he had done everything that might be expected of a rich young man, although his family had lost its inherited money during the war. The two-year tour of Europe had been financed by £200 lately bequeathed to his parents and, with their usual indulgence, passed on to him. In that way he had been rescued from dreary employment as a clerk in a family friend's business house (where, Bulfinch later remarked condescendingly, "my time passed very idly and I was at leisure to cultivate my taste for architecture").[14]

The letters to his parents from Europe showed his appetite for studying buildings and his fascination with the newest developments in architecture. Archaeological discoveries in Italy at Herculaneum and Pompeii were supplying authentic Classical motifs for modern imitation. A new, urbane style was emerging, its theatrical restraint a foil to the bustle and confusion of cities, and Bulfinch was excited by its elegance. Where Thomas Jefferson polished his taste by foreign travel, Bulfinch acquired his abroad *in toto*. He had arrived in Europe an unmarked slate, possessed by a provincial's urge to transmute everything he liked into something which could be applied at home. Anywhere but in Boston Bulfinch was always a visitor. Unwilling to compete in the centers of style, Bulfinch kept to the quiet security of home. Back from his travels he tried throughout his life to make his own town look like the sights that had beguiled him in those two years abroad.

Bulfinch returned to an unchanged Boston, but it must have looked older and uglier to him than it did before. One could walk to the outskirts of town in a short time. Narrow and turning streets crowded with wooden buildings rambled to the spots he had known as a child. Windmills drew circles above rooftops, and only the church steeples reached higher. That look of the past, Bulfinch hoped, was soon to give way to something splendid—a smaller London.

Federalist Boston's very heartbeat was a shameless quest for, and display of, money. Rich merchants traveled the old streets in japanned coaches. On the Charles River, liveried oarsmen rowed commuters from town to their suburban estates. Boston ships sailed with furs from the American Northwest to China to trade with the hong merchants for tea and silk. Bulfinch was an intimate of the richest and most powerful of these families; increasingly they turned to him for advice in matters of taste. His former employer, Joseph Barrell, gave him a free hand in designing a new suburban house; the resulting red brick mansion had oval parlors and a garden pond

Hartford, Connecticut, Statehouse, built in 1793–97, watercolor showing the 1827 lantern, inscribed
"to Miss Mary Jane Potts from her friend E. W. Clay, August 1834"

harboring four ornamental ships and a marble Neptune. Bulfinch received commissions for other houses, churches, and a theater early in the 1790's. He often accepted gifts instead of professional fees for favors done for friends.

The city directory of the day still listed Bulfinch as "gentleman," but he was already architect enough to take an interest in the actual construction of what he created on paper. He watched walls rise and smelled the new plaster with a creator's joy. Most of the negotiations about a building project in Bulfinch's time, however, were between the master builder, the client, and the various specialist craftsmen the builder hired to do specific jobs. An architect merely imagined the end result; his part of the transaction could be carried out entirely by mail.

There is no way of knowing how many schemes Charles Bulfinch drew up during the 1790's. We do know that he returned from Europe with a folio of his own drawings—and gradually added others for buildings never executed, the 1787 project for the Massachusetts Statehouse probably being the earliest. How many plans he sent to builders in other parts of New England remains a provocative mystery.

A case in point is the Old Statehouse built in Hartford, Connecticut. The structure is attributed to Bulfinch because of a letter the painter John Trumbull wrote to Oliver Wolcott, Jr., on September 30, 1792: "A new State House is to be built here next year upon a Design of Mr Bulfinch. . . ." It is certain that Bulfinch did not visit Hartford in the years the statehouse was under construction, but one of his admirers, Asher Benjamin, worked on the building in 1795, and the chairman of the building committee made a trip to Boston "for a Plan of said State House" in September 1792.[15] While these clues suggest Bulfinch may have been the architect, they are not conclusive.

It was likely enough that the Statehouse Committee of Connecticut approached Bulfinch. Hartford, always in competition with the other Connecticut capitol, New Haven, would naturally have turned to Boston for up-to-date architectural advice, and Bulfinch had become a very fashionable young man there. Certainly the finished Hartford building looked as though it sprang from one of Bulfinch's drawings. Its exterior was an English version of Federal Hall in New

37

York City, recently remodeled by Pierre Charles L'Enfant for use as Capitol of the United States. Bulfinch was present at Federal Hall when Washington took the Presidential oath, and took the opportunity to sketch the façade of the building; a woodcut of his drawing appeared in the *Massachusetts Magazine*, which often featured his own buildings.

Hartford's new statehouse was a three-story rectangle. The first floor handled daily business, the second contained chambers for the two houses of legislature, and the third housed committee rooms and offices. The blind arcading of the ground level was built of sawed brownstone from the quarries down river in Portland, Connecticut. Brick, originally intended for the whole building, was used only for the upper two stories. Pedimented porticoes with heavy arcades below ornamented the two principal façades. Through the arcades one entered a windswept open hall with a stair, reminiscent of the old statehouse in Boston and numerous government buildings in the West Indies. Great windows in the enclosed upper hall gave access to the Roman Doric portico facing the Connecticut River. The rear portico was later enclosed for use as a room. Both the Senate and House chambers were decorated with Adamesque motifs in wood and plaster, recalling plates in builders' manuals. The daintiness of the finish echoed English detailing but was more in the spirit of Asher Benjamin, the Massachusetts carpenter who was the popularizer of the Bulfinch sort of architecture and may have been employed on another project in Hartford at the time.

What is definitely known is that John Leffingwell, Hartford's most important master builder, journeyed to Boston in the summer of 1793. It is generally assumed that he consulted Bulfinch on that trip, but it is just as likely that he was only recruiting workmen and selecting materials. The interior work was undertaken two years later, when Bulfinch was beginning the new Massachusetts Statehouse. His Boston plans could by then have been an inspiration to Leffingwell, as they would be to all of New England.

Because of his constant association with the very rich, Bulfinch made the dangerous assumption that he could do as well in business as they. He wanted to make money from building speculation—an unfortunate plan, since his schemes were never based on sound financial ideas. This was especially true of the Tontine Crescent in Franklin Place, which Bulfinch fashioned after the residential crescents he had seen in England. His plan consisted of sixteen row houses in a grand programmed façade that stretched from a center pavilion, with a carriage passage below and the two floors above given free to the Massachusetts Historical Society. This great row of expensive houses seemed destined to appeal to a city then so alive with imagination. Someone advised Bulfinch to form a corporation on the tontine plan. When the legislature refused to charter his corporation, he turned to his family for money. Franklin Place, begun in 1793, became Bulfinch's obsession. Blind to the decline in shipping after the hated Jay's Treaty, oblivious to the economic implications of the growing rift between the United States and France, Bulfinch built the Crescent on the thin ice of unreasonable loans from rich friends until in January 1796 he swept his family and himself to utter ruin.

On the preceding Fourth of July, however, Bulfinch could never have suspected the impending disaster. He marched with the most prominent men of Massachusetts out to Beacon Hill for the cornerstone ceremony at the new statehouse. At last the realization of Bulfinch's dream of 1787 was beginning. His revised plan could already be discerned in the outline of the foundations on the hillside pastureland, not a long walk from Franklin Place. Most of the Beacon Hill land was owned by the heirs of John Hancock, the revolutionary, or by John Singleton Copley, the Tory, who never returned to Boston from England.

The land had never been developed in an urban sense. Except for the adventurous new people who were building on the Charles River cove, Bostonians tended to like the congestion of the town. Beacon Hill, with its wooden signal tower, had been considered remote from Boston until the tower was destroyed by a storm and a group of clever businessmen decided in 1791 to replace it with a monument commemorating Boston's role in the Revolution. Bulfinch designed the monument, a sixty-foot Roman Doric column. This was topped by a weathercock in the form of a Federal eagle clutching bunches of arrows and with a lightning rod on its head. Formed in stucco around a core of bricks, the Beacon Hill Monument became a principal attraction of Boston. The park Bulfinch had envisioned was never built, but because the monument became a popular site to visit, the public soon accepted the district as part of the city proper.

Building the new statehouse on Beacon Hill would assure that area's development. Realizing this, real estate interests set to work. In Boston, a special committee proposed that the city pay £7,000 toward the construction on an undetermined site of a statehouse to cost no more than £9,000. Negotiations were completed two years later, and the town authorized the purchase of land on the south side of Beacon Hill. Within a few days the Governor signed the bill accepting Bulfinch's plan. During the spring the small pasture adjacent to the Hancock Mansion on the slope of Beacon Hill was purchased for £4,000—an enormous sum, considering that the Mount Vernon Proprietors, the real estate developers with whom Bulfinch was involved, later paid a mere $18,450 for all of the extensive Copley holdings nearby. The Hancock heirs had certain political advantages by being residents of Boston. An infuriated Copley sent his lawyer son, later Lord Chancellor, from London in a futile effort to withdraw from the transaction.

The cornerstone was drawn up from town by fifteen horses representing each state in the Union. Behind it came a foot parade, in which old and new Boston marched together: Prominent merchant walked beside former patriot; city man lined up with rural dignitary; and the bright feathers and cloaks of Indian chiefs flashed among the dark robes of judges. Governor Samuel Adams delivered an oration. Paul Revere, Grand Master of the Grand Lodge of Masons, conducted the ceremony. Far down the hill on the Common and way up to the memorial column, picnics were spread through hayfields, cows foraged along the fence of the Hancock Mansion, armies of dogs and children played everywhere. The citizenry of Boston were celebrating the beginning of a new statehouse and the nineteenth anniversary of the Declaration of Independence.

A committee of three agents—Thomas Dawes, Edward Hutchinson Robbins, and Charles Bulfinch—was appointed by the Statehouse Act of 1795. Dawes was an outspoken master builder whose career had begun as an apprentice bricklayer. Admired for his leadership during the riots before the Revolution, he was an obvious choice as representative of the city's interests on the Statehouse Committee. As a prominent member of the Essex Junto, Robbins was also an obvious appointee. Rich and political, he brought to the committee a sound business mind and a non-British outlook.

The three agents made a good team. A contractor himself, Dawes knew the pressure the

39

current English situation had brought to the building industry in Boston. The practice of paying statehouse workmen at the close of each day was probably his idea—he knew that if he kept the craftsmen wondering whether they would have a job the next day, they would tend to do better work. Robbins handled the money, bringing cash to the hill every day at dusk. Matters of design seem to have been left entirely to Bulfinch.

The winter of the first year of construction was miserable for the architect. Franklin Place was gone, and abject poverty would have been the family's lot had not a sister married advantageously and hired her brother to remodel their parents' house. Now Bulfinch was taking regular payment for his work, and at the statehouse Robbins paid him monthly. Early on winter mornings when Bulfinch climbed windy Beacon Hill, the rising bulk of the brick walls must have reassured him. The building of the statehouse proceeded quickly, while Bulfinch saw to its every detail. Now he was living in a world removed from his capitalist friends who were planning lavish developments on the slopes of Beacon Hill. Boston's new statehouse was to Charles Bulfinch more than a step toward realizing real estate profits. When Franklin Place took his security away, the statehouse presented a challenge that carried him through a difficult time. It was with this building that the gentleman architect became a professional.

The statehouse is a very liberal interpretation of the central section of Somerset House; more accurately, it seems to follow only the basic idea of the Chambers model. The free introduction of other elements was almost certainly necessitated by the adaptation of the design to the shallow hillside site. Moreover, Bulfinch was now nearly a decade removed from his idyl abroad. The Boston dome, for example, does not follow the low, gentle lines of the one at Somerset House; instead it is a very abrupt, hemispherical crown, doubtless designed to bear some relation to Beacon Hill rising so high behind the statehouse. And the statehouse portico only faintly resembles that on Somerset House. It rather suggests A.-J. Gabriel's façades on the Place de la Concorde in Paris; yet it is so completely English in all other respects that perhaps a more probable source is the remarkably similar porch front of Heveningham Hall, the great English country house built in Suffolk by Sir Robert Taylor and decorated by James Wyatt during the time Bulfinch was in England.

At Boston the materials were of a lesser quality than those employed by Chambers, Taylor, or Wyatt. Bulfinch was working with brick and wood where the English architects had used stone. Dawes probably took advantage of hard times in the building trades to arrange the laying up of the walls in Flemish bond, a technique already so costly that it was used less and less on American buildings. In contrast to the pinkish brick of local manufacture, white marble formed the lintels and keystones. Since a large quantity of this marble was on hand and long stored in the basement, Bulfinch must originally have intended to use more marble detailing. Wood was substituted because there were excellent woodworkers in a shipbuilding center like Boston, and also because agent Robbins contributed white pine from his own lands in Maine, then still a part of Massachusetts. Carvers, in their shops on the waterfront, fashioned Bulfinch's Corinthian capitals as they might the figurehead of a ship. On May 12, 1797, Ephraim Thayer and three helpers hauled ten of the Maine logs from Tileson Wharf to his shop. The bill, paid in February 1798, after the statehouse was completed, suggests the type of architectural work

Massachusetts Statehouse, Charles Bulfinch's plan and elevation, c. 1795
New York Public Library

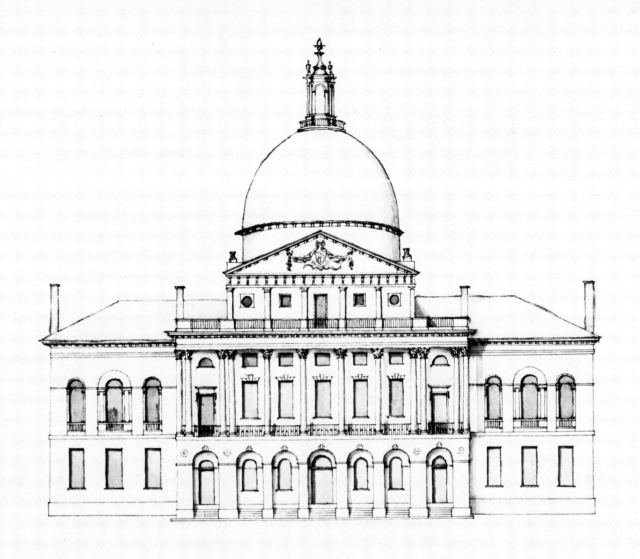

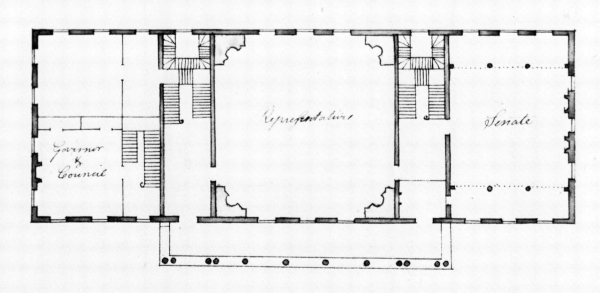

Elevation and plan of the principal Story of the New State House in Boston.

Ch. Bulfinch

John J. G. Blumenson for The Victorian Society in America
Massachusetts Statehouse, Doric Hall today

one could then obtain in Boston: "Turning twenty 28 Inch Corinthian Collums," the bill reads, "& putting on Base & Cappitals at 18 dollars . . . To turning 180 Feet of modillions at 5 cents 6 Mills per Foot . . . To turning four 18 Inch Collums for the [side] Porticoes at 9 dol . . ." At about the same time the ship carvers John and Simeon Skillin billed the agents for "Carve work done for the New State House . . . To 12 Corinthian Capitals for Columns of 23 inches Diameter . . . To 8 Corinthian Capitals for ¾ columns . . . 482 Modilions for the Outside Cornice . . ."[16]

North of the Common and its fringe of trees, Beacon Hill sloped sharply upward, with the memorial column at its peak. Somewhat more than halfway up the hill stood the new statehouse with a view of green woodlands, water, fields, and the edge of the town. The building was highly decorative. All the exterior wooden features were painted white except for the whitewashed wooden dome, which was subsequently painted, over a canvas covering, to simulate lead. The dome's only function was to ornament the exterior, for within there was no indication of its existence. At the tip of the dome's crowning lantern was a finial, a carved wooden pine cone with a coat of gold leaf that caught the sunlight; seen in relation to the blue-gray surface of the dome, it became the feature of Boston most remembered by visitors.

Bulfinch divided the long rectangle of his statehouse façade into three parts, a wide center element with a ground story arcade carrying the Corinthian-columned porch, flanked by two plainer wings. Inside there was no trace of the balanced chambers seen at Annapolis and Richmond. Instead, the middle of the building was, like Somerset House, completely filled by two

Massachusetts Statehouse seen from Park Street, as it was in 1859
Holman's Print Shop, Inc.

huge rooms, one on top of the other. The General Court, or House of Representatives, was up-stairs with a ceremonial entrance room below; here again, Somerset House was liberally inter-preted. The lower chamber, which was soon named Doric Hall, contained front and rear doors on axis bordered by two rows of Roman Doric columns set on pedestals. Except for this ar-rangement of columns, the room was nearly identical to the lower vestibule in Somerset House. It is reasonable to suppose Bulfinch originally intended a real copy; but in changing the room to a square, he was forced to place the double colonnade in the center instead of splitting it at the front and rear of the hall, as in the London model. Conceivably, the use of a single room above was first inspired by the great rectangular library over the gates to the Somerset House forecourt. There is really no evidence, however, of such a compacting of plan, and the library room is not like the Massachusetts General Court. A sure source for the decoration of Bulfinch's second-floor room was James Wyatt's Pantheon, completed in 1772 and a favorite London resort while Bul-finch was in England. The clipped corners, raised colonnades, great segmental arches, domed ceiling, and other characteristics of the principal room of the Pantheon are all present in the Boston chamber.

An even stronger influence on Bulfinch may well have been Federal Hall in New York, with which he was familiar. New York, in its effort to become the permanent national capital, commissioned Pierre Charles L'Enfant to remodel the old City Hall, the government house built by Francis Nicholson, which was quite similar to the first Capitol at Williamsburg. Head-strong and impulsive, L'Enfant had been among the first young Frenchmen interested in fighting for American independence, and since the war he had lived in the grand manner in New York on very limited funds. His remodeled and expanded interiors were rich and gaudy, the walls en-crusted with symbolic stars and sunrays, the windows festooned in scarlet damask. Most of his work was what one might call *Louis XVI*, but the domed House of Representatives in Fed-eral Hall had an even more Classical flavor.

It is very likely that many of the differences between Bulfinch's statehouse plan of 1787 and the building erected in the late 1790's did derive from the architect's admiration for Federal Hall; still only vaguely reflected in the Hartford Statehouse, it seems to have been much more of an inspiration to Bulfinch in Boston. L'Enfant had situated the United States Senate chamber immediately behind the pedimented portico that faced the street. Bulfinch put the Massachusetts House of Representatives in that same dominant position: Behind the Corinthian columns and beneath the lead-colored, gold-tipped dome, it was the heart of the statehouse.

Bulfinch made his Representatives chamber nearly square. As L'Enfant had done with his first-floor House of Representatives in New York—and Wyatt earlier at the Pantheon—Bul-finch clipped the corners of the room and sank niches into them. In place of the statues L'Enfant intended for his niches in Federal Hall, Bulfinch at Boston built fireplaces for open log fires or iron stoves. Great segmental arches sprang from one angled corner to another, creating flat-tened pendentives high above the fireplace niches on which were trophies in stucco representing War, Peace, Agriculture, and Commerce. A shallow dome roofed the chamber, again recalling Federal Hall's Representatives chamber and possibly the higher one on the Pantheon. From the dome's eye, a sunburst of stucco spread to its rim, interlaced with swags and garlands, all

Massachusetts Statehouse, Senate chamber as remodeled in the 1890's
John J. G. Blumenson for The Victorian Society in America

probably the work of Daniel Raynerd. Galleries were tucked behind two of the arches. At either end of the chamber, tall, rectangular windows opened southeast on the portico and northwest onto the peak of Beacon Hill. The play of light must have been truly spectacular.

The Senate chamber of Massachusetts was a diminutive version of the United States Senate chamber in Federal Hall. Across a lobby from the lower house, it was in the right-hand wing, a secondary location. With its barrel-vaulted ceiling, Ionic colonnades, and Raynerd's delicate stucco ornament recalling that of Robert Adam or James Wyatt, the room looked like the saloons in many Late Georgian country houses in England and resembled specifically some of Wyatt's rooms at Heveningham. Had this chamber been as large, it would have been quite as monumental as L'Enfant's in Federal Hall must have seemed to the admiring Bostonian.

There was only one other architecturally important room—the Council chamber in the other wing. The Massachusetts Council was a second and smaller Senate which served in an advisory capacity as an immediate check on the Governor. Using the theme of Corinthian pilasters, Bulfinch visually related this room to the portico. He further stressed its importance by placing it on the same cross-axis with the Senate and the House of Representatives. Behind the Council chamber was the Governor's office. It is nearly impossible to reconstruct faithfully the original appearance of that part of the statehouse, as partitions were constantly removed and renovations frequently made during the nineteenth century.

The remaining offices in the Boston Statehouse were wallpapered or plainly finished in whitewash. There was a kitchen in the basement. Glass and japanned wares were ordered for the statehouse—all inexpensive items but useful for officials who lived for any length of time in the building or entertained there, as they often did. The two-acre grounds were enlarged so that a dwelling for the messenger, a coachhouse, a firehouse, and a privy could be added. A wooden fence was built atop a parapet to enclose the yard, which was swept clean of all vegetation and outlined with poplar trees.

Bulfinch was bold when it came to color, but we know virtually nothing about how the interior was painted. Bills for the stucco work in the chambers show that "Colour and Colouring" were used in the embellishments in the Senate chamber. These rooms, requiring more light than the rooms of a private house, were probably predominantly milk-white with green, straw, stone, or Pompeiian red introduced to enliven the ornamentation. Some new furniture was made for the interiors before and during 1798, presumably under the direction, or at least suggestion, of Bulfinch. "13 pair flat brass candlesticks for New Statehouse" were delivered by Thomas Chase on January 1, 1798, the year the government moved in. George Bright made thirty mahogany chairs at $8.00 each and oiled the leather on the windowseats, which must have come from the old statehouse. Evidently the state officials brought their old chairs, desks, and bookcases for there were large repair bills for those items. To illuminate the new statehouse, candle "frames" were hung in the entries and along the outside walls. The "1 small lamp" must have been the oil lamp which for so many years blinked from the dome's lantern over the dark city and was a landmark to mariners in the bay.[17]

Bulfinch had made the dome and columnar frontispiece the principal themes of the statehouse. Here these constitutive elements, like the dominant Roman portico of the Virginia

Capitol, did not sprout from American seeds, but were imported. Yet even though its exterior was modeled on an English building, the Massachusetts Statehouse introduced in New England certain architectural characteristics already established in several other American government buildings. Bulfinch's hemispherical dome—far more than Maryland's—became in the new century the most prominent version of what would with time become the prime architectural symbol of American democracy.

There was no more popular building in the East than the Massachusetts Statehouse. It became the trademark of Boston, and rightly so. Those Federalists who ruled the city in the 1790's were not colonial Boston stock, but a new breed drawn into prominence during the Revolution. Where the Virginians found a certain literary satisfaction in the Roman temple on the James River, Bostonians enjoyed Bulfinch's frank adaptation of a modern English governmental structure. Such a building in the English style was suitable for an economy dependent upon English trade.

On January 11, 1798, dedication day, the Senate and General Court assembled with state officials at the old statehouse in Boston. Governor Increase Sumner led crowds of cheering Bostonians through narrow thoroughfares crowded with spectators. The irregular banks of dormers, shutters, and windows of the houses along the streets soon gave way to open fields and bare trees as the procession moved toward the lofty palace on Beacon Hill. Crowded into Doric Hall, their sheer numbers muffled the echoes voices always made there. It was a day Massachusetts and Charles Bulfinch would never forget.

III.

Between the close of the American Revolution and the Missouri Compromise, eleven states were added to the original thirteen. In those forty years between 1783 and 1820, Americans built seventeen state capitols and a national capitol. None of them were designed by professional architects. Jefferson and Bulfinch were amateurs; so was Dr. William Thornton, whose low-domed project won the competition for the United States Capitol at Washington City. The remaining fourteen statehouses were designed by master builders. In the 1802 competition for a new city hall in New York, the entry of the master carpenter Ezra Weeks—probably based upon Stephen Hallet's rejected proposals of 1793 and 1794 for the United States Capitol—was like the high-domed state capitols to come. It was quite unlike the winning scheme of Joseph François Mangin and John McComb, Jr.; they could both be considered architects, as could the other entrant, Benjamin Henry Latrobe, who certainly was a professional because of his English training.

Most state capitol schemes were subjected to repeated alterations at the whim of legislative committeemen in charge of their construction. The committeemen—usually lawyers, sometimes farmers—cared little about architecture; their interest in building ended as soon as questions of cost and suitability were settled. They looked to the master builder for suggestions and answers to all other problems. He could be counted upon to produce a stack of illustrated English carpentry books and a good stock of his own ideas about what was fitting and proper. The master builder of statehouses in America was nearly always by nature a patient man, untrammeled by

47

the hauteur of L'Enfant and the few other professional architects in the Eastern cities. Contracting was seldom the master builder's only occupation; he was sometimes a landowner or businessman, sometimes a city official or a surveyor. He usually traded in horses and lumber and even dry goods; he could be seen in the noisy common room of the tavern mixing with his clients, the ordinary townsmen and the politicians. Chances are he had built a local church, most of the stores, and half the best houses in town. Yet he might choose to list himself on the census in one of his lesser capacities as farmer or merchant.

The master builder was very often the local supplier of building materials, owning kilns and sawmills, or buying a quarry or clay pit for a big job. No use was made of materials already on a statehouse site. All existing trees were cut down, piled up and burned—hauling logs by ox-cart or flatboat to the sawmill cost too much, and the three months required to cure lumber properly was too long to wait. People of the new nation were in too big a hurry—and in three months the capital might be moved away.

Although the principal phrases in the architectural language of statehouses were already in existence, they were still isolated; only as individual elements had their fame spread. All the same, heightened mobility during the Revolution had broadened the influence of ideas as never before in American history. Soldiers from many colonies wandered through the statehouse in Philadelphia and even tried to appreciate it as a historical shrine. The steeple was already a legend, remembered nostalgically by older Philadelphians. Citizens passing through Annapolis often climbed the dizzying heights of the statehouse dome, which had so quickly replaced the steeple that had inspired it. Bulfinch's Boston Statehouse, as it was always called, was considered an even more tasteful pile than Jefferson's temple by the few who had seen them both. But the popularity of those first American statehouses was establishing them as sources of good ideas, not as models in their entirety. While William Thornton's winning design for the United States Capitol was a sort of overture to what was coming in statehouses, that scheme was merely a project, a proposal—a watercolor on drawing paper—for a building meant to occupy a hilltop that would remain a wilderness for a long time to come. At the close of the eighteenth century there was no universally acceptable image of what an American state capitol should be.

In practice a capitol could be modeled upon anything. But building committees, no matter how inexperienced, knew they were erecting statehouses, not private houses or churches or courthouses. They took the challenge seriously, and in thier sincere desire to build something appropriate they searched their own limited memories for ideas. Seldom had a statehouse commissioner traveled to Europe; even if he had, in those last years of the eighteenth century, he was likely to reject anything foreign as "aristocratic" and alien to republican principles. Where the Anti-Federalists were strongest, the distaste for anything reminiscent of England was growing. In retrospect, it is tempting to see those politically based emotions as determining factors in capitol architecture; but they were not, for even at their peak they were justifications after the fact. Commissioners were simply not that sophisticated; their outlook was hardly even national. Architectural influences reached them in bits and pieces, which were reflected in often curious combinations when they set themselves to commissioning designs for statehouses.

48   Columbia, South Carolina, was one of six new state capitals founded during the first decades

South Caroliniana Library

South Carolina Statehouse, Columbia, conjectural view, 1794

of the United States. In selecting central locations for capital cities, legislatures accomplished the two objectives of expressing democracy and creating advantages for individuals speculating in upcountry land. Located at Friday's Ferry on the Congaree River, Columbia's grid plan was spread over swelling hills thick with foliage, in an area believed healthful because of its sandy soil. Capitol Square was marked off at the end of Main Street on a high ridge overlooking the river.

The model for the new South Carolina Statehouse seems to have been New York's Federal

49

Hall, as L'Enfant was then renovating it. Through shipping and trading, there was a close connection between Charleston and New York; therefore it is perhaps plausible that nationalistic South Carolina should copy the national Capitol in Manhattan. Work on the statehouse began in 1788 while the surveyors and their crews were still slashing paths though the woods. Meanwhile, a woodcut of Bulfinch's sketch of Federal Hall appeared in the widely read *Massachusetts Magazine*, and may have exerted further influence on the rising statehouse. The unfinished building was used on May 23, 1791, for a banquet in honor of General Washington, who was on a Southern tour. Washington noted in his diary the "large scale" of Columbia's plan compared to the reality of its few wooden houses, including the "large and commodious" statehouse. Necessary funds were appropriated for completing the structure late in 1792, but because labor was hard to get and keep, the statehouse was not finished until 1795.

The South Carolina Statehouse was a rectangle built of wood and raised on a low brick basement. A pediment covered the portico in the center of the façade, with miniature pediments over the six front windows. The four short Tuscan columns of the portico were roughcast in stucco over wooden cores. On the rear, a simpler portico, perhaps with square piers, overlooked a yard enclosed by a high board fence that concealed a horse lot and a wooden privy. The building was painted white with green shutters. Spanish brown was applied to the shingle roof and the board fence.

Two separate doorways opened from the main portico into a cross-shaped hall of four equal arms. To the right, beyond a small vestibule containing gallery stairs, lay the House of Representatives. The House had rounded inner corners—surely an echo of Federal Hall—with niches, probably for iron stoves. Immediately across from the chamber's main door, the Speaker's chair stood against a large "Venetian" window, an element consisting of an arched opening with narrow sidelights. One center column supported the ceiling, while a row of lesser ones carried the gallery. At the opposite end of the hall was a similar but smaller Senate chamber. All the woodwork on the main floor was covered with expensive white lead paint and varnished for its protection, and the walls were whitewashed. From the back hall an enclosed stair led down to the raised basement level where brick-floored corridors separated the two or three finished offices. Apparently the interiors were not very decorative, although the contractor James Douglass noted that the chambers had "Dado Wainscott . . . Cornice and fluted Frieze."[18] Between the chambers, four committee rooms, partitioned in the hall, served until 1810, when the need for space hastened the completion of the raised basement story.

The statehouse at Columbia must have borne only a vague resemblance to Federal Hall. The portico and the arrangement of the two legislative houses on opposite sides of the building had been seen in previous government houses of this kind. Because of its size, the central lobby was undoubtedly first designed to be a place of ceremony, as at Richmond, and for joint sessions. Those committee rooms that reduced it to small cross-halls were probably added after Washington's visit. With the exception of the glass windowpanes and the iron locks, the materials came from the area of the Congaree. Clay for the bricks was dug out of the nearby hills; heart of pine for the "featheredge & lap boards" was cut and milled locally. While there is a mysterious and unfounded legend that the statehouse was the work of James Hoban—the Irish architect of the White House—voluminous documents indicate that it was the product of a collaboration between a committee and a master builder.

The statehouse served for many years and was in sharp contrast to such monumental buildings as the Boston Statehouse and the Virginia Capitol. Only its size set it apart from the better plantation houses of South Carolina. Wide and bulky, its wooden surfaces were usually peeling for want of paint. Not for fifty years was the yard around the statehouse planted. A white balustrade fence was added in front in 1810, but horses' hooves tramped anything green which might try to grow in the enclosure. Because of the danger of lightning, trees were left standing only along the fence. During the long rainy seasons, carriages and horses went to the front steps through deep and reddish mud, which members tracked over the unwaxed floors of the lobby. Strip carpets, eventually tacked down, had a maximum life span of only two years, although the statehouse was vacant every spring and summer. The building was used by the legislators from the fall when the crops were in until the spring when it was time to go home and plant; during the hot months, the officials occupied offices in the basement.

Some of the new statehouses of this period were only enlargements of familiar courthouse designs. A capitol of that sort was built in Raleigh, North Carolina, by the master builder Rodham Adkins. Work began in 1792, soon after Senator William Christmas had laid out the town amid thickets of piedmont pine. The legislators occupied the plain brick building before it was finished in 1794. They never particularly liked the new structure, even though by legislative act they ordered Adkins to add wide projections on the front and rear like those of their interim Capitol, the despised Tryon's Palace.

A new capitol was also begun in New Jersey in 1792. The master builder, Jonathan Doan, was a native of Pennsylvania who did work in New Jersey and New York. Whether Doan drew the plan as well is uncertain, but the distinctive design was in existence as early as 1789, when it appeared on a map of Trenton. Almost without question, the model was Philadelphia's contemporary county courthouse built near Independence Hall and used by the United States Congress before Federal City became its permanent residence. This courthouse, called Congress Hall, was a plain red brick rectangle with a two-story semioctagonal bay on one side. In 1792, Delaware, using plans drawn by Alexander Givan, completed at Dover what appears to have been a much closer copy of it—with the bay moved around to the back, as at Annapolis; this was to serve as county courthouse and statehouse. In its application in Trenton, Congress Hall was "doubled": In place of one court were to be two legislative chambers. The New Jersey Statehouse was wide and rectangular with matching two-story bays on each end. Windows banded the building on two levels, those below with round heads and the upper ones rectangular. A short flight of stairs led to the main entrance, which had a pediment and pilasters. The cornice was a double row of dentils and modillions; on the roof an arcaded octagonal cupola for bells stood among ten tall chimneys. Built of rough stone up to the eaves, with walls nearly four feet thick, the whole disheveled-looking mass was smoothed over with several coats of stucco, which was then stippled with paint to resemble granite. This construction was, of course, much less expensive than actual cut stone would have been, and the debt-ridden Assembly was pleased.

The entrance door led to a corridor and the stairs. The two chambers were on the ground

51

New Jersey Statehouse, by Jonathan Doan, 1794; watercolor
by A. J. Davis, c. 1830

floor, with the Speaker's chairs in the octagon bays. Upstairs the courtroom and offices were separated by a hall with a small stair to the cupola. Winds blowing over the Delaware made the statehouse extremely cold and consequently roundly disliked in winter. Various experiments improved the heating, but very little else was done to change the building for a half-century.

While the states were achieving these first substantial architectural expressions in their public buildings, the visionary city of Washington, D.C., was materializing in the heat of melodramatic controversy. Travelers and politicians frequented the Federal City, but few of them were favorably impressed, and many believed it to be superfluous. In charitable moments they would sometimes admit that, like the Bible and the Constitution, it had some redeeming features

—at least its establishment had halted the government's nomadic shifts from place to place. The new city was the butt of many jokes. Newspapers repeatedly printed humorous word pictures of the low barrens, the swamps, and the worn-out fields on the Potomac which morning unveiled and night mercifully concealed. When New Jersey offered its new statehouse as the national Capitol, nobody thought it presumptuous; indeed, it was hailed as patriotic. Other states made similar proposals. Yet Washington City prevailed, supported by powerful men like Washington and Jefferson, who had visions of an American Rome.

Dr. Thornton's plan for the Capitol had proved impractical in some respects, and one of the architects who had lost in the original competition was called in to improve the scheme. Then a succession of foreign professionals held the post of Capitol Superintendent. Thornton, who resided in nearby Georgetown, was offended that other men were given authority to tamper with his design and infuriated by their professional scorn for him. He played both social and political games to destroy them, and proved a vindictive and effective opponent. Fights perpetually interrupted the Capitol project; superintendents resigned, new ones came on, and the work went very sluggishly. Because of leaks in the completed north wing, chunks of plaster fell; but no one was there to repair them.

Money was appropriated to build the south wing for the House of Representatives, which had grown impatient with the temporary wooden pavilion it occupied on the site. According to Thornton's plan, between the two wings there was to have been a great central block with a dome. In that space one could count as many half-finished foundations as there had been architects. There were round walls, diagonal walls, square walls—altogether, a sort of architectural debate set in weed-grown footings and pools of rainwater.

As projected, the national Capitol was to be the first gathering together of all the architectural symbols which had developed in earlier American statehouses. It was to have a portico, a dome, a central public space, and the two houses opposite one another—colonial-statehouse style, but in opposite wings. As it was proceeding, the capitol incorporated numerous changes from the Thornton project. Architects with foreign training were largely responsible for the increasing addition of Roman motifs.

But while the national Capitol project was assembling all the significant statehouse symbols, it was no model for the states. If a state set out to build, its commissioners naturally sought models in existing statehouses. It was believed inappropriate for a state legislature to copy the national Capitol, even though there had already been echoes of Federal Hall at Columbia, Boston, and Hartford. The predominant opinion was that the federal government was merely an abstract association of states; consequently, there was no analogy between the central government of the United States and the individual states, which were sovereign entities. Governments on the state level often looked with contempt on the ceremonial pretensions as well as the foreign-looking architecture of federal officialdom. Those pictures of Louis XVI and Marie Antoinette which hung on the wall of the United States Senate would never have been permitted in a state capitol; the republican spirit of the states much preferred a true representation of General Washington.

Politics for most people meant local and state affairs. The average American would probably never go to the Federal City, but it was fairly certain that he would visit his statehouse, to sit in

53

the gallery which now was open to the public in every state in the Union. And state legislatures were much larger after the Revolution; delegates were not only chosen by a broader electorate, but themselves represented more of an economic cross-section. Even on a national level it soon became evident that the tidings from a local ballot box could ruin the shrewdest alliance in the Federal City. As never before, United States senators from one state carefully watched elections in other states—elections which would determine their own political strength next session in Washington.

One of the most powerful political machines in the nation was a personal party in New York State. Its leaders were the rich Federalists, united under the banner of their able Governor, George Clinton. On steamboats headed up the Hudson from New York City to Albany, one could usually recognize a "Clinton man," or so it was claimed at the time. There were always several of those well-dressed officeholders on board, lamenting their temporary exile upstate in the seat of government. The Clintonians already had an eye on their own survival in 1797 when they had removed the capital from Manhattan 160 miles away to Albany, the old Dutch city that was now the gateway to the rich Iroquois lands of the western part of the state. It was only a matter of time before the Clintonians built a monumental house of government there.

A combination statehouse and city hall was approved by the legislature in 1804, with the stipulation that the city and county pay half the $24,000 it was to cost—a price far exceeded in the final tally of $110,685.42! The local designer and contractor, Philip Hooker, later presented a bill to the commissioners for erecting a new statehouse: "To sundry services performed as per agreement in drawing a plan & superintending etc. up to the 4th day of April 1806—which was the time the foundation was laid out . . . $250."[19] Hooker was the most successful master builder in upstate New York at the turn of the nineteenth century. The son of a Massachusetts carpenter, he had been brought to Albany at a young age and reared in his father's trade. At the time the post-Revolutionary boom hit Albany, Hooker was a young man eager to make the most of the situation. His success was speeded by advantageous contracts for churches, houses, and public buildings.

New York's Capitol, finished in 1809, was only one of Hooker's early monumental buildings, and not his best. The statehouse, a strange combination of two virtually unrelated but strongly stated façades, was doubtless the result of a compromise between two disagreeing factions on the Capitol Commission. The building was essentially a rectangle three stories tall at the east and toward the river, and two at the other end because of the steeply inclined site. State Street jogged in front of the Capitol, then ran along one side. Hooker treated the narrower façade on lower State Street with a pedimented portico of fluted Ionic columns set at the top of a broad flight of stairs. The orderly lines of windows were variously arched, pedimented, or framed by heavy architraves. By contrast, the business front, or long side, had a small pedimented and pilastered doorway and otherwise resembled a town hall or courthouse of the late eighteenth century. As at Richmond, the portico was considered ceremonial—the axial ambiguity was not as successful here, but it did express the dual use of the building by state and city.

On the roof, a small domed lantern was surrounded by columns and topped by a statue of Themis. Brownstone from a nearby quarry was sawed in blocks for the walls and also used for most of the ornament. Behind the portico, tall portals opened into a hall flanked by rows of reeded columns and richly paved with gray and white marble squares laid on the diagonal. The two chambers were on opposite sides of the hall. Lavish decorations were applied in all the state quarters. The relative elaboration of these rooms with pediments, columns, and American eagles carved in wood by Hooker and his father were the means by which the builders discriminated between the state and municipal parts of the building. This was most obvious in the dual nature of the exterior, but it was consistent throughout the Capitol. The conceit was not entirely successful: From an architectural point of view, the visual conflicts gave the Capitol an air of indecision. Perhaps that was appropriate, in a way even symbolic, of the sinking fortunes of the Federalists that year.

New Hampshire's Capitol Commission was aware of the Capitol at Albany and three or four others when it began planning a new statehouse for Concord late in the spring of 1814. The United States was at war with England, and the legislature was quite occupied with the subject, but on June 22 the commissioners presented a report: "It is justly considered derogatory to a respectable and independent State, to suffer the officers of its Government to sit and transact the business of the State in a building mean in its appearance, and destitute of suitable accommodations . . . your committee . . . are satisfied that a State House, in every respect such as would correspond with the convenience and dignity of the State, may be built upon very reasonable terms, and that the money that will be required for the purpose will be very easily and cheerfully paid by the citizens of the State, as soon as the burdens imposed by the present war are removed."[20]

One year later a preliminary plan was displayed before the legislature by Stewart J. Park, a master builder who had "offered to contract for building and finishing a State-House agreeably to said plan, the outside to be built of fine hammered stone, the inside to be handsomely finished in modern style, for the sum of thirty-two thousand dollars."[21]

It was a good time to present a proposal for something new—peace had been signed Christmas Eve, 1814. Before that news had traveled the winter seas early in 1815, word of General Jackson's victory in January over the British at New Orleans raced across the nation. That the Federal City now lay in ashes and some of the issues of the war were not resolved was of no importance alongside the fact that the Americans had fought off the enemy. Where fear had lately gripped even the strong-hearted, pride now blazed. The laurels had not been won by diplomats at conference tables but by the citizens themselves. When the news came, men raced down Main Street—Concord's only street—proclaiming the victory; people came out from their houses, bells clanged from the church, and the cheering and gun firing continued into the night.

Because Stewart Park, in business in Groton, Massachusetts, could not be in Concord all the time, a building committee of three was set up for the statehouse. This committee was soon reduced to one, Albe Cady, who later claimed he had been saddled with most of the work, including "attending to the business of devising and executing plans, purchasing materials and superintending the various kinds of work connected with the building."[22] The design of the statehouse as executed can be attributed to this otherwise unknown man.

New Hampshire Historical Society

New Hampshire Statehouse, as it was in 1820

Another building committee of three was appointed to look after accounts. Concord granite from nearby Rattlesnake Hill was quarried and cut by convicts at the state prison on the outskirts of town. Convicts were also used at the building site, but after some of them escaped, residents of Concord were more and more frequently employed as workers. It was a big project for any New England town. Most of the 2,500 inhabitants turned out for the cornerstone ceremony, which was performed by the masons on September 4, 1816. Cady, a master builder, had developed a final plan that echoed the Boston Statehouse in ways he could be sure would please the legislature and the original commission, which had preferred that edifice over all they had visited.

Perhaps it is even curious that Cady did not plan an even closer copy, for Concord wanted a real monument in an effort to keep its capital status. What was more, Boston was only seventy miles away, and there was a regular stage twice a week between there and and Concord. Boston's influences upon the New Hampshire town were many and noticeable.

The exterior of the statehouse at Concord had the character of a large private house more than the public grandeur of Bulfinch's building. It did not overpower the small town, and yet it was monumental. Unquestionably, its façade was an elaboration and adaptation of Plate 37 in Robert Morris's *Select Architecture*, published in 1757. This offers the elevation of a dwelling with a tall central section and lower matching wings. Built of dark blue-gray granite set in great blocks, the Concord building also presented a tall, pedimented central block, with only somewhat smaller wings than those of Morris. The large cupola that rode the roof of the middle section was enriched with Palladian detail, its domed crown topped by a gilded wooden eagle clawing a golden ball.

There were three doors on the front, the main one rectangular with pilasters, and the other two, in the wings, roundheaded with transoms. Above the main door, the three great arched windows of the House of Representatives were set into arched recesses. Rectangular panels were incised above each of these windows, while in the pediment the wooden dentils and lunette introduced the ornamentation that was carried to a flamboyant climax in the cupola. All the windows of the façade were fashionably large. Those in the wings were square-headed, carefully space in the superbly fitted ashlar walls.

The statehouse's Doric Hall, a copy of Bulfinch's, occupied the entire main floor of the center section. The two exterior doors of the wings opened into stairhalls flanking it and connecting with various offices. Columns and stucco ornaments decorated the House of Representatives chamber, which was centered over Doric Hall. The Council and Governor's office were in one wing, the Senate was in the other. As in Boston, neither wing could communicate with the other on the second-floor level without passing through the House of Representatives.

Knowing the source of the plan increases interest in the details of the Concord interiors. Unfortunately, the building was not recorded when it was completely remodeled at midcentury, any more than was the Boston Statehouse when it was remodeled forty years afterward. There is, however, a surviving bill at Concord for supplies dated July 28, 1819, the summer the statehouse was completed. Asher Benjamin, according to this bill alone, supplied from Boston glass and, more significantly, paint for the New Hampshire Statehouse. Colors he sold Cady were white, French yellow, Prussian blue, rose pink, lamp black, patent yellow, and red lead over which to apply the "10 Doz gold leaf" surely intended for the wooden eagle. From the white lead paint ordered, we can suppose that the exterior woodwork was white or stone color, typically made with lamp black to dull the white. The yellows and blue could have been used in any way; with white lead or even whitewash they could have been thinned to the then stylish pale tints. Mixed together, they could have produced other colors for the stucco ornaments. The purchase of three "graining tools" suggests that the woodwork was grained in imitation of finer wood. Vast expanses of plaster could possibly have been painted and scored to resemble masonry blocks, then perhaps sanded with a bellows to further simulate stone. Gadgets were ordered for

57

many treatments of this sort, and there is the item "2 marking tools" among those for brushes and graining combs.[23]

Only two of the standard features inherited from previous American capitols were present in the New Hampshire Statehouse—the ceremonial central space and the two balanced wings. Americans rarely made the House of Representatives the preeminent tenant in the statehouse. It was particularly appropriate that post-Revolutionary Boston placed the lower house in so dominant a position; and in their first plan, the Capitol Directors at Richmond had tried to do the same. This had little meaning in New Hampshire or, for that matter, in any other state, for no parallel to Boston's so-called triumph of democracy had occurred elsewhere. State senates were not, after all, very reminiscent of the old Royal councils of colonial days, nor did the elected governors bear any resemblance to the Crown's agents. Those waves of popular suspicion which followed the War of Independence had by now faded. After the War of 1812, the nation was settling down to live under its new Constitution.

Bulfinch himself was a victim of a declining interest in his kind of public architecture. As Capitol Architect commissioned to complete the reconstruction of the United States Capitol destroyed during the war, he tried to alter the rotunda into a Georgian stairhall, and isolate the external dome from the interior plan as at Boston. In none of this was he successful. Only on the city, or west, front, in the pairing of columns, and in some other Boston-like details, did he succeed in maintaining his continuing taste for the Georgian design of his youth.

Architecture's authority is visual. On paper the national Capitol was the first legislative building to draw the statehouse symbols together; but it was not actually brought to completion until 1824. Before then, and before Bulfinch's taller and more nearly hemispherical dome was added, its influence was limited. New state capitols continued to be built with no deference to the one in Washington.

A case in point was the Georgia Capitol at Milledgeville, a town laid out soon after the turn of the century by land speculators in a region acquired from the Creek Indians. The Capitol seems to have been built somewhat like the old Philadelphia Statehouse, in three separate parts. A large middle section—probably similar to the South Carolina Statehouse—contained the two chambers, with the Executive Department and the Treasury Department in separate flanking buildings. The original detailing of this Capitol was obscured by subsequent drastic changes. It may even have had a strongly churchlike exterior, as did the three-part Capitol built in 1814 in Frankfort, Kentucky, with portico and cupola-steeple.

Enough documentation survives regarding the Georgia Capitol to indicate that it was elaborate without being expensive. Here again paint was employed to give grandeur through the use of marbling and mahogany graining. There were stucco columns and pediments, and American eagles were used abundantly in the chambers. William D. Lane and a Mr. Smart billed the Milledgeville Commission in 1805 for "draughting a plan of a State House with explanatory notes and references."[24] Two years later the state officials moved in. Georgia, like New Hampshire, New York, and the rest, took certain ideas from what had been done elsewhere and came up with practical solutions. At their best, these buildings were sound regional architecture. They were not intended to be more.

The first state to bring together in one building those several architectural symbols that came from the democratic movement in eighteenth-century America was Pennsylvania, where the first symbols had been born. The capital had been moved from Philadelphia to Lancaster in 1799 as a sop to the inland population. Yet another act, passed in the winter of 1810, sent the capital to Harrisburg. Delegates from the Philadelphia area fought the proposal; their defeat reveals the remarkable redistribution of authority which had changed state politics in Pennsylvania in the twenty years since the new state constitution was adopted. The Harrisburg backers took every precaution to assure that this would be the state capital's last move. October 1812 was set as the date of transfer, and it was promised that by that time two fireproof buildings would be completed at Harrisburg for the accommodation of the government offices and official papers.

It was particularly important for Harrisburg to have something finer and more modern than one could find in Philadelphia. But there was to be one major similarity between the new statehouse and the old—the three-part plan of a main building in the center, with balancing separate wings to the sides. The commissioners approached the Harrisburg master builder Stephen Hills. In consultation with the commission, Hills seems to have designed the entire master plan in 1810. A native of Ashford-in-Kent, Hills had come to America during the 1790's after serving an apprenticeship with a house-joiner. He left his business in Boston to go to Harrisburg when the advantages of Pennsylvania's new prosperity became appealing. Robust and adventurous, the 250-pound Hills was forty years of age when the commissioners engaged him to build the fireproof Capitol buildings. He already had built fine houses for Harrisburg's rich supply merchants.

From the high statehouse site, one hundred feet above the swift Susquehanna River, one could see for many miles over the hilly countryside. Harrisburg rambled along the riverbank, a village of wooden stores and houses with a brick courthouse and the several larger brick dwellings which were Stephen Hills's mark on the town. The Hills Capitol scheme called for a row of three buildings. Two small wings to be built first would be reflections on a smaller scale of the central building to be built later. Work began at once—it was important to get the legislature financially involved in Harrisburg lest a movement begin to move that body elsewhere, even back to Philadelphia. As promised, when the state government arrived at Harrisburg in 1812, it was greeted by two completed fireproof buildings set 325 feet apart.

The officials sold most of the government's furniture at auction because it was damaged on the trip from Lancaster. In Harrisburg, the two houses met in the local courthouse which Hills had remodeled for their reception. War halted the Capitol building plans, and not until the peace was any effort made to begin the main structure on the hill.

On March 11, 1816, the Governor was authorized to sell the old Philadelphia Statehouse to the city of Philadelphia for $70,000. One week later, he canceled all previous arrangements with Hills and advertised publicly for statehouse plans. If Hills protested, it is forgotten; political pressure from Philadelphia, however, dictated that there be a competition for the main building of the Capitol. The city was the undisputed leader in American architecture. Architects there enjoyed a certain status elevating them above the builder class, and they insisted upon the distinction. Like most European professionals, they preferred employment on public works; the new Pennsylvania Capitol was not only a public project, but a rich plumb.

59

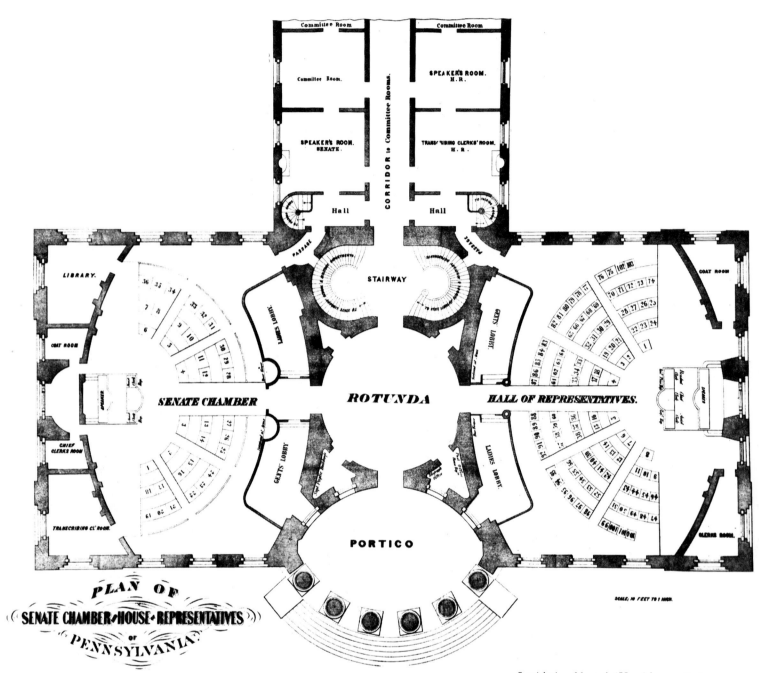

Legislative Manual (Harrisburg: 1842)

Pennsylvania Capitol, plan showing later rear wing

In advertisements in newspapers in Philadelphia, Baltimore, New York, Boston, and Washington City, the state offered a first premium of $400 and a second prize of $200. Inspired by the competition for the national Capitol, this was the first formal contest ever held for an American statehouse. Only four entrants are known: Stephen Hills and Joseph C. Laveille of Harrisburg, and William Strickland and Robert Mills, both former assistants to Benjamin Henry Latrobe, the most celebrated architect in America.

Only Strickland's written description of his own entry has survived; all other record of the competition has been lost. Because the building's architectural character had already been established by Hills, it is likely the other designs were all variations on the same theme. Strickland proposed a building rather faintly resembling the eighteenth-century courthouse on the square

Analectic Magazine, *July 1820*
Pennsylvania Capitol, Harrisburg, by Stephen Hills, 1810–1821

in Spanish Town, Jamaica, though any actual connection is very unlikely. It was to be a deeper and taller building than Hills had proposed, and was to be linked to Hills's flanking wings by an open colonnade he called a "grand avenue." The semicircular Ionic portico, a larger version of those already on the flankers, was reached by a great flight of steps. A dome almost as tall as the building crowned the roof. The main floor contained a semicircular house chamber, probably very much like the one in Washington City, and the committee rooms of that House. A stone stair in the large central rotunda, probably similar to the one in the New York City Hall, was to ascend to the upper, or Senate, floor, splitting halfway into a pair of curving arms and lighted from above by a skylight.

The competitors were uninhibited by any of their oft-expounded standards of professional propriety. They were hustling for a prestigious job that would pay the five percent fee they were demanding. A letter from William Strickland to the banker Nicholas Biddle of Philadelphia indicates the bitterness of the competition:

61

Philadelphia, February 24th, 1817

Dear Sir,

I have just this moment received information from one of my friends in Harrisburg that Mr. Mills has qualified his last proposals to the Legislature in such a manner as will perhaps be calculated to influence the vote of the House in his favor. Thus he proposes to superintend the erection of the building for *Three dollars* per day provided an *assistant* be appointed to make the necessary contracts for materials etc. Your good sense will discover at once that this is a mere *trick*, for the assistant must be paid for his services, so that the State will gain nothing by the scheme—his proposals are 200,000 dollars for the whole cost. I will thank you to state to the gentlemen explicitly the following proposals on my part.

I will agree to erect the State Capitol according to my last plan in a substantial and durable manner for the sum of $180,000., for the compensation of $5 per day for professional services, which always includes the *making of contracts, procuring materials etc., etc.* That I require no more than 30,000 dollars as an appropriation for the first year, and I will agree to accommodate the session of 1818–1819 in the State Capitol for a further appropriation of 60,000 for the year 1818.—Your dissemination of the terms among the gentlemen of the two houses will be duly appreciated by

Yours with the greatest respect and
Esteem
William Strickland

Nicholas Biddle, Esq.

P. S. I wish you would be so good as to confer with Mr. John Read as to the best plan of making these sentiments known to the house.[25]

Meanwhile, the political bickering so alarmed those who backed Harrisburg as the capital that they hurried a bill through the legislature appropriating $50,000 for the purchase of materials for the construction of "any Plan that may be adopted by the Legislature." Stephen Hills was set to this task, since he was close at hand, and he spent the money fast, piling the building materials on the ground between the two office buildings on Capitol Hill. Rough river-stone, sandstone, limestone, and cellar rubble were hauled in from the country, transported over the Susquehanna on Oglesby's Ferry at $2.00 per wagon, and maneuvered up the long incline to the site. In the summer of 1817, brick began to arrive, at a cost of 70¢ to $1.00 per thousand. Fifty thousand feet of white pine lumber came by flatboat. Hills and his handyman, Erasmus Lindy, saw that the materials were protected from the weather, but no construction was started.

An impatient legislature called for a new competition in January 1819, and by April seventeen plans, identified by numbers only, lay on the Governor's desk. We only know the names of the two winners: Stephen Hills, first prize, and Robert Mills, second.

Construction began at once, and the Pennsylvania State Capitol was occupied by the end of 1821. Inside the rising rectangle of walls was the hollow cylinder of the rotunda. That great space, which would lead up to a dome still to come, was taller than anything else in the whole Pennsylvania countryside. Unfinished, the gaunt tower looked like the ruin of a castle keep. Thin wells for ventilation pierced its walls, and the rectangular sockets of doors, windows, and joists patterned its brick surface.

The completion of the Capitol marked the greatest event in Harrisburg's history. It was an expanded version of its two red brick flankers, 171 feet wide as compared to their sixty-five-foot width, with the same two story Ionic porticoes curving outward from loggias. Identical parapets, decorative panels, and the crisp Flemish bond of the brick walls further related the three buildings. Now the center structure dwarfed the two office blocks, which themselves were almost as big as some of the early capitols. The six tall stone columns of the great portico screened a huge concave niche, in the manner of the brothers Adam and Sir John Soane. Rectangular windows filled blind arcades along the first level, and the corners were framed by pairs of giant pilasters. On the roof the hemispherical dome above a ring of columns, the full width of the portico, climaxed the novel combination of curving elements in the plan.

From the portico a door gave immediate access into the rotunda, with its one-hundred-foot view up between the several levels of cantilevered balconies to the fluted interior of the dome. On each side of the rotunda, which was decorated with pediments and pilasters, were the chambers, in both of which Hills had made front and back walls elliptical, with the Speakers' chairs sunk into round niches. Beyond the rotunda—they called it "the great thoroughfare of the interior" instead of pretending it would be for joint sessions—were a pair of partially open lobes facing one another across a narrow passage, and carrying spiral staircases to the floors above.

The master builder himself led the dedication parade January 2, 1822. At his insistence, all eighty of his workmen marched behind him two by two: bricklayers and stonecutters, carpenters and laborers. After them came the dignitaries of Pennsylvania, then a vast crowd of spectators, numbering some 1,000. The builder slipped the key into the lock and the door opened; the flag raced up the pole; musketfire and cheering and bells roared from the flatboats, keelboats, and steamers on the Susquehanna; and the people poured into their new state Capitol. Over their heads spears of sunlight crossed the dim upper reaches of the rotunda and twinkled in the glass chandeliers of the House and Senate chambers. A thick confluence threaded the circular stairs to the dome, waiting in line to see the breathtaking view from its observation gallery.

Stephen Hills's Pennsylvania Capitol has been gone now for more years than it stood, but its historical importance endures. In that statehouse, the marriage of dome, rotunda, portico, and balanced houses united for the first time the architectural symbols of American democracy. Initiated by American laymen as expressions of liberty, the individual symbols were here combined almost indivisibly by an English master builder.

III
TEMPLED HILLS

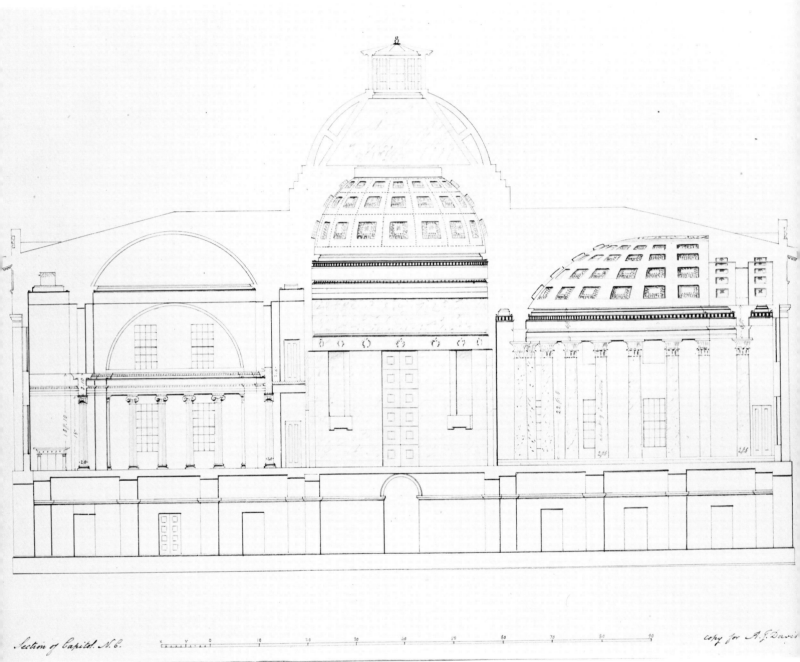

Section of Capitol. N.C.   copy for A. J. Davis

North Carolina Capitol, Town & Davis section, c. 1832

In the United States the pursuit of profit was successful so often that it gave American life a distinct character. This was fully evident in the era of Andrew Jackson. There were no old fortunes, and no laws to ensure the continuity of new ones. One generation of bad management could doom an eastern commercial estate beyond redemption; Southern planters could be obliterated by one bad crop or a fatal epidemic among their slaves.

With an upper class always on the make, there were really no cultivated patrons left to foster the arts. Businessmen generally thought about business, regardless of their wealth. Some, of course, set out to impress their neighbors with a showy house full of matched furniture and elegant plate, but even the finest American houses were considered modest and bourgeois by travelers who had seen mansions abroad.

Statehouse building fell victim to a second facet of the American character—the cult of thrift. Tocqueville wrote that "In democratic communities the imagination is compressed when men consider themselves; it expands indefinitely when they think of the State. Hence it is that the same men who live on a small scale in narrow dwellings frequently aspire to gigantic splendor in the erection of their public monuments."[1] Magnificence, yes, but only if it did not cost too much.

Time and again statehouse plans that initially delighted commissions were later drastically altered to save money. Americans were content to waste anything but money, and certainly not money on something so superfluous—"ethereal" was their contemptuous word—as monumental architecture. Yet thrift itself seemed less important than thrift's appearance. That certainly accounts for the general failure of state capitols to have accumulated fine works of American art. Only twenty-seven pieces of sculpture were purchased for the national Capitol prior to the Civil War, and much of that was no more than architectural embellishment. Still, there was a growing desire for the workings of American democracy to have richer surroundings. North Carolina's legislature, for example, finally demanded something be done about their homely brick statehouse. First the House of Commons took the cue from Virginia and decided to commission a statue of George Washington. Planned as a bust, a full-length figure, and finally as an equestrian statue, the work was to have been economically executed in plaster and would probably have been a cast of the one then planned for the Federal City.

Encouraged by a patriotic Raleigh merchant and the brief recovery of prosperity after the War of 1812, the legislature commissioned Antonio Canova, Houdon's successor as the leading European sculptor, to carve North Carolina's statue of Washington in marble. The statue was awaited with joy that built to frenzy. By 1821, when the enormous crate arrived from Canova's studio at Possagno, Italy, where the original plaster still survives, the state had completely remodeled the old Capitol.

The stinginess of this remodeling is noteworthy. In 1818 the Superintendent of the Public Buildings made a report on the statehouse, saying that it was in derelict condition, and "that Another Story should be added for the Purpose of making Suitable Committee rooms, and that there should be Projections, on the North & South sides, for Offices. . . . The Cupola should be converted into a simple Dome." One of the reasons supporting a renovation was that the awaited statue of Washington would demand "an eligible Situation within the Building."[2]

65

North Carolina Statehouse, as remodeled by Captain William Nichols by 1821

State architect William Nichols, an English-born master builder, designed and supervised the project. In a clever and practical scheme for improving the simple building, the rectangular structure was extended to form a Greek cross by attaching a new brick wing to each of the long sides. A third floor was added, and all four arms of the cross were pedimented. The existing wings were ornamented to match the new projections. Using cheap stucco lavishly, Nichols created the illusion of a heavily rusticated arcade on the first level; Ionic pilasters under the pediments gave the wings the look of monumental porticoes, reminiscent of the town front on the Hartford Statehouse. The side doors were sheltered by two-column porches like those on the ends of the Boston Statehouse. Surmounting the roof, at the crossing, was a low dome—not hemispherical and not really of the Roman saucer shape proposed for Washington, but somewhere between the two—and after 1826 crowned by a cupola with a bell.

Nichols added grandeur to the building with several inexpensive treatments in common use even on private mansions. He elaborately painted and black-spattered the exterior in imitation of granite. The colonnaded House and Senate, Nichols's own versions of Latrobe's chambers in the national Capitol, were draped in crimson fabric which the builder purchased on a special buying trip to New York. From the ground up to the dome he cut a rotunda and decorated it with pilasters—much like Hills's in Harrisburg.

In this dramatic space, lighted by oculi above, was placed Canova's heroic statue of Washington. The building was later embellished with portraits by Thomas Sully, but the statue remained the real pride of North Carolina. The Capitol seemed to exist only to house it. A traveler touring the building in the late 1820's pronounced the marble figure "well worth a visit . . . the hero is represented in a sitting position & clothed in the Roman costume however improper & inappropriate this may be it has given the artist great scope for the exercise of his talents the drapery is exquisitely done & actually seems to hang in natural folds & is only excelled by the sculpture of the limbs & body where every vein & muscle is executed to the life."[3]

Most other state capitols purchased likenesses of George Washington. A wooden effigy stood in the old statehouse in Philadelphia, and in Boston a deep niche was added at the back of Bulfinch's Doric Hall to hold a full-length marble figure commissioned by subscription in 1826 from the English sculptor Sir Francis Chantrey.

Rembrandt Peale hawked his huge Washington portraits to legislatures all over the country. Peale's unsolicited letter read:

> "Not less enthusiastic in the love of my art than for the character of Washington, my highest ambition has been to record his countenance. The success with which I have accomplished this task may be inferred from the testimony of those who were intimate with him. . . . The original itself must remain in my own hands, in order that I may execute a few faithful copies of it. As I am about to depart for Europe, I have thought it my duty, without delay, to offer to the state over which you preside, the opportunity of possessing a copy of this portrait; which I am willing to furnish for one thousand dollars. This will be considered a moderate compensation for a picture of such extent, style of execution, and the care which is requisite to insure a faithful transcript of so interesting and sublime a countenance. The time will soon come when this act, which goes at once to encourage native art, and to commemorate a nation's gratitude, will be remembered with pride and satisfaction."[4]

The painter, in a follow-up, stressed that he was "one of the last surviving artists who enjoyed the privilege of painting the portrait of Washington from life."[5] Peale's Washington portraits sold well to the capitols. But they became mere token tributes to art, a sad compromise in the name of economy, instead of initiating worthwhile capitol collections.

Americans were not so tight-fisted in business. Money was spent wildly if there was the slightest promise of return. Business deals abounded: deals in plank roads, paved roads, steamboats, canals, packet ships, new towns, exchanges, tontines, and so on and on. Money and politics absorbed American conversation. Bankruptcy counted less as a disgrace than as a battle scar. Frontiers were limited only in the eye of the beholder; the new ones of the farther west were the best and most obvious to pursue.

Americans had already gone beyond the international boundary. Moses Austin, the Virginia Capitol's unlucky roofer, was the first to gain permission to settle aliens in Spanish Texas. By the time Americans reached the West Coast, New England missionaries had already built churches in the Kingdom of Kamehameha in the Sandwich Islands.

The economic frontiers of such places as New York City and Pittsburgh drew a different kind of frontiersman, but the excitement was the same. Power looms, steam boilers, and rolling mills swept thousands of people of all economic strata into a new kind of life. Most people found the change an improvement and cast their ballots for Andrew Jackson. Enjoying what they supposed a little democracy had brought, they wanted more.

Statehouses, not the unfinished national Capitol, were the strongholds of democratic political power in the early nineteenth century. Like all American resources, this power was subject to exploitation as soon as its national potentialities were glimpsed. The Jacksonians pooled that power, making their party a sort of political corporation with a directorate representing numerous divergent interests, all full of fire.

On the other hand, the Federalists, who proved not so unwilling to compromise with one another, had sung their swan song in 1814 at New England's Hartford Convention, held in the statehouse and protesting the current war. It was a convention scheduled for good reason, but certainly under an unlucky star, so soon before the American triumphs against the British. From the Hartford Statehouse a printed pamphlet was circulated to the states, outlining the New England Federalist objections to Americans warring with England—in commerce the best friend of the United States. Wildly celebrating the victorious end of the war, the public considered the Hartford circular treasonous. For a decade or more there was only one party—the Republican—in American politics. The subsequent split into two national parties opened the Age of Jackson. But the spirit of the times was well established before the Hero of New Orleans became its symbol.

In the Presidential election of 1828, over 1,000,000 votes were cast out of an American population of about 13,000,000. Less than half that number of ballots had been marked in the election four years before. A reason for the greater participation was that the nineteenth-century trend toward universal white male suffrage was reaching its crest. Even more important was the massive alliance of various state politicians in their pursuit of the new votes.

Only in state elections was there precedent for such a universal appeal to the electorate. The sweeping climax in 1828 was the concerted effort of established statehouse organizations all over the nation. Those already hardened by local experience, such as New York's Tammany Hall, provided leadership, and their tough state election practices now spread to the national level. A national machine formed of local parts fast took shape, finding its voice through

Alabama Capitol, Tuscaloosa, by William Nichols, 1833,
as it appeared about 1890

the press or in orations on statehouse steps. The machine's year of victory was one of those strangely American milestones sometimes called revolutionary, when politics abruptly conforms to changes already well under way. During the 1820's and 1830's the bright light of reform was kindled by the common belief that democracy had awakened from a long sleep. Sometimes it was truly reform, sometimes simply a wish for something fresh and new.

State governments, buoyed by renewed self-assurance, wanted grander housing. State-house design went through a transition that led suddenly to the adoption of a new architectural style, Greek Revival. Before that, legislatures had considered various alternatives to previous models, but the choices were seldom very original: The Alabama capitol is a good example. Having decided to move their capitol from Cahaba to Tuscaloosa, Alabama legislators held a statehouse competition. The winner was William Nichols, former architect of North Carolina. (The whole incident, however, reeked of prior arrangement: Nichols was awarded the prize by the legislature in December 1827; his oath of office as Superintendent of Works was dated the previous May.) His plan, called Grecian Cross, was accepted with a construction bid of $55,-

ooo and a foolproof proposal: to copy the North Carolina Capitol at Raleigh as he had recently remodeled it. Such imitation apparently did not trouble Nichols or the Alabama politicians.

The Southerners came to know Nichols affectionately as the Captain. A gambler in business, he had improved his fortunes since he brought his family over from England. For some years he had been a slaveholder and the owner of several black carpenters and a few laborers—useful possessions for a builder. His son did part of his father's work, so that the elder Nichols was able to further his interests. By 1828 he had assets in Fayetteville, North Carolina, and Alabama, and would very soon extend them into the Mississippi Black Belt.

As the Alabama Capitol neared completion, the *Huntsville Democrat* reported: "This beautiful building is a source of pleasure to all who have the least state pride. . . . There never has been one erected in the U.S. for the same sum, half so spacious, convenient, durable, and imposing. All agree that as a specimen of architecture it stands unsurpassed, and bespeaks the extensive acquirements of Capt. Nichols, who has superintended its erection."[6]

The new Capitol was quite similar to the one in Raleigh. At the end of Broad Street, the red brick building stood high on the bank of the Black Warrior River. A cross-shape was achieved by appending projections front and rear—smaller than those at Raleigh—and decorating them with pilasters so that they resembled porticoes. The two stories rested on a rusticated stone basement; and a rather modest dome, like that at Raleigh, was placed at the intersection of the cross. At each end a shallow single-bay projection with a tall, incised arch and low porch faced the side streets.

Within the Capitol the chambers were balanced on each side of the rotunda. The House of Representatives had a circle of Corinthian columns surrounding an open well cut through the floor above. Sunlight fell into the rotunda from a lantern eighty-five feet above the floor, and straw-colored pilasters with bronzed Corinthian capitals were spaced along plaster walls painted milk white, a color popular at the time. Nichols repeated this interior three and probably four times in his career. Only the third version survives, the old Capitol at Jackson, Mississippi, dating from 1834; its somewhat un-Nichols character may well result from changes suggested by the Captain's youthful Maine carpenters influenced by their own new statehouse at Augusta.

Whether Nicholas himself devised the plan of his three statehouses or knew the rotunda at Harrisburg is not clear. Possibly he combined ideas from diverse sources—banks and the new exchange hotels, or even designs for the United States Capitol, which he might have seen in his first months in America. If some other designer was involved, the name is lost. Suffice it to say that Captain Nichols's judgment was sound in recognizing the plan as a winner. Twenty years later one of his carpenters won a California statehouse competition with the same scheme.

William Nichols's Southern career was at its peak when Maine legislators decided to build a copy of the Boston Statehouse at Augusta. They invited Bulfinch, at that time ending his career as Architect of the United States Capitol, to make a presentation. Portland politicians tried to force an alternative invitation for a local architect, Alexander Parris, who was successfully following in Bulfinch's footsteps in Boston. The older man, however, won out. Those who insisted upon employing Bulfinch for the new Capitol were the most prominent men in the state government. It was they who had achieved Maine's separation from Massachusetts, and in the course of that separatist activity had grown very familiar with the Massachusetts Statehouse. Men of wealth and education, they had grown up looking to Boston as the great center of American culture.

The Commissioner of Public Buildings, appointed in 1828, was former Governor William King. His political comet had reached its peak early in the decade when Henry Clay pulled Maine into the Missouri controversy; thus Maine statehood came abruptly to a region long torn by internal strife over the contested land titles of poor farmers. Like most of Maine's electorate, King was a devout Adams Republican. He had helped write the law which protected Maine squatters, but his faith in the common man had been shaken by the upsurge of pro-Jackson sentiment in the 1828 election. Maine shocked the East Coast states by casting one of her nine electoral votes in favor of Andrew Jackson. King and his friends hoped they had seen the last of such rampant democracy.

Bulfinch objected to producing what he called a "servile copy" of the Boston Statehouse, but amiable as always, he drew two sets of plans and elevations for consideration. One scheme was in plan a small duplicate of the Massachusetts Statehouse. The alternate design featured the chamber plan of the national Capitol, arranged in a rectangle with a broad central hall containing a grand divided staircase leading to an office floor above. It had a one-story portico with a row of Doric columns *in antis*. It was a modern building, with some similarity to the central part of the New York City Hall, but detailed in the new Greek Revival manner. Commissioner King, of course, preferred the Boston version. He took the plan to the Governor in Council and it was "Resolved, that the plan prepared by Mr. Bulfinch as aforesaid, representing the Boston State House, reduced to the demensions aforesaid, be approved. . . ."[7]

Native granite from a nearby quarry was chosen as the building material, in the hope that its use for so major a building would encourage Americans to consider the Maine product—soon known as Hallowell granite—for monumental buildings elsewhere. Ironically it was King, involved in every facet of the design, who suggested patterning the stonework after rustication executed in plaster he had seen "when passing to the South last summer." King thought the imitation made "a very fine effect" when it was marked off "to represent stones of different coulers."[8] To reduce the building's height, he suggested the removal of the dome, a change to which Bulfinch responded with delight: "I have followed your suggestion, in omitting any large dome, but propose to place on the center of the attic, a copy of the Temple of Vesta at Rome. . . . It will give a covered cupola of 12' diameter & a walk within the surrounding colonnade."[9]

His proposal—a reproduction of an ancient model on top of a saucer dome—anticipated the Merchant's Exchange built in Philadelphia soon afterward by William Strickland, and the Tennessee Capitol at Nashville which Strickland built at the end of his life. Stephen Hills had already placed a colonnaded observatory beneath the dome of the Pennsylvania Capitol. With an uncharacteristic respect for the new and more correct Classical canons of the day, Bulfinch had eliminated the dominant hemispherical dome, a major motif he himself had introduced into state capitol design.

Bulfinch had not studied the Weston Hill site in Augusta before work began, but he had probably seen it in years past; the beautiful hill lying across a rich bottomland from the Kenne-

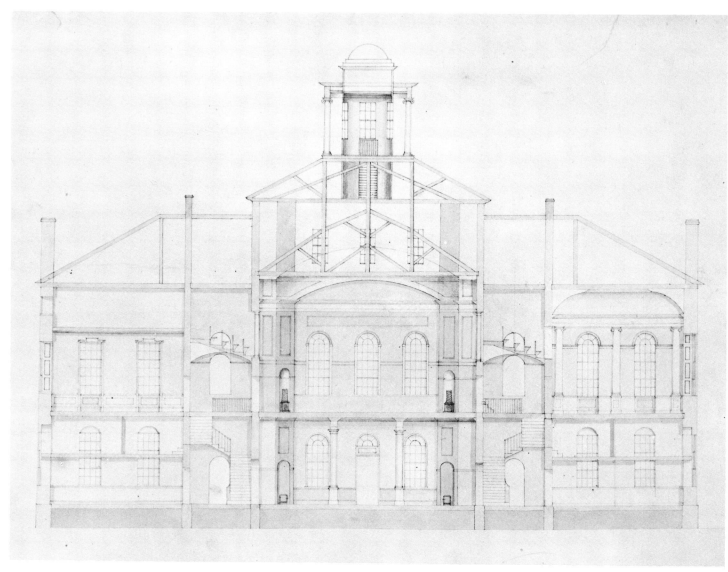

Maine Statehouse, section by Charles Bulfinch, 1827–28

bec River had often served as picnic grounds for visitors. In drawing the alternate plan, Bulfinch might well have realized that the arcaded first level of the Boston structure would be ineffectual on the steep summit of Weston Hill.

The work had progressed nearly to the roof when Bulfinch finally did visit the area. He became concerned that the treatment of the upper portions of the building was not adequate. The placement of the Capitol at the end of an *alleé* cut through a planted bottomland grove—creating America's first real capitol park—demanded more monumental verticality than the architect had originally specified. From the town only the second floor and the roof were visible.

From Thomas Moore, History of the State of Maine
Maine Statehouse, as completed in 1832

To the Governor and Council Bulfinch wrote: "The plan was designed with a platform over the East Colonnade & an Attic story and Cupola. Upon revising the plan, I take the liberty to suggest, that it would be more conformable to the simplicity of good models of Antique buildings, to crown the Colonnade with a pediment, & to terminate the building with a Dome of about fourteen feet elevation & a Cupola as first proposed."[10]

The officials not only accepted the change, but in the final outcome increased the pitch of the dome, giving it predominance in the composition. Construction moved rapidly, and for good reason: The citizens of Augusta were beginning to worry about the unfinished building, for richer cities were all too eager to take the capital away. As if to frustrate the building drive, a feud broke out between Governor King and the man who had replaced him as commissioner, an influential Hallowell lawyer named William Clark. Clark accused King of withholding some Bulfinch drawings needed for an alteration. King replied in the Kennebec *Journal:*

> I cannot consent to have my name associated with yours in the contemplated alteration, in any way whatever; for in my judgment the planning and decorating of buildings is the business of architecture—an art which obtained its highest improvement many years ago; and although professed and repeated attempts have been made to restore the orders of Architecture to their original purity in other countries, it is a fact, which from the remarks in your letter will be *news* to you, that we have very few Architects in this country—and no one to my knowledge who has any pretensions to it in this State. We have, to be sure, plenty of carpenters, stone-masons, and brick-layers, who would have about the same Architectural pretensions as the plasterers, cabinet-makers, and painters have.[11]

The granite continued to arrive on the Kennebec from the nearby Hallowell quarries, and the building was carried to completion by the devoted engineer, Joseph D. Emery. Ladies from Augusta sewed strips of carpet together, and made curtains for the windows, designing them in light sketches which still survive on Bulfinch's interior elevations. Augusta businessmen even borrowed $50,000 to ensure completion when funds ran low.

Those in power in Maine generally got what they wanted, although Bulfinch too had his way. It was the last of the architect's designs ever to be executed; he went back to Boston and lived out his days quietly in the house where he was born.

Maine's Capitol was a smaller Boston Statehouse, executed with Greek Revival detail but with the Roman Temple of Vesta perched on top of the dome. The use of local granite was an idea borrowed from New Hampshire and supported by the Council. The pale gray granite created a more monumental impression than Boston's red brick. Split into blocks at two quarries, Ballard's Ledge and Melvin's Ledge, both only a few miles from the site, the granite was cut under the supervision of Ephraim Ballard, master stonemason. Ballard stone was used where it could not be seen; the finish of the walls came from Haine's Quarry nearby; and master stone-cutter Samuel Melvin, Jr., used stone from Melvin's Ledge for the eight Greek Doric columns and the voussoirs of the arches. Maine pine was used for the woodwork inside. Bulfinch had specified the use of iron stoves in niches throughout the building; these were in various Classical shapes, such as obelisks and broken columns, their pipes threaded up through the walls to the roof.

Reuel Williams, the last commissioner, saw to the finishing of the Maine Statehouse from 1831 until 1832. He carried out the Bulfinch plan for terracing Weston Hill in ovals and enclosing it in an iron fence. On a direct axis with the center of Doric Hall, on the hill's edge, he built a compartmented "necessary house" for the convenience of tourists whom legislators believed would flock to the splendid new Capitol.

For reasons different from Maine's, the predominant Georgia Jacksonians decreed a total remodeling of the statehouse at Milledgeville. They had repeatedly tampered with the old three-part structure in the twenty years it had stood on its square in the middle of the town. Some rather pretentious houses now dotted the grid of dirt streets leading to Capital Square—wooden clapboards sheathing frames of Georgia pine, interiors elaborately carved—but even the best of them would have made a poor showing in Savannah.

Obviously the statehouse of Georgia was not to be an overblown imitation of these white-washed mansions, but rather a marked contrast. Even at that, the solution reached at Milledgeville was unexpected—indeed, at this time, unique. A traveler, passing through town after the work was done, gazed in dismay at the remodeled building: "I visited the State House. It is a brick building, which some blockhead of an architect has recently thought proper to *Gothicize*."[12] Still a second tourist said, "the Capitol or State House, seemed to us less perfect in a near view than at a distance; it being a large white Gothic structure, in bad taste and heavy proportions, though forming a very striking object in the remote picture of Milledgeville."[13]

The adoption of a Gothic design nearly always betrays the hand of an architect, but the designer of Georgia's Capitol is unknown. A possible candidate was state engineer Hamilton Fulton, an Englishman who had formerly worked as state engineer of North Carolina. It is even

74

Georgia State Archives

Georgia Capitol, Milledgeville, as Gothicized, 1827–30

more likely the proposer was one of several Georgia architects who purveyed a sketch for the remodeling to the local builder Charles C. Birch. Possibly some of the legislators, who were predominantly Masons, had seen the Masonic temples in New York City or Philadelphia, and inspired by those secular Gothic piles, had similar architectural ambitions for Milledgeville. In any event, the Masonic influence undoubtedly accounts for the legislature's unprecedented tolerance for the Gothic detailing.

The adoption of Gothic style proved a practical means of binding together a lanky build-

75

ing which had been constantly expanded since it was built early in the century. An old construction report, dated 1811 and lost for many years, lists among interior plasterwork embellishments "4 Hiptic arches."[14] If the reference was to broken or Gothic arches, the theme of the 1827–29 remodeling had its seeds in the earlier building.

While the remodeled Georgia Capitol did not resemble any American capitol before or since, it was only superficially Gothicized. Everything about it was symmetrical, with a large central block and side wings. To the front and rear of these low side wings had been appended taller towers, which were heavy but lower than the three-storied middle section. Crenelated parapets concealed complicated roofs and valleys. Along the entire second level of the central part were rows of pointed windows. It is likely that these upper levels were added in the renovations, for they housed the new legislative chambers and seem to have been more uniform in their design than the rest of the building. On the roof a great square cupola played the strongest visual role. Resplendent with traceried windows in its four faces, the cupola's clocks peered from round openings where one might have expected to find quatrefoils. A cheap coat of stucco, scored and painted, assimilated the diverse elements of the building's mass and obscured their history. Looming up among the Georgia pines, the Capitol was one of the real surprises of the American backwoods.

Six years after the Milledgeville Capitol was Gothicized—or re-Gothicized—an architect named John Lawrence, from Nashville, Tennessee, designed and actually started building a Gothic capitol at Jackson, Mississippi. Despite its original enthusiasm, the Mississippi legislature issued a protest as the high basement of Mississippi stone neared completion. A special committee demanded "the total and abrupt abandonment" of a plan "wholly unsuited" for a capitol. "The rooms intended for the Representative Hall and Senate Chamber, are in violation of all taste, and of a most undignified appearance. . . . While the interior is so devoid of every essential requisite, there is nothing in the outer appearance of the building to elicit commendation; but on the contrary, presents an exterior as equally deficient in taste, as the inner apartments are in utility: the design bearing a more general resemblance to buildings usually constructed for churches, rather than the imposing and beautiful compositions of a Capitol." That was when Captain William Nichols arrived from Tuscaloosa with an alternate plan—a proven plan—of "simplicity, beauty, and strength."[15] The committee recommended its acceptance, and the legislature complied.

The scholarly introduction of ancient Greek forms into American architecture did not begin in a statehouse, but in a commercial structure. Latrobe's Bank of Pennsylvania, built in 1798–1800 at Philadelphia, is usually considered to have been the first Greek Revival monument in the United States, though the bank was by no means a Grecian temple nor was it intended to be a reproduction of any ancient model. Architects in Philadelphia and New York, and to a lesser degree Boston, were experimentally inclined at the time. They were intentionally constructing modern buildings—antique themes were accepted as inspiration, offering valuable guidelines, but not as models for copying.

It was with the general public that a real passion for reproducing Classical themes developed. The Jacksonians made the Greek Revival their emblem. At the hands of obscure car-

Mississippi Capitol, Jackson, by William Nichols, 1838,
as it appeared about 1890

penters and builders, it was Americanized in a homespun way, while the sophistication of the highest level of professional practitioners, rivaling that of European architects, created a modern mode of design only nominally Grecian. Even the most original architects, however, still had clients to please; as a result, the determined innovators could be counted on the fingers of one hand. As soon as the laymen legislators confronted the first Greek temple statehouse, they were so captivated by the style that further architectural experimentation almost ceased.

Jacksonians in the West built the first Greek temple capitol. It was designed by young Gideon Shryock for Frankfort, Kentucky. Workmen and materials were from the country beyond the Alleghenies, and its designer, Gideon Shryock, was a native Kentuckian. The son of a master builder, Shryock had been sent to Philadelphia at nineteen to serve a one-year apprenticeship under William Strickland, the leading light among the younger generation of American architects.

Strickland was also a builder's son. At one time a youthful Strickland had turned from architecture and had made his living in the New York theaters painting stage scenery. He returned to Philadelphia in 1818 where his striking Greek design for the Second Bank of the United States won a national competition. At thirty-one, he was able to capture the imagination of the young Shryock, who knew nothing of art; Strickland was sensitive about the professional standing of architects in America and took a particular interest in his apprentices, showing attention and courtesies to them that he quite often did not accord his clients.

In 1824 the Kentucky Statehouse at Frankfort burned to the ground, leaving its two flanking buildings intact. The central structure had looked like a church—a rectangle with a portico on one end, and a steeple. An observer said that it resembled a "large Court House," with rich carpets upon which the members "continually spit and squirt tobacco juice . . . a loathsome habit, which they think nothing of."[16] It had replaced an eighteenth-century limestone state-

77

house, which had also burned. Both capitols had had substantial vertical dimensions, because the town was situated in a deep valley and was first seen from a range of hills in the surrounding forest—the direct reverse of the usual hilltop location for capitols.

After the burning of the second Capitol, the movement to build again was stunted by a predictable effort to relocate the seat of government. The battle heightened when the seminary, to which the legislature had temporarily moved, also burned down. Finally, in January 1827, the capitol reconstruction bill passed, and the local newspaper, *The Argus of Western America*, reported, "property holders have remained in a painful suspense. They now feel relieved. . . . To testify their gratitude and joy, the citizens of this place propose to give a Ball to the members of the Legislature on tomorrow evening."[17]

An issue of the *Argus* later in the month announced that in February the commission for rebuilding the statehouse would consider plans for a new capitol which must be roughly the size and shape of the old building, in order to fit properly between the surviving flankers. "Persons presenting plans are expected also to present estimates of the costs, and details of workmanship and materials. A premium of ONE HUNDRED AND FIFTY DOLLARS will be allowed for the plan which shall be adopted."[18] Encouraged by his father and friends, Shryock entered the competition and won. By spring he had moved to Frankfort from his father's house in Lexington, a three-hour stage trip to the southeast.

One sheet of drawings has survived, a neat, precise elevation of the principal façade, the very sort of draftsmanship one would expect of a pupil of the exacting Strickland. Kentucky's statehouse was to follow the Greek temple model or, more immediately, to be something on the order of the Ionic-columned Eagle Bank at New Haven, Connecticut, designed in 1824 by the architect Ithiel Town but abandoned unfinished when the bank failed. Bank, state capitol, or school—the Greek temple image was thought to suit nearly any use.

One particular feature of Shryock's elevation, however, hints that the architect's educated Grecian taste conflicted with the legislative commission's prior notions about statehouses. Mounted on a platform atop the pedimented temple roof in the Capitol drawing is a tall, domed lantern, its wall broken only by eight small sash windows. Had the commissioners insisted upon adding this rude feature so alien to the Classic temple norm, as the Virginians had attempted to do with their belfry in Richmond?

Landmark of the valley for thirty-five years had been a roof ornament of one kind or another—first an arcaded cupola, then a steeple. Just who proposed the lantern to Shryock, or whether it was his own idea, is not recorded. In any case, what was eventually built did not match the Shryock design. The architect reduced the lantern to a much smaller element, and in its final form it became a nearly separate entity: a domed ring of attached columns, not unlike Bulfinch's slightly later one at Augusta, fully glazed so as to appear open. To horsemen descending the pike into Frankfort, it looked like a little temple emerging out of the treetops; from the town's streets today, it still requires an effort to see the lantern at all.

Kentucky's Capitol was erected in two years. Labor was furnished by inmates of the penitentiary as a part of the state's internal improvements program and admirable prison reforms. The use of inmates for construction had become an accepted solution to the labor shortage. Joel

Scott, the superintendent, was permitted to conduct a liberal program of teaching trades to the prisoners, most of whom were confined for only one or two years. During the building period, the total number of state prisoners varied from eighty-seven to one hundred, of whom Gideon Shryock was allowed to employ only thirty to fifty. Several prisoners were listed as stonecutters, at least one as a carpenter, and the rest as boatmen, sailors, farmers, thieves, swindlers, and sharks. A gentlemen's agreement was made with the Capitol Rebuilding Commission instead of a contract, and all wages paid the convicts went to the penitentiary's account.

Scott played a major part in the construction. An inventive and dedicated man, he continually pressed the legislature for additional facilities from the prison, purchased and personally improved a machine to simplify stonecutting, and even as the Capitol stone was being quarried, he began work on a modern penitentiary building.

The materials were largely local. An exception was the small amount of sandstone ordered from Abner Wickersham's Pennsylvania quarry, which had supplied Stephen Hills in Harrisburg as well. A Frankfort builder named Harrison Blanton provided the rough marble from his ledge on the Kentucky River. Great hunks of marble were hauled to the penitentiary, where they were cut by Scott's marvelous device. The machine was the fascination of the countryside: "It is of his own invention," wrote one observer, "and consists of sixteen saws carried by steam. He has a large shaft, which is made to turn partly round, to and fro, having eight arms extending out on the lower side, each of which, on every motion of the shaft, is made to push one saw and pull another. The saws work horizontally. In this manner he works out marble with a rapidity hitherto unknown. . . ."[19]

After the rough cutting by machine, the shaping and polishing of the individual building blocks was done by hand. Then, in wagons hired in town, the blocks were brought·to the Capitol site. Stakes and strings plotted the dimensions of each exterior façade on the ground; under the close watch of the architect the finished stones were placed where they would ultimately lie in the wall. Before the stones were again stacked in piles, they were numbered and a key elevation was drawn. A brick structure formed the backing for the stone walls; the interior partitions were also of brick.

The legislature first assembled in the building December 7, 1829, before the columns were carved for the portico. That month, the chairman of the Capitol Rebuilding Commission announced: "I have . . . an unexpended balance . . . amounting to the sum of seven thousand and two dollars, fifty three cents in Commonwealth's Bank notes. . . . This sum will be nearly, if not entirely, absorbed in the completion of the Portico and plastering of the building."[20]

The Capitol was finished in 1830. Shryock made his reputation with that one structure, and despite all the buildings he later designed in his distinguished career, the Kentucky Capitol remained the most celebrated. His part in the actual construction is vague, but he seems to have made all the decisions concerning the design, for the surviving elevation was followed very closely except for the lantern. The Capitol represented advanced taste in the late 1820's, as well as an eye for what was going on in building elsewhere in America. The central staircase, for example, could have been a simplified version of what Shryock had read about or even seen in the New York City Hall or in Strickland's Harrisburg project.

Three years after the Kentucky Capitol's completion, the architect wrote a description for the Philadelphia magazine *Atkinson's Casket: Gems of Literature Wit & Sentiment:*

> The front elevation of the building presents a hexastyle Portico, of the Ionic order, the proportions of which are taken from the Temple of Minerva Polias, at Priene in Ionia. The exterior walls present a smooth surface of polished marble of a light grey colour. . . . The Portico is built of a darker grey marble. The columns are four feet in diameter and thirty-three feet in height, supporting a marble pediment and entablature which is continued entirely around the building . . . from the middle [of the roof] rises the cupola, the basement of which is formed by a square pedestal of twenty-five feet on each side; which rises two feet above the apex of the roof; and on which is placed a circular lantern, twenty-two feet in diameter and twenty feet high, surmounted by a hemispherical dome.[21]

Beyond the main doorway, the single opening in the main façade, a large dark hall at once established the monumentality of the building's interior. A combination of thick walls, heavy wooden doors, angular views into distant rooms, with deep doorways and window recesses, gave the desired effect of a solemn ancient place. Henry Mordecai, a black man, had executed all the plasterwork in the building; in the main hall he used the greatest restraint in order to increase the effect of tomblike massiveness. (It was to this hall a pair of crumbling coffins containing the bodies of Daniel Boone and his wife was smuggled from Missouri one night some ten years later. The Reverend Philip Slater Fall lifted into the candlelight the skull of Squire Boone; before dawn he made a plaster cast of the skull for posterity, then in a great public ceremony helped Kentucky politicians consign the original to the earth. Missouri protested the grave robbery, but soon produced another set of bones.)

A transverse hall terminated the main hall; Shryock described the point at which they met:

> . . . the stairway, which is of marble and is enclosed by a circular wall, having an entrance in front and on either side, and . . . lighted from the Cupola above by twelve large windows. The ascent is by a straight flight of steps to a large plat-form about five feet high; from each end of which there is a circular flight, which traverses the circular wall and meets in a platform at the top. The stairway leads to a lobby [on the second floor] thirty-five feet square, having a well-hole of the stairs (which is enclosed by an iron railing) in the centre . . . this part of the building is arched with a spandrel dome, the angular squares are filled with pendentives, terminating in a circular ring, on which a cylindrical wall is built, supporting the cupola. The interior of the dome is finished with raised pannels and ornamented in stucco, superbly executed; and produces that pleasing magic effect usual with a vast concave in such a situation.[22]

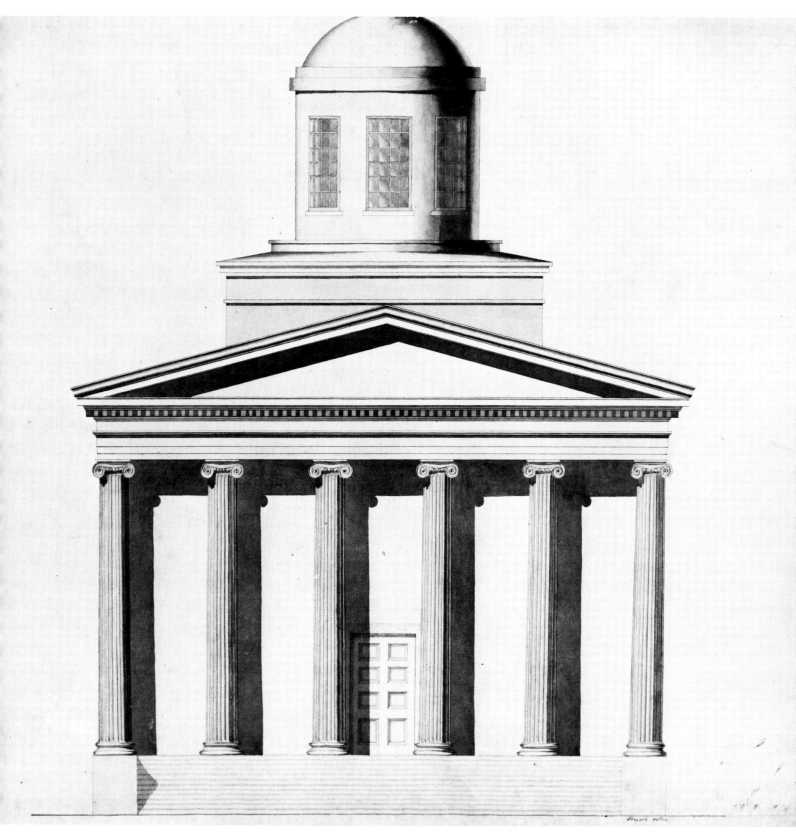

Old State Capitol Restoration

Kentucky Capitol, elevation by Gideon Shryock, c. 1827

The Senate chamber was located on the front of the building and the House on the rear. Convicts made the carpets for both chambers. Courtrooms and committee rooms were downstairs. Bluegrass soon covered the grounds, making a pretty sea on which the three separate buildings lived in harmony.

Between the two existing rectangular flankers, the Greek Revival had made its debut in American statehouse architecture. The subtle grandeur the new Kentucky Capitol gave to the plain little town helps explain why the revival was a national success. The *Argus* had written, even as the walls were taking shape: "We anticipate that this building, when completed, will be one of the most beautiful in America, and erected at less expense than any other similar structure on the continent."[23]

For public architecture, Greek temples had two particularly desirable qualities—they were splendid to look upon, and they could be built to suit nearly any budget. In the temple style, form was the principal issue; yet it was a simple form and, given due respect, it allowed for adaptation and even the addition of familiar elements. Jefferson's Virginia Capitol had demonstrated the point, and certainly the plan of the New World Maison Carrée had suggested that of the beloved old Capitol at Williamsburg. Now Gideon Shryock built a Grecian temple at Frankfort which was as traditional as it was modern. With the flexibility of a country carpenter, he had incorporated into the Classical form the architectural symbols of American democracy. The portico, faithfully following a supposed model from ancient Greece, was brought here into a composition with rotunda, balanced external wings, and dome—all revised and subdued to the predominant temple form, but present nevertheless, announcing in Kentucky marble that *architectural symbolism need not preclude change.*

The Kentucky Statehouse was well under way when another temple capitol was begun at New Haven, Connecticut. Its architect, Ithiel Town, a part-time resident of that notoriously radical little city, was an astute Yankee businessman, inventor of the celebrated Town Truss, and thereby instigator of a small American revolution in bridge-building. The Age of Jackson is perhaps most vividly personified in Ithiel Town. His own wits made him a rich man, and he was unhesitating, if not unscrupulous, in his efforts to become richer. He traveled all over the United States marketing his patented wooden truss. The extent of his business involvements may never be known. New York, Boston, and Philadelphia were major arenas for his enterprises; and he owned stock in toll-bridge companies as far south as the Carolinas. He was Connecticut's foremost architect, if a surprisingly feeble draftsman: He could hire others to develop his ideas on paper; his forte was in making the sale.

New Haven, the state's alternate capital, was only a short stage ride from Hartford, through rolling farmland. Competition with Hartford was soft-spoken but keen. The cupola on the Hartford Statehouse had only lately been added, a jewel-like miniature of that on the New York City Hall, and a warning that Hartford residents had ambitions to make their city the sole capital.

Legislators complained about the seedy colonial statehouse on the New Haven Green. A cheap wing had been added by the town many years before; rain now ran down the walls inside, and the chambers were impossible to heat. The plain brick rectangle was not big enough, nor

Kentucky Capitol, staircase as completed by Gideon Shryock about 1830
Library of Congress

was it any longer structurally safe. Local citizens began to worry about losing the capital to Hartford. A report written in 1826 urged that either a new statehouse be built or work be done on the old one. By October of the following year, the city and state had agreed to build a structure to house both state and municipal functions.

Town presented his plans to the committee in the autumn of 1827. When they were exhibited at the Tontine Building, a controversy began over the location; Town had been so thoughtless as to propose to site his building on an old cemetery. "Shall we," wrote a "relative" to the New Haven *Register*, "continue to have the solemn services of religion, the processions of mourners, pall-bearers and friends, and the tolling of bells at our funerals, and yet withhold our protection of the ground, where the remains are deposited?"[24] It was at last agreed that the site be used but that shallow foundations be laid.

As to the design, there was no recorded objection. It was a scholarly rendering of a pedimented, rectangular Doric temple with porticoes on both ends. The long dimension was to be 160 feet, counting the twenty-five-foot depth of each portico, while the width of ninety feet made the building only a little less than one-third again as large as the Kentucky Capitol. The building committee explained the design to the legislature by saying that it was "proper and necessary to exhibit in our edifices the plain simplicity of our republican institutions." At the same time, "some little regard should be paid to that style of building which prefers proportion to ornament, and in which neither should entirely be overlooked." And while the committee avoided "all extravagance," it pledged itself to build "such a building as would do no discredit to the State of Connecticut, nor the age in which we live."[25]

Town did a fine job in designing an honest modern version of a Greek temple. To his practical eye, the simplicity of the model provided an excellent opportunity to cut building costs. Cupolas, lanterns, and wings were to be omitted, he argued, for the persuasive reason that they were historically inappropriate as well as expensive. That satisfied an intellectual community like New Haven; doubtless it would have carried less weight in Frankfort. For Town it served an immediate purpose; later he would prove willing to yield his scholarly principles as circumstances dictated.

The New Haven temple cost less than half what Shryock's Kentucky Capitol had cost—a total, in fact, of $42,500, including a number of embellishments added by the legislature: a domed ceiling for the rotunda, some plaster cornices in the chambers, and a good deal of Sing Sing marble.

Town had realized that the Greek temple model, even stripped to the bare essentials, could look costly with only a modest investment. His practicalities did not necessarily mean poor construction; he was using the techniques by now known to every master builder. The New Haven Statehouse was cheaply built of rough stone up to the level of the roof which was, of course, wooden and probably framed with the Town trusses. Stucco mixed with stone chips covered all but the wooden parts of the exterior and was scored to simulate ashlar. This was painted a base color matching the woodwork, then stippled black and gray in imitation of granite.

In plan there was the obvious arrangement common to both the Virginia and New York capitols. The two chambers were set front and back and had round skylights; the low central

New Haven Colony Historical Society
Connecticut Statehouse, New Haven, by Ithiel Town,
completed 1833, as it appeared c. 1870

rotunda was covered by a sort of flattened dome not visible externally. Plaster was packed between the floor joists for insulation, and ornamented iron stoves were used for heat. The interiors were decorated by local painters with marbling and graining—familiar technical tricks that could turn a plain room into something that looked positively grand.

While the New Haven Statehouse was being built, Town initiated what became a permanent partnership with a young New York architect, Alexander Jackson Davis. Davis drew some of the details for the later stages of the statehouse construction, and may have even planned and supervised execution of the monumental Doric colonnades. Soon after the partnership was

85

formed, Town left for Europe; he toured English villages, and in France he looked at such monuments as the Maison Carrée, making special note of its connection to Jefferson's Virginia Capitol.

Meanwhile his New Haven builder, striving to stay within the budget, began using inadequate timbers for joists and rafters. The whole roof was finished cheaply, and by the time Town returned from his trip, the legislators were grumbling. A subcommittee appointed to investigate Town's work demanded and received cash compensation from the architect.

The New Haven Green was a curious site for a Greek temple. Yet the completed statehouse, in its place on the Green, became one of the most popular sights in nineteenth-century New England. The Green had been split in half shortly before the Revolution by the continuation of Temple Street. This left one part of the Green an open meadow with trees and the town well. On the other half of the Green four churches lined up parallel to one another, with the new statehouse turned crosswise to them, its side along Temple Street. The buildings of Yale College faced the other side of the statehouse across College Street. It was a site chosen for convenience and practicality, so that the building would enhance rather than compete with the churches already there: ". . . in the centre of the whole and on a line with neither," explained the committee.[26] Just the right ingredient was added to the Green by the classic pile.

"Let the stranger visit New Haven," wrote a magazine of the day, "when the fields and the forest have newly put on their green attire. . . . "[27] Elm trees lined the streets leading to the Green, screening the whole, yet allowing views of certain parts. The statehouse was fully revealed only from the vacant half of the Green. The great porticoes at the ends, the extended walls of imitation ashlar on the sides—historically accurate in the absence of antae—the broad flights of white marble steps leading up to the immense fluted columns, all gave the temple a kind of monumentality until then unknown in American statehouses. Town and Davis rather ambiguously described the building as based upon both the Jupiter Temple at Agrigento and the Haephesteion at Athens. No matter, one was literally gripped by its grandeur. In bright sunlight it cast angular shadows; it glowed in the light of early day, and a little less at dusk when the sheep and cows were being driven home through the elm groves.

Ithiel Town recognized he had a good product, and he sensed the time to market it had come. His travels in connection with the Town Truss already took him all over the United States and to many state capitals. With Davis on call in New York to draw designs, Town could devote all his time to sales.

He won his first new contract in Indiana early in the summer of 1832. The capitol commissioners in Indianapolis used the newspapers to publicize the basic rules for a capitol competition; no mention was made of architectural style, but estimates of local prices were supplied: "Stone is furnished in the wall on bridges on the National Road in this vicinity, at $7.50 cts. per perch, or 25 cubic feet. Best brick estimated at $6.50 per thousand in the wall. Lumber, from $4 to $4.50 per hundred feet. Carpenters and bricklayers, at $1.25 to $1.50 per day. Laborers, $10 per month. Boarding from $1.25 to $2.00 per week."[28]

Indiana's government had met in many places, from Territorial Governor William Henry Harrison's own parlor at Vincennes to the square-belfried courthouse-capitol in Corydon, completed in 1816. Indianapolis was a new capital laid out in the geographical center of Indiana. The town had had a hard time of it until the early 1830's; even then, the one or two rows of prosperous supply stores did not mask the village's frontier rawness.

Popular vote had been close in the Presidential election of 1828, but Jackson had carried all five of Indiana's electoral votes. The time was ripe to build a new capitol of thoroughly civilized design for the state of Indiana. Work began on the Town & Davis design in November. Jeremiah Day graded the site, hauling fill from his own cellar. At the time the commissioners paid for that task, they approved some quantities of stone and brick which had been brought to the site. The building ultimately cost $60,000. Portions of the stone came from I. Town & Company, a side operation Town doubtless put together in a hurry while he was in Indiana.

Nothing is documented concerning the negotiations leading to the approval of the Town & Davis design, but Town claimed and received the $150 premium. Davis was never officially mentioned in connection with this or any other of their state capitols, though his Day Book for October 1831 shows that he drew three sheets of designs which Town delivered personally in Indianapolis in December. It was Town, however, who was most willing to compromise his marketable temple; nearly a half-century later Davis wrote an apologetic defense of their departures from Greek models.

The yellowed pages of the final agreement at first seem to offer little that was different from the New Haven Capitol. One exception was a richer interior. Here, along the sides, pilaster-like *antae* were introduced—a sacrifice of Grecian correctness—to minimize the alien presence of the two rows of windows. Town's directions are exceptionally detailed:

> The columns as drawn are to be constructed of bricks laid so as to form their flutes in a suitable manner to receive the rough casting. . . . The columns, antae, brick walls, entablatured ceilings of the porticoes and outside of the Rotunda [drum of the dome] with its Antae are all to be Rough Cast with the best lime and cement . . . the Rough cast to be made true and regular on its surface free from unevenness in the surfaces and angles . . . the whole surface is to appear as when left by the float and straight edge. All the ornaments about the outside are to be formed with bricks and mortar and to correspond in character with the Doric Order of the Parthenon at Athens. All parts of the Rough casting are to have lines representing *joints* after the appearance of marble or light colored free-stone-Masonry: to which end the surface is to be stained with mineral colors so as to give different shades to different apparent blocks of Stone and a grain or stratification appearance to others in such a manner as to imitate the characteristic natural colors of stone work from the same or similar quarries.[29]

In the Indiana Capitol the great exception to the temple model was the prominent ribbed dome that capped the central rotunda. Whether this was in the original design drawn by Davis, or whether Town added the dome at the commission's request, is information typically unrecorded in the dealings between Town and his clients. When a transaction went smoothly, Town

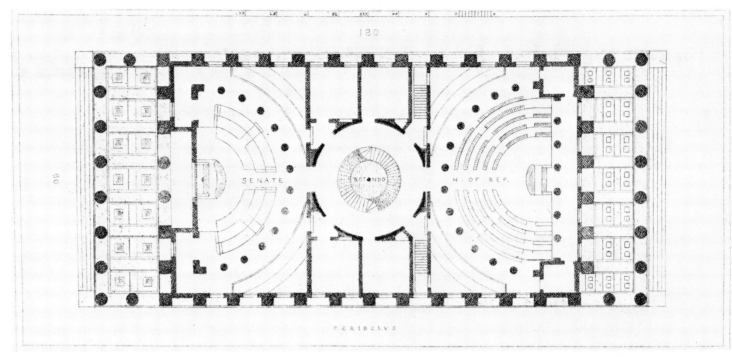

Indiana Capitol, Town & Davis's principal or second-floor plan,
as drawn and published by Davis, 1834

ordinarily kept no record beyond the minimum of terse legal documents. It is unfortunate, particularly in the case of the Indiana Capitol, that at least some opinion about the source of the dome does not survive. The addition of the vertical element here amplified the temple model even more influentially than Shryock's domed lantern at Frankfort.

Long before the Indiana Capitol was completed late in 1835. Ithiel Town was selling his temples elsewhere. A plan for a sumptuous version of the Indiana building was accepted by the federal government for its customhouse in New York City. The papers were signed in 1833, but the unchaste dome was removed from the plans for both structural and stylistic reasons, leaving the rotunda and a skylight.

Involved in a toll-bridge business in North Carolina, Town sought out and won still another capitol contract. At Raleigh, on June 21, 1831, a workman soldering the zinc roof of the state-house was careless with a burning coal. Perhaps Town, on the road, read the local *Gazette* two days later: "It is our painful and melancholy duty to announce to the public . . . the total destruction of the Capitol of the State. . . . Of that noble edifice, with its splendid decorations, nothing now remains but the blackened walls and smouldering ruins . . . and the statue of Washington, that proud monument of national gratitude which was our pride and glory, is so mutilated and defaced that none can behold it without mournful feelings."[30]

The Governor's capitol bill failed on the first try because of an effort to move the seat of government. That debate grew out of the larger economic problem common to all the older Southern states since the War of 1812. Freed from the danger of foreign invasion, the Mississippi River boomed almost before the smoke of the Tennessee muskets had cleared on the field of Chalmette. New Orleans became the economic heart of the new states, with a vigorous market from river commerce sprawling as far as western Pennsylvania. Agricultural products from the newly accessible lands poured through New Orleans and Mobile, thence to the powerful money centers of the East Coast and Europe.

88   This caused increasing financial anguish in both Carolinas. Thousands of their citizens

Indiana Capitol, by Town & Davis, as it appeared in 1871

migrated to the new states and territories, and their congressmen and senators in Washington struggled to hold what in a smaller nation had been considerable power. From the prewar nationalism that had characterized the Carolinas in prosperity, politicians turned in despair to protect the local interests of their states: American nationalism now turned into a fever of regionalism. In 1832, at the South Carolina Statehouse in Columbia, the Nullification Convention declared void the Federal Tariff acts of 1828 and 1832. Andrew Jackson vowed to hang the nullifiers from their own trees. Georgia offered its Gothic Capitol for a Southern convention. Vice-President John C. Calhoun resigned, went home to South Carolina a hero, and was soon returned to the United States Senate. During the crisis South Carolina had unsuccessfully appealed to other Southern states for help, but the event stirred every legislature in the Atlantic South.

The capitol reconstruction debates in North Carolina became a minor aspect of the nullification controversy when the opponents of rebuilding at Raleigh threatened to call a state convention, which everyone knew would mean a new constitution. Those favoring Raleigh hurried to a builder, probably William Nichols, Sr., or his son. "From an estimate I hold in my hand," a speaker told the legislature, "eminating from a source entitled, with me, to the highest confidence, I feel justified in saying that the capitol can be rebuilt, with all its original beauty and grandeur, for the sum of $42,500. Are gentlemen disposed to doubt? Let them do so no longer. . . ."[31] When the bill finally passed in 1832—the year of the Southern Nullification Convention—a ball was held by the joyous city fathers of Raleigh. The hall was decorated with a six-foot square "view of the proposed new capitol, over which floated a majestic Eagle, bearing this inscription in his bill—'The Legislature of 1832.' "[32]

William Nichols, Jr., was hired by the Capitol Commission to determine "a plan and outline of the building." The plan he drew seems to have duplicated what had burned: For his services "as architect, and furnishing drafts, ec." he was paid $350.[33]

Exactly when Ithiel Town replaced Nichols is not known, though he comes to mind immediately on reading the Raleigh orator's $42,500 construction estimate—a figure suspiciously close to the cost of the work at New Haven. Town first appears in the North Carolina records in August of 1833. But earlier drawings by Davis and events in Raleigh make it clear that the firm was planning one of its temple capitols for North Carolina well before that. It is probable that some of these temple sketches were circulated during the autumn session in Raleigh, so it was with good reason the legislature passed the act of December 1832, specifying that the new Capitol be built in the form of the old: There had obviously been some threat to the beloved cruciform structure. If law had thwarted the work of Ithiel Town the artist, Ithiel Town the businessman came through unscarred. The following spring he was appointed official architect of the North Carolina Capitol, and his partner set himself to adapting the Parthenon model to Nichols's cruciform plan.

Construction went on until 1840. The master builder William S. Drummond, apparently a friend of Town, moved temporarily from Washington, D.C., to supervise the project. Stonecutters were hired in New York and Philadelphia to prepare the hard, smoke-colored granite from a quarry near Raleigh; the Experimental Railroad was built by a highly political Raleigh corporation to transport the granite to the site. Each railroad car, down to its metal tires and its

North Carolina Capitol, by Town & Davis, as drawn in 1833 by A. J. Davis, who penciled in portico revisions a half-century later
Metropolitan Museum of Art, The Harris Brisbane Dick Fund

THE CAPITOL OF N.C.

VIEW DRAWN BY A.J.DAVIS

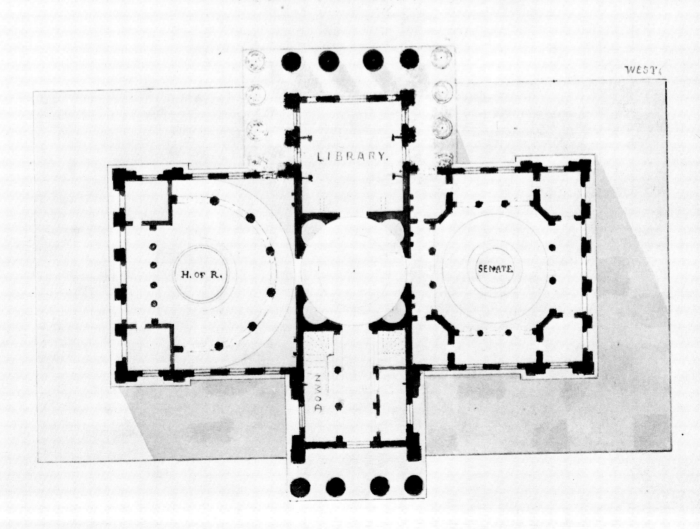

team of horses, was the responsibility of a teamster. The common laborers were mostly slaves until the eastern workmen protested and threatened to go home. A kitchen built at the quarry served three meals a day for the Yankee workers; apparently local boardinghouses were unable to offer them acceptable food.

The stonecutters did not like the Southern schedule of dawn to dusk. Drummond, who was probably accustomed to working slaves, refused to listen. Pressures intensified, and the politicians made the most of the controversy. Soon the commission fired Drummond and turned the project over to David Paton, a young Scot whom Town found for them in New York.

The walls were by that time nearly up to the eaves. Paton, who had spent most of a year as a draftsman for Sir John Soane in London, worked mainly on the interior and the dome. When the Town & Davis contract was dissolved in 1835, he was retained, but William Strickland was engaged as a design consultant and was also to pass on contracts and purchases made by the state in the eastern cities. Virtually no manufactures or skills were available in North Carolina— a telling commentary on what had happened in most of the South since the Panic of 1819 and the subsequent crash of Southern industry.

Strickland's part in finishing the North Carolina Capitol cannot be precisely determined; he had never journeyed to Raleigh. Some interior features are strikingly similar to those in other Strickland buildings; he would have been pleased with the monumental stone vaults of the ground floor and the lighter granite construction of those above. David Paton repeatedly sent drawings to his Philadelphia office for suggestions—most describing Greek details, carved first in oak as models for execution in plaster and iron—but it is equally difficult to attribute specific completed features to him.

The new dome was once fully visible from most parts of Raleigh; today, the Capitol's real magnificence is not evident until one is near enough to appreciate the granite ashlar of the massive walls. The front faces a secondary axis of the city. The ends, however, are articulated with overlapping antae at the corners, presenting one of the most distinguished and original aspects of Greek Revival design and recalling the pilastrades of Carl Friedrich Schinkel in Germany.

State governments—and their Capitols—had increased in size with the new Jacksonian democracy. In keeping with this trend, the new Raleigh Capitol was much larger than its predecessor. Still, the interior gave a feeling of compression rather than of vastness. Rows of simple offices lay behind oak-grained doors, with hinges pivoted directly in the granite thresholds and lintels. The ceremonial parts of the interior used the special order of the Temple of the Winds at Athens, which to modern eyes appears non-Grecian. This reached a dramatic climax in the chamber of the House of Commons, where the columns of the order suddenly seem of heroic size. Here they formed a grand semicircular screen, the arms of which curved to join a similar straight screen behind the Speaker, thus enclosing the chamber floor much as Nichols had done earlier in imitation of Latrobe. By contrast, in the Gothic treatment of the courtroom and library behind the porticoes graining in imitation of light oak was employed. This provided an aura of Romantic meditation which reflected somewhat timidly the advanced taste of Davis's mansions along the Hudson River.

The North Carolina Capitol was the third completed by Town & Davis, but is the only one to survive. With a freedom no struggling individual architect could have enjoyed, business-man Town continued to pursue other capitol commissions in the competitions of the 1830's. Though he did not receive any more capitol assignments, his particular talent won abundant architectural commissions of other kinds, even in hard times.

Town was not the first to introduce the Greek Revival into statehouse architecture, but its rapid spread was largely the result of a universal admiration for what he did build. Town can be considered a professional; significantly, he was one with a New York office that handled building projects throughout the nation. His pioneering career forecast the future of the architectural profession in America. Davis outlived Town and his own generation by many decades. Recognized as one of the leading architects of the United States, he nevertheless spent his last thirty years in obscurity. In the shadows of the Gilded Age he penciled changes that can still be seen on capitol schemes he and Town had devised so long before.

Practicing architects outnumbered master builders in designing capitols for the Jacksonians. Any rising profession has its Latrobes and Stricklands, but it may sometimes be better served by its Ithiel Towns. For the architectural profession, Town led the way. Dealing man-to-man with capitol commissions composed of farmers and lawyers, he taught them the advantages of employing experienced practitioners.

An advantage the Jacksonian architects enjoyed over their foreign-born predecessors such as L'Enfant and Latrobe was that they understood their fellow Americans and accepted them for what they were. The wisest architects recognized both the freedom possible with a client who had no architectural knowledge and the inhibitions a little knowledge could impose. They learned that historical accuracy in a building's features strengthened an architect's case, especially with pretentious clients, while sophisticated nuances only confused and disturbed. Jefferson had realized this when he described his proposed Virginia Capitol not as an original design but as an actual copy of a Roman temple.

After New Haven's Statehouse on the Green, the only other real temple capitol was that built at Little Rock, Arkansas Territory. It was based on a design by Gideon Shryock, but is known to have been modified locally in a practical manner of which Ithiel Town himself would have approved.

Funds came primarily from the sale of the Federal Land Donations. Considerable political power in the territory was in the hands of former Kentucky politicians; one of them, Governor John Pope, whose former home in Lexington had been designed by Latrobe, invited Shryock to Little Rock to build the Territorial Assembly Building, as the Statehouse was first called. The site overlooking the Arkansas River was not selected until 1833 because the legislature, controlled by land speculators, fought bitterly over the disposition of the federal land grant. Shryock, too busy in Kentucky to travel to Arkansas, recommended George Weigart of Lexington as architect and superintendent. Weigart, his wife, and two children moved to Little Rock in the winter of 1833.

The rough hamlet of Little Rock provided few of the facilities necessary for a major building project. A temporary population of drovers, Indians, slavers, and immigrant travelers outnumbered the more stable citizenry; and even the most successful lived in plain little houses. Governor Pope, when one visitor called, was absent in pursuit of a hog. It soon became evident

93

that any materials which could not be made locally would have to come from New Orleans and Cincinnati by way of the river.

Pope and Weigart set to work altering Shryock's design as freely as Pope had once altered Latrobe's. With all the early drawings now lost, there is no way of determining the exact extent of their changes. The only similarities between the Arkansas building finished in 1840 and the Kentucky Capitol were the pediments and the three blocks which, in the case of Arkansas, were linked by connecting colonnades. Weigart employed carpenters and bricklayers from Lexington, and work began in the spring of 1833.

Political furor erupted by summer. Governor Pope's principal enemy was Robert Crittenden, another emigrant from Kentucky. As an alternative to building a statehouse, he offered his brick dwelling in Little Rock in exchange for the ten sections of land granted by the federal government. A bill to that effect was vetoed by Pope.

In July 1833 Crittenden announced in his supporting newspaper, the *Advocate*, that Pope had spent all the statehouse money—thus far some $25,000—and construction had only barely begun. Weigart answered:

> The progress of the building alluded to has not stopped for want of funds . . . it has not gone on with that mushroom growth that some individuals might expect it should have done; but that the work is going on any man may see by viewing the premises. The foundation for the main building is laid, except that on which the columns for the porticoes are to stand; also, the foundation for the Court-house—The brick work would have been in progress ere now, but for the late high waters, and other causes beyond the control of man. . . . This brief reply, I hope, will be amply sufficient to satisfy the minds of an unbiased public.[34]

Pope's newspaper wrote of the Crittenden followers that "the whole pack of them" were "Cut-Throat Bandits."

Weigart usually worked forty men on the site. Sometimes as many as half were slave laborers, since free men in the West were preoccupied with obtaining land for agriculture. The slaves were field hands whom Weigart trained to carry brick and limestone, to steady framing timbers as the pins were driven, and to serve in countless minor ways on the job. A brick kiln was built on the site; Weigart turned it into a moneymaking operation and earned respect as a businessman he had not received as an architect.

The statehouse was Governor Pope's personal hobby; as his salty *Arkansas Gazette* put it, the project was "under the direction of the Governor."[35] George Weigart died in the summer of 1834, leaving the Governor and Lexington builders Thomas Thorn and Steven Cotter with a rectangle and unfinished walls, open to the sky. More workers were hired. Additional federal land was requested and received.

At the conclusion of Pope's second term, in 1835, in the heat of another bitter controversy, the Governor packed his trunks and moved back to Kentucky. Believing that the Arkansas legislature would honor its debts, Thorn continued the statehouse work and made a request for

Arkansas State Capitol, 1840, as it appeared about 1885–90

payment. The committee investigating the plea found that Pope had taken the building records with him. An agent dispatched to Lexington was permitted by Pope to copy certain documents. Thorn got his money, and in 1836 the legislature of the new state of Arkansas met and inaugurated its first governor in the unfinished building.

The four subsequent years it took to complete the statehouse were terrible times in Arkansas. State money was deposited in doomed banks; speculators foreclosed on the farms of settlers; cholera broke out again and again in the villages on the frontiers. The smallest issues could breed fury in the legislative halls of the new Capitol.

On December 4, 1837, the Senate sent to the House the Wolf Bill, which would allow a bounty for wolf scalps, payable by justices of the peace from state funds. This was "assailed by all sorts of ridicule," which soon enough drifted to the subject of a recent act chartering the Real Estate Bank. To an age paying the bitter price of Jacksonian easy money, such a land-funded institution had distinctly unpleasant overtones. In that particular Arkansas wildcat bank the Speaker of the House, Colonel John Wilson, was one of the principal stockholders. When brash young Major J. J. Anthony denounced the Real Estate Bank on the House floor, Speaker Wilson demanded to know if the legislator's remarks were meant to be personal. Ignored, Wilson ordered Anthony to sit down. Ignored once more, the Speaker drew a bowie knife from his shirt and cried "Sit down, or I'll make you." Slowly the Speaker began to advance toward Major Anthony, who stepped back and drew his own blade. Chairs became shields, and space was made for the brawl. Wilson suffered two slashes on his arms before Anthony fumbled his knife. Leaping forward, Wilson ripped open the major's shirt and plunged his knife "up to the hilt in his heart." Wilson pulled his knife free, and wiped the blood away "with his thumb and finger."[36]

The Arkansas temple of democracy was on the steep west bank of the Arkansas River. To boatmen, who for weeks had watched the lazy, muddy current, and the green vines and trees of the shore, the sight of the statehouse beyond a bend in the river must have been surprising. The center section, a rectangle with a pedimented Doric portico, had four fluted columns of plastered brick crowned by an entablature correctly detailed with triglyphs and metopes. An identical portico on the other end terminated the main street of Little Rock.

Lower colonnades connected the central structure to the courthouse on one side and county building on the other—flankers imitating the shape of the main building, as at Harrisburg. The stucco coating of the three blocks was scored and stippled black and white over gray in economical imitation of granite, much like the treatment used in New Haven. The New Orleans plasterer was asked to marble the exteriors but admitted that granite-like graining was what he did best. Doubtless the plasterer also carried out sanding, marbling, and wood-graining on the plain interior. The chambers at Little Rock, like those in Kentucky, Connecticut, and Indiana, were on the second floor; the Senate faced the river, the House overlooked the town. Downstairs a cross-corridor gave access to the porticoes and the colonnades at the sides. The central stairhall's two semicircular staircases rose from a stone-paved floor. Double-leaf wooden doors, milled in Cincinnati, opened onto the river portico which was, in the earliest days, the principal front.

To the optimistic, the disillusioned, and the desperate, the Arkansas Statehouse became a revered landmark on the road west. It was downstream, but still in sight, where the last of the Cherokees of Georgia left their Trail of Tears over the Arkansas River. Brazen Tennessee youths marched before the Doric pillars on their way to San Jacinto, and still later to Santa Fe and Buena Vista. The oldest surviving state Capitol built in the lands of the Louisiana Purchase, it is one of the great monuments of the new Western empire the Jacksonians pledged themselves to possess.

There was in fact only one state capitol built in the Purchase prior to the temple at Little Rock, and that was completed at Jefferson City, Missouri, in 1826. Though the walls were of stone, it looked like an ordinary, oversized house, and it might have been mistaken for a tavern. On the second floor, the Senate chamber was located among the Governor's family apartments, while the House of Representatives shared the ground floor with land offices and other bureaus —not to speak of the Governor's dining room and bedrooms. When the Governor moved out, the legislature still complained that the "contracted" state of the House chamber impeded compliance with the democratic state law that the doors must be open during all sessions. On February 2, 1837, a bill was passed providing for a new capitol. The existing building burned to its stone walls on the following November 17.

The legislature rejected one master builder's proposal to erect a new capitol in exchange for a five-year indenture of all present and future convicts of the state penitentiary and the transfer to him of all vacant public lands in Jefferson City. Other offers were doubtless refused by the commissioners until at last they decided to make their new statehouse fireproof and to pattern it on the Capitol of Pennsylvania.

They dispatched a special invitation to Stephen Hills, who had long ago returned to England. Hills sailed back to America, and by September 1838 he had made all necessary arrangements with several St. Louis suppliers and the warden of the penitentiary at Jefferson City. Work began that month with the delivery of prison-made bricks to the site. In the depths of the national Panic, with banks closing and Missouri warring against its Mormon settlers, Hills moved

Missouri Capitol, Stephen Hills, 1840, as seen in a print dated 1850

steadily forward in re-creating a building he had finished in Harrisburg nearly twenty years before. That the new Capitol was such a faithful copy increased rather than lessened its virtue in local eyes: One should never experiment with public money.

As the building neared completion in 1839, the Secretary of State wished to have its likeness engraved on an official seal. When he asked Hills for a sketch, Hills took from his pocket an old five-dollar note of a Harrisburg Bank that had long since failed. "Please take care of the note," wrote Secretary James L. Minor to the engraver. "It belongs to an old gentleman of this place (the architect of both buildings) and he is anxious to preserve it from reasons that operate very forcibly with him."[37] Two months later, when the engraver asked for a more detailed description, Minor wrote extensively of the new Capitol's commanding view of the Missouri River:

97

The building (a counterpart of the center one on the Bank Note I sent you) is situated on a hill . . . commonly called a *ridge*, that is a point of land that extends (being level and continuous on one side, and abrupt on the other three) until it is suddenly terminated . . . A man standing on the sinister side of the building . . . can [see] the river about 7 miles up, until it is lost between . . . two ridges . . . all of which are wooded, and thickly so. As the river advances from above it washes the left side, or bank, about 100 yards from the brow of the Capitol Hill . . . and as the level of the stream is about 100 feet below the said brow, you can pretty well guess at the angle of altitude at the top of the hill to a man standing on the dexter bank of the river.[38]

The work at Jefferson City was largely complete by the last month of 1840, but certain finishing touches required two additional years. Missouri looked with pride at what Stephen Hills had built. He had made few changes in the original; Secretary Minor proudly noted, "the Capitol of the State of Missouri [follows] . . . exactly after the model of the center building of the Capitol of Pennsylvania at Harrisburg."[39] He had added a high parapet wall, and here the hemispherical dome was mounted on a platform of three steps. His monument on the hill towered over the irregular line of humble taverns, warehouses, and stores that stood along the waterfront awaiting the great boats from St. Louis, Pittsburgh, and New Orleans. By turning the building endwise to the river, Hills gave his porticoes vistas up and downstream of the Missouri's meandering path between lush green banks.

"Stephen Hills, Arch^t." was how the designer of the capitols of Pennsylvania and Missouri now signed his name. Twenty years earlier he would probably not have scorned the title of master builder. In Jacksonian America, however, the masters of any craft saw their independence diminish. Carpenters had not suffered as much as the builders who had been their employers in the past. Unlike the spinners and the weavers now hopelessly lost to the clattering machines of modern industry, the carpenter was still very much on his own; indeed, some people thought times had never been better for joinery. With literacy widespread in the United States, carpenters were likely to be able to read the instructive volumes on building and design now available to them by both English and American authors. Asher Benjamin, the Boston master builder, who will be remembered here for passing involvement in several New England capitols, had already set down some directives in his first book, *The Country Builder's Assistant*, published in 1797. At Philadelphia, a decade later, Owen Biddle published *The Young Carpenter's Assistant*. There were soon many other more specialized texts. Written in plain language and clearly illustrated, they gave the ordinary carpenter information on subjects that were once the exclusive domain of master builders—how to make a Doric column in wood, how to lay out curved staircases geometrically, and so on. The number of carpenter's guides notably increased through the 1820's and 1830's.

Improvement was also sought in other aspects of the carpenter's trade. The National Carpenter's Convention in 1836 endorsed the ten-hour day. One can imagine the reaction of an old master builder like Stephen Hills or Captain Nichols to that innovation. Yet the six-to-six day became almost universal in the United States, demonstrating the power that could be mustered by craftsmen whose services were in demand. Boston carpenters went on strike unsuccessfully for seven months; but at Raleigh, when carpenters on the Capitol project struck in protest over long working hours and insolent superintendents, they were supported by commissioners fearful of losing their services.

Young carpenters, equipped with books by Asher Benjamin and Minard Lafever, went out into the world and by-passed the middleman—the master builder. There came to be less need for command performances, such as Shryock's at Little Rock and Hills's at Jefferson City. Using the right carpentry books, even an unknown amateur could often please commissioners more than an experienced builder—and at a lower price. On the most important Jacksonian frontiers—the Western lands and the Eastern cities—the master builder lost his authority. The prelude to his downfall had been the increasing competition for labor, for by the 1830's and 1840's there was already a second generation of experienced factory workers. As they began to join the drift to cheap lands on the frontiers, they were replaced at the wheels, bobbins, and rolling mills by newcomers, utterly draining the trades of possible apprentices. Even in the West, in new surroundings, a craftsman often found it unprofitable to practice his own or his father's trade or at least to do so full-time. The realization came without regret; the pioneer cheerfully laid aside his inherited tools and set to plowing the virgin lands to the west.

Change came well within the lifetime of our two master builders. Stephen Hills continued to work for several years after he completed the Capitol of Missouri. Before his retirement, he designed and erected the University of Missouri building at Columbia, of which only the file of columns now survives. Captain Nichols finished the Capitol of Mississippi; on a brief stay in New Orleans in 1835, he designed one of his Latrobian legislative halls for the Louisiana State-house, which was, ironically, a converted hospital designed twenty years before by Benjamin Latrobe's son Henry. Permanently back in Mississippi, he built the state penitentiary, lunatic asylum, university, and governor's mansion, then retired. Both Hills and Nichols ended their days as farmers.

Judged by the highest standards of their own time, the best carpenter-built capitols after 1830 were those obviously designed from the plates of the more dependable guides. But there were few of these; most of the carpenter-built statehouses attested a less than thorough understanding even of what the guides offered. They were put up in a hurry, perhaps from a scribbling by a city father, then framed and closed in a matter of weeks to secure the town's claim as the seat of government. Only in relation to their raw surroundings were these capitols monumental.

Houston City, capital of the Republic of Texas, was reached by a navigable bayou from the Gulf of Mexico. It had been adorned by its New York promoters with a Capitol somewhat resembling the unpretentious dwelling of a Louisiana sugar planter. They had engaged an Irish builder named Thomas William Ward in New Orleans in the winter of 1837 to erect the Texas Capitol. It had double galleries across its two-story wooden front, low rear wings, and the luxury of glass windows. Official balls were held on special occasions in the Capitol, and every night statesmen could be found in the nearby brothels and gambling halls. Tourists could observe street fights most days, and a horsewhipping or so was expected in the Senate chamber each session. Against the background of life in the Republic, the Capitol, in its coat of peach-colored paint, was a beautiful sight. Never technically a state capitol, it was easily converted into a hotel when the Texas government moved westward in 1839.

A more impressive carpenter-built statehouse still stands in part at Tallahassee, Florida. The first Capitol of the Florida territory had been a log building erected by Tallahassee's founders. In 1825 the legislature approved the erection of one wing of a larger Capitol, for which the commissioners of Tallahassee held a design competition. Colonel Robert Butler, surveyor-general of Florida, won the $100 prize. The originality of Butler's proposed plan has been overlooked; with the newly completed U.S. Capitol fresh in his mind, he suggested for Florida a similar long-term program, to begin with a single wing and end in years to come as a three-part composition. It would be interesting to know more about the building Butler envisioned. But by 1828 the one wing was already considered too small, and the Governor hired his own brother to begin additions to it rather than a second wing. Work was abandoned before the new walls reached roof level, and in 1832 the unfinished appendage was temporarily roofed.

On March 3, 1839, the United States Congress appropriated $20,000 for state buildings in Florida. This sum had become the standard capitol gift to new states and territories nearing statehood. The legislature ordered the existing wing and incomplete walls demolished. A new capitol was begun in 1840, but only partially covered by the winter of 1841 when the federal money ran out. Florida's government crowded into temporarily protected rooms in the basement floor until 1844, when Congress reluctantly gave another $20,000.

When the Florida Capitol was begun, the region around Tallahassee was virtually a separate state settled by Georgia planters. By 1842, while territorial officials hovered in the basement rooms of the unfinished Capitol, federal troops won the Seminole Wars, thus freeing the vast semitropical domain to the south for settlement. More cotton planters poured in, bringing with them the political ideas of an agrarian slave culture. The Capitol was brought to completion in 1845, the year Florida was admitted to the Union.

Commissioner G. C. English had hired two carpenters, Richard A. Shine and John W. Levinus, to build the Tallahassee Capitol according to plans and specifications apparently purchased in advance. Just who drew these plans is not known, but judging from the elaborate description in a contemporary issue of the *Florida Herald*, the original scheme combined various familiar elements from current architectural guides. As actually built, it was a lofty, rather well-proportioned block of plastered brick, its width nearly three times the 52-foot 5-inch depth. The basement rose ten feet above a ground-level brick floor, supporting two stories—the first for offices, the second and taller for balanced legislative chambers. There was no lantern or dome on the roof, and the temple model was rejected, for the six-columned porticoes were on the sides, as in the national Capitol, not at the ends. The Doric of the architect's drawing was changed to the plainer Tuscan; the simpler Roman order was generally preferred in Greek Revival architecture along the Gulf Coast.

The pedimented porticoes were the jewels of Tallahassee. Their simplicity was fitting. A great fire had swept the wooden shanty town in 1843, and the legislature ordered that all new

Florida Capitol, completed in 1845, as it appeared about 1875

commercial buildings be rebuilt in brick. At the foot of the new Capitol in 1845 were straggled rows of little brick buildings, painted brick-red with bright green louvered blinds. Legislators fled into the shadowy groggeries, and according to Benjamin Latrobe's visiting nephew, partook of "democratic drinks," including the mint julep, mint sling, bitters, hailstone, snowstorm, apple toddy, punch, Tom and Jerry and eggnog, in defiance of the Tallahassee Temperance Society and of the heat.[40] Set on its sandy square, the Capitol stood far taller than the other structures of the town. The columns, stark and white against the dark-painted stucco walls, rested on individual plastered pedestals, well above the weeds, mosquitoes, and sandflies that nagged the citizens. To build these enormous columns the carpenters had fashioned cores of pie-shaped brick, then encased the cores in stucco. Louvered blinds shielded the interior from the sun, and in the legislative chambers Negro slaves swayed palmetto fronds to stir the air.

Carpenters took the Grecian vernacular into other new lands of the West, but only one statehouse was as exceptional as the one still partially standing in Tallahassee: The Capitol at Benicia, California, built in 1852, was probably meant to be a city hall rather than a capitol—it would have been a very ambitious municipal building for such a small inland port at midcentury—but the building lacked a lantern or a dome. Like many towns in the state, Benicia aspired to attract the fickle legislature, which moved almost every year to the city with the best offer. The town was only a day's steamboat trip through San Pablo Bay and the Carquinez Strait from San Francisco, California's metropolis. The Benicia town fathers commissioned what they called a city hall when in 1852 certain legislators promoted the idea of Benicia as capital. According to tradition, a painting of the Virginia Capitol was the model followed by the carpenters, Houghton and Byers. This, or even a recollection of Jefferson's Richmond temple, might account for the omission of a crowning vertical feature. Two months after the foundation was laid, the last shingles were nailed to the roof.

Materials had been obtained in strange ways. When lumber ran out, the carpenters dismantled ships which gold-hungry sailors had jumped in the Strait after hearing news of the first gold strike on the American River. The ceilings of the chambers, at the rear of the building on the first and second floors, were supported by columns made from the masts of the forgotten sailing ships. Local tradition holds that other lumber was brought as ballast on ships from China, the Sandwich Islands, and the Eastern United States. San Francisco supply houses were importing millwork from the East, so ready-made doors, door facings, washboards, and probably the window sash were available to Benicia. None of the prefabricated cast-iron building elements from England, so popular in San Francisco at the time, were used.

The completed building was a modest variant of the temple type more frequently used for urban banks than for governmental stuctures. Its scale successfully approaches the massive in thick pinkish brick walls, strong Grecian details, and a broad flight of stairs from the ground to the main floor. The principal features of the main façade were the two fluted Doric columns *in antis* beneath a pediment. A possible reflection of Jefferson's Richmond Capitol was the cornice with its bold blocklike modillions simplified beyond any antique model.

Although all was on schedule, the legislators accepted an alternative offer by the speculator Colonel Mariano G. Vallejo. But by the winter of 1853, they voted to move to Benicia, both because Vallejo could not meet his promised obligations and in reaction to the terrible threats by the killers Three-Fingered Jack and Joaquin Murietta to massacre the legislature.

When the steamer *Firefly* docked at Benicia, it was greeted by a cheering populace. The legislators perhaps scanned the wharves for the twenty or thirty unmarried girls Benicia listed among its advantages. Serving as the Capitol of California for one year, the Greek Revival structure saw the inauguration of Governor John Bigler: Candles glowed in the windows of the town's low buildings, and the Capitol and ships at the docks were lit to the tips of their masts with oil lamps. The legislature's hired gunman, Harry Love, appeared soon after with the bloody head of Murietta and the three-fingered hand of his companion, thus ending the worst fears of the politicians. But in 1854 the capital was moved permanently to Sacramento.

A far more typical carpenter-built Grecian capitol was erected at St. Paul, Minnesota. The competition held for designs in 1851 was won by a thirty-one-year-old "carpenter and joiner" named N. C. Prentiss. A native of Connecticut, Prentiss shared a house in St. Paul with four fellow carpenters from the East Coast. The Capitol, completed in 1853 by the Minnesota Territory, was probably like his original design, although neither the other competitors nor the contractor, Joseph Daniels, ever shared the commissioners' satisfaction with the drawings. Prentiss had at least consulted his design books in creating the bulky rectangular building of brick, two full stories above a partially raised stone basement. The starved-looking Doric portico, too grandly mounted on a pyramid of stone steps, seemed an afterthought; the heavy dome may have been, too—a hemispherical goodwife's-bonnet on a pilastered octagonal lantern, which in turn stood in the middle of a big square base. The building, after 1858 the state Capitol, was a tolerable piece of carpentry, but suggested that Prentiss did not entirely understand what he had gleaned from Asher Benjamin's books.

Texas and Oregon were the last to complete carpenter-built Grecian capitols. The one built for the Oregon Territory was a cut-stone rectangle with an Ionic portico and a domed lantern. What Charles Bennet designed and built from 1853 to 1855, in consultation with the commission, was intended to harmonize with the prison on the outskirts of town and the unfin-

ished main building of Willamette University across the street. Capitol Yard was fenced in white palings, and native trees were planted. On the flat, green grid of Salem, the new Capitol housed a remarkable democratic legislature which had been established by the pioneers themselves only a decade before, while the dispute between Great Britain and the United States over the ownership of Oregon still raged.

Texas built its new Capitol at Austin between 1852 and 1856. The city itself was laid out for the Republic in the Texas wilderness in 1839. Its establishment in the Indian country was an expression of that curious ailment, Texas Republic nationalism, which manifested itself—like the Jacksonian fever it was—in expansionism. Indian and threatened Mexican raids gave the town a checkered history. Still, several solid buildings were constructed there, including the French embassy, a wooden cottage with walls ceiled with unbleached domestic (the cheapest quality of cotton) and painted the pale pinks and greens of Louis Philippe's France. The Texas Congress did not meet in such handsome quarters, but it was not until seven years after annexation and the subsequent Mexican War that the state legislators voted to replace their one-story wooden Capitol.

John Brandon, an Austin builder, was the architect, and the commission sent to Philadelphia and New York for furniture and oil chandeliers. In the course of construction, the scheme was repeatedly revised by the commission and the two principal contractors, Abner Cook and the partnership of Richard Payne and James Phillips. The completed Texas structure would not have been mistaken for anything but a Capitol on its hilltop at the end of Congress Avenue.

It was built of pale limestone, sawed locally from a quarry at Brushy Creek. Two full stories rose over a basement containing offices. The partially recessed portico, with Greek Ionic columns was reached by a broad flight of stone steps; an obelisk commemorating the Alamo defense stood before the main doors. Tall windows and stone quoins were the main features of the façades. On the roof, which was a near duplicate of the unfortunate one first put on the statehouse at Annapolis, was a domed lantern of eight uneven sides, pierced by Gothic windows; Payne and Phillips later told an investigating committee that they had adapted it from a church steeple pictured in Benjamin's *The Practice of Architecture* (fourth edition, 1839).

Where the Oregon Capitol was arranged on the center-hall plan of a large private house, the Texas Capitol had a narrow inner rotunda between the legislative chambers on the main floor. These chambers were designed to extend the whole depth of the building. During construction the Senate chamber was reduced in order to build a committee room on the principal floor and a courtroom above it. Apparently the interiors were plain. A Grecian building with a Gothic cap, the Texas Capitol illustrated that the nineteenth-century eclecticism of the architects was well-advanced in the world of the carpenter.

The regional mark made by the carpenter-built Grecian capitols at St. Paul, Salem, and Austin was not as permanent as might be supposed. They served only a few decades, and then were forgotten, though they were the first grand architectural expressions of their respective states. Perhaps they are not remembered because finer architectural specimens later replaced them, toward the century's end. But that was not always the case with statehouses, some of which, though long gone, are recalled today with the greatest pride. The appearance of such major monuments in localities as diverse as Little Rock and Frankfort and Harrisburg paralleled the rise of the practice of architecture in America.

And new architectural practices were increasingly evident. The Burlington, Vermont, *Free Press* of May 10, 1830, carried the following notice:

AMMI B. YOUNG
Architect & Civil Engineer
Informs the inhabitants of Burlington and its vicinity, that he has taken a room over Mr. Daniel Kern's shop in Church Street, and is prepared, to make all kinds of Drawings and Models in Architecture and Civil Engineering. He will make Plans and Drawings of Dwelling Houses, Stores & c. and superintend their erection. . . . Having been for 18 years past actively employed, either as a Joiner, Carpenter, Mechanist, or as a practical draughtsman, and having taken particular pains to inform himself in the knowledge of Architecture and Civil Engineering, the theory of building in its several parts, he flatters himself by close application of his business, to merit and receive the patronage of the public.

He will also prepare Drawings, Models, and papers necessary to the obtaining of Patents, which he is well qualified to do, by his familiarity with practical Mechanics and principles of science.

Undoubted reference can be given as to qualifications & c.[41]

Young came from a family of house-joiners, but one month from his thirty-second birthday he was the first of his kin to adopt the title of architect. Like any good businessman, he was seeking new opportunity when he went outside his native New Hampshire and opened a second office in Vermont. He was apparently successful. Basing his designs on instructions in Asher Benjamin's treatises, he built meeting houses, banks, and academic buildings.

A resolution of the Vermont legislature favoring a new state capitol was approved in 1831. The next year an appropriation was made, specifying that the established capitol, Montpelier, would remain the seat of government. Had the legislature not been so distracted by the rising power of the Anti-Masonic Party in a crucial presidential election year, the capitol bill would have become more of an issue than it did. Ambitious young politicians everywhere were finding allies in the era's passionate reformers on a fast road to political success. In other, less democratic times the national potential of reform movements was smaller. The Jacksonians, however, had early demonstrated the uses of emotional issues; the method was increasingly employed by their adversaries as well.

On October 14, 1833, the legislative committee appointed to prepare a plan for the Montpelier Capitol made its report. While they had already approached Ammi B. Young, they made no mention of him, but said that they had found a site, an expensive location which the citizens of Montpelier had agreed to help acquire. The commissioners explained that "whilst many of the other States were expending large sums of money in the erection of their public buildings—

Vermont Statehouse, by Ammi B. Young, perspective by Young, 1832

each endeavoring to surpass the others in the beauty, taste, and elegance of design and workmanship, the State of Vermont would hardly be satisfied with a building that would not compare
advantageously in point of convenience and correct taste, with those erected in the neighboring
states."[42]

Bearing that in mind, the three committee members had already made a tour to Concord,
New Hampshire, by stage, thence to Boston, and finally to New Haven, where Ithiel Town's
temple had recently been completed. They liked what they saw of the last except for the plan.
Their report continued: "The committee have prepared a plan for a building which they flatter
themselves, will be found in point of convenience, second to no one in the United States and
which, in its external appearance and architectural proportions, will be creditable to the State."[43]

It was like no plan yet seen in a state capitol, though the commissioners borrowed a little from
each one they had seen. Most of the Capitol's prime inspiration was the Boston Statehouse. Only
two years before, in 1831, Bulfinch's building had been expanded on the north side, giving the

building a T-shape. Working with Young, the committee clearly based their Capitol on the Massachusetts Statehouse as enlarged by Isaiah Rogers. This borrowed T was adjusted and clothed in a modern Greek Revival shell. Both chambers were placed on the second floor, with the House of Representatives in the center, pushed back considerably into the rear wing to allow for a transverse hallway in front of it. The Senate was in the right-hand end, and like the House, it had semicircular seating. As in Boston, the Governor's suite was at the other end. Downstairs a compressed version of Bulfinch's Doric Hall led to a long rear corridor; circular stairs were recessed from the transverse axis to permit a dramatic vista from one of the secondary entrances to the other.

The Governor appointed Lieutenant Governor Lebbeus Egerton to the post of superintendent several months after the work began on April 1, 1833. Blocks of granite were hauled by mule team from Barre nine miles away, then cut for use on the site by C. W. Bancroft, stonemason of Montpelier. The granite was a slightly darker bluish color than that of the Capitol at Concord, New Hampshire. It cost 20 cents per foot, and was cut for 34 cents per foot. The brick and stonework was done under contract with Colonel N. Sherman of Barre; for laying stone he received 10 cents per foot, payable, according to the custom, after a master stonemason had been brought in to measure the completed work.

As the building took form the legislators sang its praises. Part of a hill had been blasted away so that the Capitol could be tucked back as far as possible on its site. This gave a wide, flat expanse of lawn before the Greek Doric portico, which was a striking novelty in a region of tall hills. The building's exterior was almost entirely granite, including the mighty fluted shafts, steps, the *antae*, and the pediment. As at Boston, lead-colored paint was applied to the canvas cover of the wooden saucer dome, but here this was stippled so that the dome blended with the real granite below.

Montpelier was a small village huddled neatly in the valley where North Branch joined the Winooski River. Travelers on the road from Barre were hardly prepared for the appearance of a town in the increasing density of the hills. Now the Capitol suddenly commanded the entire scene, standing out against a curtain of green. Its massive grandeur contrasted with the dirt streets and their little white-painted wooden houses and stores, their vegetable gardens and horse lots. The meandering river sometimes caught its reflection above the usual images of the whisky distilleries and the Ithiel Town Patent Bridge. A magazine of the day described the Capitol as

> . . . beautiful alike in design, architectural character and execution . . . its design is very neat and simple, a chaste architectural character being preserved throughout the whole. . . . The interior is entered in front, from the portico, through a door eight feet wide, opening into an entrance hall thirty-two by thirty-eight feet, fourteen feet high, the ceiling of which is supported by six granite columns, eighteen inches in diameter at the base, of the Grecian Ionic order, and is panelled after the manner of the ceilings to the porticoes of ancient temples.[44]

Ammi B. Young's career is a classic Jacksonian success story. He approached building in all its aspects. He had learned joinery, and apparently he was studying the fine points of design entirely on his own. He was not an architect who learned construction, but a carpenter and technical builder who developed a sensitive eye. He wedded art and craft so completely that some of his buildings have become timeless: In the twentieth century a skyscraper tower replaced the saucer dome of the Boston Customhouse—one of his greatest monuments, and one not unlike the Montpelier Statehouse—yet Young's powerful customhouse yielded not one inch of its authority to what rose above it. His Grecian work was but one aspect of his eclectic talent in design, for his inquisitive and practical mind was constantly testing, applying, discarding, as he went from one style to another; there was a bit of Town and a bit of Davis in him, a rare and valuable combination in an architect.

Young was an architect because he had made himself one. Like a good Jacksonian, he stayed on the move, and went wherever opportunity seemed to be. In 1838, when he won the custom-house competition, he moved to Boston and opened an office on Commercial Wharf. As the immense Doric temple went up, he became friendly with Alexander Parris, who helped refine his taste. In 1852 he accepted the salaried federal post of Supervising Architect of the Office of Construction, Treasury Department, replacing Robert Mills. Thus relieved of the burdens of private practice, he became the first architect with influence throughout a nation now expanded to the Pacific.

The idea of a national practice had occurred to men and to partnerships in New York City, Boston, and Philadelphia, but the physical reality of long distances presented limitations. Young, by virtue of his position as Federal Architect, came the closest to realizing such a career in the 1850's.

Before the Civil War, the vast majority of American architects had local or at most regional practices. Directories and newspapers in every city of any consequence listed builders, carpen-ters, and often at least one architect or "draughtsman." Sometimes the title "architect" implied that the man did not have practical experience in construction, as commissioners of public build-ings too often learned through tough experience. The majority of architects lived in the rich cities of the East Coast and those along the Ohio and Mississippi rivers, where most business was transacted.

There were, however, trained architects who left the cities and, like other pioneers, sought the untraveled ways. In 1821 a twenty-two-year-old New Jersey man named John Rague, son of a French doctor wounded in the American War for Independence, set out for New York City to seek his fortune. His interest in architecture led him to the prominent architect Minard Lafever, who gave him work in his office as a draftsman. After ten years in New York, Rague moved to Springfield, Illinois, for some reason he apparently never disclosed. The Black Hawk War broke out soon after his arrival, and he was swept up by the spirit of the volunteers who, together with United States troops, were driving the Indians across the Mississippi. In peacetime Rague tried various occupations in Springfield, supposedly including that of baker. He seems to have had no local connection with building or architecture before 1837, when the Long Nine —so-called because the combined height of the nine men was fifty-four feet—in the state legislature at Vandalia succeeded in moving the capital to Springfield. Rague's friend Abraham Lincoln was one of the Long Nine. A capitol competition was held, and John Rague won it. By the close of the next year the Greek lines of the building could be distinguished. Now back in business as a builder, Rague posted an advertisement in the *Sangamo Journal*, advising the public:

> The subscriber . . . offers his services to the citizens of this country. He will execute plans and elevations for buildings in any of the orders of architecture—write specifications, receive estimates . . . and construct foundations in such a manner that the buildings will neither settle nor crack. . . . Also stucco work with enriched cornices, centre pieces & c. As wood carving for buildings has in a great degree been superseded in the Eastern Cities, the subscriber will furnish to order, and send to any part of the State composition egg and dart mouldings, stair brackets . . . for less than half the cost of carving. [The subscriber has] recently returned from New York [and has had] ten years experience as a builder in the city.[45]

Before Rague's Springfield work was terminated in 1841 over political difficulties, he had made an agreement to design a new capitol for the Capital Site Commissioners of the Iowa Territory. In the summer of 1839 Rague and two partners went to see the future Iowa City, a site which lay in the rolling green wilderness two miles from the village of Napoleon. It should have been clear to Rague from the start that Iowa City and its proposed Capitol was the obsession of one of the commissioners, a businessman named Chauncey Swan.

Someone—probably Swan—had already devised an amateurish scheme for a long, low Corinthian colonnade backed by large windows, beneath a roof composed of a pair of saucer domes which looked like umbrellas, separated by a little shanty of a clock tower. Commissioner Swan was quite as convinced of his own competence as Rague was of his own talent as an architect. A conflict began the moment Rague assumed control, and finally Rague resigned in disgust before the Capitol's walls were finished.

In order to properly evaluate both of Rague's Capitols, it must be remembered that departures from established modes were more numerous in Iowa City and may well have been due to Swan, who took over the entire operation when Rague left. Iowa's Capitol lacks the unity of Rague's Grecian composition in Springfield; instead, Iowa's has a disjointed and vernacular aspect, even though it no longer stands isolated on a barren hill.

Both Capitol buildings are rectangular blocks built of a yellowish stone quarried in their respective localities. Deep *antae* give a dramatic quality of light and shade to all four sides in Springfield but are only on the front and rear in Iowa City. The frieze in Springfield's entablature is a proper Doric one, with triglyphs, while only a molded band caps the architrave designed by Swan. Doric porticoes front and back ornament the façades of the Capitols, probably as Rague intended. At Springfield the columns were cut in sections from stone blocks; those at Iowa City, added somewhat later, are of sanded and painted wood and not so correctly proportioned.

In the vertical element on the roof Swan departed entirely from the column-ringed dome Rague had intended, giving the Iowa Capitol a steeple instead. The result resembled Strickland's

Illinois State Capitol, by John Rague, 1830's, as it appeared in 1858,
not long after the last touches were applied

"reconstruction" of the steeple on Philadelphia's Independence Hall a decade before. The reappearance of the historic steeple at Iowa City—now moved to the center of the structure in place of a dome—foreshadowed future architectural events, and, significantly, was the work of a layman. Philadelphia's original steeple had preceded the Annapolis dome, and colonial statehouses had only had lanterns. Iowa's cupola-steeple rose in three stages. First was a big square base, balustraded as an observation deck; second, a smaller pilastered block; and then an octagon surrounded by Corinthian columns carrying a small hemispherical dome.

The plans of the Illinois and Iowa capitols are similar. A series of offices in the basement and on the first floor were convenient for daily use through the year. Central rotundas contain the staircases—at Springfield a rambling affair resembling a series of bridges, at Iowa a more orthodox spiral—each rising to the second floor between the two houses. Interiors in Iowa City are restrained, at least as restored, perhaps less from preference than because Rague, the nearest source of plaster molds, was obviously unavailable. The legislature, though they occupied the   109 unfinished building for six years, moved the capital to Fort Des Moines before it was finished. Springfield's interiors were lavishly executed in plaster of Paris, strengthened with horse and hog hair, even before the completion of the exterior. The detailing was taken straight from the pages of Lafever's books, but the translation was more extravagant in the hands of the former student. Perhaps Rague, like a good businessman, was making a permanent exhibition of what he could offer customers in molded plasterwork.

Not long after he left the Springfield job, Rague took his molds and moved on to Wisconsin, where he continued a successful career as a builder. His last move was back to Iowa, where he lived to an old age, blind in his last years, supported by his second wife, a lacemaker. His old adversary, Commissioner Chauncey Swan, left for the gold fields of California as soon as he heard the news. He was lost at sea.

Even as the building of temple capitols waned, the vaulting Jacksonian dream would find its expression in Ohio and Tennessee in two monuments grander and more subtly artistic than any earlier ones, yet totally different from one another. By the 1830's architects had become more numerous, and major designs were sought through formal competitions. The laymen who set up these early competitions seldom believed such contests needed rules any more stringent than those for horse races. They contented themselves with the pious hope that the best design would win. The inherent evils of such innocence would not reach their climax until some years later. But the exacerbation of competition in capitol building had already been seen in the conniving of Strickland and Mills at Harrisburg. A more sensational competition for a state capitol design was staged by the Capitol Commission at Columbus, Ohio.

On January 26, 1838, when the new Ohio statehouse bill passed, the town of Columbus suddenly realized that its fears about losing the capital were over. Shops closed and there was drinking and dancing in the streets until late at night. The National Hotel spelled out NEW STATE HOUSE with candles over its door.

The statehouse bill specified that competition must be advertised in the principal newspapers of Ohio, New York City, Philadelphia, and Washington. (Boston, it is worth noting, was omitted.) There were to be three cash prizes, the highest $500. Early the following spring a three-man commission was appointed. The advertisements appeared, and at Columbus a broadside was printed outlining the special requirements of the state, including the suggestion that the Greek Doric order be used. Considering that the Panic of 1837 had not subsided, the number of entries in the competition—over sixty (including one Gothic proposal)—was hardly surprising to the commissioners. As businessmen, they must have realized that the flood of entries was an indication of hard times in other parts of the United States, caused by Jackson's fiscal policies.

At an October meeting that year the Capitol Commission awarded three prizes: the first to Henry Walter, a house architect from Cincinnati, the second to Martin E. Thompson, sometime associate of Town & Davis in New York, and the third to the leading painter of Romantic landscapes, Thomas Cole, a resident of Catskill, New York. In December, however, the commission reported to the legislature that any one of the three projects would be suitable for the Ohio Statehouse.

The winning designs were somewhat similar, each with balanced wings and legislative cham-

Iowa State Capitol, Iowa City, by John Rague, 1840–42, as in use today
by the University of Iowa

bers, external porticoes, and large domes. Two of them used the Doric order as suggested, and the other the Ionic. Exactly why the commissioners became uncertain of their decision is not clear, but there are provocative possibilities. The third-place winner, Thomas Cole, was a friend of William A. Adams, a member of the Capitol Commission. Adams had once loaned money to the young Cole during his brief and impoverished career in Ohio as an itinerant painter. Cole in his later success never forgot the man who had shown such faith in him, and Adams was always proud of their relationship. On the commissioner's parlor wall hung a Cole painting of Tivoli. In his letters to Adams, Cole was clearly irritated that he placed only third in the capitol competition. His nephew, William Henry Bayless, a former draftsman for Ithiel Town, had given him professional help in making the plan. "I think in justice," wrote Cole, "I ought to have a *first* premium."[46]

In spite of the indecision about which design to follow, the commissioners built a wooden

111

wall around the site, right on the National Road that ran through Columbus, and began construction of a great rectangle that could serve as the foundation for any of the three. Convicts did the work under heavy guard. From a spring on the outskirts of town, water was conveyed by wooden pipes into the compound. Several days a week the commissioners scrutinized all three sets of plans and elevations. Meanwhile, a lively correspondence continued between Adams and Cole. The commissioner sketched animals and faces in the margins of his letters for Cole's criticism. Sharing a special affection for Grecian architecture, they deplored the public's ignorance of it, though Adams confessed that he had not always been so knowledgeable himself: "When I was first convinced that the greeks painted their temples with various colours it made me melancholy for a month, those divine forms on the metopes of the Parthenon painted blue, and red, and green, and gilt like Dutch toys, this was too horrid."[47]

Legislators began to complain about the slow pace of the work. "This delay," wrote the commissioners, "was occasioned by numerous unforeseen minor arrangements . . . the adjustment of the several details and modifications of the plan."[48] When construction had proceeded as far as it could without a definite plan, two of the commissioners went to Philadelphia to consult with William Strickland, who, though now hard up, was still known as the leading exponent of Greek Revival; they also met with his former student, Thomas U. Walter, who would one day make his own mark in the history of capitols. Still apparently unsatisfied, they made a number of calls in New York, including one to Ithiel Town's office. Town and Davis characteristically began to pursue the job.

Cole had admonished Adams not to take the three designs to Davis: "you will find that the premium plans will be treated with contempt as childish & impracticable works—he will talk about violation of first principles in erudite phraseology And will offer you some fresh drawings one of whose excellence will certainly be beautiful execution."[49] The two commissioners permitted Davis to do a revision that combined some features of the three premiums; for this they paid $140. The large sepia drawings by Davis covered six sheets of blue atlas paper; back in Columbus a succession of men from stone contractors to the captains of the convict teams studied the proposals. To the last man they pronounced them too expensive. It was probably Adams who now took the lead, and Thomas Cole's design was modified locally. "My plan," wrote Cole, "is the one adopted."[50]

The commission finished the foundations on its own, before hiring Henry Walter as supervisor. Walter was undoubtedly given the job to compensate for the abandonment of his first-prize plan. But he proved useful only in matters of design, so a supervisor of construction was hired as well. William S. Sullivant directed the operations at his nearby limestone quarry, where teams of convicts, dressed in blue stripes, were sent to labor six days a week.

By Christmas 1839 the commissioners could stand on the mighty foundation wall and point out the rectangular shape of the building. In their report to the legislature three days later they said:

> We have commenced a work, not for ourselves only, but for future generations; posterity will view it as the work of a former age, the en-

lightened views and intelligence of which will be clearly indicated in the structure—it is thus that the architectural monuments of a country cherish national pride and patriotic sentiments, and contribute, in a great degree, to identify the citizen with his country. A state destitute of great public works . . . is not likely to have its institutions cherished and sustained, and its soil defended, with that zeal and tenacity which has always distinguished those regions adorned with monuments of art and architectural magnificence, to which the citizen can, at all times refer, as lasting evidence of the glory of his ancestors.[51]

Heavy snows in Columbus halted the work until early spring. Columbians with time on their hands often passed idle afternoons in the old brick statehouse at the House of Representatives—called the Bear Garden—observing legislative activity that daily became more frenzied. The Panic had hit Ohio late; the reaction intensified the mutual hatred of the Democrats and the Whigs. On March 10, 1840, in one of those furious controversies, the Statehouse Act was repealed.

The mighty stone foundations of the Ohio Capitol, on their deep bed of quarry chips and mortar, were now completely covered over with earth. Eight years passed; nearby residents were allowed to graze their milch cows on the Capitol mound. In 1843 a resolution to move the capital from Columbus passed the Senate, and was stopped in the House only with the greatest effort. The next year a commission was appointed to reconsider the statehouse plans, but no action was taken on its proposals for modifications.

Columbus finally secured the capital in the winter of 1846 with the Act to Provide for the Erection of a New State House. Instead of appropriating money, the legislature turned the entire work force of the state penitentiary over to the Capitol Commission, effective whenever that penal institution had satisfied its current business obligations. There was a protest from the penitentiary officials, who rightfully asserted that theirs was the only paying institution in the whole state system. In 1845, these same prison officials, recognizing the possibilities of the quarry for profit, had bought the riverbank site from Mr. Sullivant. The first money from the sale of stone was used to make initial payments for a railroad spur. A thriving business had resulted, and the commissioners of the prison resented intruders, insisting it would be two years "before any very efficient aid can be expected . . . under existing liabilities."[52] All the same, further burdens were placed on the penitentiary by the legislature the next year.

Still, the weeds and saplings grew undisturbed over the statehouse square in Columbus. Henry Walter estimated that it would take one hundred men 275 days a year for ten years and $250,000 cash to complete the building. The delays continued: The penitentiary had commitments; the Democrats were preoccupied with their campaign in Mexico. Not until the spring of 1848 did the commissioners, employing two new architects, William Russell West and J. O. Sawyer, make further modifications in the plan and set the convicts to digging out the buried foundations. When the volunteers came home from the war that summer, the basement walls were already begun.

Meanwhile, the state of Tennessee was building its own monument for the ages. Not surprisingly, the legislature of 1843 made Nashville the permanent capital. The city had long been the economic center of the region, and it stood out boldly in the history of the United States as the symbolic fatherland of Jacksonianism.

On the Lebanon Pike outside Nashville the peeling entablature of Andrew Jackson's Hermitage could be distinguished among the branches of cedars and hickory trees. The Hero of New Orleans was still alive. He hardly knew Nashville any more, although he kept abreast of current events through newspapers, letters, and the crowds of callers who had assaulted his privacy and his pocketbook in the years since he left the White House. The announcement that a capitol would be built must have amused him. Tennessee politicians—including Jackson—had always been too busy to bother with any kind of building. They had housed themselves in many places; one of the favorites, especially not the least after sessions, was the old Nashville Inn where, it was said with some truth, Jacksonian democracy had been born. The inn had finally gone broke—in one of the General's own little depressions, ironically—and the parade of Jackson's political creators had gone on to Washington.

In the first weeks of 1844 the capitol bill passed the legislature as expected. Soon the commission of Nashville businessmen was meeting with penitentiary officials about purchasing a limestone quarry. Mayor Powhattan W. Maxey bought a property for the state known as Campbell's Hill; from there the residence of Judge George W. Campbell enjoyed a remarkable panorama of the countryside across the Cumberland River. Letters were sent to various architects who in some way had connections with the board. The commissioner with business interests in Louisiana was probably the one who approached James H. Dakin, a former Town & Davis associate then active in New Orleans; Gideon Shryock was reached in Louisville, Kentucky; and a Nashville architect, a German immigrant named Adophus Heiman, was also invited to submit a plan.

Shryock's proposal for Nashville seems to have been the one most seriously considered. An economic depression in Louisville had cut short his prosperous career there, and he contemplated moving his family to St. Louis. The invitation from the Tennessee penitentiary in the winter of 1844 brought him some hope that he could end his monetary problems by undertaking this large public project. On two occasions he visited Nashville, under the sponsorship of the incorrigible old Governor Billy Carroll. Shryock later wrote that he was assured that "a majority of the board were in favour of engaging my services as Architect."[53]

While Shryock was refining proposals he had already made, presumably based upon his design for the Kentucky Capitol, the commissioners bought copies of the plans for the new North Carolina Capitol and also made "various inquiries . . . in the northern and eastern cities." They were astonished to learn that it would be possible to engage a certain celebrated architect of Philadelphia, a man "who had devoted a life now somewhat advanced, to this profession—that he had commenced it on the Capitol at Washington under LaTrobe, its architect, had superintended many of the public buildings in this country, and had personally visited and examined the most remarkable public edifices in Europe."[54] So William Strickland supplanted his old pupil as architect of the Tennessee Capitol. The delighted commission flattered itself before the legislature for finding a man of the "utmost good taste," and one who "never sacrificed solidity for show—the useful, for the merely ornamental; and that his estimates of cost were to be relied upon."[55] Gideon Shryock demanded and was paid $150 compensation for his trouble.

It cannot be supposed that Strickland would have left Philadelphia at the age of fifty-five if he had been in a position to enjoy the fruits of past frugality or even commonsense economy. He had never had a knack for either. When he had returned from his youthful exile as a scene painter, he mounted the swelling wave of a Philadelphia building boom which ran uninterrupted until the Panic of 1837. As the reigning architect of the city, and one of the major architects and engineers of the nation, Strickland commanded big fees. For twenty years he and his family lived in fine style in Philadelphia; then the Panic brought the harsh reality of no new contracts. Typically, the architect turned to the bright side. He packed his trunks and with his wife and children sailed for Europe, where living was said to be cheaper. But six exhausting months of touring and calling on professional acquaintances made the Stricklands anxious to return home. The prospect of planning a new city brought them back to America, but the promised job and other possibilities came to nothing. Strickland then went after federal work, unwisely becoming a political supporter of the luckless President John Tyler. What work he got did little to ease his situation. The inquiry from Nashville came none too soon.

But the architect still knew how to deal with commissioners, and dictated his own terms: a fee of $2,500 per year, payable quarterly.

Strickland arrived in Nashville, and it was a little as though good times had returned for him. He was a striking figure, with his brown hair brushed back from a high forehead, wildly framing his long and handsome face. The look of a hard-muscled workingman was combined with the Byronic visage of an aristocrat in William Strickland. That dichotomy echoed the dual nature of his personality, which made his stonecutters and bricklayers quite as devoted to him as his intellectual equals.

On the Fourth of July 1845 Strickland—whom the Southerners had already dignified with the title of Major—marched in the parade with the Tennessee Governor, militia, and officials to the peak of what was then called Capitol Hill to lay the cornerstone. After several orations, and the presentation of the sealed glass jars filled with mementos, Strickland addressed the crowd, then placed in the hands of the Grand Master of the Masons the plumb, square, and level. The occasion was more solemn than most of its kind; a profound sense of beginning anew must have impressed that confluence of thousands, who only three weeks before had stood in silent awe at the graveside of Andrew Jackson.

By 1848 the Ohio and Tennessee Capitol projects were at about the same stage. Each of the programs was funded by successive appropriations, and each ultimately cost a great deal more than the original estimate. The commissioners lay in wait for the legislators when they arrived for sessions; there was always the need for more money or more complete participation by the penitentiary. Had both commissions not been deeply involved in politics, their projects would not have succeeded.

In 1853 the Tennessee Capitol was ready for use by the legislature, though still in an unfinished state; Ohio's chambers were not occupied until 1857. By that time the Ohio commission had hired several more architects. William Russell West took the building the farthest, then resigned after unpleasantries in 1854. He was replaced by N. B. Kelly, who served for four years. As consultant on the interiors, one of the original competitors, Isaiah Rogers—then in practice in Cincinnati and later to be Ammi Young's successor as Federal Architect—was brought in to work full-time. All three men suffered political attacks of the kind that had driven Henry Walter away.

Strickland in Nashville seemed immune to attack. The unity of the commission and the popularity of the architect helped ward off enemies of the Tennessee project. When Strickland died, the legislature already occupied the building, and Strickland's son Francis became its architect. A rich Nashville merchant named Samuel D. Morgan, a commission member from the first, increasingly forced his ideas on the other commissioners. At last Morgan virtually took control of the work and young Strickland was fired. H. M. Ackeroyed, then a mere draftsman, was employed to develop on paper Morgan's demands, in the apparent belief that Morgan had watched the work for so long that he had absorbed a knowledge of how to proceed.

The capitols of Tennessee and Ohio were completed in 1860. One was the product of the efforts of many men, the other the design of a single architect. No other buildings belong more to the Age of Jackson than those two, although they were not like any earlier state capitols.

Ironically, a more typical state capitol of the period was Louisiana's Gothic statehouse, built between 1847 and 1849 by James Dakin. Moving the capital from Creole-dominated New Orleans to Baton Rouge was an expression of the Anglo-Americans' final victory over the Creoles. Dakin sold his castle design on the premise that it was more economical to build than the Grecian kind, but one suspects that his commissioners liked it because it looked radically different. In any case, the Gothic shell was really only another example of Jacksonian eclecticism, here expressing growing weariness with the Greek Revival.

Strickland and the various other architects involved at Columbus and Nashville had designed neither castles nor temples. The two buildings, based on traditional abstract symbols—balanced houses, the porticoes, rotundas, and most of all, vertical external elements—transcend "style" and historical models: They are uniquely American state capitols.

Every state capitol by this time had the traditional American elements in some form; indeed, the Philadelphia architect John Notman was called to Trenton in 1845 to add a rotunda, dome, and Greek portico to the front of New Jersey's eighteenth-century statehouse, which already had balanced chambers. Architects had become resigned to using the democratic symbols demanded by their clients. But Tennessee and Ohio achieved a synthesis of the architectural symbols of American democracy—a synthesis which was at last the basis of design instead of a burden imposed on those more interested in creating historical curiosities. The two statehouses were more monumental than the national Capitol had yet become and more intrinsically coherent than it would ever be.

The view of Tennessee's Capitol heralded Nashville as it was approached on the pike, by steamboat on the Cumberland, or by the new railroad trains. Most of the scene spread out below the Capitol terraces was bare farm country, beyond the town's few streets of one- and two-story houses and three taller church spires. When the Capitol was finished, some of the brick outbuild-

Louisiana Capitol, by James Dakin, 1849, as drawn by architect Adrien Persac
as a part of a much larger lithograph of the Baton Rouge waterfront, 1860

ings of Judge Campbell's residence still remained, together with litter accumulated from fifteen years' construction. The rectangular Capitol seemed even larger with such small things at its feet. It is a temple, in a sense, but lifted very high on its rusticated basement, it is no mere cultural trophy.

Strickland related the huge pedimented Ionic porticoes on the ends to shallower ones on the sides with fewer columns and no pediments. The windows are narrow and tall, paired along walls of smooth, rubbed Tennessee limestone. Mounted on the ridge of the roof is a great lantern, a feature modeled on the Choragic Monument of Lysicrates. (Strickland used that model before to top Philadelphia's Exchange, where it gives a certain antique cachet to what is otherwise a very free adaptation of Grecian design.) In Nashville, Strickland perhaps avoided building a dome by relying on his reputation and repeating something generally recognized as successful in one of his major earlier works. There is little carved decoration on the Tennessee Capitol other than the Ionic columns on the porticos and the Corinthian columns on the lantern. Otherwise the building is very simple: Two forces, one vertical, one horizontal, are balanced by the careful coordination of the parts; the basement notably increases the height of the whole, yet is vigorously striated with horizontal rustication.

The Nashville and Columbus interiors are somewhat alike. In both buildings one ascends spectacular divided stairs to very loosely defined central areas. From there dramatic barrel-vaulted halls stretch with much of the lofty grandeur of a medieval cathedral. These central areas are not really rotundas; their round shape begins far above the floor to follow the outline of the vertical elements on the roof. One notices the cylindrical climax of this space only on second look, for the grand transverse axis first commands attention. In Tennessee's Capitol the halls are vacant, three of them terminating in the great Ionic porticoes that frame views of the

Ohio State Capitol, as completed in 1860

landscape and the fourth at the doors of the House of Representatives. The transverse halls in Ohio are plugged with long and narrow divided staircases of iron and marble. Contrasting darkness and light in Ohio results from small skylights and the indirect glow from utilitarian lightcourts. In Tennessee the full glare of sunlight from great hall windows provides a play of light that seems brighter than day.

Both the Capitol at Columbus and the one at Nashville were revised and modernized somewhat as they neared completion in the 1850's, and were made more flamboyant through the available technical advances in iron decoration. Stucco ornament was also added, particularly in the Ohio House of Representatives—adornment more gaudy than sumptuous. Tennessee re-

118

United States Army Corps of Engineers
Tennessee Capitol, by William Strickland, 1845–59, as it appeared in 1865

mained truer to Strickland's ideas, and the interiors seem to date from an earlier period than the fifties. After the architect's death, Samuel Morgan, apparently inspired by fireproofing then going on in the national Capitol, ordered considerable ironwork for Nashville. Full-size iron figures, allegories of Morning, Noon, and Night by Wood & Perrot of Philadelphia, were grouped on the great terraces around gas lamps. Lavish iron decoration converted the library into a fantasy of vines, twigs, and flowers, with a spiral stair, balconies, and gas jets. In the chambers, the giant gasoliers from Cornelius & Co., also a Philadelphia firm, had tinted glass moons to protect eyes accustomed to dimmer light.

The completed Ohio Capitol was essentially what had been adapted by the commission from

119

Thomas Cole's competition twenty-two years earlier. The building has none of the lofty quality of the Capitol of Tennessee; it does not crown a remote hill but has been from the start a monument within a city. There are four loggias of Doric columns *in antis*, wide ones in each of the sides, and narrow ones set into the ends. These porticoes continue the rhythm of the ranges of powerful *antae* that completely surround the building. Between the antae the rectangular windows are set in sunken two-story panels, a favorite A. J. Davis motif. The play of rectangles becomes the dominant feature of the design, its geometric severity modified by the continuous Doric entablature with its triglyphs and metopes.

The Columbus building is seldom the object of criticism except for its radical roof treatment. Over the loggias on the front and rear are small, pedimented attics, in the Bulfinch manner, set back from the plane of the colonnades. Looming above those attics is a heavy cylinder ringed with *antae*, a vertical element at odds with the horizontal proportions of the building below. Two bands of windows encircle the lantern; a smaller cylinder supporting the nearly flat roof is barely visible. The three original winners in the Ohio competition had proposed domes, but the completed building has none.

No designer of monumental buildings was more profoundly impressed by a sense of his own place in history than William Strickland. Though in poor health, he regularly walked from the City Hotel up the steep hill to the construction site. He petitioned the legislature in person for specific legal considerations in the event of his death; they were granted outright. A small boy later remembered playing in a "cavity" the stonecutters were chiseling, under the architect's supervision, in a wall within the north portico.[56]

Strickland's condition deteriorated, and his son assumed most of his duties as the project's architect. As the need for money increased, Strickland took constant advances on his own salary and even intercepted his son's pay. He collapsed on the post office steps one spring afternoon, and died in his bed before daybreak the next morning.

Several thousand people attended the Major's funeral at the Capitol. His coffin was placed in the cavity in the portico; on the marble block that sealed the opening his stonecutters carved:

WILLIAM STRICKLAND, ARCHITECT
DIED APRIL 7, 1854. AGED 64 YEARS
BY AN ACT OF THE LEGISLATURE OF TENNESSEE
HIS REMAINS WERE DEPOSITED WITHIN THIS VAULT.

The architect's estate was valued at $26. Thirty years later the corpse of a second, far richer man was entombed in Tennessee's Capitol: With the end in sight, Samuel Morgan, too, had demanded and won his place in history.

Tennessee's lofty tower, like Ohio's cylindrical lantern, was a striking departure from the dome, initiating a new sequence in capitol building which promised the complete reinterpretation of the architectural symbols of democracy. Anyone who had considered the matter in 1860 might well have said that the dome—something of an interloper, anyway—was dead. But a civil war was soon to bring changes to the American nation and to its state capitols.

IV
THE TALISMAN

The United States Capitol in 1847, unchanged two decades
after its completion by Charles Bulfinch

By 1850, several great cities had developed in the United States, but the national capital was not one of them. A passenger on the stage traveling from Baltimore to Washington gazed out the window at "dark woods and an uncultivated country; and, after passing a single bullock-cart, on lifting up my eyes, I saw before me, on a bare plain, the great dome and the massive pile of the capitol . . . with a few inferior houses all round it, and hardly a living object moving on the silent scene . . . it reminded me of a Russian city; the streets of great length and breadth, the houses inconveniently scattered over an open and treeless plain, and no bustle of commerce."[1]

A few years later, another traveler wrote: "On every side the distances stretch out in apparently interminable lines, suggesting to the stranger who walks through the city at night, when the gas lamps show their fairy radiance at long intervals, a population of at least a million of souls. But at daylight the illusion vanishes. . . . All is inchoate, straggling, confused, heterogeneous, and incomplete."[2]

It was a dirty, wanton place where nobody liked to stay for long. Most of the inhabitants lived near Pennsylvania Avenue, the ceremonial street L'Enfant had envisioned to connect the Capitol and the White House, but in whose path General Jackson had built the Treasury Building.

Mud ruts and cobblestones on the avenue worried the pedestrian less than vehicular traffic. Hacks, the most numerous carriages on the street, slowed down for no man. On the south side of Pennsylvania Avenue cheap lunchrooms, saloons, and boardinghouses clustered among the stores. Across the street were establishments of the better sort, including the hotels, a relatively new feature on the Washington scene of 1850. Politicians, who rarely brought their wives to the capital, used to live in small taverns with dining rooms. Now the big hotels, particularly the Willard and the National, claimed most of the business of the predominantly male population. Their bars and lobbies were very large, built in the owner's hope that they would become gathering places, like the famous exchange hotels in the larger cities.

Terminating the view eastward along the avenue from the thickest part of the business district was the national Capitol. An enthusiastic lady tourist in 1850 climbed to the top of its dome and wrote, "I felt a little thrill of joy when, in the evening of yesterday I beheld from the top of the Capitol of the United States the glorious panorama of the surrounding country, through which wound the Patomac River, the whole lighted up by the golden light of evening; it was a magnificent sight . . . certainly the most beautiful that can be met with."[3]

Washingtonians tended to agree with her. The Congressional Library was the most popular resort for people wanting a quiet place to relax. Just adjacent to the west portico of the Capitol, it had a splendid view of the city below, and on clear days the eye could discern the Blue Ridge Mountains forty miles away. Sofas and cushioned chairs on Brussels carpets filled the reading rooms and the carrels which were open to the public. The west piazza was littered with benches and rocking chairs always occupied by men reading newspapers and chewing tobacco on summer afternoons. Downstairs in the Capitol the politicians could buy whisky cocktails in their private club. Old ladies sold Indian trinkets, flowers, and guidebooks in the rotunda. Until the advent of gaslights, evening sessions were seldom held.

The Capitol, unaltered since Bulfinch left Washington twenty years before, had never been very popular. A tourist observed as it neared completion: "The architecture of this building partakes too much of the old French school to please the present taste. The architect appears to have taken Versailles for his model, and to have made a copy of it, preserving all the defects of the old style without adding the improvements of later times. Ornaments are seen, as if sprinkled without calculation over the walls, and pillars are crowded together . . . a kind of patchwork."[4]

From the first the Capitol had seemed out of fashion. Just as it was completed in the 1820's the Grecian mania got under way. Washington public architecture had long been controlled by Robert Mills, a faithful Grecian, and beside the city's chaste temples, the Capitol seemed dull and tawdry.

No state had seen fit to copy the Capitol, although, ironically, the Capitol could have been taken for a big statehouse. The wings, rotunda, dome, balanced chambers, and portico were the architectural symbols borrowed by a young government whose only traditions lay in the individual states.

From a distance the Capitol was bright in the sunshine. Up close it looked like a stage-set palace of crumbling pudding stone painted white. Foreign visitors complained that they expected a more magnificent seat of empire; the United States Capitol was in fact small compared to monumental architecture abroad. Americans themselves were seldom very critical of the building, perhaps because it was bigger than any state capitol they had seen, and because they were frankly uninterested.

From time to time the House and Senate took a notion to do something exceptional with the Capitol, but their attempts were always thwarted. A vault had been built in the crypt to receive George Washingon's remains; but the Washington family would not allow the body to be removed from Mount Vernon. In the rotunda there were spaces for heroic pictures; John Trumbull had already painted four, but the other spaces remained bare. Fine furniture and carpeting were abused by constant use.

Considered as a whole, the Capitol was not very impressive, except that it had housed the machinery of American democracy for a half-century.

In the 1850's and 1860's the United States Capitol underwent changes which transformed it into the most monumental building in the nation, and one of the most monumental in the world. Like the historic colonial and state capitols which preceded it, the national Capitol's remodeling started out as a solution to practical problems. Yet its single most striking feature, the unique feature of its monumentality, would appear later, and would be purely ornamental.

The alterations of the United States Capitol were instigated in 1850 by Senator Jefferson Davis's Public Buildings Commission to satisfy the pressing need for additional space. While the political history of the decade was unfolding in a way no one expected, the Capitol scheme changed drastically as the concept grew broader. A building which had been merely the outdated seat of American government became a symbolic embodiment of the American Union.

Expansion was long in the making. Since 1840 there had been movements to add more space; by that year the lower house already had three times more members than when its Hall was designed. Congress had become concerned with the danger of fire and wanted better protection against it. Nowhere had the problem been dealt with more casually than in the United States Capitol. The fireplaces and stoves were kept brimming with big fires—there were men who did nothing else but feed them—and oil lamps and candles were in constant use. Carpets or straw matting edged the hearth, tinder beneath chandeliers and Argands. Spittoons on squares of oilcloth were provided for cigars and cigarettes, but seldom used. Increasing numbers of people crowded the halls, committee rooms, library, and galleries; and offices and conference rooms were utterly inadequate.

Though the Public Buildings Commission in 1850 approved the official plans of Robert Mills for enlarging the Capitol, the Senate insisted upon a public competition. In December three alternative plans were chosen, which the seventy-year-old Mills was to combine into a final design for the remodeling. His scheme called for an elongated dome carried by a colonnaded drum on the central block. He then proposed to decorate the flanking pair of low saucer domes with lanterns, and to add beyond them, to the north and south, new saucer-domed wings for the Senate and House.

President Millard Fillmore threw Mills's plan out. In the summer of 1851 he appointed Thomas Ustick Walter of Philadelphia as Architect of the United States Capitol Extension. As Vice-President, Fillmore had already taken a great interest in the Capitol; elevated to the Presidency in the summer of 1850 by the death of President Zachary Taylor, he lost no time in reminding the Public Buildings Commission and the Congress that the act authorizing the Capitol expansion made all plans subject to Presidential approval.

President Fillmore did not want to disturb the existing building any more than necessary. The new wings were connected to the old only by narrow passages, but the wings themselves were huge rectangles set transversely with their ends to east and west, somewhat as at Harrisburg. Walter, who might well have preferred using Grecian motifs, was constrained by the President's demand that the wings conform to what already existed. Few architects in America were as well-qualified as Walter for the assignment. A self-educated student of architectural history, he had practical experience in building dating back to his boyhood training by his father, a Philadelphia bricklayer. At various periods in his youth Walter had worked for Strickland. Besides being recognized as a leader in the Greek Revival, Walter's reputation as an engineer was international.

He brought two inexperienced assistants from his Philadelphia office, then had the good fortune to find a German draftsman, August Gottlieb Schoenborn, in Washington. During the entire building campaign, when the forces of politics and public opinion badgered the architect, Schoenborn remained at the Capitol office and kept the work going. A multitude of contracts for materials were signed in the summer and early autumn of 1851. The Library of Congress was gutted by fire Christmas Eve; early in 1852, Walter's domain was extended into the central body of the Capitol, where he began to reconstruct in iron the main part of the Library. By spring, all the foundations of the two new wings had been completed.

As these extensions were being planned and built, other changes were making themselves felt in the U.S. Capitol. Every year the representatives of a nation of small farmers, with more or less the same interests, had arrived in Washington. Thirty years before, under the Jacksonians, they had cast their deepest sectional differences aside, led to compromise by the challenge of new national goals acceptable to all or most Americans. With the end of the Mexican War in 1848, the most potent feature of the Jacksonian Promise had come true—the wilderness had been acquired, or at least enough of it to satisfy all but the most ambitious. But the fulfillment of the Promise had introduced a fresh sting in the old and dreaded issue of Negro slavery. If the Missouri Compromise restricted the spread of slavery in the Louisiana Purchase, what of the lands that were the spoils of the Mexican War? Would slavery's geographical limits be extended? It was a question which had to be answered, and in the face of it, what was left of the old Jacksonian spirit of give and take collapsed before the moralistic demands of sectional opinion. The 1850 Compromise, growing out of heated debates, attempted to calm the waters by granting territorial options on slavery in the lands acquired from Mexico. But the slavery question did not disperse—as the Compromisers wished—into local issues. Those who had supported the Compromise for love of the Union saw their hopes vanish into more insoluble controversy and even bloodshed.

Congressional conflicts in the decade following the Compromise brought back the political excitement of early Jacksonian days. Now the participants were more reckless, and their audience nearer. Steamboats, railroads, and telegraph wires carried the drama of congressional debates. Newspapers served up the issue front page—a place once reserved for advertisements—and by the close of the 1850's over eighty per cent of American newspapers were political in nature. Suddenly the average citizen felt very close to national events. He had previously gotten his information largely from his own state politicians. In the ruin and rebuilding of national party lines, the local politician saw some of his independence dwindle, as an increasingly dominant national Congress brought issues directly to the American public.

For all that foreboding of doom which is so hauntingly clear in retrospect, the 1850's were, all the same, years of optimism. Everything was colored by the brightest hopes. The little fires lighted by reformers in the era of Jackson came into full blaze when the reformers were at last polarized around the issue of slavery, and made their grand united entry into politics. But the cotton planters of the South who were extolling slavery's virtues realized many victories in Congress and in the Supreme Court.

An estimated one-third of the American population was supported directly and indirectly by manufactures; their value actually increased eighty-six per cent in the ten years after 1850. This affected every aspect of life; in farming, for example, the value of agricultural implements swelled to 160 per cent of its appraisal at the beginning of the decade. Iron production all but doubled, and doubtless would have done so if the Depression of 1857 had not intervened. Businesses new to the decade—such as the production of ready-made clothing in New York, Philadelphia, Cincinnati, and Boston—knew the wildest prosperity. Gas jets lit thousands of places that had only known candlelight or oil lamps. Farm production increased at least fifty per cent with every crop, and more in some years, over that of the 1840's.

Most Americans were still farmers. Statistics show that they quickly adopted the new in the purchase of farm machinery and the use of improved methods. Their world, however, had not broadened so much that they could grasp the fundamental changes taking place all around them.

The optimistic spirit, evident in the ambitious expansion of the Capitol in Washington, was also seen in such politically diverse places as Vermont and Alabama. Both state Capitols burned from unknown causes and were rebuilt by public demand. Neither project was merely a reconstruction; each, when completed, bore the stamp of current fashion.

Little is known about the Capitol built by Stephen Decatur Button at Montgomery, Alabama, in 1847, because it did not stand for long. The only known visual record was made by a daguerreotypist who set up his camera on Dexter Avenue one day in 1849 and photographed the flaming building after its dome had fallen into the rotunda. The original structure had a broad façade rising two stories above a high basement with a wide stair leading to a pedimented portico. Button, a Connecticut native who first made his reputation in Montgomery as a master builder, had been careful to note the sources of his design. A newspaper reported when the building was new that the "Grecian composite style" columns of the portico came from Minard Lafever's *Beauties of Modern Architecture*, published in 1835.[5] The lantern on the dome was copied from the Choragic Monument of Lysicrates.

After the fire, capital removal became a hot Democrat and Whig contest in Alabama, but finally, on February 11, 1850, Democratic Montgomery won out. Mayor Nimrod E. Benson talked to several builders before he employed John P. Figh, a builder who had worked in Tuscaloosa in Captain Nichols's day. J. D. Randolph was hired as carpentry contractor.

Politicians arriving home from Washington, still grumbling about the 1850 Compromise, were doubtless surprised to see the old foundation already braced for reuse. Button's original plan was not followed, however. The resulting Capitol, completed in 1851, was larger and more gangly than its predecessor. In the portico now dropped to ground level, six massive columns with capitals—again taken from Lafever—supported a flat roof. The drum beneath the hemispherical dome was surrounded by detached Corinthian columns. Above its basement the building had three very tall stories. Two levels of iron balconies receded behind the giant columns of the portico, and rows of great windows cut the stuccoed walls. A pair of circular stairs—ordered perhaps from a Cincinnati mill—twisted up from a marble-paved vestibule to the spectator galleries on the third floor. On the roof of the portico a big-faced twenty-day clock in a curious little cupola gonged the hours loud enough to be heard in the cotton fields across the river.

The rebuilt Capitol seems too awkward to have been the work of an architect. Its mail-ordered iron parts are poorly fitted into the stuccoed brick shell; where present, decorations were too lavish; and about the interior one felt the hand of the experimenting builder fascinated with such things as roof-clocks and the "new plan of accoustics [with] angular instead of spherical walls and ceilings."[6] The building was finished in time for the meeting of the legislature in the autumn of 1852.

Vermont's rebuilt Capitol was not a duplicate of its original building either. Rival towns began a relocation feud in the winter of 1857, soon after the fire. Pages of frivolous testimony ranged in subject from Montpelier's fog to state patriotism to nostalgia for the old wooden statehouse that preceded the one designed by Ammi Young, and had once been "an object of wonder for its size, in a State where everything, for most of the people, was on a humble scale."[7] The legislators were taking a holiday from the usual topic of abolition in their statehouse orations.

A young architect from Boston, Thomas W. Silloway, who was also a Unitarian minister, was invited to Montpelier to investigate the ruins. He reported the foundations "as perfect as they have been at any time since their construction," and the remainder of the building as needing major repair only around the portico.[8] The new Capitol could be built within the surviving walls of the old one. On February 27, 1857, the legislature passed the Capitol Bill, appropriating

Alabama State Capitol, as rebuilt by 1851 after the fire

$40,000, on the condition that the town of Montpelier raise a sum equal to the entire cost of the project. The village unhesitatingly set its bond at $100,000.

By autumn, Silloway had completed drawings for the reconstruction. But the stone walls were found to be defective, and "many of them at the height of forty or fifty feet, from the slightest disturbance suddenly and unexpectedly fell to the ground with frightful crashes."[9] Only the foundation was retained.

Dr. Thomas E. Powers of Woodstock, who had worked with Silloway on his home county's courthouse, was the superintendent appointed by the Governor to direct the statehouse work. The other commissioners, apparently not interested in the project, gave free rein to Dr. Powers. In his first report to the General Assembly, Powers acknowledged the "deep obligations which I feel myself under to Thomas W. Silloway, Esq., of Boston, upon whom has been conferred the appointment of architect of the work, for his very valuable professional services."[10]

Powers soon began to worry about Silloway's design for the roof trusses, and called in Joseph R. Richards, another Boston architect who for nine years had served as an engineer in the office of Gridley J. F. Bryant. At that point the friendship between Silloway and Powers ended. Finally replaced by Richards, Silloway went in a huff to stir up his many friends among the Unitarians; they demanded and got a legislative investigation into the project.

Thomas Powers had his reply printed in a booklet:

> At the request of many who are indignant at the report of the famous "Committee on Public Buildings" made at the last session of the legislature of Vermont, a portion of the evidence used before that *august tribunal* in justification of the acts of the Superintendent, is here published, as an antidote to the poison so widely disseminated by that delectable and spotless document. . . . For instance, the "cracks in the walls," which, at one time during the investigation, certain heartless *accusers* trumped up and sought to invest with a sort of seriousness, and for which the gentleman with *tin ears,*

Vermont Historical Society
Vermont Statehouse, by Thomas W. Silloway, Senate chamber as it appeared in 1870

Vermont Statehouse, by Thomas W. Silloway, in the village of Montpelier,
as it appeared on completion in 1857

and some other with *"long ears,"* were suddenly seized with alarm for the safety of the building, suddenly sank into insignificance, and was far more even than the *Reverend* gentleman . . . could magnify into importance enough upon which to bestow even a passing remark in their immortal report!

Gridley J. F. Bryant, who had recently added a rear wing to the Massachusetts Statehouse, had come up from Boston to inspect the work—"notwithstanding the criticism of the rejected architect," Powers wrote, Bryant had approved the drawings of architect Richards, and *"does not* endorse the *silly* idea advanced by *Silly-*way, that the presence of an architect is required at the work, *all* or *most* of the time . . ."[11]

Bryant offered a complete proposal for the reconstruction, but it was Silloway's designs that were followed after all. The new Capitol was not altogether unlike the old one, but beyond the Doric portico and heavy ashlar walls, the buildings were similar only in plan. Features in the new Italianate taste had been added, notably an edicular treatment of the windows with entablatures and pediments. The interior was heavily ornamented with stucco rosettes and filigree, 129 and the furniture—all of which survives and is still in use—was walnut in the cottage version of what was then known as French Antique.

A new and larger hemispherical dome with a pilastered drum almost canceled out Young's basic Grecian temple image. On the dome was the statue of Agriculture carved in wood by Larkin Goldsmith Mead, a twenty-three-year-old Vermont prodigy.

As a unified architectural composition, the new Vermont Statehouse was no match for the one it replaced. The size had been so much increased that both Young's popular version of the temple form and Silloway's Italianate modernizing were diluted. Silloway himself would probably have been the first to point out the weaknesses, since he had little to do with the actual execution of his design. He lived a long life as architect, author, architectural critic, and Unitarian minister. In old age he proudly authorized the statement that he had designed 400 churches. Dr. Powers gave up the practice of medicine when his work in Montpelier was finished. For his services as superintendent, a special committee awarded him a large settlement, which did not receive much public notice, in the first year of the Civil War.

In those tempestuous years of the 1850's the United States Congress was meeting amid noisy construction. Behind high board fences, building materials in mountainous heaps were being catalogued under military guard—a protection not even afforded the White House. Boardwalks and paint-marked paths guided visitors and politicians through the building area to the Capitol.

Work was not going rapidly, so Walter had time to reconsider some of his first decisions. He had wanted the interiors to be similar to the old building, with whitewashed walls, some decorative plaster detail, brick floors, and wooden trim for the windows, washboards, and doors. More and more, particularly since the Library fire, Walter had turned to the use of cast iron, a material which encouraged the introduction of more intricate architectural ornament. Once iron had made its first appearance in the United States Capitol, it became increasingly important in the overall scheme.

Political pressures on Walter also increased, and he was obliged to draw plans for politicians' houses and other federal projects. The protection offered Walter by the Presidency ended when Fillmore left office in 1853. Jefferson Davis succeeded in reasserting his authority over the Capitol by convincing President Pierce to place the work under the Department of the Army: Davis was the new Secretary of War.

Captain Montgomery C. Meigs of the Topographical Corps was appointed general supervisor of the entire Capitol extension project. Born in Georgia and reared in Philadelphia, he loved strict military ways. The engineer and the architect soon clashed. Meigs, claiming that all decisions now rested with him, demanded drastic changes in the scheme for the wings. He listened to the criticisms of the congressmen and senators, and military man that he was, he tried to please all his superiors. In a very short time, however, he infuriated the various contractors. Some of them walked out when Walter seemed powerless to help, making it necessary to find other sources of materials. And that Meigs did with amazing promptness and efficiency. He was abrupt in his dealings and bored with pretense. Walter, full of pretensions and accustomed to professional deference in Philadelphia, could not conceal his anger when Meigs referred to him as his "first draughtsman."[12] As the wings rose, the contempt between Walter and Meigs grew frenzied. Confrontations outside the Capitol sometimes matched the political furors within.

The wings were very much in evidence the winter the Kansas-Nebraska debates began. That legislative session of 1854 would be remembered in American history for the act that reopened the slavery question in lands the Missouri Compromise had decreed free. Throngs of people had come to Washington to protest the bill.

Passing over the boardwalks each day, between the high fences, visitors often paused to consider the Capitol itself. They must have thought it a rambling pile resembling a row of fancy candy boxes, uncomposed as a whole and somehow foreboding. But Walter had already begun to make drawings for the architectural feature which would eventually unify the disjointed Capitol.

His proposal was sufficiently in hand by March of 1855 for the Congress to appropriate $100,000 for continued construction. Work began at once with the ripping away of parts of Bulfinch's dome of wood and brick. As Maryland had done in the 1780's, Walter set out to give the existing building new monumentality through the addition of a grander dome; his structure would also be a splendid, even fantastic, one, although its exact details were not yet clear even to the architect. On the advice of Walter and Meigs, August Schoenborn began plotting a giant skeleton of iron. Many years later he remembered Walter in the office laboring over a nearby drawing table to perfect the design of the outer shell: "he had before him copies of St. Peters, St. Pauls, St. Isaacs, Dome of the Invalides and the Pantheon in Paris," wrote Schoenborn.[13] (Of these, only St. Isaac's in St. Petersburg was of iron.)

In the 1850's, the South Carolina Statehouse of wood and brick housed the most publicized legislature in the nation. Radical to its core, that legislative body had not deviated from its flamboyant path since nullification days, when the battle was won against Andrew Jackson. And for nearly a quarter century it had refused to meet with the national Democratic party.

In a fenced circle before the statehouse in Columbia stood a giant palmetto tree, the state symbol, executed in cast iron at the close of the Mexican War to commemorate the heroic Palmetto Regiment. Also of iron were the busts of South Carolina heroes already adorning the House and Senate chambers; that of General Jackson was defaced by vandals when word of his death reached Columbia.

For many years governors had worried about the safety of the South Carolina archives, the thousands of pages of manuscripts going back to the earliest colonial times. One proposal called for a fireproof duplicate of the statehouse to house the archives; the pair of buildings, placed not far apart, would present a minor Acropolis for the government, on the order of Jefferson's first scheme for Richmond. When a committee was appointed in 1851 to consider alternatives, it recommended that the basement story of a new fireproof building be begun which, at a later date, might be completed as the north wing of a future fireproof statehouse.

The legislature approved, and assigned to the committee certain funds from city-lot sales still being conducted in Columbia. This went so well that in 1853, acting largely in response to public opinion, the committee requested money to proceed with construction of the new statehouse. Bonds were issued in the amount of $250,000; the commission was instructed to preserve the old statehouse for use until the last, but to transfer the archives into the fireproof basement of the new as soon as posible. P. H. Hammarskold, a Charleston architect of Swedish birth, already in the employ of the commission, drew the master plan.

Professional movers from New York lifted the eighteenth-century statehouse from its brick basement and rolled it onto a new, taller basement. Iron railings were attached between the columns, and a pair of semicircular iron stairs was fixed to each end of the portico. The iron elements of the palmetto tree were unscrewed, cleaned, and reassembled out of the way of the new construction.

Just as the rainy weather yielded to summer sun, in mid-May 1854, cracks appeared in the brick and granite work of the fireproof building. The project, which had gone so smoothly, now became accursed; few major crimes in South Carolina received the press coverage of this blunder. Hammarskold was suspended. He asked the Governor for an unbiased professional to be brought in to inspect the work. John R. Niernsee, of the Baltimore architectural firm of Niernsee & Neilson, was summoned.

Niernsee, a Viennese, was a hard-working romantic who had achieved a personal reputation as an engineer while serving several years as a draftsman for the Baltimore & Ohio Railroad. He was probably about thirty when he arrived in Columbia, and saw that the city of so much notoriety was no more than a country town slumbering in groves of China trees. The foundation for the Capitol, with wings flanking a central block, was spread over the hilltop. Niernsee gave a highly unfavorable report; he found the scheme already obsolete in its very sparing use of iron. Knowing that Hammarskold would leave, Niernsee said a few words in behalf of his own abilities before returning to Baltimore.

Advertisements were placed in newspapers in Columbia, Charleston, Baltimore, Philadelphia, and New York detailing the competition for the new South Carolina Capitol, to be held August 2, 1854. By the time that day arrived, Niernsee had been in continuous contact with the commissioners. Meanwhile, several South Carolina architects were exerting as much political influence as they could muster in their own interests.

A wicked little conflict ensued, involving men who had once worked for a Charleston architect named Colonel E. B. White. Each of them, including Hammarskold, had previously entered a competition for the Charleston Customhouse. The vote of the local commission for White's project was overridden in Washington in favor of Ammi B. Young's Grecian plan. When Hammarskold left in disgrace and moved on to Tennessee, his former associates battled among themselves for his job. On the morning of August 2, Colonel White and his draftsman and assistant, George Edward Walker, were on the train bound inland to the state capital. While the commissioners deliberated for twenty-four hours, White and Walker called on politicians, White loudly declaring that his name must be withdrawn from the Capitol competition if Niernsee remained involved in any way; otherwise it would be a "breach of professional etiquette."[14]

On August 3 the commissioners announced their decision: George Walker would be Supervising Architect, and Niernsee would be retained as Consulting Architect. This unexpected solution was reached because the false start by Hammarskold had "engendered a distrust in the public mind in this State of all professional architects and especially of strangers of foreign birth." Niernsee, the commission later hastened to explain, was a naturalized citizen, and people had written from the "land of his nativity" the "highest testimonials" to his professional stature.[15]

Walker was a South Carolinian, and Colonel White had disqualified himself by his own statement. The two architects of the Capitol project were destined to agree only on one thing—the inadequacy of Hammarskold's scheme. They reported to the commissioners that the plan was incomplete, "containing no details of any part of the work internally or externally, no finish of stairs, galleries or decorations for the Senate chamber, Representative hall, or Library; none of the important constructions of their iron ceilings galleries, roof or in short any other mater beyond the base elevation and the general and unfinished plans of the building."[16] Some redesigning of the original was done, but Walker's proposals were set aside in favor of one of at least four proposals submitted by Niernsee. Enraged, Walker set out to destroy Niernsee.

Controversy still exists as to whether Niernsee may in fact have been copying Walker's design. But whoever was responsible for the design, the building was intended to be grandly monumental, inspired mostly by the Charleston Customhouse and the new Capitol of Tennessee. It was raised a full story above the ground, with a broad stair in front as on the Alabama Statehouse and the national Capitol in Washington. The Corinthian order was used for pilasters and columns on the great pedimented porticoes. Local granite rusticated the basement story, while the same material was used in ashlar on the upper two floors. The façades were rich with pedimented windows and other Italianate motifs. From its balustraded terraces the view would extend for miles across the pinelands beyond the Congaree River.

Above the roof, not a dome but a gigantic lantern rose in three mighty stages. Beginning with a great colonnaded square base—recalling Cuthbert Brodrick's tower on the town hall at Leeds, England, more than Strickland's at Nashville—the lantern was reduced to a smaller octagonal section pierced by bull's-eye windows, and at last a round tower, with a ring of Corinthian columns, capped by a spindly bell-shaped element.

In some ways the proposal for South Carolina was reminiscent of the wings Walter was adding to the national Capitol. Niernsee was certainly aware of the work in Washington; indeed, he could even see it from the train on his trips from Baltimore. His repeated changes in plans frustrated Walker, for foundations had to be demolished after work had progressed for several months. Walker blamed his troubles on Niernsee. Friction grew until Walker decided the hour had come to rid himself of the consultant.

In the spring of 1855 he wrote to his former employer Colonel White: "Come up as soon as you can and we will kill Mr. Niernsee as dead as possible. . . . Niernsee['s] plans are a disgrace to any man who calls himself an architect, they are not any better than Hammerskold's in fact when the committee asked him for his elevation he stated that it was the same as Hammerskold['s]."[17] To a commissioner Walker wrote that Niernsee wanted "to choke me off." The commissioner replied: "I am at a loss how to advise or what to say in the matter."[18]

At its next meeting, however, the commission wrote Walker a letter of dismissal. Niernsee was offered total responsibility. In the autumn of 1855 he and his family established permanent residence in Columbia. The walls of his project stood only a few feet above the foundation level,

Archives of The Church of Jesus Christ of Latter-day Saints
Utah Capitol, project by Truman Angell, 1851

but in a short time, he organized a team of Italian stonecutters, built a railroad to the granite quarry across the Congaree, and pushed the work forward.

South Carolina's rather abrupt decision to build a splendid new statehouse was a manifestation of only one of many different kinds of nationalism in the disjointed America of the 1850's. To a large degree the nationalism of that decade was regional and often local, flickering in little separate fires all over the country, with only vague and occasional reference to what would later be the almost spiritual sense of American union. The labels "Northern" and "Southern" are a convenience of hindsight; regional nationalism was far more varied.

Hot coals were increasingly borne from one hearth to another. Southerners in Kansas, for instance, used devious means to gain control of a constitutional convention at Lecompton City, the capital of the territory, to the outrage of equally aggressive abolitionist settlers from the North. Pictures of a proposed Lecompton Capitol with four Corinthian porticoes were dispatched to the Eastern newspapers for publication. The proslavery constitution created less disturbance in Kansas than it did in Washington, for its approval by the President cracked the Democratic party irreparably, and stirred unrest elsewhere, to the advantage of the new Republican party. The antislavery majority was ultimately triumphant, however, and both the Lecompton Constitution—and the ambitious Capitol plans—were rejected in 1858.

At about the same time, California's legislature, having weathered the floods at Sacramento for two years, decided to build a permanent capitol. Rich and self-confident by the late 1850's, yet remote from the rest of the nation, California was ready to have a monumental government edifice. Sacramento was a rambling hamlet of fifty-five hotels, several fine brick buildings, and innumerable wooden shanties. In its center was a block called Capitol Square.

A statehouse competition was won in 1856 by Reuben Clark, a Maine carpenter who had worked for Captain Nichols in Mississippi twenty years before. Clark's life had taken many turns since those days in Jackson. He had formed a little company of his own in New Orleans, then abruptly boarded a schooner in 1848 for the gold fields. Considerably the poorer for his effort, he became a house carpenter, then an architect in San Francisco. His winning design for the California Capitol closely resembled the one in Mississippi, except for Italianate detail in place of "antique Roman." The House of Representatives was located at the rear, like the one Nichols had appended at New Orleans. It is interesting to suppose that Reuben Clark and other Maine carpenters had recalled Bulfinch's Augusta Statehouse when they assisted Nichols in designing the Capitol in Mississippi. If that was so, the Bulfinch idea, mingled with the Captain's own foolproof plan, had reached the westernmost edge of the American nation.

The most original monument of regional nationalism in the West was designed by the Mormon architect Truman O. Angell for a capitol deep in the Indian country of the Utah Territory. In 1849 visionary members of the Church of Jesus Christ of Latter-day Saints had conceived a State of Deseret to be a religious promised land sprawling from the Colorado Rockies to the Pacific Ocean. A suspicious United States Congress created a more restricted but still ambitious Territory of Utah one year later.

In 1851 the territorial legislature, with the future in mind, decreed that the capital must be located central to all of Utah's lands. A commission of four and a party of settlers, accompanied by Territorial Governor Brigham Young, left Salt Lake City immediately to select the site, with seven teamsters, three servants, two cooks, seven carriages and wagons, eighteen horses and mules, equipment and medicines. They journeyed for sixteen days. The resulting report, dated November 27, 1851, read:

> We located the site for the seat of government . . . on the East side
> of Pauvan Valley . . . as nearly central as the nature of the country will ad-

mit. . . . At the suggestion of your Excellency the seat of government . . . is called Fillmore City & the county in which it is located Millard & in the survey of the city, agreeably to your request, a square block of 10 acres, near the West brow of the table land, with a beautiful lone cedar upon it, is reserved for the State House . . . the inhabitants have passed a law that no *green* tree shall be cut in the city, nor within two miles of it.[19]

Long before the expedition left Salt Lake City, Brigham Young was searching his maps for the perfect site; the statehouse he envisioned was one Truman Angell had painted in watercolor for him. Angell, the brother of one of Young's wives, had been a close associate of Young on trails that had led to Illinois and Missouri, then westward. As official architect of the Mormons, Angell had designed temples, dams, mills, barns, and houses; fences, machines, and corrals were all a part of the daily fare of his Salt Lake City shop. He had been a carpenter in Providence who had followed his impassioned mother in taking up the gospel of the Saints; the romance of his religion inspired his architecture. Grecian and Gothic rules of his boyhood became no more than points of departure for the mature architect. The new country of the American West freed him from the restrictions of wood construction, introducing him to adobe and its plastic possibilities. His eyes surveyed a landscape of powerful horizontals and diagonals, of great distances and fierce colors. To the established Greek forms of Asher Benjamin and Minard Lafever, Angell added the soaring dimensions of his Promised Land.

The statehouse he painted for Young's delight was, for its time in history, the most eclectic of all capitols—a carpenter's fantasy, the likes of which had not been seen in state capitols since the Annapolis dome. Its central block was a tall, ponderous octagon, with four major sides, all broad and pedimented, and four narrower ones. Wings were connected to the wide faces of the octagon, producing a Greek cross plan. Above the octagon base rose a giant dome which Angell labeled Ottoman, and near its peak a balcony encircled it, like the one at Annapolis, supported on scroll brackets. Single-story colonnades shaded the wings. The decks on the roofs of these colonnades were spiked with Gothic pinnacles and fenced by Baroque balustrades. Oval windows, fan lights, louvered blinds, bands of arabesques, and panels of anthemions appeared in endless profusion. The building looked like a palace in one of the ladies' literary magazines of the day, lifted from its lush fictional setting of palms and flowers and placed on barren ground. As in his greatest works to come, Angell took into complete account the particular grandeur of the Utah country: The towering levels of his statehouse provided promenades encouraging the contemplation of lands yet unplanted that lay between it and the horizon.

Actual plans were not drawn until after the location was established. "This plan seems urgent," wrote Angell in his neat little diary, "and makes extra labor."[20] In the meantime Young instructed the settlers at Fillmore to devote themselves to improving the site as much as possible.

A construction crew was sent out in 1852 after the spring thaw; the foreman, William Felshaw, wrote home to Angell: "We arrived here the 8th day of May and found nothing done at the state house and mill or dam, and no road made to the timber in the canyon."[21] He estimated that it would be one hundred days before a single nail could be driven in the statehouse. Angell directed him to build the south wing only. He began construction immediately, but progress was slow because of the cold winters and the reluctance of local people to interrupt work on their own projects.

Young arrived by coach in Fillmore in May 1855, demanding to know the reasons for the delay. He put the town on notice that the legislature would be there at Christmas. When the politicians arrived, they faced cramped living quarters and plain fare, but a completed south wing. The session was pleasant, for the participants were not strangers to the frontier, the most seasoned of them having migrated west only seven years before. Several dances were held in the Hall of Representatives, and the Saints passed laws about ranching and school lands. By the session's close in the prescribed forty days, heavy snows made travel arduous. One year later, fearing the blizzards, the legislature was called to order at Fillmore, then adjourned immediately to the rented Council House of the Church in Salt Lake City.

The last attempt to utilize the Fillmore Capitol was in 1858, the year the United States troops entered Utah to establish the federal authority Brigham Young had repeatedly defied. Truman Angell's statehouse was thereafter abandoned. The one wing stood solitary and wind-blown, a great cedar tree its sole companion. Finally, the building which was to have been the capitol of a Mormon empire was converted to use as a public grammar school.

Angell's Capitol was not the only unrealized scheme. None of the capitols born of regional nationalism were finished in the forms first proposed—most, in fact, were never even begun. The town of Omaha in the Nebraska Territory courted the legislature by hiring the St. Louis architect William Rumbold to design a capitol with Classical columns. City and federal funds hurried the roofing of the building for the 1857–58 session. In the process, however, the Corinthian colonnades were left unfinished. Governor Mark W. Izard, who always credited himself with drawing the plan, added a little dome.

At Santa Fe, New Mexico, the territorial Governor, legislature, and military occupied the ancient Adobe Palace. Rough boards were laid over its packed earth floors, and muslin stretched over the ceiling caught some of the dust from above. Wanting something better, the legislature petitioned Congress for money to build a capitol. Funds were granted, and the project began at once. The building was well into the second story when money ran out. But Congress refused another cent, and the territorial legislature disclaimed any responsibility for providing funds. So the building stood, like a ruin, for nearly thirty years, while officials patched the Adobe Palace, put glass in its windows, and regularly hauled loads of dirt to thicken the leaky roof. For the use of these historic quarters—use required by law, oddly enough—$500 rent was deducted from the Governor's salary.

During the decade of regional nationalism, Capitol construction in Washington moved ahead, in spite of the battles between Thomas U. Walter and Captain Meigs. The genteel mutual contempt with which they started was transformed into heated conflict between the two paste-board generals, each with his army of supporters.

For four years Meigs had the advantage of having Jefferson Davis for his ally. When a new administration sent Davis back to the Senate, Meigs found President Buchanan's Secretary of War not only disinterested in the Capitol war, but annoyed over being so frequently drawn into its verbal cannonades. In January 1858, when Walter was out of town, Schoenborn was ordered by Meigs to transfer all his drawings to the office of the Captain of Engineers. "I refused," the draftsman later wrote, "and as a result earned a reprimand from Meigs and an approval from Walter."[22]

But work on the Capitol went well. The House of Representatives was already meeting in its new hall, and the Senate chamber was nearly completed by that autumn. Much of the marble veneer had been applied to the brick exterior. A scaffold extended up through the opened eye of the old dome, supporting a steam-powered mast and boom that one could see from far away, bobbing and turning, lifting and setting the iron members of the new dome.

Both Meigs and Walter made contributions to the rising structure. In Walter's designs Meigs made structural modifications and even added some ornamental embellishments. Supported by his patron, Senator Davis, Meigs was successful in urging the purchase and commission of artworks for the Capitol. Walter remained on the verge of resigning, muttering how Meigs was infringing on his professional jurisdiction.

It was Meigs who finally lost. During the autumn of 1859 he rudely demanded help from the Secretary of War, who was preoccupied by now with more important events at Harper's Ferry. Sensing from the Secretary's silence that his superiors had turned on him, Meigs addressed the President directly, and was dismissed the same day for his insolence.

Walter, whom Meigs had dubbed a "rebellious assistant" in a year haunted by the word rebellion, was the architect triumphant. His enemy's replacement was a gentle soldier, Captain William B. Franklin. Franklin did not consider himself a designer, and the temperamental Walter knew that he would have a free hand. When money ran out one month after Franklin came to the job, Walter calmly returned to Philadelphia, where he remained until an appropriation of July 1860 reopened the project.

At their April convention of that same year, the Democrats at last split apart over the issue of slavery. The Republicans nominated Abraham Lincoln for President in the following month. That summer politicians came forth from all sides offering to save the nation, each in his own way, and for his own reasons. By fall, it seemed all the forces of the past decade were converging in the Presidential election.

The two Capitols under construction—in Washington and South Carolina—that summer of 1860 were miles and, indeed, worlds apart. Niernsee's granite statehouse was up to the second story. His new town was such a hotbed of Southern nationalism that he may well have wondered if a new Southern nation might soon be governed from his marble halls. Walter, on the other hand, might have wondered if the town his dome was to dominate would always be as empty as it was that summer, with the politicians all at home stumping. Under the scorching sun one could walk from the Capitol down to the Willard bar and meet few people besides the cursing hack-drivers.

The outline of the rising peristyle of the new dome could now be seen from the woods and fields across the Potomac. But for all its burgeoning majesty the national Capitol did not serve as an inspiration for statehouses in the 1850's. Architectural symbols must be seen in order

Wisconsin Capitol, by Kutzbock & Donnell, in 1861, when construction
was interrupted by the Civil War

to influence; the Capitol was still only a collage of unfinished pieces. Its decorated windows and profusion of Corinthian colonnades were merely a part of the increasing taste for richer membering—ornamentation was even used in the cast-iron fronts of commercial structures. The appearance of such detailing on the new Capitol of Wisconsin in 1857 and in a building proposed for Hartford, Connecticut, represented no effort to copy the national Capitol.

At Hartford, F. S. Jewett apparently proposed a modernized version of the state Capitol of Ohio, at the time an incomplete but well-known project. His Corinthian colonnade around the dome's drum doubtless came from one of the variations on Ohio's first design, particularly from Isaiah Rogers's currently published modifications of that statehouse. Jewett presented his scheme to the Connecticut Capitol Committee in the form of a painting, but the committee was unable to raise sufficient funds, and the proposal never materialized.

A. Kutzbock and S. H. Donnell, partners in an architecture and contracting company at Madison, Wisconsin, began construction of a Capitol that Kutzbock had designed with exceptional imagination and freedom. The German-born "Arch^t & Civil Engin^r" did business in Madison as one of John Rague's successors. His daybook, written in German, records payment for the designs of houses, academies, churches, and a summerhouse, for which, incidentally, he was paid $1.00. The Capitol was at the foundation stage when Donnell died, so the building can be considered entirely the work of Kutzbock. It was in the shape of a Greek cross; one axis terminated at each end in semicircular Corinthian colonnades, while the other ends were framed by romantic octagonal towers. A source in Washington, D.C., for this building could have been James Renwick's Smithsonian Institution; the national Capitol was certainly not the inspiration.

For the center of the nearly flat roof Kutzbock designed a dome which would please the most tradition-minded of his clients and yet express his own taste for the exotic. Its style was variously described as Oriental, Moorish, Turkish, or even more precisely, Ottoman. From a tall and highly ornamental cylinder, its walls lively with pairs of arched windows and columns, the dome swept upward to a smaller, bell-shaped cupola crowned by an elaborate finial.

Kutzbock's Capitol was only up to the level of its tin roof at the outbreak of the Civil War.   139

Putting their plans aside, the commissioners decided to wait for better times, when they would tear off the temporary cover from the rotunda and attend to the dome.

The year 1860 was a turning point for many currents in American history, and it proved to be so in capitol design as well. During the spring of that year, Reuben Clark paced the corridors of the Sacramento Courthouse awaiting the decision of another capitol commission. On a technicality, the state supreme court had called a halt to his work on the new Capitol four years before. Clark had gone home to San Francisco, leaving his plan at the foundation stage. Nothing was done to rectify the situation until 1860, when Governor John Downey instructed the legislature that his state needed a fine capitol.

California had been good to Downey, and the Irish immigrant loved his adopted United States with the passion of the truest patriot. News from the East now traveled fast; it went from St. Louis by telegraph to Saint Joseph, Missouri, then by pony express it raced to Carson City, Nevada, thence by telegraph to Sacramento. While everyone else was fretting over troubled times, Downey so pressed the legislature that $500,000 was appropriated to complete a capitol for which new designs would be sought in a second competition. The bill itself was a monument to the Irishman's ability to get what he wanted.

Seven designs, including Clark's, were entered in the competition. The San Francisco *Bulletin* favored the Clark plan from the first: "To obtain a complete and correct idea concerning its appearance, you have only to look at the Custom House and Post Office in San Francisco—leave out of sight those ugly chimneys which ornament each end, imagine a dome similar to that on the Merchant's Exchange over the centre, and place a statue of Liberty, and another of California on the two ends of the front, with a flagstaff between them."[23]

Newspaper accounts of the judging in May 1860 indicate that the new Board of Capitol Commissioners, under Governor Downey, had no interest in the Clark design. They were giving serious consideration to quite a variety of drawings. Four plans were for cross-shaped capitols with domes and Classical motifs. Another design showed a group of one-story buildings resembling "one of the old colleges in New England." The winning scheme by Miner Butler, said the Sacramento *Daily Union*, "differs from all the preceding ones . . . it appears to be better proportioned, with more of the 'modern improvements' of public buildings."[24] Butler had hardly been informed of his triumph when five of the other architects raised an angry protest and a member of the commission resigned. Fearing that the public too would think the competition weighted toward Butler, contestants were given a two-week extension "for the purpose of perfecting or improving" plans already entered.[25]

The commissioners knew no peace during those fourteen days. At cafés, saloons, hotel lobbies, and in the interim Capitol the architects sought them out, rolls of plans in hand, to plead for more time. Taking as hints every word the commissioners spoke, they revised their plans. The new drawings were inspected on the appointed day, and Butler won over his own former entry, with a new scheme modeled on the United States Capitol as he envisioned it in its finished form.

Butler was accused of copying another designer's façade, and an investigation followed. In mid-July, at the hearing, three witnesses confirmed the report that Butler had been seen closely inspecting his opponent's design. A single witness appeared for Miner Butler: Reuben Clark. On July 14, 1860, "Butler's 2nd Plan" received the prize and Clark the post of Superintendent of Construction at a salary of $300 per month.

A bigger site was needed. As more city blocks were added to Capitol Square, obstructing buildings were razed. About two weeks after construction began, news of Lincoln's election arrived. In December, South Carolina was the first state to secede from the Union; Georgia followed in January.

All through the first months of 1861, with work going slowly on the foundation of the California Capitol, sensational accounts burned over the telegraph wires. At Montgomery, Alabama, a unifying constitution was written for the seceded states. On February 18, on the new iron portico of the Alabama Capitol, Jefferson Davis was inaugurated President of the Confederate States of America. When Lincoln took his oath in Washington in the following month, the unfinished Capitol loomed behind him, its great ring of Corinthian columns complete, its third stage well under way. Still, its upward movement was entirely vertical, for there were as yet no curved members to indicate whether or how the ascent would end.

After the attack on Fort Sumter, the War Department fortified the Capitol by stacking sandbags around loose iron members intended for the dome. An army bakery was built in the basement. On the main floor 1,500 hospital cots were installed. Troops passing through Washington were billeted in the Capitol in rooms where the few statues and paintings had been crated for protection. Walter and the Commissioner of Public Buildings objected to the War Department's utter disregard for the work of remodeling.

Safety was still another question, since at no hour of the day was the building ever completely vacant. Construction finally came to a halt. As the December meeting of the·second session of the 37th Congress was approaching, President Lincoln issued an executive order removing military personnel from the Capitol.

Jurisdiction over the Capitol was transferred from the War Department to the Department of the Interior in April, and the Capitol funds were frozen, except for those spent to protect the building from the weather or used "to complete the Dome."[26] Later on, in the bitterest depths of the war, Lincoln was criticized for continuing the building program on the hill. He replied: "If people see the Capitol going on, it is a sign we intend the Union shall go on."[27] By Christmas 1862, the iron skeleton of the dome stood completed, awaiting the plates which would enclose it. Down beneath the framework gaslights glowed all night in the windows along the marble walls.

From the noisy, crowded confusion of Washington's mud streets, thousands of men watched the Capitol's dome grow. The iron web was the last sight of home to soldiers marching south, and the first welcome to those returning. Each passing month saw it nearer completion, in a city so suddenly the crucial point between North and South.

On the other side of the divided nation, Reuben Clark was completely cut off by the war from the building materials he had ordered from the East. Finding the proper materials in California or the Sandwich Islands was not easy, and the suppliers overcharged. Clark's dealings with his commission were not always happy either, and he was in turn hard on his subcontractors.

Early in the winter of 1862 the Sacramento River flooded the Capitol's foundations, ruining the files and all plans. The Commission paid Clark $500 to redraw the whole Butler scheme. Because of the flood, Clark increased the height of the foundations six feet, a change put into a legislative act by the new Governor, Leland Stanford. The former New York lawyer, who had made a fortune as a Sacramento merchant, was California's first Republican Governor.

Like Downey before him, Stanford attached great importance to the rising Capitol. With other prominent citizens, he had stood in the Sacramento telegraph office in the fall of 1861 and sent the first transcontinental telegraph message to President Lincoln in Washington. On the morning of his inauguration, January 10, 1862, Governor Stanford climbed into a boat from a second-story window of his mansion and was rowed over flood waters to the site of the new Capitol to be sworn in. He urged Clark to get on with the work, despite the war, as soon as the foundations were drained.

Under official pressure—and swept up in Stanford's enthusiasm—Clark accelerated his pace. When money ran low, the Governor forced a new five-cent property tax through the legislature to replenish the fund. Almost every day he called at the superintendent's office, which was first in a brick house, then moved into a temporarily finished basement room in the Capitol. Clark's big drawing board on trestles, his "squares" and "angle boards," and some other drawing boards and various small instruments comprised all the furnishings. On the walls the plans and elevations Clark had redrawn were available for inspection. It was reported that these plans were exactly like Butler's original ones. The building, brought to completion eighteen years after the work was begun, must have pleased Stanford in its obvious similarity to the national Capitol.[28]

Revised specifications were completed by Clark in May 1862 for Stanford's approval. The rectangularity of the principal façade was broken in relief by slightly projecting terminal bays and a central pedimented portico of considerable size, above an arcaded basement recalling Bulfinch's. Subsidiary porticoes with flat roofs on the ends of the building had the same iron Corinthian columns as those on the main front; *antae* along the four sides were decorated with Corinthian capitals in iron. Instead of a portico, there was a great semicircular bay originally on the rear containing the courtroom and library, a feature somewhat like the small semioctagons on some earlier capitols.

From the windows of that bay, the eye would one day view Leland Stanford's dream, an uninterrupted stretch of four blocks of the finest flower gardens ever executed for a state capitol. Dominating the elevation was the dome, rising behind rich rooftop balustrades and lines of Classical statues and urns, a diminutive reflection of the one being built in Washington.

Meanwhile, the dome on the United States Capitol neared completion. Its growing presence had a profound effect upon everyone who saw it. Years after the war a Michigan minister recalled how, as a young and homesick soldier, he had wandered on Pennsylvania Avenue that first night his company arrived in Washington:

> As I approached the Capitol . . . it was shrouded in the deepest gloom, so that it was scarcely visible. . . . Presently there was a rift in the shifting shadows, and I caught sight for the first time of the new dome—in all its

towering height, its immense proportions, its sublime magnificence. As I peered curiously through the mist, it seemed . . . as if in utter defiance of the rebellion and laughing treason to scorn, and daring their united power to do its worst, the mighty symbol of our national authority was steadily advancing to its completion. . . . Then as never before I felt that my first loyalty was to THAT DOME—rather than that of Michigan, Pennsylvania, or any other State—to that dome in the mighty shadow of which all other domes could safely rest.[29]

At the close of 1863, the bronze statue of Armed Freedom made its formal ascent to the peak of the dome. In spite of the uncertainty about the war at the end of that year and the first months of 1864, several thousand spectators wildly cheered when, from above the statue, the Stars and Stripes unfurled in the wind. In Sacramento, a mysterious woman climbed the scaffolding to the highest point on the Capitol's unfinished walls and tied a United States flag to a timber; thereafter workmen raised the flag on that Capitol every day before their labors began.

An older capitol flaunted a different flag. Overlooking the James River and the fallow Virginia farmlands, Jefferson's Roman temple housed the government of the Confederate States of America. The stuccoed walls were painted a yellowish stone color, with lighter trim; otherwise nothing much had been changed since the building was completed. Jefferson Davis had moved the capital from Montgomery soon after Fort Sumter in an attempt to appease what was being called the "Virginia Party" among the Confederates. The Confederate goal of taking Washington, like the Union's objective of Richmond, had been continually discussed since the beginning of the war. Not until General Ulysses S. Grant was given command of the Union armies in the spring of 1864 did the realization of the Union aim bring the war to its end.

Grant's program called for the conquest of strategic places in the Confederacy, and a campaign against Richmond began in May. In the same month, a mighty thrust of 100,000 men under General William T. Sherman began the march from Tennessee, along the Western and Atlantic Railway, down into Georgia.

Since 1862 the Union's flag had adorned the Choragic Monument on the Tennessee Capitol. Cannon were placed along the terraces, among the iron figures of Morning, Noon, and Night. Louisiana's castle Capitol was a blackened ruin. A Yankee soldier's family showed their neighbors back home an old French volume with the following inscription penned on the flyleaf:

When the troops of the Union occupied the capital of Louisiana . . . the state-house was garrisoned by a company of Mass. soldiers . . . the building took fire, doubtless it was set on fire, perhaps by some reckless & unprincipled Union soldiers but probably by some secession sympathizers. . . . The flames were subdued by the persevering efforts of the soldiers, the townspeople keeping well aloof; but . . . the interior was utterly consumed. The books of the library were thrown in great numbers from the windows. . . . This is one . . . and it is sent as a reminiscence of the events, and the winter campaign in Louisiana.[30]

143

Union forces took Little Rock in 1863; in the Arkansas Statehouse local pro-Union men set up a state government to replace the Confederate government which fled. The Mississippi Capitol at Jackson overlooked a ruined city the Union soldiers nicknamed Chimneyville. The bloody summer of 1864 for the Union army was followed by an autumn of victories.

From conquered Atlanta, Sherman's troops marched to Milledgeville in November. In a brief respite the soldiers held a mock Confederate session in the Gothic Capitol. In Richmond that warm season, a city by now accustomed to the distant noise of war, there was rising hostility between Confederate representatives. President Davis proposed to employ 40,000 slaves as noncombatants and to promise them pay and freedom. The end of the war was near.

In February 1865, Sherman's army marched on Columbia. A young rebel wrote in her diary:

> I ran upstairs to my bedroom windows just in time to see the U.S. flag run up over the State House. Oh, what a horrid sight! After four long bitter years of bloodshed and hatred . . . flames broke forth . . . Imagine night turned into noonday . . . a copper colored sky across which swept columns of black, rolling smoke glittering with sparks and flying embers, while all around us were falling thickly showers of burning flakes. . . . The memory of it will haunt me as long as I shall live.[31]

Far above the ashes of the old South Carolina Statehouse the Union flag had been fixed to the unfinished and long-abandoned walls of the new.

On April 2 the Confederate government and the army garrison fled Richmond. President Lincoln entered the city on April 4 and wandered through the silent, vacant chambers of Jefferson's Capitol. For all practical purposes, the American Civil War had ended.

Ten days later Abraham Lincoln was dead. The city of Washington solemnly expressed its first and greatest public emotion. On a roofed and columned catafalque, decorated with black and white silk, the coffin was exhibited to mourners who passed in endless lines beneath the new iron dome of the Capitol. A three-week period of national mourning followed, as Mr. Lincoln was returned to Springfield. April 21, at eight o'clock in the morning, the funeral train left Washington, to begin a journey of 1,662 miles through an American landscape so unchanged that it seemed the war had never been waged. The corpse would lie in state in the major public buildings along the carefully charted way. Most of them would be state capitols, themselves by now monuments of quite a different America.

At Harrisburg the catafalque was carried into Stephen Hills's landmark Capitol, where there were thousands of townspeople and farmers who had risen early and waited in line. From Harrisburg the body was taken to Philadelphia and from New York City to Albany, where Philip Hooker's Capitol was festooned in black crepe and the catafalque set in a bower of lilies. The leaders of Tammany Hall had ridden on the train from Manhattan to stand in quiet ceremony in the old-fashioned Capitol whose own fate had been sealed in a special legislative act during the war.

At the great statehouse in Columbus, its Doric columns resembling black peppermint

The Grand Review of the Armies of the Union on Pennsylvania Avenue,
Washington, May 1865, as photographed by Mathew B. Brady

sticks in their crepe wrapping, the coffin was placed in the dramatic central space with officials standing on the flower-banked stairs in the transverse halls.

Six thousand mourners awaited the train at the Indianapolis depot, and almost three times that number filed through the rotunda to see the martyr's face. Wooden barracks cluttered the lawn around Ithiel Town's Indiana temple, and the soldiers of two wars had written their initials on the temple's walls; but as a Capitol it had held its own, through thirty-five years.

On May 2, the funeral train arrived in Springfield. A Chicago newspaper reported, "The mourning decorations of the exterior of the State House were marked by an excellent taste. The building itself most certainly presents little architectural beauty, and can lay no more claims to stateliness or elegance of finish than any ordinary warehouse; but draped in the symbols of mourning, it assumed an appearance of solemnity, and, contrasted with the remainder of the city, had a somewhat imposing effect."[32]

Lincoln's body lay in state in the Hall of Representatives John Rague had made so elaborate with his plaster molds. A party of Springfield businessmen, on first hearing about the assassination, had purchased a tract of land several blocks from the Illinois Capitol to build a tomb for Lincoln there, somewhat on the model of Washington's tomb. His widow refused the offer. On May 4 Lincoln was buried on the outskirts of town in a new cemetery Larkin Mead, the Vermont sculptor, would soon adorn with a tomb.

Meanwhile, the faraway city of Washington was awakening to spring. The mourning crepe, faded now by the rain that had fallen in the weeks since the train had departed, was being removed from the buildings. Trees had budded and the spring flowers lingered. The lively pace the city had reached during the war had by no means vanished with peace. On the contrary, the streets were crowded with a larger population that only lacked an expanded city to house it. War had broadened the scope of government service; new federal bureaus squeezed into converted houses and over shops and stores. Many years of Jacksonian spoils had been brought to an end with the advent of the Republicans. The new party had brought a liberal attitude toward bureaucracy, and the war had made it necessary for the government to hire so many men that even big-business Republicans from the greatest Eastern cities were astounded.

The finale of the war era was the two-day Grand Review of the Armies of the Union in May. Two hundred thousand soldiers marched down Pennsylvania Avenue. Flags and bunting and garlands of flowers adorned the streets. Bands played, and stirred by marching feet, clouds of dust rolled on the masses of cheering spectators.

At the end of the avenue the Capitol was almost overpowering in its splendor. It loomed far taller than anything in the whole countryside; its whiteness dazzled the eye. Hundreds of thousands of Americans were brought to Washington by the war. Most of them would never visit the city again, but the triumph and tragedy of what they had lived through was unmistakably summed up in the memory of the dome: The symbol of faith was reborn a talisman of union.

V
THE UNION'S
EXALTATION

Several days after the Grand Review, Thomas U. Walter submitted a bitter resignation to the Department of the Interior, and with boxes of Capitol drawings, boarded the train home to Pennsylvania. In his fourteen years on the national Capitol he had never understood the workings of politics.

Reuben Clark, on the other hand, refused to leave his post at Sacramento, even for a rest. Night and day he labored at the working drawings, fretting over the delayed shipments of cast iron, taking too much to heart the criticisms of certain legislators. Finally he went insane and died in 1866 in the state asylum. His widow and his doctor asked if he, like Mr. Strickland, could be buried in his last work. Because of rough conditions at the site, the Commissioners declined; they suggested that the matter be brought up later, but it was soon forgotten. The duties that had driven Clark mad were immediately taken up by a younger man, G. P. Cummings, who carried the building most of the way to its completion in 1878.

Thomas U. Walter returned to private business, and actively pursued a career as a professor at the Franklin Institute. He grew to loathe official Washington. Time and again he pressed for additional payment he felt was due him. His remodeled national Capitol was now unquestionably the country's most famous building. Even those who scorned its elements as heavy and crude were captivated by its monumentality, its command of the landscape, the spectacle of its dome. And that dome soon made its impression on state capitol architecture.

At Concord, New Hampshire, two years before the end of the war, the old granite state-house was remodeled by G. J. F. Bryant and Arthur Gilman of Boston. A wing was appended to the rear, on the order of the one they had added to the Boston Statehouse but with a mansard roof, and a large hemispherical dome on a tall octagonal base replaced the cupola of forty years before.

In the summer of 1866, the same year the work in Concord was completed, an even clearer example of the influence of Washington's dome was a decision made in Madison, Wisconsin. As Kutzbock prepared to build at last the exotic dome which would bind together his eclectic Capitol composition, the commissioners rejected his design, insisting instead on a dome like the one in Washington. Kutzbock appealed to the Governor to no avail, then wrote a sarcastic letter of resignation. Colonel S. V. Shipman came forward with an acceptable drawing based upon what he had seen many times in Washington during the war. Within a few years Shipman had completed the patriotic symbol, a hemispherical dome over a colonnaded drum, all built of iron framing and plates and painted white—a little souvenir of the national Capitol.

On a more elaborate scale, similar revisions were proposed by Bryant and Alexander R. Esty for Bulfinch's Boston Statehouse. First in the 1850's, then in 1865 and 1866, Bryant had drawn various studies for enriching the façades and adding mansard roofs, over which would loom a tremendous dome reaching high above Boston's new commercial buildings.

The end of the war witnessed a building boom in state capitols. Old states needed more space, and wanted more grandeur, and the new Western states, in spite of their sparse populations, wanted to build proud emblems. Americans wanted shrines to house their blood-stained regimental flags and marble rolls of soldiers lost. The Grand Army of the Republic, which had virtually supplanted the Masons and established official quarters in the state capitols, demanded heroic rooms to house their meetings.

California Capitol, Sacramento, as completed in 1878

More than ever before, architecture was the poetry of the American ability to apply invention to practical uses. In the twenty years since James Bogardus introduced cast-iron fronts for commercial buildings in New York, cast iron had come to play a part in every aspect of architecture. Iron was cheap, it was thought to be fireproof, its elements were endlessly reproducible, and it was light in weight. Walter's dome, a marvelous giant erected on walls built to

149

support only a light wooden dome of brick and wood, was cast iron's grandest American expression.

Once the safe passenger elevator came into use in office buildings, cast-iron construction could be carried ever higher. The lesser structural costs made it possible for builders to afford richer materials as the surface veneer. Liverpool tiles, Italian marbles, mahogany balustrades, and parquet began to appear in reality where they had been pantomimed in paint. The ancient architectural models—so well suited to wood and brick—were too simple for cast iron. Architects tutored in the eclectic currents of the second quarter of the nineteenth century now joyfully anticipated a horizon of new possibilities. Though the architect still thought in terms of historical models, and clients still wanted the safe justification of established precedents, both were eager to experiment with the new ways.

Seeds of inherited eclecticism sprouted as the awareness of the potential of new inventions increased. The architect's forward step was hesitant, beginning with modest departures from such a familiar theme as the Italian Renaissance. Very soon the pace quickened. As architecture entered unbridled the age of the entrepreneur, American eclecticism entered a particular florescence nearly a century in preparation. Trained and untrained architects now had equal chances for success.

The spatial needs of insurance companies, hotels, and stores were usually no match for those of the state governments housed in the capitols. Those quiet, paper-strewn basement offices of the prewar days had become overcrowded hives of activity, and on upper floors and in attics state employees occupied partitioned corners. Bureaus of taxation, land grants, transportation, pensions, agriculture, internal improvements—many of them never heard of before the war—had created jobs for department heads, section chiefs, clerks, and assistants.

State government's machinery had only begun to grow. The Republican spoils system was more far-reaching than the Jacksonians could have imagined. Many officeholders were forced to contribute money to the party whose leaders had appointed them, and it was very common to require civil servants to work in election campaigns. Civil War heroes of any celebrity at all could demand as good posts in government as in business.

Once forgotten in those months when the legislature was absent, capitols became places of buzzing activity all year long. Everybody had business at the statehouse; and of all statehouses in America, New York's was the busiest.

For ceremonial occasions, Philip Hooker's columned hallways could be cleared of desks and temporary canvas partitions, but his double-faced building was considered an eyesore—out of style and unbefitting the Empire State. An 1863 resolution authorized the Trustees of Government Buildings to procure plans for a new capitol. Advertisements were placed in various newspapers the following summer. The plan was to include a suite for the Governor and "his Civil and Military staff, The Senate and its Officers and Committees . . . the Assembly . . . The Court of Appeals, the Judges, Clerk and Officers of the Court, The State Library, The Superintendent of Public Instruction, The Keeper of the Capitol, Store Rooms and Rooms for miscellaneous purposes needed in a building of this character . . ."[1]

Of the three plans submitted, the trustees preferred the entry of Thomas Fuller and Chilion Jones, architects of the new Gothic Parliament building in Ottawa. Perhaps this project was Gothic as well. Whatever the style, opposition to it is suggested in the subsequent act of May 1, 1865; while authorizing construction to begin, it made the plan subject to the approval of the Commissioners of the Land Office as well as the trustees.

A new competition was announced in July 1866, probably at the instigation of indignant New York architects home from the war. Thirty plans were entered. Thomas Fuller, taking on two partners in Albany, entered a second scheme. The commissioners deliberated for nearly a year, deciding at last to give the premiums but not to execute any particular entry.

Arthur Gilman was by this time famous not only for his early critical writings, but for the recently completed Boston City Hall, the first echo of Napoleon III's New Louvre in American public architecture. Though he had been a partner of G. J. F. Bryant in Boston, the commission summoned him personally to Albany to combine the desirable features of their various plans into one final design. While he worked on this, the politics of architecture raged in the halls of the old Capitol.

At an appointed time, Gilman's sheets of drawings were exhibited, along with drawings from two other firms, in what might be called an informal competition. Thomas Fuller had meanwhile added to his Albany firm of Fuller, Nichols & Brown the architect Augustus Laver, newly settled in New York City. Like Fuller, Laver had been trained in his native England and had gone to Canada to seek his fortune. They had been friends in Ottawa; both had worked on Canadian government buildings, and both believed they knew how to deal with politicians.

Laver's sudden removal to New York had been timely, in the very months of the selection of a final state capitol plan. Both Fuller and he knew that being residents of the state could only help their case with the commissioners. But this time the commission selected the plans of another firm, Schultze & Schoen, a firm working at various times in Philadelphia, Boston, and New York.

The winning plan, however, was soon thrown out by the Commissioners of the Land Office because it had no central dome or tower. The lay board apparently did not care which dominant vertical element the Capitol had as long as one of them was included. Gilman was invited back to adjust the design by adding the desired exterior feature, and Fuller at once formed a partnership with Gilman, by now considered a New Yorker.

After an unsuccessful attempt, the partners arrived at a design acceptable to all members of the two commissions, with one exception, Obadiah Latham, who criticized the impracticality of the plan and doubted the estimate of cost. Most of his demands were met, thanks to his noisy campaigns and his published pamphlets.

Nobody seems to have really worried about the estimated cost, which was nearly $4,000,000. New York State was living through an era of the greatest extravagance. William M. Tweed from New York City had risen through Tammany Hall, and in 1867 his election to the state senate ratified his decision to extend his domain. The Governor whom he placed in office in 1868 appointed a new commission consisting of the three original members and five Tweed men. That

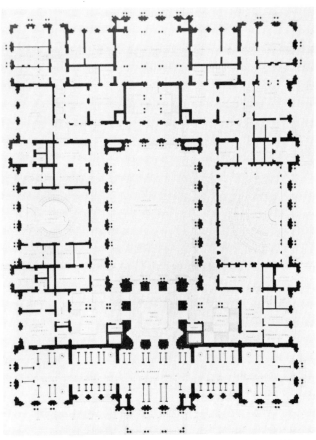

New York Capitol, Fuller & Laver plan, 1871

commission met several blocks up State Street from the hotel where Boss Tweed was weaving with audacious bribes the Tweed Ring he would subsequently use to control Manhattan, the financial capital of the United States.

Architect Fuller's talent for making alliances was only slightly less than that of Senator Tweed. He appeared before the new Capitol Commission on behalf of his latest firm, Fuller & Laver. But despite his pleas, the Commission does not seem to have been pleased with the latest winning design. It was too aristocratic for the Court of Tweed. Gilman gave up and went back to New York City. He signed the rights to the dubious winning capitol design over to Fuller, who thought there was still a gleam of hope. Fuller judged correctly, for on August 14, 1868, he made a contract with the Board of New Capitol Commissioners.

The history of the Capitol scheme is a tangle of modifications proposed and effected. A fire in the commission's office in the early 1900's destroyed almost all the original papers; the only existing records are the commission's own reports of their activities. If these carefully edited publications agreed exactly with the original masses of letters, receipts, and books of minutes, it would be the only example of such faithful documentation in American capitol history.

According to all reports, only one entry in the second competition attempted to copy the United States Capitol as a whole, and that scheme was crude and artless. Fuller's proposal at that time was of academic Renaissance design, in the vein popular in England for monumental public buildings. His dominating portico, however, was a near replica of the pedimented one in Washington. Even Laver's "French Renaissance," or Second Empire, project was crowned with a dome based upon the one in Washington.

New York State Library
New York Capitol, model of the accepted Fuller & Gilman design, 1871

As the accepted design developed, it drifted away from dependence on the national Capitol, a fact that accounts for many of the troubles that ensued. The Fuller & Gilman design included a dome on a great columned and pedimented base, several heavy towers, and a principal entrance portico very closely resembling G. J. F. Bryant's most elaborate proposal of 1866 for remodeling the Boston Statehouse. This was similarly heightened by a recessed and pedimented attic story in the Bulfinch tradition. Once Gilman was gone, Fuller changed the dome to a tower rather like that of the Leeds Town Hall (which Niernsee seems to have had in mind in his

153

South Carolina project). Still later that was changed, and the Second Empire spirit revived along the lines still evident in the lower stories which Fuller was able to execute.

The New York plan was a descendant only of Ohio's statehouse; it bore no resemblance to any other state capitol built before. The stone rectangle had heavy corner pavilions simulating towers, much in the manner of those on the New Louvre. On the four sides the porticoes were recessed, but their columns projected somewhat more than the colonnades in Columbus. Where Ohio's Capitol had an unconfined central space beneath its dome, Albany's proposed capitol went farther in opening its great central court to the sky. Moreover, this court was meant to be adorned with plants and fountains, adding what was indeed a new—but ill-fated—variation on democracy's architectural concept of the ceremonial saloon or rotunda. There was a large columned foyer of the Doric Hall type; monumental staircases led up to the principal story into realms of decorative stonework illuminated by skylights; long vaulted corridors linked the ceremonial parts of the building—all attempts to give grandeur to what was really a huge office building for a large bureaucracy.

Because it was being so richly executed, because its design seemed foreign, and because New York politics were storm-tossed in the years of its construction, the Capitol was cursed by controversy. Boss Tweed's new New York City Courthouse was investigated in 1871, the year of his downfall, and an Aladdin's cave of graft was exposed. A Manhattan contractor, for example, called the "Prince of Plasterers" by the New York *Times*, was paid nearly $3,000,000 for less than a year's work. When the Tweed empire fell, anything even remotely associated with it was in danger. For New York's Capitol project, so exciting in its introduction of up-to-date European design, so clearly the next radical step beyond Ohio and Tennessee, scandal was inevitable. Soon Fuller, for all his machinations, was out.

The postwar architectural ambitions of the state of New York were frustrated by many forces, not the least being conflict and indecision about style within the capitol commissions. Statehouse building went faster in the new states, farther from the constantly changing taste of the style centers. In Topeka, Kansas, the Capitol Commission, at its first meeting March 26, 1866, elected Colonel J. G. Haskell of Lawrence to the new office of State Architect—a post unique for its time. Originally, however, Haskell was more concerned with construction than design, and he functioned as what in every other state was called Superintendent of Buildings. The commission resolved to build a capitol in three parts—a central section with east and west wings. The east wing was to be the first, with one end "thirty feet removed from the main building with an attachment after the manner of the new wings of the National Capitol."[2]

A Milwaukee architect, E. Townsend Mix, partner in the firm of Mix & Boyington, presented a perspective and plan for a capitol wing the following morning. It was not at all what the commissioners had in mind. Mix, though a New Englander born in the very shadow of Ithiel Town's New Haven temple, had designed a Second Empire block, rusticated and pilastered, with convex mansards and a portico of small, paired Corinthian columns above high basement piers. He was apparently inspired by the New Louvre, in proposing three mansarded pavilions on a wide principal façade. The commission rejected the plan and ordered Colonel Haskell to revise it completely, changing the placement of the wings, the interior plan, and even the architectural style, by omitting the mansarded pavilions.

Kansas Capitol, J. G. Haskell's accepted project, 1866

Construction began that summer. By May 1867 the basement was almost finished, and a contract was signed with Dow Bogart and John Howison to carve the Corinthian column capitals in stone. In August the iron structural members arrived from the Phoenix Iron Company in Philadelphia. A Kansas geologist, Professor Mudge, selected local yellow limestone from Junction City.

155

Kansas Capitol, east wing as it appeared in 1879

The legislature moved into a Capitol wing—minus all its stone ornaments—in December 1869. An impudent editorial in the *Kansas State Record* of Topeka noted that the "architectural wonder," the temporary stairs outside, bore "a remarkable resemblance to the 'shoot' up which the pigs march to certain death in a slaughterhouse." The reporter found the Governor's office so rich, with its bathtub, Brussels carpets, and gasoliers that "we expect the office of Governor will be hereafter in greater demand than ever."[3]

Fully finished three years later, the wing must have been striking on the open prairie amid the little stone buildings of Topeka. Even as a solitary wing, it was the biggest building in Kansas. To ascend the gradual incline of the stair to the portico was to rise above most of the rooftops of Topeka; to look toward the horizon through the screen of Corinthian columns of stone and iron was to enjoy an architectural experience unequaled between St. Louis and Sacramento.

It was probably Colonel Haskell who drew the perspective of the projected Capitol that the Governor hung in the upper hallway. The building he proposed was to be in the shape of a Greek cross, with other magnificent colonnades at the terminus of each arm. On the roof would rise a dome like that on the national Capitol. While this was stylistically revised, it is in effect what the state of Kansas built over the next fifty years.

Architects entering statehouse competitions began to face a real dilemma. The postwar boom in building had reached every city, even many of those in the ruined South, and the changing architectural fashions of the day were being seen everywhere. Capitol commissioners were not unaware of the current changes in design. Like most Americans, they viewed with both suspicion and overwhelming admiration the new character of national life and its abstract promise of extravagant personal fulfillment. Much of that promise was symbolized in architecture, and when people thought of public buildings, they thought of a splendor appropriate to abundance.

They wanted buildings on the patriotic model of the national Capitol, but they also wanted

Kansas Capitol, Senate chamber as completed in 1870

urban stylishness and grandeur befitting their booming nation; little whitewashed and marbled temples were no longer enough. They wanted their legislative chambers to blaze with gas light, and their steam-heated marble halls to be as fine as those in the grandest metropolitan hotels. All this was to be done, of course, at the lowest possible cost.

Architects cringed at the prospect of erecting mere copies of existing buildings, but short of trying to reeducate the commissioners, they had to design whatever might win competitions. The Second Empire style, nominally based on the French Renaissance popular in the Eastern cities, was the obvious answer to lavish and inexpensive building. Dollars went further in pavilioned and mansarded structures, because ornament could be used or abandoned as the budget dictated.

In 1864, Bryant was the first to successfully propose a Second Empire design to a capitol commission. He wrote the following to the Governor of New Hampshire:

> The style selected is one which is of a public character and which grows naturally out of the size and requirements of the structure. It will be at once recognized, by all those conversant with such matters as the prevailing style of modern Europe,—a style which the taste of the leading architects of Paris in particular have largely illustrated under the patronage of the present Emperor, in most of the great works of the French capital . . . it has now been so successfully naturalized in other countries as to have become the prevailing manner. . . . I have earnestly desired in this respect, not to fall behind the progress of art . . . but to present a design which . . . will be found to commend itself to the legislature and its constituents, as graceful and harmonious . . . cheerful . . . without any very elaborate or costly decoration.[4]

The commissioners in Concord permitted Bryant to give their existing statehouse a modest Second Empire character by concealing the new top story in a mansard. Otherwise, the main changes were in the addition of a two-story portico and a tall dome. Within, the House of Representatives was elaborated with cove ceilings and pilasters, and Doric Hall was faithfully rebuilt; the only new embellishment permitted there was a simple plaster cornice.

Even the persuasive Bryant could not sell his Second Empire designs to the remodeling commission in Boston. He certainly tried, for the second and last time in a decade, even to the point of privately printing a costly folio edition of the several proposals and distributing it to the legislators. In Boston, as in Kansas, the introduction of the new richness and "foreignness" was acceptable only if it did not obscure the established architectural symbols of American democracy.

Some of America's best-trained architects were slow to grasp the nature of public works commissions. Architects with less training learned more readily that radical architectural concoctions must be made palatable with familiar spices. Like any businessman, the architect belonged to this age of enterprise, an age making up rules as it went along. A small group of Eastern architects, considering themselves professionals, were the only ones reluctant to compromise. Consequently, in the Gilded Age, only two state capitols came from the drawing tables of leading eastern architects.

The first architectural school in the United States was opened at the Massachusetts Institute of Technology after the end of the Civil War. Training in America was still more typically through apprenticeship, usually in New York, Philadelphia, or Boston. The system was slightly more regimented than it had been earlier in the nineteenth century, requiring an unprescribed period of service as a draftsman, at low wages, in the office of an architect or designer-builder. Precisely when the apprenticeship ended was decided by the architect, who was then expected to write letters of recommendation to the prospective clients of the former assistant. Some men entered the field of architecture through engineering; others rose from carpentry to contracting, and eventually to architecture. Designers of the state capitols of the Gilded Age had, in fact, the most varied sorts of previous experience.

Capitols were among the most costly architectural projects of the nineteenth century. It took nerve, some design talent, and a clever tongue to win jobs. Mingled with the lure of profit was the prospect of expressing oneself in mighty spaces and material lavishness.

For several people, the announcement in 1871 that Connecticut's two statehouses would at last be replaced by one enduring structure of stone was the siren's song. Hartford, the business center of the state, would be the permanent capital. The regional fever of the ante-bellum period had been strong in Hartford, where in the arts, education, and humanitarianism a dozen busy citizens took the lead and were supported by generous gifts of money from dozens more.

Horace Bushnell was a prime civic instigator. That opinionated little man was a familiar figure in Hartford. Congregational minister, author, and thinker of national reputation, he was rewarded in old age with abundant evidence of his own contributions. His favorite achievement was City Park, a green expanse of rolling land on which the city's worst slum had stood. Quiet negotiations had already begun for the purchase of the contiguous Trinity College, whose existing buildings were to be torn down to make room for the new Capitol. When he realized that Connecticut's halls of state would overlook his park, Horace Bushnell took an interest in their design.

On the five-man Capitol Commission, only two members could be considered active. The most vocal, if sometimes confused, was the chairman, Governor Marshall Jewell. Second in command was General William B. Franklin, the Captain of Engineers who succeeded Meigs at the national Capitol. His distinguished service in the war had won him the presidency of the Colt Firearms Company of Hartford. A third local party was James G. Batterson, Hartford businessman and friend of politicians. He owned a granite works in Rhode Island and had his own reasons for wanting to become involved in the Capitol project.

In September 1871, the Governor invited selected architects to enter a capitol competition. The building was to cost no more than $1,000,000; it was to be of granite; and the winning architect would be offered the position of superintendent at a good salary. On New Year's Day 1872, four sets of competition drawings were presented in the Governor's office; the fifth entry, on its way from the San Francisco office of Fuller & Laver, was held up by a snowstorm in the Rocky Mountains. James G. Batterson and the Scottish-born Hartford architect George Keller proposed a Gothic castle. George B. Post, a young New York engineer whose star as an architect was already rising, entered a Renaissance scheme. G. J. F. Bryant and Lewis P. Rogers presented a Second Empire project, printed especially for the commission on expensive paper.

From New York, Napoleon LeBrun, a former Philadelphia student of Walter, sent a design based on the national Capitol. Fuller & Laver's plan, described as a great quadrangle and probably like their Albany scheme, seems never to have arrived; no record of it exists today.

The commission could not reach a decision. An Illinois man named Elijah E. Myers wrote: "I am informed through the press that the board of Commissioners have rejected all designs submitted for your State Capitol. My plans have been adopted for the Capitol of Michigan and should your board desire I will forward the designs to them for their consideration. . . . I wish you would let me hear from you."[5]

Each of the five architects was compensated with $1,000, and a new competition was announced, which more architects were invited to enter. The commission's list is puzzling. Some, but not all, of the nation's architectural leaders were invited, along with others now forgotten: Peabody & Stearns, Charles B. Atwood, Hammatt & J. E. Billings, all of Boston; New York's Richard Michel Upjohn, and again George B. Post. The Hartford partners Batterson & Keller were included from the former competition, together with the obscure Elijah E. Myers from Illinois. Of those seven, only Myers failed to enter. Bryant & Rogers were excluded, along with Napoleon LeBrun and Fuller & Laver.

Because of the rather unrealistic deadline of three months, five of the eleven invited architects declined to submit plans. They were replaced by four Boston firms, Sturgis & Brigham, Emerson & Fehmer, William T. Hallett, and T. O. Langerfeldt; and the last to be invited was the Paris-educated Henry Hobson Richardson, in practice at the time in New York with Charles Gambrill, a former partner of George B. Post. On March 1 the commissioners cut open eleven postmarked parcels. As a safety measure, several of the architects had submitted two alternatives—one pious Gothic and the other worldly Renaissance, but both fitting the same plan.

But the commissioners were no better off than before. The plans submitted were not of chaste Grecian temples, but confusing complications of towers and steep roofs, superimposed arcades and irregularly spaced openings. The architects were asked to make oral persentations of their designs. The drawings were exhibited in the Senate chamber for public inspection, then taken to New Haven and displayed for six days in the Street Art Gallery at Yale.

Most of the architects appeared personally before the commissioners in their deliberations in the old Senate chamber. The question of a dome had already arisen, although none of the projects had one. George B. Post denounced any scheme in which the "mass was dwarfed by its own dome." Instead, he explained, "The style of architecture which I have adopted is that which has developed in the erection of . . . many . . . public buildings of France—And is, I think, far more appropriate, and know it to be more economical, than the huge mass of columns, cornices, & pediments usual in such structures—whose great projections cast a dark shade into the windows and whose effect is rather showy, than dignified and elegant."[6]

Peabody & Stearns advised a minimum of ornament in their Gothic design: "The pointed arch in itself gives an effect and picturesqueness which would outbalance many carefully carved & expensive classical mouldings, pediments & cornices—we should depend entirely upon these arches & the several groupings for our effects, only adding certain variations in the tints of the stone—some polished shafts, a few carved capitals & the like."[7]

The proposal of T. L. Langerfeldt featured a tall clock tower. "The style chosen," he wrote, "is Modern Renaissance, distinguished from the other Renaissances in finding its new birth in an understanding and study of the spirit of Classical Masters and ages, and not a mechanical copy of their monuments."[8]

Gambrill and Richardson presented a small printed book outlining views, not dissimilar to those of the *Néo-grec* circle in Paris with which Richardson was in contact while working there for Henri Labrouste's brother Théodore. The ideas put forth in the Hartford pamphlet shed considerable light on Richardson's thinking at this critical point in his career, only a few months before he entered the competition for Trinity Church in Boston that was to make him famous:

> In selecting the style for a monumental work such as a State House is, or should be, the architect should have in view, *first*, its historical character, as illustrating the architectural history of the country; and, *second*, its adaptation to the material, or to the material and the proposed outlay combined. Having no architectural type of our own, as distinctively American to follow, we have a greater latitude of selection than would obtain in any of the countries in the Old World; for, without any national traditions to maintain, we can choose among all styles and all ages. . . . In the design herewith presented, we have had recourse, therefore, to the principles of design and construction of [the] builders of the middle ages. . . . It is difficult to give a name to this style, which has grown out of the "Gothic Revival," but to which the term Gothic cannot be applied without misleading· those to whom the name suggests pointed arches and delicate tracery . . . this *new* style is in reality a Renaissance of those characteristics of the meridian period [presumably Byzantine and Romanesque] of sound and beautiful building which common sense suggests as most appropriate to the social and practical wants of our own day.[9]

The Connecticut Capitol Commission had yet to be convinced. Pressures intensified on all sides, and the commissioners merely increased their problems by openly discussing modifications with their favorite architects. By April, Richardson, who had agreed to make some changes in the entrance suggested by General Franklin and Judge William D. Shipman, wrote, "after considering the matter [I] hardly feel that I would be acting rightly toward my fellow competitors if I, having seen all the other designs present in this state of the competition altered [my] sketch. I can only assure you that the alteration had suggested itself to me before my drawings were forwarded and only a lack of time prevented me carrying it out—"[10]

Richard M. Upjohn wrote to Governor Jewell, "Allow me to congratulate you on your succession to the gubernatorial office. Being a kind of a rabid republican myself I naturally sympathize. . . . I met Post the other day he told me that you would adopt one of those plans on Tuesday last. Did you do so—if not when will you? You recollect when I saw you last that was before I made a plan you said I should be *your* man—OK then I hope you will vote for me as the architect of the building."[11]

From Richard M. Upjohn, State Capitol, Hartford, Connecticut (*Hartford: 1886*)
Connecticut Capitol, by Richard M. Upjohn, 1873–79, Senate chamber as completed.

Such letters flew particularly between New York and Hartford through the spring of 1872. Horace Bushnell, who had been silent, strolled down to the statehouse and perused the lines of plans along the walls.

At the end of his patience, he wrote to the Governor, "I am under a vow not to meddle with the public in the papers any more. . . . I find two good, very good plans in Battersons and Richardsons. . . . The front entrances of both are faulty—Battersons in being too Church like, with a spire too spiritually thin. Richardsons has a small uncovered doorway and I don't see how it can have any other. . . . Excuse me for this obtrusion on your patience." Ten days later he added: "My dear sir Pardon me as a meddler just once more. I saw Richardson here in town yesterday and he told me that he has an entrance already planned—also an amended form for the low projecting part. . . . But he will not consent to show what he has got, lest it should not be honorable. But I think Batterson is not satisfied with his entrance and would like to amend that also. Now if it should be the mind of the commissioners that they will take one or the other of these two, I suggest that they say so, and dismiss the others."[12]

On April 18, 1872, Upjohn's plans were unanimously selected by the Capitol Commission. This announcement was the opening trumpet of a war which lasted until the autumn, when there was a silence which could best be described as no more than a cease-fire.

The majority of the competitors packed up their plans peacefully and went home that April, leaving the field of battle to Batterson, Richardson, Upjohn, countless local figures, and, oddly enough, G. J. F. Bryant, who brought his plans back to town. With the exception of Batterson, every man presenting proposals was considered a professional architect; while they all talked about ethics, their competitive conduct was ruthless.

The English-born Upjohn had been taken to America as a child. His father, Richard Upjohn, was by midcentury the most famous church architect in the United States, and the son

From Richard M. Upjohn, State Capitol, Hartford, Connecticut (*Hartford: 1886*)
Connecticut Capitol, by Richard M. Upjohn, as completed in 1879

studied and worked in his father's New York office for many years before they formed a partnership.

While no innocent, Upjohn was surprised by the precariousness of his appointment as State Capitol Architect of Connecticut, and family friends in New York were astounded. Upjohn received a note that summer from the very successful Paris-trained architect Richard M. Hunt:

> A few days since Mr. Batterson sent a person to me to make arrangements about preparing a design for the state house at Hartford Ct.! I said I thought Commissioners had awarded the work to you, he replied that it was so but that opinions differed about the matter. & that the question would be brought up before the Legislature & he wanted a design already to shew—I expressed surprise & said . . . that what he proposed was outrageous—and that there was not enough money in the United States to tempt me . . . besides I thought that no contractor should offer designs. . . . I drop you this line to post you—His designs are boxed in my office but are to be returned to him in Hartford.[13]

Upjohn was directed by the commissioners to make certain changes in his elevations, and was given until May 1872 to produce the new renderings. Meanwhile, Bushnell and Batterson collected political allies, including—ironically—Governor Jewell. It was summer before Upjohn realized that his one true friend on the commission was General Franklin, who felt that the architect was being abused. The more the battle raged, the stronger Franklin became in his support of Upjohn.

On September 16, 1872, after Franklin had gained public admiration by reprimanding Batterson and Bushnell, Governor Jewell resigned from the Capitol Commission. His resignation was only too cheerfully accepted, but the commissioners knew that in so doing, they had numbered their days. Jewell and Batterson conducted a campaign of slander against Upjohn. On October 10, in spite of it all, Batterson's construction bid proved to be the lowest, and the commissioners signed a contract with him.

Seven days later construction began. By Christmas, politics had done its work: The commission was dismissed, with no provision for the future, while Batterson's workmen proceeded with the foundation of the Capitol.

A new Capitol Commission was not appointed by the legislature until midsummer 1873. General Franklin, its chairman, had obviously been doing some politicking on his own. His old employee from national Capitol days, James A. Brown, was elected Clerk of the Commission. Since the war Brown had appeared whenever the General needed him. In Hartford he had supervised the construction of the Colt factory and E. T. Potter's Church of the Good Shepherd. Now he had left "a good position in New York" to help again.[14]

On August 7, 1873, the architects appeared before the new commission: Bryant & Rogers from Boston, Gambrill & Richardson from New York, Upjohn, and of course Batterson from Hartford, now with an alternative plan. This time there was none of the noise of the previous competition. Dr. Bushnell stayed away. A new silence had fallen over Hartford; so much of the town's economic lifeblood, flowing through the insurance companies headquartered there, had been drained by the Chicago fire two years before and the recent one in Boston. The general downward spin of business, soon to be called the Panic of 1873, was already jarring nerves.

Upjohn's plans were adopted, pending revisions, which the architect made within a few days. Bryant & Rogers and Gambrill & Richardson went home for good, but Batterson made one last unsuccessful try for his and Keller's Gothic scheme. General Franklin stepped down as chairman to take the job of Chief Engineer. Feeling the financial pinch of the Panic in New York, Upjohn requested a salaried superintending position on the Capitol project. But too many people were already employed on the Hartford work, and the architect's application was refused.

Connecticut's Capitol was not finished until eight years after construction had started. But the conflicts, and even scandals, by no means ended with the final selection of Upjohn as architect. The High Victorian Gothic design was radical for a capitol. This was the largest public building in that extravagant mode ever erected in America, and it continued to ignite controversy with each new legislature and each new politician who gazed with conservative horror on the rising granite walls. Even to the sophisticated, the arcades, the polished columns, the rich carving, the sharp-pointed towers were still strange and foreign (though they were already going out of fashion by the late 1870's).

Before the ultimate form of the Hartford building was comprehensible on its hilltop, Albany erupted in renewed political turmoil over the New York Capitol, resulting in the dismissal of Thomas Fuller. Construction scandals had been the deciding straw; but there were deeper reasons, both in the dislike of Fuller's Second Empire design and in personal ambition on the part of the New York City architectural circle. Fuller was replaced by an Advisory Committee under Lieutenant Governor William Dorsheimer. Members included the landscape designer Frederick Law Olmsted, Leopold Eidlitz, a long-established New York architect, and H. H. Richardson, whose reputation was then being made with the construction of Trinity Church in Boston.

The committee changed the Fuller design so that at the second-story level the Second Empire yielded to a massive and plain medievalizing mode closer to Eidlitz's Germanic *Rundbogenstil* than to the new "Richardsonian Romanesque" that would soon be so fashionable nationally. The alteration touched off a great controversy spearheaded by Manhattan professionals.

Surprisingly, most of the criticism at Hartford tended toward praise. While Richardson, Eidlitz, and Olmsted sucessfully presented a united front against the construction of a dome on the New York Capitol, Upjohn in Connecticut was willing to yield. He proposed modifications in the design, which were quickly approved. The greatest difference would be on the exterior: "the square tower of 20 feet in diameter [is] to be changed to a domed tower of marble and iron, 56 feet in diameter and 240 feet in height."[15]

The completed building is still Hartford's crown. From a distance the massing appears crisp, almost Renaissance in character, despite the sumptuous and abundant Gothic detail carved in stone. But the upward slash of granite arches, columns, and steep towers belie the dominant horizontality, giving a dramatically animated sense of contrast to the whole. Most of the rich exterior carvings recounted some aspect of Connecticut history. Upjohn, an amateur local historian, envisioned statues of heroes to fill the many round niches above the porches; he temporarily ordered the openings plugged with stone, as most of them remain today. On the interior, a tall central space rose between giant L-shaped piers up into the inner shell of the dome. Like the rest of the public rooms originally, this is frescoed in deep tones of red, gold, green, blue, and ochre, with fields of sky blue spangled with gold stars. Flanking the central space were two glazed light-courts banked by three levels of Gothic arcades. Such courts, monumental expansions of the small ventilation and light-courts in Ohio, would appear in many later state-houses. The legislative chambers were not balanced, but were arranged asymmetrically as in the earlier New England statehouses at Boston and Montpelier. Curiously, this is the only example of characteristic Gothic asymmetry in a building that is basically symmetrical throughout.

Richard M. Upjohn had gone further than any capitol architect in creating that romantic ambience based on history that was so revered by the age. He had freed himself to do so by adding the dome his critics wanted, though he went to considerable effort to show that it did not belong above the mass of a Gothic building: The thin web of its exterior decoration—a ring of statues and Gothic carving—gives it the superficial feeling of a temporary pavilion built for a festival, a Field of the Cloth of Gold. Within the central saloon Upjohn made no effort to conceal the mighty piers supporting the dome. On the contrary, he designed them with such functional simplicity that they appear to be intruders, forced in between the two very open staircases. The dome was Upjohn's compromise; it was for him what the Choragic Monument of Lysicrates before it had been for Strickland. Once the building had been given the familiar culminating feature that made it understandable to the lay commissioners, Upjohn never again had to defend the merits of his design.

In Hartford, at the close of an argument with his commission, Upjohn exclaimed: "I hope the cause of art will prevail."[16] Even in Hartford, which had valid claims to being a leading intellectual community, Upjohn was considered impractical and, in some matters, foolish. That attitude is reflected in the commission's repeated refusal to permit him to be more than an adviser.

The Gilded Age would end before architects finally adopted Ithiel Town's maxims about marketing architecture as a product. Bizarre, complicated, and unfamiliar designs confused and frightened public works commissioners. Architects were expected to provide guidance; those who invited conflict moved fast to their own ruin. Even by the end of the century those various people building the Capitol at Albany had not yet learned to compromise, and their project was a history of recurrent dissatisfaction and alteration for thirty years.

Of the thirteen new capitols built from the close of the Civil War until 1890, only Hartford's and portions of New York's were designed by architects whose names have been remembered. On several occasions, however, rather well-known men served as consultants or were concerned with remodeling. For example, in 1871 and 1872, a Philadelphia architect, Samuel Sloan, further enlarged and redecorated in gold, red, and imperial blue the venerable 1792 statehouse at Trenton, New Jersey, adding new sky-lit legislative chambers and deliberately covering up what anyone had done before, including Doan and John Notman. And Bryant, of course, had remodeled the statehouse at Concord.

166   Leading architects did not avoid the competitions. On the contrary, they were very much

in evidence, sometimes in person, for any job of the large scale and great cost of state capitols. As in New York and Connecticut, they fought among themselves, all the while denouncing men of lesser stature or training as "nonprofessional" for using orthodox business tactics. But the lesser-known architects repeatedly won, generally pleasing their legislative clients and the public by speaking a language both parties understood.

For the most part the capitols of the Gilded Age followed the monumental pattern of the national Capitol, incorporating the dome, rotunda, temple portico, and wings at the ends. Other features, such as colossal orders of columns, were incidental. By the end of the century the syndrome had even spread to some of the Canadian provinces and to Europe. Although those architectural symbols had long been familiar in American statehouse design, capitol builders of the late nineteenth century believed what they were doing was making bold improvements on what existed in Washington.

During the whole period there were only five exceptions: New York, Nevada, Idaho, and two in West Virginia. In 1875–76, the city fathers of Charleston, West Virginia, hoping to attract the seat of government away from Wheeling, built a round-arched structure, towered and mansarded. Like its rival in Wheeling, built in 1869, it was erected hurriedly and at private expense, free from the influence of public or legislative criticism. Charleston's Romantic State-house—a distant echo of the one in Albany—finally won out, largely because of the town's location on the Baltimore & Ohio Railroad, and served for many years as the state Capitol.

What Nevada and Idaho built were really oversized courthouses. Both were smaller than many metropolitan city halls. Nevada would probably have postponed the erection of a capitol had the new United States Mint not been built in Carson City at the close of the war. Supervising Architect of the Treasury Alfred B. Mullett designed the Mint as one of the numerous public edifices in the rising tide of governmental construction that had begun in the 1850's. It took five years to complete this Italianate structure; in 1870, one year later, Nevada proudly dedicated its own Italianate Capitol on the same dirt street. The modest, round-arched villa, all of fine local stone, was erected in eight months and soon dominated the landscape—as it still does— by its quality, though not its size.

Joseph Gosling, a San Francisco architect, had submitted the winning plans for Nevada. He had undoubtedly been familiar with the new Mint; the kinship of his design to that Federal structure is obvious.

On New Year's Day 1871, the *Daily State Register* rolled off the presses in a snow-covered Carson City with this headline: "A SPLENDID EDIFICE." Its style, the article went,

> is of a modern order of architecture, compounded of the Corinthian Ionic
> and Doric . . . all the openings are exteriorly finished with rustic coines,
> window jams and heart-stones, incourses to suit the random-tooled ashlar
> stone work of the front. The cornice around the entire roof and base of
> gables is formed of heavy foot mould and modillion or Ionic cornices. . . .
> The cupola rises 48 feet above the roof, octagon in form . . . and is sup-
> ported by 16 ornamental pilasters and buttresses. . . . Altogether Nevada's

new Capitol is an ornament to Carson City. . . . The flag staff was raised on the new Capitol, yesterday afternoon, for the first time, and the Star Spangled Banner was thrown to the breeze.[17]

Not until summer was the velvet-lined cornerstone laid in a Masonic ceremony. Miners, volunteer companies, and firemen from all the little towns and diggings of the region filled the day and night with revelry. Gamblers and sharks did business, and the madams from Nevada's best houses sent their girls. On Capitol Square two grandstands accommodated—and protected— dignitaries. The two houses of the legislature lay at each end of the second floor. The kerosene chandeliers, lambrequins of silk brocade, Brussels carpets, and Corinthian columns of painted tin were splendid beyond what most local people had ever seen. And to view such grace in the new country brought a sense of great accomplishment. A little stair ascended from the upper hallway to the cupola, "which drinks in the day," noted a reporter "through forty lights of crystal sheet glass."[18] From there the dedication parade of 750 could be seen in the street weaving through a crowd of many thousands.

Carson City's Italian Villa Capitol, exceptional for its small scale, is like a private mansion. Except for its Romantic mood, it was a reversion to the simple town hall type of American statehouse. It was not unlike the original Trenton Statehouse or the Maryland Statehouse before the addition of its historic dome. For a brief period, fifteen years later, it would have a kinsman in the "Norman" courthouse Capitol built in 1885 at Boise, Idaho, by Elijah E. Myers—who, it might be remembered, had offered his assistance to the Connecticut Capitol Commission in 1872.

Other states had grander ambitions. The Springfield, Illinois, businessmen whose offer of a tomb for President Lincoln had been rejected now proposed the same site for a new state capitol. On February 25, 1867, the Governor signed a bill authorizing the transfer of the old statehouse to the city and county in exchange for the land where the tomb stood and $200,000 in cash. An attempt by Chicago investors to win the seat of government was deftly turned by Springfield politicians into a big-city-against-small-town fight; but the rural villages of Illinois had such voting strength that the Chicagoans timidly withdrew.

The relatively peaceful open competition began with a notice in selected newspapers, and inquiring architects were sent a printed circular outlining what would be required:

> Stone will be the principal material. . . . No "style" or "order" of architecture has been decided upon. Each architect will consult his own taste; select such "order" as he may deem most suitable for a building of this character, but avoiding extreme or superfluous ornament, the Commissioners preferring simplicity and solidity. The great desideratum is a Hall of Repre-sentatives, with the capacity to seat not less than three hundred members; each member with a separate desk, two desks between each aisle; main aisle five feet, others three feet. The general plan and size of the building must conform to that one idea, AMPLE ROTUNDA AND HALLS.[19]

Considering the appropriation was $3,000,000, it is surprising that the competition at-tracted so few entries. The press, covering the current New York competition, had made the

Nevada Capitol, by Joseph Gosling, 1872

public aware of the big money involved in capitol buildings. Still, even the Albany competition was limited to a largely regional response. Springfield was beginning to show the first signs of change; all but two of the entries were architects from the East, for whom Illinois meant a journey of several days by train. Thomas Fuller and Walter Dickson, the Albany architect whose awkward adaptation of the United States Capitol had placed in the second competition in New York, were among the competitors. Also represented were one firm from Massachusetts and two from Pennsylvania, and individual entries from Macon City, Missouri, and Chicago. John C. Cochrane of Chicago submitted the winning design.

The Cochrane office was by no means Chicago's largest, but some maneuvering in Springfield during the competition suggests Cochrane had influence in Illinois politics. As a youth he left the New Hampshire builder under whom he had served an apprenticeship and made his way west, attracted by Chicago's postwar boom. He successfully built small houses and stores, and won a contract for a church before the capitol competition in 1867.

Two employees in Cochrane's office probably were the authors of the Capitol design. Alfred H. Piquenard, a forty-year-old naturalized citizen, born a few miles northwest of Paris near the town of Bernay, was a civil engineer, a graduate of the Ecole Centrale. He had come to America in 1849 on the second expedition of Etienne Cabet's communistic Icarians, and for most of the decade before the war he had lived with them in the Illinois town of Nauvoo, sold

Illinois State Archives

Illinois Capitol, Springfield, J. C. Cochrane's accepted project, 1867

to the Icarians by the Mormons. Restless, Piquenard had escaped now and then to St. Louis to work as an architect, then served the Union in the war before settling in Chicago. His fellow employee in Cochrane's office was George C. Garnsey. A headstrong twenty-seven-year-old, Garnsey took full credit for the Illinois Capitol design, and admitted contempt for the Frenchman. Piquenard later said of him: "He is a young man, and I suppose he will be called a good architect if he lives long enough."[20]

170   On February 5, 1868, Cochrane and Piquenard formed a partnership and signed the con-

Iowa Capitol, Des Moines, Cochrane & Piquenard's project, 1872

tract with the state of Illinois. Work began at once. The basement was complete in the fall of 1869 when several legislators from Chicago demanded an investigation of what the building would ultimately cost. A long hearing proved that everything was satisfactory, and the commission was actually urged to make some costly changes in the plans.

The enemies of Springfield had their chance to sabotage the Capitol in 1870; they added a clause to the new Constitution of Illinois that in appropriations exceeding $3,500,000, the electorate must make the decision. The additions to the original design had already placed the

171

projected cost higher than that. Shrewdly, the commissioners remained calm; if necessary, they would demand more money. They believed in the design, which they engraved on their letterhead, and decided to see it through to the last cent of the amount allowed by the Constitution.

Piquenard moved to Springfield, where he took personal charge of the work. He made changes in some of the details, exhibiting, as one architectural periodical was to write about him several years later, "the free exercise of his exuberance in ornamental designing."[21] His partner now turned his attention to getting jobs for the firm elsewhere in the Midwest and Chicago, and was seldom involved to any great extent with the Illinois Capitol.

It was probably shortly before his move to Springfield that the talented Piquenard drew the winning plans in the competition for the Capitol of Iowa at Des Moines. He called his grandiose scheme "Palladian," though the name hardly applied to the style.

The commission sent that and three other proposals for evaluation to Edward Clark, Capitol Architect in Washington. September 24, 1870, Clark wrote to the commissioners that he liked the elevation of Palladian, but preferred the plan entered by J. C. Farrand, a Des Moines architect. On October 5 the commission of businessmen made a predictable resolution: "*Resolved,* that the Superintendant and Architect to be selected be directed to modify the ground plan of Mr. Farrand as reported . . . and also to modify, the elevation of said plan so as to correspond with the so-called *Palladian Plan* now before this Commission."[22] Cochrane and Piquenard were given the jobs of superintendent and architect, Farrand won the prize money, and nobody was displeased with the decision.

Construction on the two capitols continued into the late 1880's. Cochrane & Piquenard maintained offices in Chicago, Springfield, and Des Moines. To an investigating committee in 1871, Piquenard described the demands the Illinois Capitol alone made on his Monroe Street office in Springfield:

> I have had as high as twelve men employed upon this building. I have now four men. Sometimes I have three, four or five—depends upon how the work is going on. Upon the average we have certainly had four men employed all the time since we started. For months we had as high as twelve. . . . They work in the drawings after I pencil them out; occupied in tracing and so forth. The best thing for you to do is to go to the office and see what they are doing. They are making plans for each stone in the building. Each separate stone has to be marked out; a drawing has to be made of every stone, one above another. The size, length and height, with every job, and every piece has to be marked out, so the stone cutter cannot possibly mistake one stone for another. There is not one stone in that building that is not drawn five times. . . . I work day and night. I didn't sleep more than four hours any night while I was making those drawings.[23]

The great Chicago fire of 1871 created so much business that Cochrane resigned both Capitol jobs, writing to the Illinois Commission that the stricken city "has called into requisition the immediate service of her architects . . . considering the small compensation received for

Services as Architect of your new Capital, I feel it my duty to . . . tender my resignation to take effect as soon as consistant with the terms of our Contract."[24] He apparently dissolved the partnership as well. Several months later he withdrew his resignations, writing to the commissioners at Des Moines that he had returned "upon the urgent request of many of the citizens of the State of Iowa."[25] The two commissioners then took him back, and when he resigned for good in the autumn of 1872 the Iowa Commission resolved "to place on record a recognition of his abilities in his profession."[26]

Piquenard was more constant, remaining at the Springfield and Des Moines posts until his death. After Cochrane's departure, the commissions granted Piquenard a leave of absence to travel in Europe to study domes. Upon his return he enlarged the design for the Iowa dome. His own copy of the *Specifications and Description of the Materials and Workmanship Necessary in the Erection of the New Illinois State House* had the state name marked out, and the word "Iowa" substituted above it, indicating that while the designs were only somewhat similar, the building specifications were approximately the same. He died in Springfield November 19, 1876, when the capitols of Iowa and Illinois were no more than unfinished shells.

One of Piquenard's assistants, M. E. Bell, formed a partnership with W. F. Hackney of Des Moines and they became the architects for the Iowa Capitol Commission. Bell revised Piquenard's dome and roof, and modified the interior ornamentation. In Springfield, W. W. Boyington of Chicago, sometime partner of E. Townsend Mix, assumed the duties of capitol architect. For Boyington there was little but the interior finish to be done; at Des Moines, however, much of the construction had yet to be started.

The commissions were the sources of endless trouble to the architects, and there were further legislative investigations. Work in Springfield was carried to within about $60,000 of the limit set by the Constitution before construction was halted. The great building stood without its porticoes for six years, while the legislature, in unfinished chambers within, debated the structure's faults. Not until 1883 was the electorate willing to vote the funds needed to finish the job.

M. E. Bell was entirely responsible for the manner in which the Des Moines building was finished, although he left in 1884 while construction was still in progress, to take the post of Supervising Architect of the Treasury Department. After Bell's removal to Washington, Hackney completed the Iowa Capitol, seeing to the last minute details of its furnishings in the spring of 1887.

These capitols of Alfred Piquenard are among the unforgettable sights of the Midwest. They once stood taller than anything else in the region; train passengers said they seemed to grow from the land, long before the rooftops and chimneys of Des Moines or Springfield came into view. The architect had given them a cosmopolitan touch befitting a maturing state, and at the same time he followed the outline of the national Capitol.

At Springfield the Washington model is more evident than at Des Moines, where the ends of the wings are heavily stressed in an English Baroque way by corner towers each crowned with its own small dome and lantern. Some collaboration between Piquenard and Cochrane probably went on at Springfield, judging from that Capitol's similarity to the one in Des Moines. Bell's

173

particular contribution at Des Moines was the dome, which he completely redesigned on the pattern of St. Peter's in Rome; Piquenard's associated towers recall ones on Vanbrugh's monumental country houses. The choice of such European models was unusual for the 1870's and 1880's, if not for succeeding decades.

The two Midwestern capitols were variations on the same scheme. The projecting blocks of the five-part façades recall the New Louvre, which Piquenard admired. Colossal orders formed the porticoes. Fine native stone of a yellowish-gold gave a quality of powdery softness to the exterior walls with lighter stone for all the trim, and the connecting sections were designed to suggest very tall glazed galleries behind three-story arcades. The dome in Springfield was like a separate structure; its four axial porticoes were hoisted on a towerlike tapered base under a tall drum and dome. Reminiscent of the Paris Invalides, it was, all the same, quite as pointed as Upjohn's in Hartford. Mansard roofs capping only the end pavilions were covered with fish-scale zinc shingles pierced by round dormers.

Within the capitols, the long halls, great rotundas, and legislative chambers were given the richest treatment with a limited use of marble and a lavish use of scagliola, the secret of which Piquenard had taught the local plasterers. The big gasoliers were adorned with gold leaf and brown, mustard, and maroon paint; etched glass moons over their flames were tinted pale pink. From the grand ceremonial spaces, lines of office doors opened to reveal simple rooms with domestic gas brackets and radiators.

Commenting on the Capitol in Springfield, the editor of *The American Architect and Building News*, addressing himself to the architectural profession, wrote: "Of the exterior of the building the impression given is not so favorable as that of the interior; and one cannot help feeling that this is one of the last domed State Houses of what may be called the 'vernacular American type' that we shall see erected."[27] The judgment was hasty. In these legislative palaces architect and layman commissioner had found a common ground of agreement. The stage was set; the Gilded Age of state capitols awaited its prime protagonist.

A few blocks out on Monroe Street in Springfield, beyond Piquenard's office, lived the architect Elijah E. Myers, who would soon become the greatest capitol-builder of the Gilded Age. He was forty-two in 1870, when Cochrane & Piquenard's main office was moved from Chicago.

Springfield was a small town, so Myers must have known the successful architects of the new Capitol. He was brassy anyway, and he had always made it a point to know the best people or at least a useful few wherever he lived. Each morning on his way to his own office downtown in the Lewis Block, Myers passed the windows of the tireless Piquenard; through them could be seen the six-foot square linen sheets weighted with dowels on which the Capitol's elevations and plans were being meticulously drawn in lines of India ink and washed with watercolor. Piquenard's heavy accent was not alien to Myers's ears; he had lived among many tongues back in Philadelphia, in the days when he still practiced the trade of carpenter. He had gone home each day from his work to a dwelling in the working-class Frankford district. His neighbors were coachmen, housemaids, washerwomen, and laborers. Nearly all of them were immigrants from Europe.

He had abandoned that world of monotonous brick row houses, noisy streets, and long hours of hard work when he left Philadelphia at the beginning of the war. It can be said of Myers that in the 1860's he leaped from the old into the new. The transformation from carpenter to architect took place on the way from Philadelphia to Illinois. In a loft over Chaterton's Jewelry Store in Springfield he opened his first architectural office, and in the nine or so years since then, his fortunes had improved. His worth of $200 in Pennsylvania in 1860 had already grown in Springfield to $19,000. E. E. Myers had earned every penny of it.

No one would have guessed that such a dandy as he was ever a carpenter. He was a boyish-looking man, narrow-shouldered, with a short thick neck, prominent nose, and a little mouth pursed behind the fringes of a theatrical-looking moustache. An old photograph shows him with his long hair slicked back, forming curls. His light, probably flannel, jacket, and silky striped cravat have not a single wrinkle.

How Elijah Myers came to architecture is not clear. He is known to have had a long friendship with Samuel Sloan, who had himself risen from the trade of carpentry and for most of his career listed himself in the Philadelphia directories both as carpenter and as architect. Myers and Sloan frequently recommended one another for jobs. Myers's toughness, aggressiveness, and lack of artistic pretentiousness were like Sloan's, and he seemed intrigued by the business world's reckless competitiveness in the 1870's and 1880's. He was a superb draftsman, though where he got his first lessons remains a mystery. One thing seems certain: It was on Piquenard's drafting table that he first saw the splendidly monumental elevations which fired his own ambition to build capitols.

Before long, Myers was a competitor of Cochrane & Piquenard. He was among eighty architects who inquired about the new Michigan Capitol Competition, announced through the press June 6, 1871. Myers had already made a reputation for himself as a designer of public buildings. His most ambitious project thus far was the Freeport, Illinois, Courthouse, a decorative and costly Second Empire structure still unfinished at the time of the Michigan competition. Myers's stationery had a printed perspective of this courthouse beside the following legend:

E. E. MYERS
ARCHITECT AND SUPERINTENDENT
Plans Furnished For

FIREPROOF COURTHOUSES   SUBURBAN RESIDENCES
School Buildings, Churches, Jails, Etc.

"My Dear Governor," he wrote on April 24, 1871, responding to an earlier letter from Michigan, "I expected to visit your city before this time, My business engagements requiring my close attention has prevented me from carrying out the proposed visit. I see in the Chicago papers that you propose to visit our city this week. Should you do so please call and see me. I have several designs I wish to show you and to ascertain your views in regard to your State House design. I wish to submit a full set of designs for your consideration."[28]

The Chicago fire destroyed numerous plans being prepared by Chicago architects, so as a courtesy the deadline was extended to the end of December. Twenty designs, packed in huge pine crates and tin containers, were assembled in the commission office in the old frame Capitol at Lansing by January 1872. On January 24 the E. E. Myers project was unanimously selected. Myers had entered the usual minimum of sheets to indicate the general layout and design. Now he was faced with completing an entire set of working drawings, for the commissioners wanted work to begin as soon as possible. Myers seems to have had no assistance in his office, and as an informal part of the bargain, he had agreed to move to Michigan.

"I have all the detail drawings completed of the stone work and one half of the detail finished for the Carpenter work," he wrote to Governor H. P. Baldwin, commission chairman, in April 1872. "I am drawing all of the several parts of the work full size. So far I have all the detail every minute every part of the several connections clearly shown will write you soon again and let you know how soon I will get through, the work has occupied all my time upon the Capitol."[29] One month later he wrote that he was ready to "ink up the drawings" and send them on. "I will remain in Lansing several days," he added, "in order to get the location of the building on the ground and ascertain the grade line that we can fully determine the depth of excavation and foundation in order that there will not have to be made any changes after the contract has been let."[30] The architect had made contacts with suppliers in Philadelphia and New York, and the construction firm of N. Osborne & Co. of Rochester, New York, was awarded the main contract.

The Myers design won out over at least one Second Empire scheme with mansard roofs and towers. His Capitol project was a monumental version of the courthouses he completed over the next thirty years, especially the ones in Carlinville and Freeport, Illinois. Michigan was to have a statehouse of considerable grandeur, but without ostentation; it was, in fact, simpler than at least three of the other entries—the Second Empire runner-up and two designs based on the rising Illinois Capitol.

Myers designed a five-part plan, consisting of three parallel rectangles connected by subsidiary elements. In his scheme, an elongated bottlelike version of the national Capitol dome rose over the central and largest rectangle. The colonnade around the dome was not continuous as at Washington, but varied by projections on the four sides, rather like the porticoes at Springfield. This became a favorite Myers theme. From a low, rusticated basement, three stories of equal height extended to the terminal cornice on the wings and connecting links; there was even a fourth story over the central section. On the principal façade, pilasters defined the levels: Doric on the first floor, next Ionic, and then Corinthian, but the corners of the central section had broad chains of rustication. Windows on the first story were arched, with those above pedimented, repeating again and again the theme already established by the pediments of the three main sections. A ceremonial stair ascended to a balustraded double portico, itself on a shallow projection from the main block with columns of the same orders as those on the corresponding wall surfaces.

It is a building of almost academic restraint, though the roof decorations are lively, with the ventilators of the two legislative houses disguised as tin imitations of the dome. But it was in such trivial features that Myers often revealed uncertainty about his own designs.

Michigan's Capitol was not Elijah Myers's most representative building, for his destiny

Michigan Capitol, winning project by E. E. Myers, 1871

was to build other more splendid edifices. Yet its historical sources are so obvious that the Capitol stands apart from others of the Gilded Age. The New York City Hall comes immediately to mind in the delicate scale of the portico and the strong, forward projection of the wings. Elements of the central section recall Boston, both as built by Bulfinch and in one of Bryant's proposed remodelings. For such borrowings one might expect intellectual explanations from a more sophisticated designer; Myers's reasons are still a matter of conjecture.

On the architect's suggestion the commission employed O. Marble as assistant superintendent. Every step of the construction was carefully watched, and the state of Michigan was rewarded by having exceptionally fine stonework and interior finish, as well as some money left over in the budget.

On October 3, 1873, the cornerstone was laid in a Masonic ceremony. Women's rights groups protested in the press that not only was the ceremony dominated by men, but that the bleachers were made with men in mind. A very proud E. E. Myers marched in the parade beside the Governor. He had moved his wife, two children, and office to Detroit, where he would remain for the rest of his life. When asked to describe the style of the new Capitol, Myers, perhaps remembering Piquenard in Springfield, replied, "Palladian."

While the capitols under construction in New York, Connecticut, Illinois, and Iowa were constantly in the news because of their problems, the Michigan project attracted attention because its progress was free of trouble. Myers's career blossomed accordingly. He was considered a practical man, not an artist, and an honest one. Myers himself heartily agreed with both appraisals. The questionable shortcuts he sometimes took in the name of these traits brought accusations of unprofessional conduct. But Myers never considered himself a professional. He was first of all a salesman; public buildings were his product. His promise to clients that he could design, plan, and superintend in an efficient manner painless to commissioners and legislators infuriated other architects, who branded him a liar and a fraud. Yet he could produce what he promised. Hospitals, churches, schools, city halls, and over one hundred courthouses took form on his drafting table in the heyday of his architectural career.

From his Detroit office he issued a printed leaflet explaining his position. "DO YOU INTEND TO BUILD?" was the initial headline, with a second caption, "SHALL I EMPLOY AN ARCHITECT?" To that last he replied that "circumstances" should govern:

> This country is filled with self-styled architects—Picture peddlers, with no practical knowledge of building,—young men, who have learned something of draughting in an architect's office, and put up a sign, and solicit patronage; and lead those who employ them into embarassment, and perhaps ruin. . . . Do not employ an architect unless he can refer you satisfactorily to *work which he has already done*. . . . Require your architect *to guarantee his work to be correct*. . . . If he objects . . . do not employ him. . . . If you have a neighbor who contemplates building, kindly show him this circular.[31]

Elijah Myers thus offered to commissioners everywhere the safe alternative of a packaged deal. Few competitions escaped his watchful eye. In 1873 he entered one sponsored by the state of Indiana. The old temple Capitol had become crowded with offices, structurally deteriorated, and inadequate for the enlarged legislature. Of the four sets of plans entered, G. B. F. Cooper's of Indianapolis was chosen. But the Panic of 1873 hit Indiana hard and put a halt to the building program.

It was not until March 14, 1877, that a new capitol bill was carried to victory in the legislature. The commission at once prepared for a second competition, and the four former competitors brought out their plans again. The commission, to accommodate Myers, agreed to travel as a body to Lansing to inspect the still-unfinished Capitol there. Certain features pleased them, notably the sky-lit transverse halls, which Myers had probably adapted from Upjohn's in Connecticut. Indiana's Capitol commissioners, however, still wanted a competition, and there was pressure from all over the state to proceed. Myers revised his plans and entered the new competition.

Of the twenty-four entries, most were Midwest firms, like Cochrane's, but there were also interesting competitors from the East. Richard M. Upjohn entered a Second Empire design; Samuel Sloan's firm was represented; a mysterious entry from the "Hartford Combination" proved to be none other than James G. Batterson, now in partnership with the Philadelphia architect John McArthur, Jr., designer of the City Hall there.

Indiana State Capitol, as constructed, 1878–88

First place was awarded to a local man, Edwin May, whose Swiss draftsman, Adolf Scherrer, had designed an academically Classical version of the Capitol of Iowa. The fighting began at once. Indianapolis architects shouted their objections on many grounds, and Elijah Myers pitched in with relish. Upjohn and the other outsiders were so shocked that they quietly withdrew. The spokesman for the local objectors was Isaac Hodgson, whose entry, entitled "Architecture," had been a finalist with "Finis Coronat Opus" by Myers. Hodgson told a news reporter that he and his friends had in mind only the need for a "proper building" for Indiana. To that the editor replied:

> Was such disinterestedness ever before exhibited? What they wanted was a reconsideration of the plans by the Board and we reckon they'll wait a precious long time. But here's where the joke comes in—Hodgson actually had the effrontery to assure the reporter that "they did this for the benefit of the State more than in their own interests." Did you ever? We never did in all our born days. Does Mr. Isaac Hodgson think the public are such consummate asses as to believe for a moment that those disappointed architects are making all this fuss and enacting all their tom foolery for the benefit of the State? . . . We had given Mr. Hodgson credit for better sense than this.[32]

179

Elsewhere in the state, the press disliked the May plan. The editor of the Madison *Courier* announced:

> We have never been able to endorse it. Take the one feature of extrav-
> agant and useless ornamentation for instance. What mortal man can frame an
> excuse for a public building [to] have five domes? It seems simply preposter-
> ous to the heathen on the Ohio. Imagine five additional domes puckered out
> of the National Capitol at Washington! It would utterly destroy the sym-
> metry and sublime appearance. . . . We have concluded that these domes
> are an insidious artifice employed by [the] architect whereby to sweetly flatter
> the honorable Commissioners to accept his plan. . . . A statue of each of the
> worthies . . . will surmount "his dome" . . . and the four commissioners
> will be clothed in bland smiles, to be interpreted by the common herd as
> equivalent to the beautiful sentiment of the Attic poet, "How we apples
> swim!"[33]

May, who was politically influential in Indianapolis, suffered from these assaults. While some of the local architects were beginning to lose interest in the battle, Myers engaged the Indianapolis law firm of Harvey, Galvin & Huff and filed suit against the Capitol Commission on charges of fraud. The commissioners hardly had told news reporters that Myers was "in-sane" when Samuel B. Tibbetts sued the commission for bribery.

The entire feuding cast of characters was present October 15, 1878, when the Myers trial opened. Crowds flowed from the jammed courtroom out into the street. Headlines proclaimed "MYERS ON THE WARPATH." The suit was for $45,000, alleging that portions of his plans had been copied by an architect hired by the board, and that when his drawings were returned they were seriously damaged. The hearing opened up a Pandora's box of clandestine activity. W. C. Tarkington, secretary of the commission, had taken mysterious train trips and had given away secrets; he had made private offers to various architects. Court was recessed, and Tarkington was fired by a unanimous decision of the commission.

Months passed, and ground was broken for the new Indiana Capitol. Edwin May served as salaried superintendent. A builder of courthouses and public buildings in Indiana for thirty years, he was the same sort of a self-made architect as Elijah Myers, though unlike Myers, by now he farmed out most of his work to his staff. His health had suffered from the ordeal of public testimony; most of the work at the Capitol was directed by Scherrer, an architect trained at the Vienna Akademie. Scherrer had designed the building for May. In the winter of 1880, before court reconvened to hear the Myers case, May boarded the train for Florida to escape the cold weather. He died in a hotel at Jacksonville in February. The commission appointed Scherrer Architect and Superintendent in his place.

Few changes were made in the original plans. The influence of Viennese academic de-sign reveals Scherrer's hand in the executed building—a hand much better trained than that of May. Developing the sort of tight and gangly towered massing of Iowa, Scherrer designed a large building of powerful blocks, broken outline and various advanced academic motifs seen in no other capitols at that time. He had been in the United States only about five years. His experience as a draftsman in various European offices, together with his familiarity with the vast Ringstrasse development in Vienna which rivaled Napoleon III's Paris boulevards, had more influence on the design than any mandate—tacit or otherwise—to follow the national Capitol. European aspects of the Indianapolis Capitol design—the correct Corinthian order, the statuary, and the rich surface decoration—were more palatable to those commissioners who remembered the academic Classicism of Memorial Hall by the German architect H. J. Schwarzmann at the Philadelphia Centennial Celebration of 1876. Ironically, the Centennial building had been envisioned by some powerful Philadelphia businessmen as the core of a future state capitol complex for Pennsylvania.

By the spring of 1880, when Myers returned from Detroit to Indianapolis to pursue his lawsuit, the walls of the Capitol were only halfway to the top of the basement. It was still too early to discern or judge the building's design, but those men commonly called the "unsuccessful competing architects" still denounced the May-Scherrer plans as adamantly as ever. In their impassioned legal arguments, the real basis of their criticism—jealousy—does not appear, although it is not improbable that they honestly disliked the design.

There were other people who were somewhat wary of the adopted elevations: "Our State-House," wrote one newspaper, "is not a German building. In many respects it shows the effect of the German school. It has also in it the marks of the French revival renaissance, and there is in it traces of the 'New Greek,' which is one of the more recent French productions . . . we find at times a studious, mechanical hardness in its composition."[34] Interestingly, Upjohn's "New Greek" proposal had been rejected nine years earlier at Hartford, as had Richardson's, which was more subtly *Néo-grec* in the best French manner of the Labroustes and Léon Vaudoyer.

After Edwin May's death, the court testimony became more pointed. The Capitol Commission had originally employed three architects as advisors to help judge the competition: C. M. Allen, Jr., J. K. Wilson, and the venerable Henry Walter of Cincinnati. Wilson, who was retained full-time by the commissioners after the initial plans had been received, admitted that some of Myers's accusations were true. Several members of the commission had reserved the May-Scherrer plan for special consideration; Wilson had been ordered to add the best features of the other entries to that plan—which, he said, was unquestionably the poorest of the four finalists.

"I felt exceedingly uneasy and reluctant in doing this because I thought it was not exactly the proper thing to do," Wilson recalled under oath. General T. A. Morris, one of the commissioners and a friend of May, had ordered Wilson to do the revisions with the full approval of the others. Instead of merely revising, Wilson completely redesigned the building because "I was afraid it might get us all in trouble if I didn't."[35] Among other things, he moved the chambers from the central block into the wings, and the commissioners were "perfectly delighted" with the results. This confession swayed the court in favor of the Capitol Commission. Myers fired his lawyers and took the next train home "in disgust" on March 22, 1880.

But Elijah Myers had other irons in the fire. By now his young son George was working in his office, and he had taken on additional draftsmen as well. His firm worked in the Midwest, 181

Far West, the South, and even Brazil. When Texas announced its plans to build a new Capitol, Myers sized clean linen sheets and set to work. The Capitol of Michigan had already been dedicated. Its columned halls, great rotunda, and original detailing were greatly admired. That would be to Myers's credit in Texas; the cattle and land-rich state, spared the panic suffered elsewhere, would be a fertile field for the former carpenter's imagination.

At the north end of Congress Avenue in Austin, the Grecian statehouse, not yet in its thirtieth year of use, was obsolete. The halls were lined with makeshift bookshelves, and offices were partitioned within offices. A shabby array of cane-bottom chairs and mahogany desks furnished the Hall of Representatives beneath portraits of Stephen F. Austin and Sam Houston. Oil lamps had puffed soot on the whitewashed walls, and in places the graining on the doors was worn through to the Bastrop pine. Across the hall in the Senate was a portrait of Washington, with even bigger ones of Austin and Houston.

The General Land Office, a Romantic crenelated building at one corner of the barren Capitol Yard, housed thousands of documents. There the elected Land Commissioner managed and distributed the empty western wilderness: Public lands were the unique inheritance permitted the state by the terms of annexation. From the windows of that building, Texas Republicans, in the last hour of their power, had watched the elected Democratic Governor and his armed supporters march down Congress Avenue and take over the Capitol. President Grant had offered the Republicans no help, and the Democrats achieved a signal victory in the remotest part of the old Confederacy.

The new government called a constitutional convention at Austin. On November 20, 1875, a resolution was passed setting aside 3,000,000 acres of the public lands, the sale of which was to pay for the construction of a new Capitol. Three months later the Constitution was approved by a vote of the people.

Long before it considered actual plans, the Capitol Commission faced the task of identifying its funds by ordering a survey of their vacant lands. Two surveyors were hired, and in 1880, after five years' labor on the High Plains, field notes and plats were presented to the commissioners.

The commission then announced a competition with such naïve rules that it was denounced by architects throughout the country. Complete working drawings were required, "worth at least twenty thousand dollars apiece," an architectural periodical mocked, "and from among these one was to be chosen for purchase by the State at the lavish expense of twelve hundred dollars . . . and with the additional proviso that payment should be made out of the proceeds of some future sales of public lands."[36]

While the professionals thought it "marvellous that even an apology for a design should have been received in response to such an invitation," Elijah Myers, back home from his Indianapolis fiasco, had a different attitude.[37] It was, after all, a matter of business. He slipped his drawings into the shiny tin container marked "Tuebor," the motto of Michigan and the lucky pseudonym he had used for the Lansing competition, and shipped them by railroad freight to Texas.

On the appointed day in the spring of 1881, eleven entries were counted. Myers was the

Texas Capitol, E. E. Myers's elevation of dome, 1881
Texas State Archives

one competing architect with any claim to even a regional reputation; he and a Mrs. Banting of Burlington, Iowa, were the only contestants from outside the South.

The commissioners felt more at home with land surveys than with capitol elevations. For weeks the plans hung on the walls of the Senate chamber and the public gawked, preferring, of course, the several local entries, and one in particular entitled "Pay as you go," by F. E. Ruffini. An impatient legislature passed a bill authorizing the employment of a consultant. The commissioners approached Napoleon LeBrun, apparently on the recommendation of Thomas U. Walter, and LeBrun, who had recently taken his son into partnership in New York, agreed to come for $3,000. Arriving at Austin by train, after the ten-day sail from New York to Galveston Island, LeBrun was an immediate success with his employers. For several weeks he studied the drawings. At last Myers was summoned by telegram from Detroit. He was agreeable to LeBrun's suggested changes, which were apparently minor and of a mechanical nature, and returned home to begin the working drawings in May 1881.

The following November a fire completely destroyed the Capitol. The remaining stone walls and a row of columns were eventually pulled down for use as rubble fill, long after the Capitol Commission had completed a temporary Capitol across the street. Some considerable distance behind the terraces of the old Capitol, Myers helped stake out the site of the new building early in 1882.

He stayed in Austin until the last week in May. During those months the Capitol Commission made a contract with Mattheas Schnell & Co., of Rock Island, Illinois, to build the Capitol, taking the western lands as full payment. Schnell, a promoter, wanted to subcontract the whole work. This did not seem proper to the commissioners, and they withheld approval until Schnell agreed to sell most of the contracts to the Chicago firm of Taylor, Babcock & Company in partnership with Farwell Brothers & Company. That combination of Chicago investors and contractors assumed responsibility for the whole work.

Colonel Abner Taylor and Colonel Amos C. Babcock established offices in Austin. The 3,000,000 acres, distributed by the commission in portions, was ultimately developed by the Farwell Brothers into the legendary XIT Ranch, one of the most fabulous business ventures of the Gilded Age.

The Texas Capitol Commission began and ended its career on the same dictatorial course, entertaining interference from no one. A worthy effort to commission statues from a new resident of Texas, Elisabet Ney—who had worked for Ludwig II of Bavaria at Linderhof—came to nothing. No authority was delegated to superintendents, contractors, or anyone else, including Myers; his title, Designing Architect, merely meant he was an adviser and interpreter of his plans, much as Upjohn had been in Hartford. Now and then he was asked for assistance in hiring draftsmen for the Capitol office in Austin. Otherwise, everything that went wrong was blamed on him, and his presence was constantly demanded on short notice. His patience seemed endless.

At the close of the first year, the commission boasted that the new Capitol, "Of all similar structures in America . . . is second in size only to the National Capitol at Washington, D.C., and is larger and finer than the German Reichstag or English Parliament buildings."[38] Copies of the report were sent to those in charge of the still-floundering project at Albany.

Texas Capitol, E. E. Myers's brick vaulting and iron-construction detail, 1883

Early in 1884, however, some of the contractors began to balk at the commission's annoying demands. Several contracts were torn up. Myers grew irritated with repeated requests for the redesigning of heating pipes and other technical features; he assured Colonel Taylor that kind of work involved stock equipment and could be handled by draftsmen on the scene.

Shipments of limestone from Round Rock and elsewhere began to show serious differences in color. A group of speculators offered a large supply of red granite seventy miles west of town as an alternative in exchange for building a railroad to the site. At first the proposal suggested graft, because one of the owners was N. L. Norton, a developer very recently resigned from the Capitol Commission. Norton issued a statement: "I am not ·. . . *directly or indirectly interested or concerned with any contractor* as inhibited by my oath. The material has been tendered *to the people of Texas* freely and without price or consideration or understanding as to present or future remuneration of any kind with any party whomsoever."[39] Senate and House delegates convinced the commissioners to change to granite.

Myers pointed out the impracticality of the decision: "The Texas Capitol Board," he wrote, "have concluded a contract with Col Taylor to use Granite for the Capitol Building. I made the estimate of the difference in cost. The granite work costs Seven Hundred Thousand dollars more than Limestone for which the State furnished to Col Taylor the Labor of 500 convicts. Taylor has to build a rail road 17 miles long to the quarry through a very hilly and almost unapproachable country which will cost about $100,000 dollars."[40]

Such statements displeased the commission. In that body's behalf the new supervisor of construction, General R. L. Walker, of Richmond, Virginia, denounced Myers as an incompetent engineer. On the plans he called attention to a wall thirty feet high and ninety feet long, which Myers had left unsupported by partitions or beams. An alarmed Texas official stated, "the board ought to send for Col. E. E. Myers and tell him he had made a very bad job of it."[41] Governor Ireland added that if the plans were faulty, "I want to know it."[42] It is tempting to wonder whether General Walker, politically oriented and a builder himself, was bitter toward Myers for defeating him in the competition for Richmond's new City Hall.

In other aspects of the Texas work, Myers increasingly found himself vulnerable during his long absences in Michigan. "So-called stonecutters" in Austin had written circulars to the Georgia Capitol Commission at Atlanta "for the purpose of influencing . . . [them] against Col. Myers" in that competition.[43] Typically, Myers was unaware of local friction; he was too much on the move to notice until small problems had become big ones.

When the Capitol Commission finally decided to use Texas granite, the Governor ordered 1,000 convicts to the quarry. Colonel Taylor protested that the labor union men would then force him to supplement with "every single solitary granite cutter in Texas at union rates."[44] As he predicted, the Knights of Labor publicly condemned the Capitol Commission. One of the subcontractors thought of a way to circumscribe the union men: "I learned some very important facts this morning," an Austin stonecutter wrote in high excitement to the Granite Cutters of America, "regarding the cutting of the granite on the new capitol of Texas. Mr. Gus Wilkie the subcontractor is to employ no man who can speak one word of English, hence he will import foreign pauper labor. These same fellows are to teach convicts how to cut granite and then they are to be discharged. Do you see?"[45] There was nothing the union men could do.

Wilkie sent George Berry to Germany and Scotland to hire teams of workers. "Wilkie's pimp," as the union men called him, returned by way of New York, where a United States Deputy Marshal protected him from a mob at the dock. Union men who planned a protest march at the Austin railroad station the day the foreign workers arrived were warned by the Texas Rangers to stay out of town. The commission felt that it had won a great victory, and by the close of 1886 the German and Scottish stonecutters had filled out the massive outlines of the new Capitol.

In spite of the new device of blueprinting, which made it simpler for Myers to comply with the constant requests for changes and additional sets of working drawings, the architect was growing exhausted with the insolence of the Texas Capitol Commission. He wrote to the Governor that he would "not consent to any further changes in the plans and specifications."[46] The commission's almost immediate reaction was to demand drawings for a stone dome; Myers sent his refusal by telegram. Several commissioners moved to "eliminate him entirely," and the architect had no protection against them. Myers's letters of protest arrived daily in Austin; the commission's response was always a command that he appear in Texas. When Myers refused, on the grounds that he was too busy with other work, the matter was turned over to the Attorney General. Myers was removed from the job of Designing Architect at Austin. He later designed the hospital for the deaf in that city, and he always expressed his great pride in the fact that the Capitol closely followed his original design.

Of all the capitols of the Gilded Age, Austin's—with its tall dome rising over a colonnaded drum, and its sprawling wings—was most like a parody of the national Capitol. The iron parts of the building were painted to match the reddish granite the commission had decreed would form the walls. Sharp of line, sensitive in texture, the huge mass is even more impressive because of the rough quarry finish. There is a mountainlike grandeur and variety to the Capitol. Evening brings a purple cast to the earth-red surfaces; at daybreak the granite is the gold of the sun.

Myers had recessed a columned porch into the central block, within an enormous stone arch extending up through three stories and into the attic—a unique feature on a capitol. Still higher, a second attic, brought fully forward, recalls on a giant scale Myers's earlier references to the Boston Statehouse. Colossal pilasters along the walls, mostly in pairs, contrast in their smooth simplicity with the texture of the granite walling. The wings terminate in broad corner pavilions beneath convex mansards. From high on the naked hill the windows of the Capitol's nearly 250 rooms survey a landscape which rolls out to the horizon; even the principal story is higher than were the rooftops of the stone buildings then lining Congress Avenue. The commission's effort to copy Indiana by building a masonry dome over an iron substructure was stopped by the stonecutters after Myers left. Colonel Taylor agreed with that decision, saying that such a dome would require crowding heavy piers into the rotunda as Upjohn had done in Hartford. The commissioners reluctantly consented to build the iron dome Myers had designed to roof the thick limestone cylinder ninety feet above the ground. The decorative skin of the wrought-iron frame is of molded zinc.

Texas Capitol, by E. E. Myers, 1882–88, as completed in 1888

On February 26, 1888, the day the homemade Goddess of Liberty was raised to her perch on the lantern, the commissioners proudly proclaimed that now the Capitol of Texas was seven feet taller than the Capitol of the United States.

Elijah Myers may have lost some peace of mind on the Texas project, but his career did not suffer at all. He had designed, the Texans boasted, the seventh largest building in the world. If that claim to size was only Texas talk, the words fell sweetly on his ears. It was the elevation of the Texas Capitol he now printed on his letterhead.

Had he been able to flaunt the Texas triumph earlier, Myers might have been successful in the 1880 Georgia competition. "Permit me to suggest," he had written to the Governor at Atlanta, "[that your] architects should be required to guarantee the accuracy of their plans and estimates and if they should make any mistakes . . . either in omission of material or artisan work or to design of any work . . . he should be held liable. . . . I furnished the plans for the Michigan State Capitol building and now engaged on several large public buildings [all courthouses], one . . . in Indiana one in Ohio and one in Illinois."[47] But the Georgia Governor and commissioners gave the premium to Edbrooke & Burnham of Chicago, overlooking James G. Batterson as well as Myers.

In 1883 Myers entered the Colorado capitol competition. His design, "Corinthian," was one of five entries chosen from the twenty-one submitted. But a prohibitive restriction on funds forced the commission to cast aside the results of the contest. A second competition was provided for two years later by a more realistic capitol act. As in the first competition, a dome and wings were specified. Myers revised his original plans and reentered them. He was chosen as one of three finalists and immediately boarded the train for Denver. But the commissioners, he found, were unable to decide between the three plans before them. The Attorney General's office

advised them to pay premiums to all three, thereby becoming the legal owners of the plans and leaving them free to make their own mix.

In August 1885, Myers was selected to combine the plans. This had obviously been decided beforehand, for already in July Myers had written to the secretary of the commission:

> The cost of the iron work . . . with the approved machinery and appliances now in use . . . can be executed at much less expense than a few years ago. . . . The iron beam pool of this country is very difficult to contend with as all the manufacturers are in one Combination, they ask 82 dollars a ton for Beams delivered at Denver. We can get the foreign beams delivered at 70 dollars a ton, Yet the American beams are protected by a duty of 25 dollars a ton. . . . I have carefully read the law and do fully understand that if the building cannot be let for my estimate I must loose all my work, it will cost me several thousand dollars yet to prepare the full detail plans so that bidders can figure on the work, when all the plans are completed there will be an outlay of at least 6000 dollars incurred in addition to what I have already expended . . . the time allowed to prepare these plans was entirely too short to accomplish so much work.[48]

He took his finished drawings to Denver in February 1886, just as the little Idaho Capitol, mentioned earlier, was reaching completion. The commissioners were delighted with the designs, but the bids came in staggeringly high.

Myers did his revisions in the Hotel Windsor. The rowdy and lavish surroundings in this noisy high noon of Colorado's silver kingdom seem not to have hampered his work. Although Myers loved the decorative glitter of the age, nothing in the scant surviving information about his private life suggests an interest in high living. In Detroit he built and sold houses almost yearly in middle-class neighborhoods. His wife and children were accustomed to moving, and his son George paid board at home. One of the rare glimpses of personal feeling in his surviving correspondence is in a letter to a member of the Colorado Commission: "During the Grant obsequies here our city was first crowded, the appearance of the city was Gloomy everything black with emblems of mourning, the Countenance of the People seemed sad. Instances of any mirth I did not see. All seemed to feel the sadness. I doubt that if ever again in this country will be seen so much mournful decoration and sadness."[49] More typical were occasional outbursts of an economic nature: "Business of all kinds will be utterly prostrated if the Knights of Labor keep on with their system of strikes."[50] In his impassioned harvesting, Myers seems to have seldom stopped to reflect; so in love was he with work and its rewards that he never seems to have realized the field of his labors was changing in the 1880's. When he was nominated for the post of Supervising Architect of the Treasury late in the decade, Myers was flying too high in private practice to consider becoming a salaried bureaucrat.

The Colorado Capitol Commission was satisfied by 1886 that Myers had made the best plan possible. Myers recommended W. D. Richardson, with whom he had worked on the Grand Rapids City Hall, for the job of contractor. Richardson's heavy construction machinery was

State Historical Society of Colorado
Colorado Capitol, by E. E. Myers, 1886–1908, as it appeared in 1900

loaded on railroad cars and sent to Denver, and work began on the foundation. Back in Detroit, Myers laid the Colorado work aside and busied himself with other projects; fickle Austin commissioners had taught him to wait for final decisions before executing the working drawings.

Time, however, caught up with Myers. By 1887 Richardson was complaining to the commission: "In our own contract, you undertook that the plans and specifications for the building should be complete. It is a notorious fact known to you from the first, that the plans and specifications for this building were not complete. . . . Your building so far as it has progressed has not been according to the plans and specifications embodied in our own written contract, but 191 according to the plans prepared and drawn by myself."[51] Myers, using the title Supervising Architect, Colorado Capitol Building, called Richardson a liar.

The quarrel between Myers and Richardson lasted for close to two years. Work on the sandstone walls nearly stopped. Scaffolds and boardwalks led among partially finished foundations to the tall cylinder of brick exposed to snow and cold winds from the Rockies. After the first snow, Richardson loaded some of his equipment on the train and went on to a new job in the Midwest. Angry and embarrassed, the Capitol Commission found itself in a controversy which had dangerous political implications. Attendance at meetings declined—a matter of increasing interest to newspaper reporters.

The commission withheld all payments to Richardson and Myers. For Richardson the problem seems not to have been serious, but Myers was in trouble. He had borrowed from banks to maintain his Detroit office and seven draftsmen, while on the road he pursued new work in person. The outlay of cash to keep Myers & Son going appears to have been astounding; George Myers now took residential work on his own, perhaps to help support his mother's household.

Richardson, Myers, and the commission all threatened to sue one another. But on April 1, 1889, the legislature abruptly dissolved the Capitol Commission of Colorado. A new commission met the following month and honored a legislative direction by changing the Capitol building material from local sandstone to Colorado granite. A new contractor was hired, and Myers was dismissed.

It is suspected that the small compensation paid Myers by the Capitol Commission barely saved the architect from bankruptcy. Two banks, one in Springfield and one in Denver, filed suit against him. Settlements were made, leaving him financially stricken. Work he had done in 1886 trying to win a capitol competition in Wyoming had come to nothing, and the six weeks of hurried traveling between Denver, Cheyenne, Austin, and Detroit had cost heavily.

Now Elijah Myers, at sixty-one, went home to start over again. In a smaller office he and his son and an occasional part-time draftsman drew up proposals; a Myers design could still delight a commission or a school board, and even a committee of church elders. And for all Myers's difficulties with commissioners, its members never had serious complaints about his capitol designs. Though some of his fire was gone, American architecture had not heard the last of him.

The Colorado Capitol, twenty-two years in construction, was not completed until 1908. Certain changes naturally came with the introduction of granite, but they were very few, mainly omissions of zinc and iron decorations for economic reasons. The colossal Corinthian porticoes, parapet, and tall dome all came from Myers's first proposals. Pilasters with plain capitals, like those at Austin, surrounded the exterior walls. We can suppose that Myers would have taken fuller advantage of the rich materials than did the commissioners who decided to use the same sort of rustication for the entire exterior, from the ground to the cornice through four monotonous levels. A rather abrupt entrance stair ascends beneath the portico, through arches on piers, into the vestibule.

Soberly Classical features were added here and there, the marks of "improvement" in the later and more inhibited academic period of architectural design, and one that was reaching its peak at the turn of the century. The Capitol's sharply defined central block and wings lack the broad spacing that the height of the building demands. Yet the interior arrangement—the House in the central block, as at Hartford and Indianapolis, and the Senate in the East wing—precludes any but symbolic justification for the flanking wings. In balancing the Senate and the Supreme Court, Myers carried out an innovation first proposed by H. H. Richardson for Hartford. No objection was recorded in the minutes of the Colorado Commission.

Because of inappropriate changes made after Myers's departure, Colorado's Capitol has a piecemeal look not characteristic of Myers, and the interior lacks the grandeur of the architect's work at Lansing and Austin. He had learned in the Michigan competition that in spite of the wish for state splendor, the only political justification for building new capitols was the need for office space. Myers seems to have willingly accepted the fact that he was hiding big utilitarian buildings within his symbolic and stylish piles. He grandly bound together the functional spaces of each of his capitols with monumental and imposing ceremonial areas, even though there were few state ceremonies to fill them.

Each Capitol had its equivalent of a Doric Hall as a prelude to the central rotunda. The most magnificent of the rotundas is the constricted one in Austin, which jumps up a full four stories through rings of balconies to a frescoed dome. To enter or to cross the Texas Capitol is to walk constantly in the presence of that stunning upward—or downward—view. At Lansing, the lesser upward sweep is tighter—a foretaste of the showmanship to come at Austin. The three window-less rotundas were theatrically lighted first by gas, later by hundreds of bare electric bulbs. Myers never intended his grandest interiors to be naturally illuminated; the architect was too infatuated with the inventions of man to allow nature's intrusion. Perhaps the darkest of all his rotundas was to have been in Denver's Capitol. The energetic Colorado Commission, however, filled the space with an overscaled divided staircase, completely obliterating the sense of spatial surprise that Myers provided elsewhere at the end of his columned entrance halls.

According to Myers's plan for Colorado, staircases were to have been built in the two balanced light-courts. But the commissioners decided to leave the courts unobstructed like those at Hartford. Lansing and Austin have narrower transverse halls with staircases of iron occupying well-lit alcoves on the sides. The few decorative elements of the halls, endlessly repeated in long rows—the caramel colored doors with brass mountings and etched-glass transoms, the bronze gasoliers—become, by their repetition, decorative borders parallel to the axes. Wall surfaces were sometimes treated with a simple swirling design, almost Art Nouveau in character, pressed into the wet plaster by a special cookie-cutter kind of tool. Myers delighted in such inexpensive detailing.

On his gasoliers at Lansing, bronze stags romp among clusters of gas jets. Brass door locks and escutcheons at Austin are decorated with the Lone Star of Texas. Court and committee rooms at Denver once had stenciled borders in Pompeiian red, gold leaf, and powder blue. Portraits of Colorado's greatest citizens still peer from stained-glass bulls's-eye windows.

To view one of Elijah Myers's capitols from across the open land was to feel the immensity of its scale and the vigor of its decoration; to push through its doors even today is to vanish from the world outside into fantasies of vines and maidens and state flowers in glass and bronze. 193

Polished walnut, brass, nickel, green glass, and the marbles of the floors gleam in dim interiors seemingly unlimited in dimension and linear continuity.

Myers was actually copied at least once. The Wyoming Capitol at Cheyenne was a small version of his Texas Capitol. Myers and David W. Gibbs of Toledo, a man of about Myers's age and background, were invited to submit proposals at Cheyenne in the spring of 1886. A deadline of May 1 was set, and several more architects were soon added to the restricted invitation list. Only three entries were submitted, and Gibbs won with a design he described as "Classic Renaissance."

On his way to Denver, Myers got off the train in Cheyenne to find out why he had failed. He was in town only briefly, but heard a rumor that some of his elevations and photographs had been sent to Gibbs in Toledo. The Capitol Commission claimed it had not the least knowledge of any such shipment, and their secretary explained in a letter: "Mr. Myers [wired] last evening that he heard Mr. Gibbs had the photographs at Toledo. If I thought so I should be inclined to be a little put out about it, but the fact is I think he only said it on acct. of his suspicious disposition."[52] At about that time the secretary wrote to Myers, "I assure you that no advantage has been taken of you . . . there was no undue influence acted, and . . . the [competition] was acted upon fairly and honestly and made by the board without any interference. I write this which might otherwise be improper for the reason that I understand you have written a letter here speaking rather infamously of the action of the board."[53] There were several other architects who had reasons to complain about the conduct of the Wyoming competition. When a real fight seemed certain, they withdrew, Myers last of all.

Completed in 1890, the Wyoming Capitol faced the Union Pacific Depot down the long stretch of Capitol Avenue. Cheyenne was nearly always entered by train, over the windy plains. Through the massive stone arch of the Richardsonian station, passengers saw the Capitol at the far end of the street. The sight was as memorable then as it is today. The dome, a slender structure in stages, overlooked a dusty hamlet of red brick buildings, wooden sidewalks, corrals, and shingled cottages painted yellow and maroon. Below the pedimented attic a great arch reflects that of the Austin Capitol. Rusticated piers sheltered by the great arch frame wide stairs leading to the entrance, much as at Myers's in Colorado. Inside, the rotunda is not very tall, terminating in a domed ceiling stenciled like a gilt-edged bond. The transverse stairhalls beneath skylights were built well before the Colorado Commission decided to remove its stairs to the rotunda, so again Wyoming reflected Myers. While the design Myers entered in the competition is forgotten in Cheyenne, the indications are it was similar to what Gibbs built.

The Gilded Age in state capitols ended only when Myers left Denver, but in many respects its decline had begun long before. There would be no more palaces of his kind. The architect was still putting final touches on the Michigan design in the early 1870's when H. H. Richardson proposed for Hartford a simpler, more massive, and high-minded architecture. By the end of the decade it was already making a considerable impact on Eastern architects. Even as the architectural Gilded Age peaked nationally, in the late 1870's and early 1880's, there were strong currents of opposition to it.

Louisiana, for example, more or less reconstructed its old Gothic Capitol, which by 1882

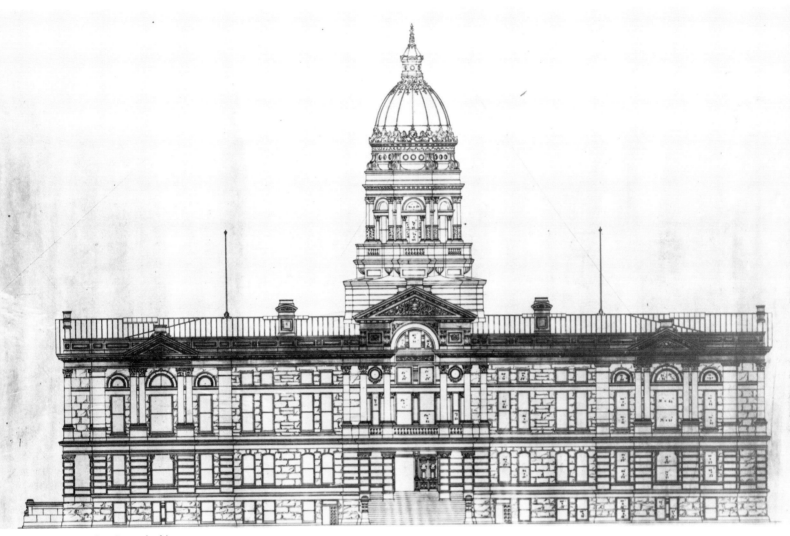

Wyoming Capitol, David W. Gibbs's elevation, 1886

had stood for over twenty years a vine-covered ruin on the Mississippi River at Baton Rouge. The capital, which had been taken to New Orleans during the war, was now returned to Baton Rouge for good; by rebuilding the Gothic Capitol in 1881–82 certain political cliques reconstructed the triumphant symbol raised by their fathers only a generation before. Except for the addition of a fourth story and some iron lanterns on the towers, the James Dakin Capitol reappeared much as it had been. The architect was William A. Feret of New Orleans, later Supervising Architect of the United States Treasury Department. According to an issue of *The American Architect and Building News* at the time, the Capitol was "conceived in a species of Americanized castellated Gothic, which closely recalled if it did not actually reproduce the structure destroyed during the Civil War."[54] In the great central court, Feret placed a new spiral staircase of cast iron entwining a clustered column that burst open at the top in a spectacular umbrella of stained glass.

The age in general was not concerned with historical monuments. Yet Chicago, its own past lost in fire, went on a curious quest for a tangible piece of history. In the 1880's Chicago businessmen tried to purchase the old Statehouse in Boston and move it to Illinois. This created an uproar in Boston, perhaps more because of Chicago's impudence than any attachment to the Statehouse, and lit a spark of public piety: Besides a restoration of the Boston building, a fine history of it, *The Old Statehouse Memorial*, was published and widely distributed.

After a disastrous fire in Trenton, the 1885–88 renovation of the New Jersey Capitol by Lewis H. Broome made that historic pile into a modern building. Now it received, among other modifications, a façade in belated Second Empire style. Exceptionally heavy in its detailing, this was doubtless intended by Broome to be even more florid than it actually turned out. Broome, a Jersey City architect, was principally a builder of schools and municipal buildings. He was so willing to please the commissioners that in the name of economy he gave Trenton what was no more than a stripped-down version of a Gilded Age scheme, yet one not unworthy of comparison with Myers's in the West.

The new Capitol of Georgia also evoked the spirit of the Gilded Age, but its rather naked look again indicated that the flamboyance of the era was dying down. Georgia's Capitol Commission had engaged the services of George B. Post, by now a top New York architect, as adviser in its nationwide competition. Among the ten proposals submitted was the one by E. E. Myers. Post, a man esteemed both for his capacity as a designer and for his expertise in structural matters, found the Myers plan admirably done: "It is most elaborately executed, and is thoroughly illustrated by details. It is excellently arranged." But he gave the premium to Edbrooke & Burnham because their project "is more academic in its plan than the other designs. It is very dignified and more simple & elegant in detail than that of Myers; less picturesque but more monumental. . . ."[55]

Edbrooke & Burnham's structure was more like the Indiana Capitol than any others of the era. It lacked the uninhibited touch of the Myers capitols, and stood stiff, uncertain, and seemingly incomplete behind its hesitantly academic façades.

Willoughby J. Edbrooke and Franklin P. Burnham were primarily courthouse architects, with headquarters in Chicago and projects all over the Midwest. They were among the many architects who had found a real economic and professional frontier in Chicago after the fire. The population of architects and builders had been quite large in those years of the 1870's as one boom had merely faded into another. Postfire needs in Chicago, moreover, had led to specialization.

The individualistic world of the Chicago architect varied according to business demands. Edbrooke & Burnham formed what was called a "loose" partnership, in which they were moderately successful. When the Georgia Capitol was completed, Edbrooke served briefly as Supervising Architect of the Treasury in Washington. Burnham moved to Los Angeles after his partner's departure and opened an active practice which continued until the early twentieth century.

New Jersey Capitol, as revised and remodeled by Lewis Broome, 1889,
with one end of 1794 statehouse visible to the right

The Civil War transformed Atlanta from a small railroad town into the financial center of the state—"a legitimate offspring of Chicago," they liked to call it. It was associated with other Southern cities in trumpeting the "New South." Atlanta's pride was money, and the city manifested it in strange ways: A team of German artists had begun a 400-foot cyclorama, *The Battle of Atlanta*, designed to mingle actual war artifacts with bloody scenes in oil. It was originally proposed for the new Capitol but installed instead in a park pavilion, where it stands today. There was a last-ditch effort among some legislators to return the government to the Gothic statehouse at Milledgeville. Atlanta businessmen urged the contractors to hurry; and the limestone walls of the new Capitol now rose faster.

Begun in 1884 and finished in 1889, Atlanta's Capitol was only one of the many sights of the phenomenal inland city. Among Southern capitols, it was exceptional in its modernity. At Columbia, South Carolina, for example, Niernsee's great statehouse was scarred from Sherman's shells and cheaply roofed over. Poverty and remorse still haunted most of the South, including the better part of Georgia; Atlanta alone seemed to stand bright and new, and even more than Birmingham and Richmond considered itself a vital part of the American nation.

Edbrooke & Burnham had given the Capitol Commission what it wanted. In the context of its counterparts in other states, Atlanta's statehouse was advanced in design in a certain superficial sense. Its exterior showed a definite tendency toward the academic Classicism still to come. The interior, however, was drab and utilitarian except for the galleried light-courts. Most other big cities would have found the building unacceptable, but somehow it satisfied Atlanta's strange brand of nationalism in a way the old Gothic pile at Milledgeville could no longer do.

In plan it has something of the cross shape of the Indiana and Colorado capitols, but with the halls of the legislature balanced front and rear instead of on the sides. A colossal pedimented Corinthian portico, raised on rusticated piers, defines the principal entrance; a parapet partially conceals the skylights in the roofs of the wings. The Renaissance dome, ringed with pedimented

Nolan Ninabuck for The Victorian Society in America
Georgia Capitol, by Edbrooke & Burnham, 1884–89, more or less as completed, 1889

windows and detached Corinthian columns, commands the cityscape; the rotunda beneath the dome is sunlit. There is nothing remarkable about the interior except the arrangement of the legislative chambers. Light-courts form large transverse stairhalls with ponderous divided stair-cases ascending to colonnaded galleries. These stairs were banked in evergreens when Jefferson Davis's body lay in state in the rotunda in 1893.

An era of material excess, the Gilded Age had followed close on the heels of moralistic excess. The leaders of the major historical currents that culminated in the Civil War were no greater in number or less ambitious than those who played the prime roles in the Gilded Age. But the war period's strong sense of community was followed by an ideal of individual achievement. Those who made the war were ready to destroy to get what they wanted, but the younger men who fought it came home to build. In the postwar years and until the end of the nineteenth century, the private businessman had all the romantic—even mythical—appeal of the cavalry captain who had gone before him. Even at the time of the Panic of 1873, when businessmen drew in their horns a bit and purged their ranks, their new righteousness matched their father's earlier moralism; and they were even more the era's heroes for confessing their sins.

Triumph and not defeat finds expression in monumental architecture. The builders of the Gilded Age sought grandeur. The new race of reformers after the Panic of 1873 began to scorn

Georgia Capitol, by Edbrooke & Burnham, left-hand light-court

public edifices such as Piquenard's and Myers's for being superficial and tawdry. The new "honesty" in architecture—brought to real excellence by Richardson—could be quite as affected in its aesthetic aspirations as its more glamorous predecessors were in theirs.

While projects were repeatedly entered in capitol competitions by architects who extolled worthy materials and simplicity of design, commissioners hesitated. The Richardsonian Romanesque was often so somber that it had an even smaller chance of succeeding against the boldness of Gilded Age luxury than had the Gothic over the Greek Revival in the years gone by. A capitol, it was felt, should not be dark and brooding, but optimistically bright. Only when

American architecture returned to the more familiar Classical themes would state capitols come into accord with contemporary "high style." Some of them would even lead the way.

The Gilded Age did not end all at once. It was over in New York when it was only reaching its crest in Colorado. Not until the mid-1890's—after the Panic of 1893—can its demise be considered universal; and even then, some of its maxims were merely reworded.

Reactions to the businessman's rampage appeared in many areas of American life. Urban labor and the newly organized farmers of the West, curious bedfellows indeed, are only two examples. Where basic political controversy had been set aside in the decade and a half since the Civil War, it now came back with a fury not seen since the 1850's. Live issues of taxation, tariff, and Federal control now challenged the old-line politicians.

Business was at first able to beat back its opposition. The protective laws sponsored by farmers were repealed in Iowa and Wisconsin. In the national Capitol battles against restrictive business measures were also victorious many times over through the 1880's. Yet progress was eventually made. President Grover Cleveland signed the Interstate Commerce Act in the winter of 1887; enforcement of the Federal act was slack, however, and the hallways and galleries of the American state capitols resounded with cries for strong state laws. At Topeka, in the now completed Capitol, fist-fighting broke out between the Republicans and the Populists in the House of Representatives, and the National Guard was summoned. Then in 1889 the first antitrust act in the United States was passed by the Kansas legislature.

Long after the Gilded Age faltered, the New York Capitol project was still in progress. It had been a political pawn every step of the way. Eidlitz and Richardson finished most of the exterior before Eidlitz's death and Richardson's dismissal in the early eighties. They were, however, constantly attacked by Manhattan professionals on stylistic grounds, and in 1877 the legislature actually voted that the work be continued in Fuller's original "French Renaissance mode." Responsibilities were divided between the two architects. Eidlitz completed the House of Representatives by New Year's 1879, and Richardson's Senate was occupied in 1881.

The House chamber, a Gothic interior with immense arches springing from giant granite columns and carrying masonry vaulting, was unlike anything in the country. The Senate chamber, powerfully membered as well, but less blatantly grandiose than the House, is an intimate room—a full statement of the piety of the political reformers, yet with the sensuous luxury of a private theater. Neither of these halls is as superficially splendid as those in Kansas, or any of Myers's. By comparison they are simpler but far more monumental and sumptuous in their materials. A reporter described the House chamber in the late 1880's:

> Ascending . . . the Grand Staircase (and one needs strength and endurance for these lofty flights), we find the Assembly Chamber, one of the noblest halls in the world, eighty-four by one hundred feet. Four great pillars four feet thick, of red granite, sustain the largest groined arch in the world, the keystone being fifty-six feet from the floor. . . . The coloring is intended to be Moorish. The architect and the internal decorator have evidently been thinking of the Alhambra. . . . The allegorical pictures of William M. Hunt, on which he spent the last days of his illuminated life,

New York Capitol, Assembly chamber as completed by Leopold Eidlitz, 1878

remain here to praise him. That on the northern wall represents the allegory of Ormuzd and Ahriman. . . . The Queen of Night is driving before the dawn; her chariot is drawn by three plunging horses, one white, one black, one red. On the right of the goddess, and in deep shade is a lovely group— a sleeping mother and child. But the strangest figure in this group is the floating dusky guide, who holds the head of one of the horses. . . . It is intensely poetical and full of suggestion; and to the thoughtful, what more lovely and exquisite picture of that future for which Capitols are built than is conveyed in that shadowed sleeping mother and child?

And of Richardson's Senate:

Its acoustic properties are good, in great contrast to its sister Assembly Room. In the lower western wall-space is a dado of Knoxville marble, giving great solidity to the wall . . . arches are supported by four massive col-

New York Capitol, Senate chamber by H. H. Richardson,
completed 1878, as it appeared in 1890

umns of a dark, red-brown granite, with capitals of white marble exquisitely carved. The arches are of yellow Siena marble and rails of gray marble, the projections of the galleries being supported by long flat corbels of gray stone elaborately carved . . . the fireplaces of this room are constructed of marble, as are the spaces between them. The openings of the fireplaces are about six feet in height and something more in breadth. The cheerful effect of these when filled with burning logs can scarcely be exaggerated . . . bas-reliefs illustrating the legendary character of the room, filled with historical and legendary scenes, will cover the broad faces of the chimney-breasts.[56]

The carving over the fireplaces was never executed. In 1883, after Eidlitz's and Richardson's connection with the Capitol had ended, the reform administration hired Isaac Perry to finish the job in a hurry. Perry, an architect with considerable experience in the state's service, was efficient, but no designer. Everything he had done over the years reeked of his willingness to compromise. In front of the State Street side of the Capitol building he now added a gigantic ceremonial staircase, but his attempt to sheathe its bulk with a skin of shallow stonecarving only increased its clumsy relation to the building as a whole. Defects in the design of the Capitol were pointed up again and again by the superiority of certain of its parts—Richardson's and Eidlitz's chambers and three grand staircases, two at the front and the one at the rear which Perry developed from Richardson's projected design. Eidlitz's stairs and stairwells are even more sumptuous examples of High Victorian Gothic than his Assembly chamber and are unrivaled indeed by any other secular interiors of that character in America. New York's was the most costly state capitol of the nineteenth century, and one of the most expensive buildings in the United States. The least talented of all the architects associated with the job carried it to a quiet completion in 1897, thirty years after work had begun. Perry's success was the triumph of bureaucratic adequacy. Even if it had escaped damage by maneuvering politicians and the grasping egotism of powerful Manhattan tastemakers, it is doubtful that it would have become an influ-

New York State Library

New York Capitol, as completed by Isaac Perry, 1898

ence on other state capitols. It still belonged to an unfinished sequence of innovating capitols that had begun in Ohio and Tennessee but was cut off in its infancy by the Civil War. And by the time it reached completion, its incoherent design had to face the blinding light of a new architectural era in which Americans would again seek perfection by following in the footsteps of the ages.

VI
MONUMENTS
OF THE
AMERICAN
RENAISSANCE

Minnesota Capitol, by Cass Gilbert, begun in 1895, as it appeared in 1905 before
installation of most of the exterior sculpture

The scientific discoveries and inventions that were to make twentieth-century life so different from all that had gone before came largely between the Panic of 1873 and the next panic twenty years later. During those years, as the forces of the new made their mark, the belief in progress became a sort of religion of perfectability.

The bigness and individuality which had fascinated the generation of the Gilded Age was by the 1880's seen as merely a raw product in drastic need of improvement from within. A belief in the importance of groups returned to American life; on all levels people were banding together. Even in business, for example, more than a thousand railroad lines consolidated during the 1890's into six giant companies. A decade later, three great Eastern financial houses owned assets far greater than the total value of all the land west of the Mississippi River. On another level, workers formed a succession of associations. So did the farmers, who were still in the vast majority, with dual objectives of protection and self-betterment.

Weary of the complex polychromatic monuments of the past two decades, architects longing for something bright and simple turned again to the Classical. But they were not to be content with past interpretations of Greek architecture in America, for theirs was a grander vision than that of their grandfathers. Now was the age which would perfect all that had been inherited. The architect had a mission. He no longer hesitated to call himself an artist, and he seriously contemplated his particular place in the world of art. In picture books or in actuality he wandered the ancient streets of Rome and Florence; more and more he came to believe in a spiritual link between the buildings of those places and the common inheritance of Americans. And he began to look into the architectural past of his own country.

In the postwar years, when individualism uncontrolled was still at its peak, a Colonial Revival first appeared, as one of several themes in a broad reaction to superficial luxury. This was on a rather sophisticated level, with only a scattering of people actually enjoying the novelty of things quaint and innocent. Exactly when large numbers of Americans were smitten by the architecture of their past remains uncertain. There were Colonial Revivals in nearly every part of the New World, but the one in the United States came relatively late.

Americans were influenced by a contemporary English movement known as Queen Anne, with which the Colonial Revival converged in the United States around 1880 and then superseded. Almost immediately after the 1876 centennial festivities at Philadelphia, the old vernacular elements of colonial buildings began to be more commonly imitated. Pediments, balusters, columned mantels, dormers, and pilasters of an eighteenth-century American sort now appeared under thick coats of dark green or ivory paint. These first Colonial Revival houses, usually oversized, were designed as irregular compositions to capture the picturesque quality that made the originals attractive. A more scholarly approach to the style developed by the mid-1880's as authentic oblong blocks displaced the initial hybrids. It has been the pattern of all revivals to become more "correct" than the original, although few have ever remained so self-assured in that respect as has the Colonial.

There was a concurrent interest in historic sites. Societies for the preservation of antiquities in different regions were founded by people in whom patriotism and ancestor worship mingled. The site of the colonial Capitol at Williamsburg was purchased, a barren plot in a forgotten town, where the existing remains were well hidden under several feet of earth. The citizens of Annapolis stood watch as a state commission planned the expansion of the old statehouse. In 1878, the architectural elements of the Senate chamber had been ripped out and the furniture thrown away. When a committee inquired into the propriety of such vandalism, the architect George A. Frederick of Baltimore said of the items in question: "Well, I wouldn't have taken them if presented to me as a gift."[1]

Frederick's attitude toward antiquities was still typical of Americans of his period. In 1886, however, a Maryland minority had its say, and a Colonial Revival annex was built on the rear of the statehouse. Its carefully correct design made it seem more colonial than the century-old structure nearby, itself recently modernized by the introduction of new four-pane windows and decorative chimneys. Within a few years restoration was under way in the Senate chamber.

The Boston Statehouse had never been so hallowed a structure. Changes had been made in the building almost since the day Charles Bulfinch stepped back from the finished product in 1798. Because of seepage through the walls and the resultant rotting plaster, the red brick exterior had been covered first with white paint, then with paint of a pale straw color.

Two additions had been put on the rear of the statehouse after the removal of the beacon and the peak of the hill it crowned. The dome, which Paul Revere had sheathed with copper in 1802, was gilded during the Civil War. To further mark its importance at the apex of a growing city in an era of domes, it was covered with gold leaf in 1874.

Twelve years later there seemed to be no hope for the building. Battered and worn from overuse, the partitioned halls and rooms housed only half the state bureaucracy. Rented row-houses in the area provided additional offices, always uncomfortably out of the way across streets deep in dust, snow, slush, or mud. Not only was Bulfinch's Statehouse too small and poorly built, it was also a fire hazard. The two fireproof additions attached to the rear before the war by Isaiah Rogers and G. J. F. Bryant were all that kept the building from being considered a dangerous firetrap.

Many architects and many commissions had tried to sell proposals for remodeling to the Massachusetts state legislature. In the 1850's J. D. Towle and Francis Foster had made careful plans for a further addition on the rear that would not have damaged the old Bulfinch building. The scheme was refused, as was Bryant's for a virtual reconstruction in the following decade. Edwin Brown, when invited somewhat later to make suggestions for emergency relief of the space problem, recommended that the portico be enclosed with glass, to provide a new lobby for the House of Representatives.

Other similar ideas proved unacceptable. The technical reasons given were numerous, but the real dilemma of the statehouse was politics. For thirty years there had been a strong interest in moving the Massachusetts capital westward. When the building of a new statehouse was brought up, Boston's city fathers, realizing that certain legislators meant to follow a capitol bill with a removal act, responded in the name of history: The statehouse with which Charles Bulfinch had crowned their city must not go. In that way Boston had long managed to hold its enemies in check, but by 1886 it was clear something had to be done about the governmental facilities.

Bostonians came up with a last-minute solution. After consulting with Charles Brigham, a prominent Boston architect, the Statehouse Commission suggested the extension of an annex from the back of the statehouse on fill land across Mount Vernon Street. The forty-seven-year-old Brigham had worked for Bryant & Gilman on the Boston City Hall, and in the years since had built a considerable reputation as the business member of a partnership with the English-educated John Hubbard Sturgis. Their work consisted largely of Victorian Gothic public buildings and private mansions. When Sturgis returned to England, Brigham formed a partnership with another talented designer, John Spofford, a former Maine carpenter. Since that association had just begun when Brigham first met with the Statehouse Commission, the annex idea might well have been Spofford's. Its deeper implications, however, suggest a subtler man.

Letters were written to members of the Maryland Commission, for the Boston commissioners admired the Colonial annex then under construction in Annapolis. That the commissioners would think of Neo-Colonial design as compatible with the Bulfinch Statehouse is not surprising: The term "Colonial" was applied indiscriminately to all relics of America's past up to —and even later than—what is now called the Federal period of Bulfinch. But well before they had settled the issue of style among themselves, the commissioners held a competition in the autumn of 1888, specifying that the annex be connected to the statehouse by a covered bridge over Mount Vernon Street. The firm of Brigham & Spofford won over twelve other entries. For all practical purposes the contract was made exclusively with Brigham.

Charles Brigham faced several challenges in making his design. In the first place, he hoped not to offend the commissioners' taste for the Colonial; secondly, he had to contend with his own natural aspiration to design a building which would be more than a handmaid to the old statehouse; and third, the new must blend with the old. The material he selected was yellow brick, matching the yellow-painted surfaces of the original building.

Classical architectural motifs were used in the annex in greater abundance than on most real colonial buildings. On the exterior they were executed in stone, thus lacking the delicate scale of Bulfinch's painted wooden trim. Brigham designed a grand stairway of a very regal and ornamental sort, to be seen from the main entrance once the back of Doric Hall was knocked out and the Washington statue moved aside. A new chamber for the greatly enlarged House of Representatives was located on the second floor of the annex, with a library, new offices, lounges, committee rooms, water closets, storage rooms, and vaults.

The hallways of the annex were lined with pilasters and enriched with colored tile floors, marble balustrades, and marble wainscoting. Everything about the new addition was richer and more sophisticated than the old structure facing the Common, but the public readily accepted it.

Work was well along by the late fall of 1892. Several weeks before Christmas of that year, the commission and its architect issued a statement:

> The commissioners feel it their duty . . . to suggest whether the whole
> State House should not be made new. . . . It is some hundred years old.
> Its outer walls and wooden finish will not be in keeping with what, while
> called an extension, will really be five-sixths of the whole building. . . .

> it is to be considered whether this renovation cannot be made better and cheaper now in conjunction with the work of the extension than hereafter. . . . It is recognized of course that no change would ever be permitted in the now historic and always admirable contour and architectural effect of the State House; but we believe the time has come when the front should be rebuilt.[2]

All Massachusetts now saw what the city people had in mind: The commissioners and the architect had built the annex as an anchor to hold the capital designation in Boston. Now that the anchor was dropped, they were proposing demolition of the old Bulfinch Statehouse in order to "reconstruct." Anyone could foresee that once the original building was gone, its historic value would no longer be an issue, and the commission would then decide to build an elaborate modern front to conform with the annex. Newspapers published verbose editorials in opposition. Politicians from distant towns, irritated that they had been duped, rose in defense of the Bulfinch Statehouse. The cause was taken up for sentiment's sake by hundreds of citizens, and the movement rapidly spread.

Now the commission summoned consultants to examine the structural state of the building. "The life of the timbers is gone," one engineer wrote, "every wind has its effect."[3] Demonstrations of potential dangers were devised by the commission, only to be scorned by a public already committed to preservation. When heavy books were ordered removed from the overloaded attics at the base of the dome, the dusty old volumes, placed on exhibit in Doric Hall, became relics of the greatest interest to the people. Professor George Swain, an engineer from the Massachusetts Institute of Technology, urged state officials to also clear the attic of a heavy tin tank, placed there for fire protection at about the time of the War of 1812. Crowds of spectators gathered on the statehouse lawn to observe in utter fascination that forgotten device, as its painted parts were lowered to the ground.

Alarmed by the reports of the engineers, the Sergeant at Arms of the Senate wrote a note to the Governor asking that the building be locked lest somebody be crushed beneath falling plaster. He requested, however, that his note be kept in confidence: "I have found it very embarrassing to say anything against the Old House."[4] Finally, on October 6, 1896, Acting Governor Roger Wolcott notified the commission that he had patiently listened to the "arguments of Mr. Brigham," but that the legislature wanted the old building preserved. Hereafter the original statehouse was to be treated as "a distinct building," known as the Bulfinch Front.[5]

A restoration program was planned by the architects Charles A. Cummings, Robert D. Andrews, and Arthur G. Everett, and carried out in the mid-1890's. Crumbling plaster and decorations were carefully removed. Steel beams strengthened old walls and floors. Worn or rotten wood was replaced. The old decorations were reinstalled and other decorations were added, elaborating portions of the structure beyond the Bulfinch design. The old House of Representatives in particular received a more ornamental treatment. As long as the additions passed for "Colonial," nobody seemed to mind.

208 Work was finished in time for the one-hundreth anniversary of the original building's com-

Massachusetts Statehouse, Brigham & Spoffold's competition project
for the addition, 1888

pletion. At the dedication, against a background of bunting fluttering from the old Corinthian portico, the Honorable Alfred S. Roe of Worcester, one of the saltiest champions of the Bulfinch Front, made a jubilant victory address. Boston, he said, wore a "halo of history," and "selfish interest" had tried to take it away with a "wholly false notion that gaudy colors and glittering tinsel are better than that which had withstood the test of time." Perhaps some Boston citizens had momentarily forgotten the historical value of the Bulfinch Front; no matter, Roe said with a political wink: "The farmers came in as they did at Lexington."[6]

Brigham's annex met universal approval. In its decoration he showed more restraint than the restorers of the Bulfinch Front. Around the new House of Representatives, paired pilasters stood on a high wainscot of polished oak. The ceiling's circular skylight filtered colored sunrays onto plain desks and deep floral carpets, and dark velvet portières hung limply from burnished brass rings. Principal offices were paneled in oak, glowing under coats of pumiced lacquer. Colonial motifs—wooden urns and balusters and paneling—were used in these offices, giving a cozy, unofficial look; fireplaces were little nooks, framed in oak columns, their fireboxes decorated with sea-green and yellow tiles.

Brigham, in the end prohibited from opening the back of Doric Hall, had to make other arrangements. In 1895 the space was filled with two impressive but totally un-Colonial courts. One was a square basilica-like stairhall; the second was called Memorial Hall, a circular shrine for the relics of the vanishing Grand Army of the Republic in Massachusetts. The blending of marbles on the walls, floors, and in the ring of columns rising to a balustraded mezzanine was thoroughly Italian Renaissance. In this section of the Boston Statehouse the academic current came to full fruition. What was more, Bulfinch's Statehouse at last had a rotunda.

Construction continued during most of the 1890's, and as American architecture changed in those years, so did the Bulfinch Statehouse. The annex must be considered transitional. Because they were better suited to the scale of the annex, formal Renaissance themes were used instead of vernacular ones from the American past. Brigham may well have explained—as other architects would be doing to other commissions—that he was returning to the European ancestry of eighteenth-century American design. In his introduction of academic detailing, he anticipated a whole era of Renaissance Classicism that would be full-blown before work on the Statehouse had passed his final inspection.

Not a long walk from the Bulfinch Front, beyond the Common, lies Copley Square, where scholarly Italian Renaissance design made its American debut in public architecture. Facing each

209

other across the square are two of the most influential buildings ever constructed in the United States: H. H. Richardson's Trinity Church and the Boston Public Library by McKim, Mead & White. Trinity was built first, in the mid-1870's, and though the library was designed only a decade later, they differed markedly. In designing the library, the architects met the challenge of creating an edifice to stand in balance with the pyramidal bichromatic mass of Trinity, for which Richardson had borrowed features from Romanesque buildings of the past to produce his mighty romantic composition. Such historicity had rarely been seen in American architecture since the Greek Revival. McKim, Mead & White's solution was to continue such historical borrowing, expanding the concept. Their library was Trinity's antithesis—a plain block of palest pink granite in the formal style of fifteenth-century Italy. It was praised for its abstract qualities, and history blessed its Renaissance clarity. But it was not a reproduction of a particular building. The concept of a library with a low, ground story, heavy and solid, and a great arched range of light-giving windows above it came from Henri Labrouste's Bibliothèque Ste. Geneviève in Paris, completed less than forty years before. The Italian sources for the detailing were great Renaissance monuments, the Tempio Malatestiano in Rimini and the Palazzo della Cancelleria in Rome. To the epochal work Charles McKim called some of the most famous artists of the day—the world's leading muralist Pierre Puvis de Chavannes of Paris, the portrait painter John Singer Sargent, the illustrator Edwin Austin Abbey, and the sculptor Augustus Saint-Gaudens.

The architects and the artists were all friends, either as neighbors in the Worcestershire Village in New York or as members of the Century Club, and some of them through longtime New England family connections. They were an aggressive lot, in love with art itself and with their own art as a profitable business.

Those who worked on the Boston Public Library were among the foremost creators and passionate believers in what they liked to call the American Renaissance. That such a renaissance should find its expression in generically Classical terms showed the innocence of its creators; instead of liberating themselves from the eclecticism of the nineteenth century, they reaffirmed it by initiating what was really a new Renaissance Revival. Rejecting any suggestion that they were copyists or imitators, these architects believed they were spiritually reliving the creative experience that had given birth to those famous monuments of the European past.

The Neo-Renaissance discipline recurrently sponsored by foreign academies was late in reaching the United States. In state capitols it first appeared in the 1870's at Indianapolis in the work of the Vienna-trained Scherrer and in Bell's Michelangelesque revision of Piquenard's dome at Des Moines. A special sort of Renaissance Classicism dominated at the Ecole des Beaux-Arts in France. What Americans came to call "Beaux-Arts Classicism" was by no means revivalism in the strict sense of copying Renaissance buildings; the new sort of revivalism was intellectual and subtle, employing a vast vocabulary of forms and details from the past in what was otherwise "modern" monumental architecture.

American students at the Beaux-Arts brought their French experience home with them, but once the American movement started, the alumni proved less possessed by it than the American architects who stayed home and knew Parisian work only at secondhand.

210   The American Renaissance had its roots deep in the art world of New York. For nearly

fifty years New York had proclaimed itself the style center of the United States. Ambitious architects had gravitated there since the Civil War; H. H. Richardson represented a rare reversal of the trend by moving the headquarters of his national practice to Massachusetts. New York architects developed friendships and tacit professional rules. They created a forum for their ideas about professional conduct in the American Institute of Architects. Founded in the 1850's, by the early 1890's A.I.A. had only a small membership, most of it Eastern, and was beset by the politics and the machinations of inner cliques.

This American Renaissance in architecture symbolized less an artistic rebirth than the maturing and organizing of the profession. As a style, it was introduced to Manhattan in the Villard House, five town houses built together in 1882–85 by McKim, Mead & White to form one great Italian *palazzo*. Here was architecture as fine art—an intellectual reaction against the utilitarian elevator buildings and the first skyscrapers which were becoming the peculiar trademarks of American urban life. Features once the work of common stonecutters were now assigned to sculptors. Murals replaced stenciling and tapestry replaced wallpapers. Suddenly artists of many kinds were working together on the same structure, and a parallel was hastily drawn with the days of the Medici.

All this is very interesting in retrospect, but at the time no one outside the Northeast knew anything about the American Renaissance. By 1890, however, the design of the Boston Public Library was receiving national acclaim. Such monumental works required ambitious clients and big budgets. It was inevitable that the American Renaissance, even before it was really defined as such, would find its greatest domain in public architecture. While big houses at Newport and the city mansions were good jobs to get, the big money was in public buildings. Even before the completion of the Boston Public Library, Italian Renaissance architecture was recognized as proper for them. All architectural firms aspired to public work, first for the money, but certainly for prestige as well. Classicism was once again a marketable product. It would live longer this time in public architecture than any other style; its aura of aesthetic perfection stood out in a pragmatic age.

An old lesson in the practice of architecture in America was that the best partnership was between a salesman and an artist—a businessman to go out and find the jobs, and an artist to stay in the office and do the work. As far as is known, Town & Davis was the first partnership of that kind in the United States. Through the decades since their heyday, New York architectural firms had grown considerably larger, sometimes employing as many as forty draftsmen full-time. But the formula for success—the proper balance between architect and businessman—remained the same. Just such a perfect combination was the firm of McKim, Mead & White, whose office at 160 Fifth Avenue had beyond any doubt the most prestige in America from the mid-1880's until World War I by which time only Mead was still alive.

It became the largest firm in the country once its reputation was made—a veritable plan factory for houses and commercial and public structures. After the Boston Public Library, the three partners were celebrities: McKim the architect-designer-businessman, Mead the businessman-architect, and White the master of architectural and particularly interior detailing.

Charles F. McKim was old enough to remember the 1850's, when his parents had been devoted workers in the cause of abolition. They had accompanied John Brown's widow to what is now West Virginia to claim the martyr's body. During the 1860's McKim was an outstanding athlete at Harvard, then spent several years abroad as a student at the Ecole des Beaux-Arts. Back home in 1870, he had many opportunities in New England, but instead went to work for Richardson in New York. In a year or two he opened a little private office several doors away. McKim did not like working for other people, but he soon found a sympathetic partner in William R. Mead.

Mead, a native of Vermont, was the firm's organizer. He delighted in the minutiae of operating the Manhattan office, which grew to be huge, with teams of draftsmen and a business staff. Usually he was the front man of the firm, meeting business clients, church committees, and commissioners of public buildings. Even in the worst economic times, Mead could still find work for the firm. As a young man he had spent a year and a half living at the Florence studio of his sculptor-brother Larkin Goldsmith Mead, the artist responsible for the wooden Ceres on the Vermont Capitol. His understanding of the Italian Renaissance was deeper than that of McKim or White, and he was committed to creating such an age in American architecture.

Stanford White, the last to join the firm, was destined to be the best remembered. He was the socialite, devoted to big city life, yet obsessed with his work, and remembered as a Renaissance man of his day. A native of New York and a drama critic's son, White had wanted to be an artist, a painter. But instead he went to work in Richardson's office while still a youth, and became fascinated by the art of architecture. He gained a vigorous, practical exposure to every aspect of design and construction. Richardson delegated detail work to him on Trinity Church, and he supervised some important projects for the office. By the time White first traveled to Europe, he was an experienced young man. His artistic interest knew almost no limitation; his enthusiasm was often the motor force of McKim, Mead & White.

In May 1891, when the Capitol Commission of the state of Rhode Island was authorized to obtain plans for a new statehouse, McKim, Mead & White were among nine firms invited to participate in a selective competition. Obviously they were expected to submit something that looked like the Boston Public Library, then well along toward completion, which occurred in the next year. Rhode Island already had numerous buildings by the firm. Socially and professionally recognized in Newport, the partners had designed numerous seaside houses for rich New Yorkers there and on the New Jersey shore. The fanciful Shingle-Style Casino in Newport was their one semipublic work.

While the New York office set to work on the Rhode Island Statehouse drawings, McKim and Mead boarded their private railroad car and headed for Rhode Island to make proper appearances on the scene and lay the political groundwork.

The act authorizing a new Rhode Island Capitol at Providence was sponsored by the city's Public Park Association, one of the civic groups characteristic of this era of perfection. Strangled by railroads, with streets filthy from sewage, Providence was a likely place for a beautification program such as those being formed in cities all over the nation.

The association members were dedicated to all things new. "The State," they wrote in 1891, "has stultified itself long enough by occupying the present ancient, inadequate, incon-

Division of Methods, Data Processing and Central Services, State of Rhode Island
Rhode Island Capitol, Providence, McKim, Mead & White's competition project, 1891

venient and insecure legislative building over one hundred and thirty years old, with less architectural pretensions than a county court house. . . . Why should the State appear poor and parsimonious when she is rich and ought to be generous to herself?" They urged that a new statehouse be built on Smith's Hill, to be approached by "an area three hundred feet wide from the passenger station to the Capitol . . . converted into a magnificent boulevard. What an ornament this would be to the city, to the State! It should be designed in the perfection of landscape architecture; with a wide avenue . . . transversed by electric cars and vehicles of every description, and the one hundred and ten feet on each side ornamented with foliage, lawns, promenades, beds of flowers, fountains and other works of art."[7]

Most entries were Renaissance—five Italian, one Spanish. There was also a Richardsonian Romanesque one, and another that was Victorian Gothic. A Second Empire scheme recalled Piquenard's Midwestern capitols. It can be supposed that it and the Gothic essay were passed over quickly: Perhaps a little more consideration was given the Spanish project with its tall, balconied central tower, for this was proffered by the local Providence firm of Stone & Carpenter and was intended to become the great landmark of the region.

McKim, Mead & White's Italian Renaissance elevation was the only design with any clear commitment to the new. The others lingered safely in the spirit of the 1880's, most of them picturesque compositions with their busy façades and clumsy silhouettes. McKim, Mead & White's scheme had the desired aura of the Boston Public Library, expressed through the features that were expected in a state capitol: the prominent colonnaded dome, the portico—though without pediment—the matching wings, and the monumentality that befitted authority.

But it was more than that. The massing of its series of crisp rectangular blocks made it appear to have been sliced from the stone itself. Rows of tall French doors on the wings opened on to balconies lit by electric torches and overlooked expansive terraces with balustrades. In the center was a great cube weighted by a dome and lantern based on Christopher Wren's on St.

Paul's, with domed *tourelles* at the corners. A loggia behind tall Corinthian columns formed a ceremonial gallery over the severe entrance doors. Wide flights of stairs ascended between bronze torchères. Groups of sculpture were to stand at intervals on the projecting terrace below the loggia.

Mead was in Providence on January 14, 1892, when the commissioners voted unanimously in favor of his firm's entry. He also hoped to gain the salaried position of Capitol Architect, but the commissioners were authorized by law only to select plans. The drawings on linen were rolled up on their sticks and deposited with the Secretary of State to await further action by the legislature. Mead welcomed a postponement, for his firm was already busy with the Chicago Fair.

Several cities, including New York, had badly wanted the 1892 international exposition which was to commemorate the four-hundredth anniversary of Columbus's discovery of America. Chicago had won, and the work had been put into the hands of one of those perfect architectural partnerships, that of Daniel H. Burnham, the promoter, and John W. Root, the artist, which had been the leading firm in Chicago for several years and among the greatest builders of early skyscrapers. The fair commission had engaged Frederick Law Olmsted to devise the layout of the fairgrounds. Burnham & Root encouraged the commission to invite the nation's most important architects to design the exhibition buildings.

Mead and some friends went to Chicago for the first meeting in the winter of 1891. He expressed some doubts, but after the sessions with other architects, he brought his enthusiasm back to New York, and the sketching started. Soon after, the talented Root died, a very significant loss that threw most of the responsibility for design to the New York firms, under the leadership of McKim.

In May 1893, one year late, the World's Columbian Exposition opened on the once sandy and ugly site beside Lake Michigan, and soon New York's appetite for Renaissance architecture reached the entire country. Along shimmering lagoons, through the spray of fountains, colonnaded façades rich in statuary conjured up a dream city in white plaster. Tourists hardly noticed the vast glass and iron roofs inside or the exhibits, so resplendently novel were the vistas outside the promenades—the electric lights, the banks of flowers, the overpowering consistency of the Classical façades.

Architects learned something in their association with one another during the exposition—there was a real need for businesslike cooperation among the big firms on a national basis. Joint efforts had brought rewards. During the three years of the Fair's preparation, the nation's most successful architects had worked under the direction of Burnham through the heretofore powerless A.I.A. to make truly far-reaching changes. Burnham and Mead had sought out Republican senators and congressmen in Washington to discuss with them the Treasury Department's building programs. Some of the biggest public jobs in the country were Federal ones, all now handled directly by the Supervising Architect of the Treasury through a well-staffed office in Washington. This meant that from thirty to fifty buildings a year were designed and nominally supervised by one man. Sanctimoniously, the architects of perfection set out to destroy a bureaucratic agency that had enjoyed the approval of even the entrepreneurs of the Gilded Age. Federal projects should be awarded in open competition, argued the A.I.A., and the winning architects should be given salaried posts as supervisors of the work. A loud controversy began, laced with harsh criticism of Cleveland's Secretary of the Treasury. The architects maintained that the office was overworked, and pointed to examples of what they considered consistently poor taste in Federal design. Only a few blocks from the Capitol, McKim, Mead & White's train car stood by for entertaining; different architects arrived weekly to take their turn at politicking in Washington.

The Tarsney Act, passed three months before the opening of the fair, was a signal triumph in America for the great private firms. In the bitter battle to push it through, the tone of the act had to be softened several times after Burnham and Mead's original draft. The approved text reflected the act's wholly political conception: At the discretion of the Secretary of the Treasury, federal building projects would now be open to architectural competition, and the winning architect might be employed to supervise construction.

By the time the Fair opened its gates, however, the Secretary of the Treasury had absolutely refused to stage competitions. Open conflicts with the architects rambled on for months after Chicago's winter wind had begun to blow plaster acanthus leaves over the empty park. An official statement of the American Institute of Architects to the Secretary of the Treasury made an appeal in behalf of the public: "The people are no longer ignorant regarding architectural matters. They have been awakened through the display of the World's Columbian Exposition. . . ."[8] Finally, in 1897, a new Secretary of the Treasury was appointed, and the A.I.A. managed to get one of its own members, James Knox Taylor of St. Paul, appointed Supervising Architect.

The producers of Chicago's great show changed the history of American architecture, extending, if only nominally, the professional climate of New York and Chicago to the whole of America. In turn the fair sold the public on Beautiful Architecture, with the corollary that real beauty could only be created by established professionals. The Chicago exposition also proved that a city could be clean and safe and lovely. Americans willingly accepted the idea that architecture would lead them into the Age of the City Beautiful. Over and over again, in the remotest places, mayors and businessmen pored over pictures of the White City and imagined what their own towns might become.

Such was the idea of the Capitol Commission in Minnesota, when it met at St. Paul in its first session of 1893. The state needed a new capitol and had planned to build one since 1881 when the old statehouse, damaged by fire, was replaced by a high-roofed, round-arched temporary building. Inspired by the Fair, the legislature finally appropriated $2,000,000.

One of the Minnesota architects taking a special interest in the coming competition was Cass Gilbert, the thirty-four-year-old partner of James Knox Taylor. Their office in the Endicott Building was the most successful in St. Paul. Gilbert's single year of working in New York had made him acutely aware of the professional status architects enjoyed in that city. He was an ardent member of A.I.A. and had founded the Minnesota chapter, though he never severed his connections with New York. Taylor assisted Gilbert in his often daring efforts in behalf of professionalism in Minnesota. As soon as the capitol act was published, Gilbert led the A.I.A. chapter in opposing several of its restrictive clauses.

Gilbert was a native of Ohio but grew up in St. Paul. He was witty and easy with close friends, but he never stopped selling himself long enough to seem very relaxed with anyone else. There were those who considered him obnoxious; still others—Charles McKim, for example—counted him among the finest men they knew. He had been attracted to architecture through his love for sketching and making watercolors. No blank sheet of paper remained empty in his presence, if he had a pen or a soft-lead pencil at hand. Little scenes with sky and birds over sloping rooftops were begun in the margins of letters while he contemplated the contents. Even his signature was a complete composition, one of staccato strokes struck parallel and fitted tightly into an invisible oval.

After attending public schools in Minnesota, he worked as a rodman and draftsman for a railroad company in Wisconsin. He spent a brief period with the United States Coast Survey, then a year as an honor student in architecture at the Massachusetts Institute of Technology. Too restless for the classroom, Gilbert left for Europe and traveled in England and on the Continent.

On his return, he served one year, 1880, as a draftsman in the McKim, Mead & White office. At that time the commissions were largely for picturesque residences. It was a ten-man firm, including the three partners, and growing; White had joined the firm only five months earlier. Gilbert was sent to supervise the Ross Winans house in Baltimore, which was the earliest reflection of Hunt's and Post's two *François premier* Vanderbilt houses in New York. From there the opportunity of a job with Taylor brought Gilbert back to Minnesota. He had made a wise decision: His knowledge of popular Eastern architectural modes soon established his reputation in St. Paul and won him a full partnership with his employer.

There can be no denying that Cass Gilbert wanted passionately to be the architect of the new Minnesota State Capitol. He was not the only one to oppose the legislature's restrictive compromise bill, stating the precise dimensions of the building and limiting the architect's fee to two and one-half per cent, when five per cent was the fee specified by the A.I.A. On May 29, 1894, the Capitol Commission agreed to meet with representatives of the state A.I.A. at the office of Channing Seabury, a rich St. Paul wholesale grocer and importer.

Seabury, vice-chairman of the commission under a chairman who preferred as Governor to remain uninvolved, had been one of the local people most in favor of building a new capitol in St. Paul, for fear of losing out to some other city. His interest had increased on the commission's capitol tour, which included railroad trips to Des Moines, Lansing, Indianapolis, Hartford, and Richardson's Allegheny County Courthouse in Pittsburgh. Lansing had so impressed him that he wrote to E. E. Myers for photographs. Myers returned them autographed, with a note suggesting the advantages of hiring a practical man. Seabury was also a good friend of Cass Gilbert. They knew the same people, and Seabury admired Gilbert's Richardsonian and Shingle Style houses in St. Paul.

The Commission, however, was immovable. Its members refused to honor Gilbert's request that they lobby en masse to "amend the act that the architect of the building shall receive payment for his services to the amount customary and usual."[9] After some argument Seabury convinced the other seven members that a committee of three architects should be appointed to study the competition rules. Gilbert was the only one of the three to appear, but once his foot was in the door he became a fixture at commission meetings, talking continually, interrupting, objecting, at last demanding that the fee be raised. Both the commissioners and the Attorney General refused and sent Gilbert a copy of the original act.

The competition was advertised in Chicago and Boston and in the city newspapers of Minnesota. From a list of twelve architects, the commission selected Henry Ives Cobb of Chicago and Edmund M. Wheelwright, the City-Architect of Boston, as the competition judges. Gilbert, annoyed because he did not know Wheelwright or have any connection with him, hurriedly sent inquiries to friends in Boston. The replies assured him of Wheelwright's integrity.

Fifty-six sets of drawings were in the commission office by October 15, 1894, when Wheelwright, Cobb, and the commissioners began unwrapping the entries. Barred from the meeting, Gilbert registered professional objections and declined to enter the competition. Eleven other Minnesota architects felt fewer scruples and submitted schemes; they were invited, as a courtesy, to join seven outside finalists in making personal presentations of their proposals. Gilbert implored Seabury to reject them all.

Several months of silence followed, and no decision was made. On April 11, 1895, the commission announced that five premiums would be paid and the plans returned to their authors. The conditions for a second competition were then formulated.

A vacancy created by the death of one member of the commission was filled by Daniel Shell, a shrewd insurance man from Worthington. He was a friend of Seabury and of Gilbert. This time Gilbert was a competitor.

In October 1895, an unrecorded number of plans stood stacked in the commission office. Wheelwright, now the lone judge, ordered them hung on wires from the picture molding, where they remained three weeks for the politicians to inspect. On October 23, each architect spoke on the merits of his design. Gilbert was one of the five finalists chosen late that night.

The next day all but the five schemes were ordered removed from the room, and the commissioners set themselves to the task of making a decision. An informal vote was taken; of the seven votes cast, Gilbert got two. Shell called for another ballot. This time Gilbert and George Mann of St. Louis, also a former draftsman with McKim, Mead & White, tied for first place with two votes each. Shell called for three more ballots. When the last count still showed a tie, Shell called for adjournment.

Two days later Gilbert's support fell to one vote, with a three-vote majority going to Bassford, Traphagen & Fitzpatrick, a hastily created firm of Duluth and St. Paul architects. Harry Jones of Minneapolis placed second, with Gilbert and Mann now tied for third place. Shell demanded a recount and a revote. After a four-day recess, Seabury recommended that the commissioners reconsider taking another ballot. The suggestion was accepted, and Seabury made a motion, seconded by Shell, to award first prize to Cass Gilbert and appoint him supervising architect of the work.

The vote was unanimously in favor of the proposal, and small awards were distributed to the losers. On January 16, 1896, Daniel Shell resigned from the commission. That same week Gilbert signed a contract with the remaining commissioners, specifying a five per cent fee for himself.[10]

There was little public reaction to the sequence of incidents leading to the final selection. Gilbert continually assured the commissioners of his professional rights, almost as though they were a holy writ revealed only to him. Of the numerous losers, it can be supposed that many had never been serious about the competition. A Redlands, California, architect named Lyman Farwell, another onetime draftsman for McKim, Mead & White, wrote to him:

> Having nothing better to do, I went with [the competition] for the fun of it, as I do most every competition. . . . I had too short a time in which to do justice to the problem, or even to myself. I had no photos, no books . . . nor . . . any numbers of *American Architect* showing the R.I. State Capitol. I remembered the "type" of McKim's design. . . . I know how McK. took his ideas & his exterior treatment from the little city hall in N.Y.C.— Tom [Hastings?] and Harry Bacon both told me of that and I took my pendentive dome treatment for the Rotunda, from St. Peters. . . . I like the proportions of my Rotunda better [than McKim's].[11]

Many of the serious entries were published through the remainder of the 1890's in *The American Architect and Building News*, which, since the Fair, had become an established and lively spokesman for the architectural profession. All the schemes showed that academic Classical design now dominated American public architecture.

The Capitols of Minnesota and Rhode Island were both completed in the first decade of the twentieth century. They became important models which were never really copied, but which loomed behind every other project of that kind for a whole generation. If any American capitols ever represented the high style of their period, it is these two. The New York world of taste and fashion pervades their grand interiors. New York artists and craftsmen were kept busy on the site, at the architects' insistence, despite legislative protests that local talent was being ignored.

Both were also monuments to good management. Try though they might, legislators were unable to dig up scandals. Powerful commissioners dealt personally with the astute architects, ironing out difficulties behind closed doors and rarely permitting any differences to appear, even in the minutes. Newspapers longing for headlines had to be content with the controversial question in Providence of whether the state's own Roger Williams or a Manhattan nymph should crown the dome. At St. Paul, editors fretted over mounting costs, but the remotest counties did not object when their representatives appropriated more and more; the loudest opposition was a stone's throw away in envious Minneapolis.

On September 16, 1895, a little group of men walked together up Smith's Hill, huddling together in black coats to break the bite of the Rhode Island autumn. Between two dwellings and around the side of a barn they filed shivering through the mud of last summer's vegetable gardens to the piece of ground on which a crowd was collected. With little ceremony the Governor scooped a shovel of dirt and turned it over; there were three cheers, and Smith's Hill was left to the wind. Henry Bacon represented McKim, Mead and White. He had been their superintendent at the fair, and took the lead in the construction of the Rhode Island Statehouse, which began in the first warm days of spring. The following summer, a good part of Minnesota attended the opening ceremonies for their new Capitol, as nearby residents who had refused to sell their land looked grudgingly on from vine-covered porches.

The original scheme for Providence had to be enlarged sixty feet, increasing the width so much that the architects wanted to omit the *tourelles* that weighted the corners of the central block. They found, however, that the commission had no intention of giving up what was one of their favorite features of the design. On the recommendation of Richard M. Hunt, the commission's consultant, Georgia marble was selected as the principal material. Hunt, who died in 1895, was the high priest of taste to Rhode Islanders because of the Vanderbilt palaces he had built in Newport. He insisted that white marble, and particularly Georgia marble, was "indispensable"; and Mead had added that in chemical composition Georgia marble was "almost exactly like that of the famous Grecian marbles."[12] The commission in St. Paul also selected Georgia white marble over Gilbert's preference for granite. And both commissions changed tooled marble to "sand-rubbed" surfaces which would have the plaster-white look of the fair.

A certain competitiveness existed between the two projects. When the Rhode Island Commission decided to have a masonry dome, Minnesota demanded one too, though it required one of much less weight. Gilbert did the exterior design; then the commission hired R. Guastavino & Co. of New York to make working drawings and to execute the dome in the lightweight Catalan tile technique, a layered method popularized in the Boston Public Library. Norcross Brothers, contractors at the Providence project and for many of Richardson's past works, devised the structure of the masonry dome McKim had redesigned.

Considered as finished structures, the two Capitols were rather similar. In its stark white simplicity, Rhode Island—even after its revision—kept alive the image of the Chicago Fair. At the commission's suggestion and without opposition from McKim, Mead & White, some carving in marble was added to the bull's-eyes and the loggia. At St. Paul, however, as the work progressed the effect became very lush; after Gilbert moved to New York, he became obsessed with decoration, and the Minnesota Capitol was a biographical record of the development of his taste.

His decision to leave St. Paul was made when he won the competition for the United States Customhouse in New York. Gilbert knew full well that by moving to New York he was entering an arbor of sour grapes, for the big Manhattan firms—his old A.I.A. friends, the losers in the competition—were accusing Supervising Architect Taylor of favoritism. But controversy never frightened Cass Gilbert.

Now his field was the entire country, and Gilbert was making the best of it. He was always on the move, and his matchless enthusiasm for what was new was manifested in constantly changing ideas for St. Paul. At lunch in Kinsley's Restaurant in Chicago, he saw stone pavements he liked; they were perfect for St. Paul, and he made arrangements that day with the contractor who had installed them. On to something else: The stub-point pen fiercely sketched a better *torchère* than McKim's, a finer marble bench, maybe like the one he had seen in that house near Florence so long ago, or was it Siena? He must go again and see. "I am very tired with incessant hard work," he wrote to a Boston friend in the spring of 1899.[13]

The Minnesota Capitol, completed in 1904, seems from a distance to float above the town,   219

Minnesota Capitol, Senate chamber, photograph by Cass Gilbert, 1905

yet at the foot of its terraces, which Gilbert patterned after those by Brigham in Boston, it appears to be on level ground. St. Paul had developed from the bank of the Mississippi on natural land shelves that descended from hills in steps down to the river. The new Capitol, far from the old heart of town, did rise above most of the country around it, and Gilbert planned grand avenues to accentuate its place as a focal point in a City Beautiful scheme.

Except for its greater size, the Minnesota Capitol immediately brings to mind the one in Providence. The three heavy blocks decorated with pilasters are connected by fully detailed links. An arcaded loggia, once again without a pediment, pierces the central block and is suggested in each of the outer wings beneath shallow domes. The main dome is a slightly more conical version of St. Peter's in Rome. Counting the basement, there are four full floors, carefully articulated on the façades by the surface treatment of the white marble. Statuary and garlands in marble testify to the legislature's generosity but seem lost in the varied plasticity of the exterior treatments. Daniel Chester French and Edward C. Potter had created for the base of the dome a group sculpture in bronze, a chariot drawn by four leaping horses with figures of a youth and two maidens. This Quadriga was covered with gold leaf at Gilbert's insistence.

There is little similarity between the interiors of the two Capitols. Gilbert's interior is much more sumptuous and far grander, if only for the reckless waste of space. The rotunda, a dark region in Pompeiian red with green and gold borders, is lined with bronze electroliers. To each side stretch great light-courts, barrel-roofed in glass to illuminate marble staircases rising between files of Corinthian columns with golden capitals. The best contemporary New York muralists decorated the dozens of blind lunettes with heroic scenes. Colored marbles dimly glow in a perpetual twilight from the skylights and the windows in the dome, but the dark interiors become monotonous in their endless repetition of pattern. The Senate chamber in one wing is balanced by the Supreme Court in the other, with the House of Representatives in a wing to the rear of the rotunda. Most of Gilbert's reception rooms are Neo-Colonial, although one is Renais-

Rhode Island Historical Society
Rhode Island Capitol, by KcKim, Mead & White, 1895–1905, as completed

sance, its original curtains purple damask, embroidered in silver with the *M* of Minnesota. The interior is a confusing maze of an interior in spite of the seeming orderliness of its plan.

McKim, Mead & White followed no precedent at Providence, but there are some touches which they may well have called Colonial. Unlike St. Paul, where the transverse halls thrust out from the rotunda with a grandeur all their own, in the Providence interior all parts are arranged centripetally around the central space in a tighter composition.

Completed in the same year as Gilbert's Capitol, the Providence building was under the heavy influence of the latest Hunt houses of Newport. But the light-court and rotunda, compressed into one feature, actually provide a ceremonial space reminiscent of that in the Ohio Capitol.   221

This space at Providence is filled to overflowing with a rippling pair of staircases in white marble that ascend on either side to encircling galleries. The commission wrote: "By means of this central rotunda, immediate access is gained to all parts of the building, thus avoiding the usual costly and inadequate light wells."[14] Sunlight from clear glass lunettes and windows in the dome fall on the white interior, decorated on the landings of the stairs with bronze *torchères* and some inlaid brass. The even starker simplicity of the balanced chambers is slightly relieved by murals which resemble eighteenth-century French tapestries in their pinks and lilacs.

Only the Governor's Reception Room contrasts with the plainness of the rest of the building. Opening through tall French doors onto the loggia, the room is the *Louis quatorze* style of the expensive Fifth Avenue houses of the time. Glass chandeliers, frescoes, and "antique gold" reproductions of seventeenth-century French court furniture give the room the contrived luster of a New York salon.

Gilbert's work at St. Paul was far more illustrative of the American Renaissance than its contemporary in Providence. From the first, Gilbert had intended to fill the Minnesota Capitol's ceremonial areas with works of art. In the truest spirit of the American Renaissance, the architect set out to wave his magic wand and create, in one grand stroke, a palatial monument of the kind it had taken Europeans centuries to build. With a big state budget and the blessings of both Channing Seabury and the Fine Arts Commission, Gilbert hired the artists who were considered in Eastern architectural circles to be the best. The works of these men were never supposed to interfere with architecture; painters and sculptors were expected to be content to play a benign supporting role.

Gilbert made friends in Manhattan studios and gave out contracts. A bitter Minnesota artist wrote to him:

> I have watched with interest the efforts of the local artists of this state to just secure the crumbs that fell from the tables of Public donations, also the heartless manner in which hundreds of thousands of dollars of the State's money have been spent *"presenting"* commissions for Works of Art for the new Capitol without any competition whatever . . . personally I have nothing to say against Mr. Guernsey or Mr. French. I think that if anyone else was "presented" with contracts to the amount of $150,000 and $35,000 respectively without competing for it they would gladly accept it and consider themselves one of Fortune's favorites.[15]

Gilbert was worried about commissioners who tried to grant their own friends the contracts for serious works of art. To one commissioner he wrote:

> You have accepted, tentatively at least, the services of two persons, estimable as they may be in their private life, who have never, so far as I am informed, executed any kind of a statue much less a heroic statue of such importance. The work is one which should enlist the best services of the best men, and I have constantly advised you toward this end. My advice in this

Rhode Island Capitol, by McKim, Mead & White, great central crossing in 1905
Rhode Island Historical Society

respect has been ignored and you now have before you models for this important work by persons who are naturally ambitious but who, so far as I can ascertain, utterly lack training and experience to execute the work. You would not employ a foreman in your factory upon such principles.[16]

Minnesota commissioners visiting New York with visions of the proverbial starving artist were surprised to see such a painter as John La Farge living in luxury in a huge studio on West 10th Street. What was more, they were jarred by such modern devices as photographic slides used to project fragmentary sketches on bare canvas for assistants to fill in with oil paint. Men whose greatest exposure to sculpture was in the selection of family tombstones looked with disappointment upon the steam and electric tools used to carve marble statues.

At Providence, the more experienced McKim, Mead & White consciously avoided any changes which might involve the commissioners in new aesthetic decisions. They remembered that the selection of the exterior marble alone had taken Mead months to resolve and required building numerous mock-ups. Gilbert, on the other hand, out to make a national reputation with his Minnesota Capitol, made continual demands on his commission to approve additional works of art.

Sometimes in amusement, sometimes in rage, but always with patience, Gilbert guided his commissioners along what he considered the right path. Privately he was in constant contact with the artists, getting his own way. "You will be glad to know," wrote Daniel Chester French, "that I have begun a model for the central figure [in the chariot] of the Quadriga. The other figures are already designed, as are the horses, since we are to follow the Quadriga which presided over the Columbian Arch at Chicago."[17] The muralist Kenyon Cox wrote:

> Your letter . . . with its most courteously put criticisms and suggestions for the St. Paul Lunette came on Saturday. . . . I hasten to say that I appreciate your point of view and shall try further sketches. . . . I had thought of the swirl of drapery for the upper part but did not use it because it seemed to me to introduce too much restlessness and movement where I wanted immobility and stability. . . . I shall now try an entirely new scheme, which seems to me preferable to tinkering with this one, and shall endeavor to get more massive and sculpturesque qualities. . . . I shall consider your suggestions . . . though I hope you will not expect oriental costumes. I have rather an objection to "local color" and prefer abstract draperies as much as possible.[18]

Capitol commissions met in great excitement as the works of art arrived, relishing every detail. The last entry of the minute books of the Rhode Island Commission records rather sadly that each of the commissioners then had to surrender his keys to the Capitol: McKim, Mead & White, no less than Cass Gilbert, had spun a web of American Renaissance romance over their project. Gilbert kept his commission so busy thinking about details that they seldom meddled in larger matters. When Seabury wrote a criticism to John La Farge, the artist snapped back in a long letter that he hoped would "make you understand how irrelevant many of your observa-

Rhode Island Capitol, McKim, Mead & White, Governor's Reception Room in 1905

tions are. . . . You may not be to blame for not understanding matters outside of your habit and knowledge, but in such matters . . . it is dangerous to go outside of one's experience and against the opinions of experts."[19] Gilbert would have agreed.

If the secret of creating the American Renaissance was only for the few, the glorious finished product was for everyone. The guidebook at St. Paul contained the following passage even before the golden horses were in place:

> Time flies so fast in this building. . . . Three, four or five hours may slip away while one is thinking that hardly sixty minutes have fled . . . within these walls are blended so much of art and religion, so much of science and literature, so much of romance and history, that one must needs forget the time and space element till, passing through the great rotunda out toward the main entrance, the fine old De Laittre benches invite a second rest and give rise to reflective and historic musings: These benches, with their curious carvings, are Italian and a thousand years old! The work upon them is exquisite, and they could have adorned no mean building. In what public place

225

were they? They need be Italian and a round half a thousand years old to have given a resting place to Savonarola, to Catherine de Medici, Raphael, Michael Angelo and how many others whose lives were weft for our warp or whose achievement our noble capitol wears like a crest? But you must leave the building sometime . . . you pass out and down the great approach . . . you turn to take another look at the stucture. By this time you will feel a thrill of friendship for the White Temple.[20]

Such were the enchantments of Providence and St. Paul. Through the several depression years of the mid-1890's sketches of the two buildings, then barely begun, were published widely in magazines and newspapers. The extravagant and ornate structures at Albany and Denver, and others like them nearing completion, only recalled the long season of excess that Americans believed was over.

Renaissance Classicism as a national style began its conquest in the swell of optimism that followed William McKinley's election in 1896. There had already been efforts to apply the architecture of perfection to other state capitols besides Providence and St. Paul. A capitol competition was held at Olympia, Washington, before the Chicago Fair locked its gates in the fall of 1893. It was won by the Brooklyn-born Ernest Flagg only, five years after he finished his studies at the Ecole des Beaux-Arts. The design was so academically self-assured that it turned its back on the beautiful Puget Sound. At the foundation stage, with the full appropriation of $200,000 spent, work came to a halt. The bulk of the additional money was to come from the sale of land bonds funded by a large federal land grant to the state. If the Federal government had little success in its own bond sales through the 1890's, the state of Washington met complete failure. Roadblocks were built over the muddy path to the bare foundations of the Capitol, and state officials turned their attention to troubles more pressing.

After McKinley's election in 1896, the horizon seemed brighter. The Republicans had won their victory by scattering wild promises, more effective than the fearful Cross of Gold of the Populist opposition. But fortune also smiled on the Republicans. Farmers harvested the best crops in years, and the quarrel over the gold or silver standard was settled by the fabulous gold strikes that year in the Yukon. Prosperity returned with the Republicans, and suddenly there was every expectation that the nineteenth century would end on a happy note. Legislatures were ready to accept the new. Secure in their authority after 1896, Republicans and Democrats alike, rid of the Populist invaders, had a strong sense of their own endurance. The idea of monumental architecture, then, had a natural appeal in its permanence. Americans believed that in the nineteenth century's last breath, their architects had created a timeless style for public buildings. No capitol in the United States went unaffected by the American Renaissance. Whether in the form of annexes, wings, murals, or sculpture, the era of perfection made its mark.

Giant white marble wings were added at the sides of the Bulfinch Front in Boston. In Richmond Jefferson's temple, hardly touched for over a century, was gutted and rebuilt with porticoed wings added on either side, stuffy Renaissance parodies of the original building. Maryland's

John H. McGrail, Caroliniana Library
South Carolina Statehouse, begun in 1853, as completed in 1907

Statehouse was given an overscaled rear wing with the pedimented portico the old front lacked. The new wing, replacing the earlier Colonial Revival one, provided executive offices and legislative chambers. McKim, Mead & White, summoned to Alabama, sent McKim, whose persuasiveness rescued the historic Capitol at Montgomery from virtual demolition. This son of Yankee abolitionists argued that the columned structure must be preserved as a shrine to the memory of the Confederate States of America. He only added rather simple wings with academic Ionic porticoes at the sides. South Carolina cheaply finished at last the Niernsee building by capping it with a Classical iron dome.

Florida now remodeled its unique and untouched state Capitol by adding a dome and wings, and Beaux-Arts detailing was stuck on the whole of it. The state of Maine replaced the building Bulfinch had designed at Augusta with an enlarged copy and added a great Renaissance dome. In Washington, D.C., under the influence of Burnham and the New York architects, the turn of the century witnessed a dramatic return to the L'Enfant plan recurrently disregarded since 227

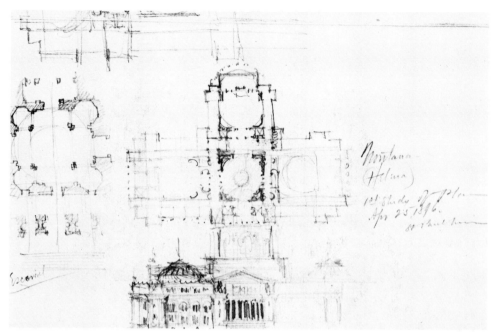

Montana Capitol, Cass Gilbert's studies, 1896

Andrew Jackson first defied it seventy-five years before. The national capital began to take on the special glow of the American Renaissance.

State capitol architecture of the era of perfection was seldom characterized by such sophistication as at Providence and St. Paul. Even when presented with various competition entries, the commissions sometimes turned from high-style design in favor of some frankly provincial and backward proposal. This was particularly true in the late 1890's, when the new style was first becoming familiar to the general public. Consequently some capitols not really as advanced as Brigham's annex at Boston were built well into the twentieth century. These buildings can perhaps also be considered transitional in their particular regions, even though the American Renaissance was by this time in its palmy days in the East.

Just such a transitional building was erected by the state of Montana at the conclusion of a national competition held in the heat of the 1896 election. The economic situation was still so bad that Montana had 400 inquiries about the competition and over 150 plans were supposedly sent in. Gilbert was one of the entrants. He was well-known in Helena as the designer of several houses, and the picturesque Governor's Mansion is locally attributed to him. Not long after his first appearance in Montana in 1884, he joined the exclusive Montana Club in downtown Helena. Many years later he rebuilt the club's headquarters after a fire destroyed the old building.

"A classic treatment has been most generally followed," wrote the competition judge, "and with a few exceptions, the buildings surmounted with a dome or cupola."[21] George R. Mann of St. Louis won the first premium, Cass Gilbert the second, and Charles L. Strange and Thomas Stent of Los Angeles the third.

The judge was Seymour Davis of Philadelphia, about whom Gilbert had already sent an inquiry to his A.I.A. friend, Frank Miles Day. A reply came by telegram at about the time Gilbert received the results of the competition: "Never heard of him before," the telegram went. "Studied two years in Paris, practiced in Topeka."[22] Soon after that, one of the third-place winners, Thomas Stent, who had worked with Laver on the government buildings in Ottawa

Montana Historical Society

Montana Capitol, by Bell & Kent, 1898–1902, later extended
by Frank Andrews, 1909–12

in the 1860's, wrote to Gilbert: "I never knew such a dirty transaction as this competition presents, from beginning to end."[23]

Scandal erupted in Helena. The state architect was found dead of an apparent heart attack and buried so quickly that the Masonic Order refused to pay the widow's insurance benefits until the coffin had been exhumed and rumors dispelled that it was filled with rocks.

A new commission was appointed and opened a second competition. Gilbert entered again, and again placed second, this time to Charles E. Bell and J.H. Kent of Helena.

Montana's Capitol is a good example of the way high style was revised far from the national centers. Helena was a rich little town, where cattlemen's wives ordered their lace curtains from Davenport's in Boston and organdy dresses from Chicago. A brief walk down its streets shows that in residential architecture earlier picturesque modes were not so diluted; but many of those houses were erected from plans purchased from architects in Chicago, New York, Boston and, it is suspected, even in Great Britain. The Capitol is a mountain state's version of the Eastern

Renaissance. Bell and Kent had obviously studied the published perspectives of Providence and St. Paul.

Three heavy connected blocks make up the Montana structure, with a rather low central dome lifted up on a square platform framed by pediments. A broad-columned loggia forms the principal entrance. Simplicity here does achieve grandeur, but the continuity of the smooth ashlar walls of Montana sandstone is broken up by too many windows, and the parapet is too tall. The beautiful landscape outstrips the architect's best efforts. Originally there were to be several forlorn bronze maidens gathered on the roof over the loggia. Those were never commissioned, but an allegorical statue—a big, vulgar woman, like the one at Austin—was purchased for the dome.

The interior of the Montana Capitol belongs to an earlier time. The halls and public rooms are merrily adorned in a flowery opera-house style common in the Gilded Age. F. Pedretti's Sons, interior decorators of Cincinnati, were engaged to do the entire job. Painted tapestries, mahogany and Golden Oak furniture upholstered in green cut-velvet and stamped Morocco arrived in boxcars. The *Montana Daily Record*'s front page noted on January 14, 1902, that C. A. Pedretti was in Helena to install and supervise the work and "will remain . . . until it is completed."[24] Some of the decorative panels were executed in Cincinnati, then applied to the walls with lead paste, varnished, and framed in plaster moldings. Arabesques, filigree, rosettes, and exotic faces frosted the main walls approaching the grand stair.

Little gilded niches above bigger ones make the rotunda resemble a theatre with boxes. Scagliola columns with gold-leaf capitals were ringed with electric lights. A barrel-roofed stair-hall at the back of the rotunda, lighted by stained-glass skylights, was a variation on E. E. Myers's original proposal for Colorado and Gilbert's design for Minnesota. The Pedretti company sent furniture, "french silver chandeliers," and curtains from Cincinnati. This was the American Renaissance expressed in the language of the Gilded Age.

Ranchers and businessmen strolled after lunch the ten blocks up 6th Street from the Montana Club to observe Professor Pedretti at work on the pastoral vignettes for the walls. The profusion of side arms must have made the professor long for the peace and quiet of Cincinnati. Several times he was asked to add certain cattle brands, wagons, and even a railroad train to one or another of the romantic murals. The commission protected the artist, who nervously brushed the final blushes on the cheeks of his cherubs the day before the dedication.

Montana's Capitol has always been popular. The legislators of South Dakota in 1907 were so impressed with it that they chose it as a model for their new Capitol at Pierre. C. E. Bell, leaving Kent behind to practice in Minneapolis and occasionally in Seattle, agreed to do the design, but the Capitol he built was no reproduction of the one in Helena. He set out to improve the original with more correct academic detail, a more forceful massing, and a striking colonnaded dome rising above pediments. Inside he built simplified marble halls, furnished only with sconces and electroliers of the plainest sort. Several murals by New York painters adorned the public spaces—in recent years one of these murals, the Liberty Goddess as Betsy Ross Sewing Stars, was nearly destroyed by a legislative act because the flag was touching the ground.

In comparison with Helena, the South Dakota Capitol reflects Bell's advancing knowledge of

Montana Capitol, by Bell & Kent, rotunda and grand stair
as they appeared in 1904

academic Renaissance design. It is a finer composition, situated on a gently sloping hill and mirrored in a famous pond for wild ducks. The Pierre structure shows that Bell had obviously profited from working on Federal projects in the intervening years. Because Federal competitions exposed architects to expert criticism, they offered unequaled formative experience to young architects, even in remote places.

George R. Mann was hired by the Arkansas Commission outright for reasons different from those that led South Dakota to hire Bell. In the habit of getting to know the proper people, Mann had opened an office in Little Rock and met the new Capitol Commission, even before the funding bill was passed. Those working to authorize a new Arkansas Capitol in the late 1890's had obtained a set of Mann drawings to use in their arguments with the legislators. Unquestionably these were the same plans with which Mann had won second place at Minnesota and the first premium in the original Montana competition. He was determined, in any event, to have the Arkansas job, even though the 1899 appropriations bill established a disappointing $1,000,000 budget—on which the legislators expected the finest capitol anywhere to be built.

South Dakota State Historical Society

South Dakota Capitol, by C. E. Bell, begun in 1907

Before the governor signed the bill that spring, Mann had begun drawing final plans. The commission accepted him at its first meeting. Frank P. Milburn, the only other competitor, was a North Carolina railroad architect who offered proposals for remodeling the Capitol at Raleigh, made additions at Tallahassee, and who actually completed the Niernsee building at Columbia.

Back in St. Louis, Mann was roughing in the foundation drawings when a member of the Little Rock Commission, George W. Donaghey, took it upon himself to go to the new capitol site, which was still enclosed in the high walls of the old state penitentiary. He drove stakes in the ground, to establish the building's specific location so construction could begin. The dapper little man was a contractor; the commission elected him "representative . . . to remain in continuous charge of the State Capitol work."[25] He took his fellow commissioners at their word. As long as things went his way, the project could not have wanted a dearer friend.

Office of the Secretary of State of Arkansas
Arkansas Capitol, by George R. Mann and Cass Gilbert, 1900–17, as completed

When Mann returned to Little Rock after a long bout with typhoid fever, he saw to his bewilderment that the foundation was more than half completed. According to his figures, the foundation that Commissioner Donaghey had begun without specifications was not strong enough to support the building. Work stopped one month before Christmas, and early in 1900 convict laborers were put to work tearing down the old prison walls. As the walls fell they revealed another problem: Fifth Street would never offer a straight vista to the new Capitol. Donaghey's calculations had been several degrees off.

No sooner was the cornerstone laid in the autumn of 1900 than hostility broke out between Donaghey and Mann over the structure of the foundation and the very nature of the architect's design. Donaghey began a correspondence with E. E. Myers, nearing seventy, who proved more than willing to help by offering to make "full and complete plans and specifications details, and working plans, full size of all construction plans of the building and ten copies of the entire plans and a large size color perspective design of the building for $14,000 and to give three years supervision and inspection once a month for $4,000, and traveling expenses."[26] This was not agreeable to the other commissioners. Donaghey then attacked Mann on the basis of the A.I.A. standard professional fee of five per cent. "The building of State Houses is not confined to the

American Institute of Architects," Donaghey sneered. "All will agree that there are many distinguished architects that are not members of this organization. Mr. E. E. Myers of Detroit is not a member of the Institute, but he is the Architect of many of the finest buildings in America."[27]

A new Governor, the tough Populist Jeff Davis, was inaugurated early in 1901. Urged on by Donaghey, Davis launched accusations of dishonesty at Mann, and halted construction with a predictable explanation that the Capitol was a monument to the elite few. The money, he said, should be for the poor. Davis was arbitrary and ruthlessly political, but the public cheered him on. Both the commission and Davis finally agreed to summon an expert. There were numerous replies to the advertisement for advice, and the application of Frank Miles Day was accepted. Day arrived from Philadelphia in July. His conclusion was that it was a good plan, thus far well built, but that it would never be completed for an even million dollars. He suggested certain alterations in the quality of the materials that could shave the costs; on that basis, Mann went home and set to work revising his specifications.

But an unexpected meeting between Governor Davis and Mann interrupted the architect's progress. Mann later told how Davis had, "with a good deal of bluster," informed him that if the Capitol "must be built he wished me to make a new set of plans for a building that would be one-half the size." Mann declined, voicing concern about the needs of the future, to which Davis replied, "Damn the future; it is the present I am interested in." Then he offered Mann a bribe of $10,000.[28] Mann refused it, and the enraged Davis began to build up a case against Mann in Little Rock. Between the Governor and the Attorney General, the Capitol work was halted by technicalities from which it seemed it would never be extricated. The legislature meanwhile used the temple statehouse on the bank of the Arkansas as temporary quarters. A group of heroic statues made for the Arkansas Pavilion at the Centennial celebration of 1876 now adorned the roof, but inside, falling plaster had become a common danger.

In 1900, the year construction was stopped on the Arkansas project, one new Capitol was completed and another begun. The Arizona Territory had held its competition in 1898. Since the maximum expenditure was to be only $100,000, the competition attracted little national notice. Of the eleven schemes presented, J. Reily Gordon's of San Antonio and Dallas was granted the $500 premium. His design was a little Italian villa planned so that it could be expanded into a great Renaissance capitol as the fortunes of Arizona improved. Gordon was a successful practicing architect, a member of the New York chapter of A.I.A. He had built the Texas Pavilion at the Chicago Fair and owned a manufacturing company in Texas, but his professional associations were in New York. He had worked with his father, a civil engineer, and had spent two years in the engineering corps of the International & Great Northern Railroad. Success as an architect and builder had afforded him the opportunity to travel in Europe.

The ten-acre Capitol site at Phoenix had already been landscaped as an oasis by the English gardener George Hough Smith. "It appears as though every part of the world has been ransacked to furnish the plants and trees," wrote the *Arizona Republican*. "The driveways are bordered with hedges of beautiful scented myrtle, Monterey Cypress and evergreen Japanese privet . . . a profusion of roses and oleanders, chrysanthemums, jacaronda, with beautiful fern-like foliage,

State of Arizona

Arizona Capitol, by J. Reily Gordon, 1899–1900, with legislative wings
by Associated Capitol Architects, 1957–60

magnolia grandeflora, grevilias, bananas and many others but little known to the general world
but all beautiful and seemingly flourishing."[29]

Gordon's little territorial Capitol was built of smooth tufa, a soft, porous stone to which
the wind and weather of sixty years have given the worn look of age. The Ionic columns on the
loggia are separated by deep louvered blinds. Along the walls pedimented windows cast sharp
afternoon shadows across the pinkish stone. A low dome of tin, once painted red, was decorated
with a metal statue called Victory. The interior, before the addition of wings at the time of
World War I, consisted only of a rotunda with flanking rooms, all small and simple. Seen

235

through the lush plantings, over the flat ground of combed sand, the Arizona Capitol had the look of a medium-sized Italian villa.

The commission had exceeded its budget by $25,000. In an effort to save expense the cornerstone was eliminated. Yet on the dedication day in February 1901, no money was spared. Several thousand people crowded into the building beneath strings of electric lights. A "comely" singer performed in the rotunda, and the audience "listened with rapture to her melody."[30]

Mississippi's Capitol Commission advertised for plans in the spring of 1900. The fourteen entries opened at Jackson on April 9 included three familiar names: J. Reily Gordon, George R. Mann, and E. E. Myers. Lost letters and incomplete files of the commission leave some questions unanswered about the competition. It would be interesting to know something about Myers's entry, and also about his feelings concerning the new Renaissance capitols, for those were providing in the hands of others an even more marketable product than his "Corinthian" capitols of twenty years before.

Even younger men were using his tactics: In the first Mississippi competition, held in 1897 by a previous commission, J. Reily Gordon won with plans originally intended for a Texas courthouse. Early in that competition, A.I.A. members had banded together under Gordon's leadership to insist that the commission accept a plan only from an A.I.A. entrant. These dubious actions prompted the Governor to veto the appropriations bill, effectively dissolving the commission. The second capitol bill, passed just after the turn of the century, provided an appropriation of $1,000,000 and called for a new competition. Some of the former contestants entered again, but the conditional winner was the German-born Theodore C. Link of St. Louis.

The Link plans were "most excellent," according to the commission, although "certain alterations . . . had to be made before the building would be . . . the kind of structure which the present and future necessities of the State demanded." One change required was the removal of the "campanile or bell tower about three hundred feet high," which stood at one end of the building.[31] The reappearance of the tower, though already proposed by Stone and Carpenter a decade before, was sudden here. Not surprisingly the commission ordered it replaced by a dome like the one George Mann projected. Link wrote to Mann, "a warm personal friend," asking permission to copy his dome. "Of course," Mann later wrote, "I told him I would be glad to have him use it and sent him the design of the dome I had on my drawings."[32]

Construction was started on New Year's Day 1901. The site was then still occupied by the state prison Captain Nichols had built in the 1830's; the walls of the prison were crumbled into the new foundation. Several blocks away the state legislature still used the Nichols Capitol, and the Governor's Mansion he built had undergone few alterations.

Work went very fast, and the legislature met in its new halls before the close of 1903. In a state and region still suffering from the effects of the Civil War, Reconstruction, and its own cold-blooded politicians, the Capitol seemed very splendid. From a distance, through the dust of the streets, one could see in it lingering traces of the romantic Italianism of the original project. The long and low planes, the red tile roofs, and round-ended wings were retained. All that was missing was the campanile. The Italian features were adjusted to proper capitol uniform, yet with a touch of originality.

Mississippi Capitol, by Theodore C. Link, 1901–03

Link gave the building a showy air of luxury without overspending his budget. A native of Heidelberg, he had served a youthful apprenticeship in London as a draftsman before entering the Ecole des Arts et Métiers in Paris. He was twenty when the Franco-Prussian War broke out, and the poverty that gripped France afterward drove him to the United States. His Romanesque Union Station in St. Louis has the same sort of free monumentality he later achieved in the Mississippi Capitol.

On the exterior the Capitol was essentially a simple arrangement of three connected blocks. On the ends of the wings, however, Link had added semicircular Corinthian colonnades and saucer domes. This magnified reflection of the first Williamsburg Capitol and the original Trenton building is all the more remarkable since Link's design had started out clearly echoing the Philadelphia tower-steeple. A lofty Roman portico with a pediment, a feature abandoned in several of the first Beaux-Arts capitols, here again projects from the main front; above, heavy stone finials weight the corners of the central block around the base of the colonnaded dome, somewhat as do the *tourelles* in Providence.

With extraordinary deception the architect made the Capitol's interiors wondrously sumptuous. Wherever the human hand could reach, the walls and columns are real marble, cold to the touch. Above that, marbled wood and scagliola replace marble in arches, friezes, colonnades,   237 bull's-eyes, and keystones. These elaborate details lead to an inner dome executed in plain white plaster. Stained-glass ceilings, necklaced by electric bulbs, cast natural light from above on the balanced legislative chambers, whose differing curved shapes were expressed externally in the identical round ends. Columns, gold leaf, extensive use of black walls, and the dark mahogany furniture created an atmosphere some said was even richer than the Saint Charles Hotel in New Orleans.

On dedication day, June 3, 1903, the cornerstone was also laid, a unique economy move decreed by the commission. The papers reported that large crowds attended "from every farm, village, town, station, crossroads store . . . on wagons, trains and some a-foot, and all day long they have made the streets of Jackson like a moving river, a living tide."[33] Masons from all over the South marched in the parade, followed by carriages filled with delegates from the United Daughters of the Confederacy. A thunderstorm boomed overhead, chasing the parade under black umbrellas and the tin awnings of the few nearby stores. But it would take more than soaked bunting and wilted cape jasmines to dim Mississippi's pride that day. Theodore Link's success was so great that he moved his office to Jackson and spent twenty years building public edifices in the Deep South.

In the same year, the state of Pennsylvania passed a General Appropriations Act, authorizing, among other things, the expenditure of surplus moneys on furnishings and repairs in state government buildings. There was no difficulty passing the act, because its financial implications were seen only by a few. Those were the days of Matt Quay, Pennsylvania's late-nineteenth-century boss, a man whom Republicans all over the nation knew as an effective political manipulator. He had made big corporations pay privately and publicly for every favor they got, and the surplus cash piled up in the Pennsylvania treasury—Quay's particular darling—amounted to many millions.

The historic Stephen Hills Capitol had burned down in 1897, just as final decisions were being made about its restoration and Neo-Colonial additions. Both flanking wings survived, and a battling legislature appropriated a mere $550,000 for a new Capitol to go between them. The competition was won by Henry Ives Cobb, a former Chicago architect who had designed the Fisheries Building, the lone Richardsonian structure at the Fair. He had become an active and well-known professional in New York, and his presence in this unpopular competition is surprising.

Work on the Capitol started immediately in a storm of controversy: Seven of the competitors sued the commission for a long list of unfair practices. Two different courts wrote decisions favoring the commission. In the spring of 1899 Cobb finished the shell of his design, a great brick rectangle crowded between the columned flankers Hills had completed nearly a century before. The money was gone, and politically this could not have happened at a worse time. Senator Quay went on trial that spring for fraud, a charge he fought and won, not by claiming innocence, but by the statute of limitations. While the trial was still in progress, Cobb was fired, leaving his unfinished Capitol only far enough along to suggest that it adhered to the traditional capitol form. The commission ordered sheets of canvas tacked over the interior walls, and timbers covered the gaping hole where the dome was to have been.

Mississippi Capitol, by Theodore C. Link, 1901–03, looking toward the eye of dome
Gil Ford Photography

The next legislature provided a $4,000,000 appropriation and appointed another commission. A new competition was announced for completing the building, as decreed by the legislature. Though denounced by the national A.I.A. for being restricted to Pennsylvania architects, the competition got under way in the fall of 1901.

A socially prominent residential architect from Philadelphia, Joseph M. Huston, was the winner. He was asked to resign from the Philadelphia T-Square Club, a local professional group; and the A.I.A., which had forbidden its members to participate, filed a formal protest against the commission, the competition, and the architect. Nobody important particularly cared. Huston was later accused of locking one of his draftsmen in the attic of his office and instructing him to copy blueprints of Cobb's design for the Capitol. But by that time he was being accused of many things.

Whatever the circumstances, both the work and the money went fast. The new Governor, a Philadelphia judge and Quay man named Samuel W. Pennypacker, was more than enthusiastic about Huston's Renaissance scheme. As Governor he became chairman of the commission and also of the Board of Grounds and Public Buildings, which had the blanket authorization to use surplus state funds for the furnishing and repair of state buildings.

The Harrisburg project was well under way when a fire seriously damaged the Wisconsin Capitol on February 27, 1904. The legislature had already appointed a Capitol Commission to make unobtrusive expansions in certain parts of the crowded building. Now that same commission was ordered to restore the very popular Capitol to its former appearance, incorporating wherever possible the new additions.

Robert M. La Follette's governorship was in its third year, and his progressive state had made the "Wisconsin Way" a lesson to the whole nation. La Follette and his Progessives were using legislative investigation as a means of purifying the state government. They amassed testimony and statistics that became lamps to light their political road to perfection. Most Progressives were not opposed to publishing the scandal they found in national magazines like *Cosmopolitan, Collier's* and *Everybody's,* that were printing sensational exposés in lavishly illustrated detail. Wisconsin had already uncovered its share of sin, as would a score of other states, including Arkansas and Pennsylvania. Likely hiding places for misdirected funds were in costly building projects. The Wisconsin Capitol Commission, for example, found itself constantly badgered by busy politicians.

In the autumn before the fire, the commission had tried without success to interest several of the big New York firms, particularly McKim, Mead & White and George B. Post & Sons, in an invitational competition for enlarging the state Capitol. None of the well-established Eastern offices wanted to compete for a $150,000 job, much less deal with a state so investigation-happy as Wisconsin. Cass Gilbert, however, saw the Wisconsin project as something to occupy the office he still maintained in St. Paul. A Wisconsin commissioner, one of Channing Seabury's friends, received an unsolicited letter from Gilbert, and sent a copy to the commission's secretary with a note: "Mr. Gilbert . . . assumes to give us some advice about how we should select an architect."[34] What Gilbert wanted was a competition in which the winner would become supervisor and the fee would meet A.I.A. standards. The commission was uncertain, and in the true spirit of the La Follette administration, invited local advice.

When he heard that the Capitol had burned, Gilbert stopped by at Madison on his way from St. Paul to New York. He wrote to Seabury:

> I went through the ruins of the Capitol building—which were very cold and damp. . . . The Madison Capitol was not so completely destroyed as I expected. The central section was gutted, but only one of the wings was damaged, and that was not beyond repair. The commission seemed to be all right, but they are persistently opposed to employing an expert to review the drawings or to prepare a program, consequently the program will probably contain conditions which cannot be met, and without an expert all the fine points in the design will be lost sight of. . . . Of course I would like to be architect of the building.[35]

All the same, he entered the competition in November 1904; the only other participants were two Milwaukee firms. Professor Allan D. Conover of the University of Wisconsin—Frank Lloyd Wright's instructor in engineering in the 1880's—was a member of the La Follette "Brain Trust." The commission paid him $1,000 to select the winner, and his choice was Cass Gilbert.

Opposition came in every imaginable guise. The Milwaukee firm of H. C. Koch & Sons demanded an opportunity to present capitol proposals to the assembled legislature; and by February, 1905, the competition controversy had vaulted into the headlines, with accusations of graft aimed at Gilbert. The charges were unfounded; if they were intended to frighten him away, someone had seriously misjudged the victim. One by one the principals of the conflict began to air their views in print; Seabury urged Gilbert to hold his temper. Suddenly La Follette requested a legislative appropriation of nearly $3,000,000 for a new Capitol. The motives of his critics then became clear to Gilbert and he proclaimed himself heir to the job by virtue of having won the competition.

In a courteous letter to La Follette, Gilbert stated why he thought the legislature's interference in the competition was wrong and how Koch "well knows" that what he is doing is "quite unprofessional and most unusual."[36] La Follette seems not to have cared. A political friend of Koch's in the state senate was not content until he had publicly defamed Gilbert beyond redemption. At Seabury's wise urging, Gilbert stayed in New York. Early in May, Gilbert was invited to London to discuss the possibility of his designing a major commercial structure there, probably Selfridge's Department Store. Just before he set sail in July on the *Wilhelm II*, he engaged a Milwaukee lawyer to speak for him in Wisconsin, and wrote to Seabury: "I am disgusted with the whole matter. I don't care a damn for the Wisconsin Capitol; but I am exasperated beyond endurance at the fact that a very respectable body of gentlemen would sit all winter long and listen to that blatherskite senator libel me, and *I am done with it.*"[37]

He did not enter the new competition held in February 1906. The two Wisconsin firms of the first competition were invited—or, as the commission so carefully put it, employed—to enter, along with three prominent out-of-state firms: George B. Post & Sons of New York; Shepley, Rutan & Coolidge of Boston (H. H. Richardson's old firm); and Peabody & Stearns, also of Boston. Both Wisconsin offices, H. C. Koch & Sons and Ferry & Clas, were from Milwaukee, and Koch was still working hard politically to get the job. Originally, Governor La Follette had wanted to limit the competition to Wisconsin architects. He was apparently dissuaded on learning of the scorn Pennsylvania's second competition had aroused nationally in the profession. La Follette, then the most publicized governor in the nation, had vaulting national ambitions. He could not afford to alienate professionals and artists; nationally the intelligentsia had been among the most vocal supporters of the Progressives.

The purpose of the Wisconsin competition was not actually to obtain a final plan. All the commission expected to do was to select an architect whose ability promised to satisfy the needs of Wisconsin. Details would be determined later. The Milwaukee men were disqualified immediately because their proposals lacked sufficient monumentality. Boston firms had no better luck. Peabody & Stearns submitted a "beautiful and scholarly" project, but it was considered too "stilted" for the site. "Grandiose approaches" would be necessary for the Shepley, Rutan & Coolidge proposal, a City Beautiful scheme neither Wisconsin nor the city of Madison could ever build.[38]

Several Wisconsin architects met with some of La Follette's Brain Trust. Their report was considered with the major consultant report made by Daniel H. Burnham, who during the American Renaissance was so busy on the City Beautiful program in Washington that he never competed for a state capitol job. The winner of the competition was George B. Post & Sons.

Conscious of its complicated history and anxious to prevent any further trouble, the Capitol Commission protected Post and his sons from the outset. All conferences regarding the plans were confidential; only final decisions were made public. The senior Post was represented in Madison by his sons, William S. Post or usually J. Otis Post. On the rare occasions the seventy-year-old George Post journeyed to Wisconsin to inspect the site, there was a long advance notice and he was treated like a visiting dignitary.

Post's project was in plan a Greek cross, like the old building which still partially occupied the small hilltop. It was described as being in the Italian Renaissance style; the commission decreed that it be built of white marble and filled with works of art. Beautifully executed drawings enchanted the commissioners and the public, calling to mind the Court of Honor at the Chicago Fair thirteen years before. Otis Post took the train back to New York on Christmas Day 1906, with pencil notations for a final version of the west wing, to be built first, while the state government still occupied the remains of the old building. Ground was broken the next month.

Work at Little Rock and Harrisburg had progressed steadily during these years. By 1906 Harrisburg's new Capitol was in the last stages of construction. In that same year the production schedule at Little Rock suddenly came to a halt when the legislature, in keeping with the current vogue, ordered an investigation of the quality of the materials. Coincidentally, at that moment the big cutting machines at the granite quarry broke down. To solve these problems, Frank Miles Day was again invited to Arkansas; he endured the political pedantry of the long investigation, helping Mann where he could. Other experts were called in to advise on the granite-cutting machines. The Capitol had just begun to resemble the form it would ultimately take.

On the day after the session closed, the Attorney General, with no advance warning, ordered the arrest of several of the Arkansas legislators on charges of bribery. After interrogating those few, the entire legislature was legally detained from leaving Little Rock; but they did leave, and fast, some of them crossing state lines. That summer a series of trials was held in the old Capitol. It was hot and humid, and during recess defendants and plaintiffs crowded into the saloon across the street for sandwiches and cold beer. Ultimately only one man was convicted: Legislator Festus O. Butt was sentenced to prison for accepting a small bribe in exchange for favors to the Capitol contracting company, Caldwell & Drake of Indiana.

For another two years the inquiries continued. The politically ambitious George Donaghey delighted in what was happening. He managed to keep himself clear of liability, but persecuted figures in the Capitol scandal long after the public had lost interest. At the state Democratic Convention of 1906 he righteously demanded, as a contractor, that experts look into the soundness of the new Capitol; the masonry, he observed, was covered with cracks. An alarmed public put pressure on the Governor, who pressed the contractors. In a rage, Caldwell & Drake called a public meeting; they stacked sacks of cement and thousands of bricks on the upstairs floors of the unfinished rooms, then ordered some sixty workmen to mount the tall piles of heavy material. Donaghey was unimpressed.

All the investigations resulted in reports favorable to the contractors. Persistent Donaghey, however, told a spicy story from an opposite viewpoint, and it was widely believed. Largely on the basis of his Capitol platform, he was elected Governor of Arkansas in 1908. By 1909 he had successfully rid himself of George Mann. E. E. Myers died that spring in Detroit of "nervous prostration," so Donaghey had to look elsewhere for a practical man. In the late summer he made a contract with Cass Gilbert.

Two years before Donaghey's election, Joseph M. Huston had expressed mixed feelings of his own to a newspaper reporter. "I have been living in a dream," he said, looking over the glistening marble rotunda in Harrisburg. "It was my first public building, and, please God, it will be my last."[39]

A second reporter visited the completed building alone. "Mr. Huston has put himself squarely on record as believing that every great building erected by and for the people should be a monument of the national union of the sister arts, sculpture and painting. . . . Standing beneath the dome, I believe that the architect's ideal was that of a shrine, conceived as a habitation for the spirit of this utterance—great, as befits the magnitude of its significance; soaring high, as with its aspiration; strong, serene, and beautiful as the faith that is in it."[40]

Special Saturday and Sunday trains from Philadelphia were scheduled in October 1906, for the dedication ceremonies. By public demand the excursion trains were retained indefinitely on weekends, and thousands stood in lines on the steep hillside waiting to enter the sprawling mass of the Capitol each week.

Although the building followed the lines Cobb had established, it was much too decorative for the more cultivated exponents of the American Renaissance. The general impression remains more reminiscent of the Second Empire than of the new ideals of academic restraint with touches of Neo-Colonial delicacy. Large-scale ornamentation in the form of paired columns,

243

pilasters, pediments, rustication, and balustrades in marble is scattered over an episodic mass composition consisting of three principal blocks connected by sections that house the two chambers. Rows of Corinthian columns band all the walls, with pedimented windows and bull's-eyes. Elaborate little subsidiary domes poke up from the wings; the main dome is, like many others, a version of St. Paul's in London, but covered with green glazed tiles that give a Latin rather than an Anglo-Saxon flavor to the whole.

Great bronze doors in the deep arcade beneath the central portico have entwined in their decorations the faces of Governor Pennypacker and his late patron, Senator Quay. These huge portals fall back into the richest rotunda in any state capitol. A heroic staircase of white marble —perhaps the grandest in America—ascends between bronze angels to a landing, where it divides two ways and sweeps up to a balustraded gallery. The total effect recalls the palaces of Rococo Germany. Marble putti dance through lines of tall columns, trailing garlands among golden clocks, brilliant electroliers, and above benches deeply cushioned in green damask. Amber glass filtered the light and, as an ecstatic reporter wrote: "The delicate harmony and suffused radiance [gives] the dome, as it spins up above the massive rotunda, an effect quite aerial."[41]

Three celebrated artists had been engaged to further enrich both the interiors and the exterior. The muralists Edwin Austin Abbey and Violet Oakley were finishing patriotic scenes for the public spaces; the sculptor George Gray Barnard had been told by Huston, "You are perfectly free to do what you please on this building. I consider you the greatest and I want you to do just what you will."[42] Some of the statues were in place, and sixty more were under way in Barnard's studio in France.

Along the halls gilded electroliers prepare visitors for the big ones of gilt and crystal in the legislative chambers. The carpeting was so thick it made walking difficult, and people saw mirror-true reflections in the surfaces of the mahogany tables. In a side hall, the shoeblack's stand was mahogany and brass. The post office was mahogany, silver, and stained glass, all lit by Baccarat electroliers and softened by the carpeted floor.

Pennsylvania made no effort to conceal its pride in the new Capitol. Editorials printed statistics to show that the state had obtained a real bargain in what was undoubtedly the newest wonder of the world, a "palace of art." Jealous criticisms from New York and Philadelphia architects were disregarded; after all, hadn't A.I.A. members far exceeded their budgets at St. Paul and Providence?

Stephen Hills had made architectural history with Pennsylvania's first Capitol. Joseph M. Huston's Capitol was to make a different kind of history. Since before the death of Matt Quay, the Republicans had faced an opposition that grew more formidable each election year. People were dissatisfied with the Democrats, too; but they were more willing to vote for them than for members of the Republican machine. Good evidence of a restless electorate was the choice of William H. Berry, an outspoken renegade Democrat, for State Treasurer. This had been engineered by men with Progressive sympathies but calling themselves Independents—a loathsome and fearful word to men of either party. Berry at first caused little trouble, but by the autumn of 1906 he turned on the Independents and was openly campaigning for his Democratic friends.

244 The Republicans had hurried the work on the Capitol so that the building would be ready

Pennsylvania State Museum
Pennsylvania Capitol as completed by Joseph Huston in 1909

for dedication at the peak of the campaign that October. President Theodore Roosevelt honored a party invitation by coming to Harrisburg to make the main speech of the day. In his oration he did not mention the Capitol at all—a politically surprising and provocative omission in view of his current association with McKim, Mead & White on the White House extension. But the cold shoulder, intentional or not, was hardly noticed.

Several days later, State Treasurer Berry, on the Democrats' campaign trail, turned to the matter of the Republican Capitol. He had personally examined the books: "It will surprise the

245

taxpayers to know," he announced, "that their Capitol cost nearer ten millions than four." Within a week, he was telling a huge crowd at Reading: "Yes, the State Capitol cost nearer twelve millions than ten!"[43] Bit by bit Berry teasingly tossed details to the press. Headlines now proclaimed the "Palace of Graft." Architect Huston and the Philadelphia interior decorator, John H. Sanderson, could not be reached for comment. Governor Pennypacker, always willing to comment, said: "I know of no graft. I do not believe there has been any. I do not like the term."[44]

Two additional excursion trains and extra Pullman cars were added on weekends. The shoeblack's stand, now nationally famous, had to be roped off so that the maintenance men could keep its brass footrests polished—curious fingers longed to touch a $1,619.20 throne for blacking boots. The bill for the beautiful electroliers had come to about $2,000,000. In some cases, objects were not even what descriptions claimed they were. Chairs, for example, had painted putty-on-wire spindles instead of mahogany. A crude sort of scagliola had cost as much as real marble.

That was the sort of political fuel guaranteed to ignite the taxpayers' fury. The Attorney General's hasty dismissal of the charges against Huston, Sanderson, and the contractors was all the more justification for the new administration to order an investigation. Political reasons were just as strong—the investigation would be a broom to sweep out the last dust left over from Matt Quay.

The artists and sculptors involved made voluntary statements assuring the state of their innocence. The painter Abbey was left in dire straits because he had been promised a commission of over $100,000 and had borrowed heavily against it. He made his public statement so that the press would not present his removal to England as the flight of a criminal. Miss Oakley issued a statement through her agent in New York. The sculptor Barnard threw his cape over his shoulders, took the train to Harrisburg, and basked in the drama of the investigation. On the stand he told how the Capitol job had left him marooned in France. He had been forced by need to give up his "magnificent studios," and was faced with having "no place to live except perhaps a peasant's house, with an earthen floor . . . fourteen months . . . I was without money and twelve months of those I spent in the Southern part of France collecting antiques in order to make a living. I have been in almost every village and almost every yard in France collecting fragments of broken cathedrals and taking them to Jew merchants in Paris and selling them for what I could get. I made enough money out of that so that I was able to send my wife and children over and come over myself and also to settle up all I owned. . . . I came back from France to give my life to American art."[45]

The hearings opened in the Capitol late in the spring of 1907, making the front page in every major paper in the country. They were held in the Capitol, in a paneled committee room on the fourth floor. Sometimes the newsmen were admitted; other times they sweated through scalding summer days in the dark hallways outside. Almost all the men summoned to testify were by now celebrities. Before his appearance, Huston issued a letter to several newspapers saying, "The cost of the Capitol furnishings exceeded my expectations and those of the members of the board. But wherever the money has been expended it was in accordance with the law and

Pennsylvania Capitol, grand staircase as completed by Joseph Huston in 1909
John J. G. Blumenson for The Victorian Society in America

John J. G. Blumenson for the Victorian Society in America
Pennsylvania Capitol, House of Representatives, by Joseph Huston,
with murals by Edwin Austin Abbey, completed by 1910

in the only manner permitted by law. As a result of it all the State has got, by actual comparison, the cheapest, biggest and best building of its kind in the country or in the world."[46]

Slowly, the details surfaced. Technically there had been no limit on what could be spent by virtue of the 1903 General Appropriations Act. In 1904 the Board of Grounds and Buildings, along with its customary advertisement for bids to purchase coal, stationery, and similar supplies, had quietly added several items: "Designed furniture, fittings, furnishings and decorations of either woodwork, stone, marble, bronze, mosaic, glass and upholstery, 'per foot' maximum price, $20"[47]—sculpture, flooring, chandeliers all to be bid by the foot or the pound.

It had been decided, but not officially announced until later, that all furnishings must be included in one blanket bid. There was a single successful bidder, John H. Sanderson, whose prices were a few dollars below the maximum. The occupants of the committee room listened quietly three years later as Sanderson explained the method of measurement: a mahogany table with a surface eight by four measured eighty feet; that is, considering that it was also two-and-a-half feet high, it would occupy a space of eighty cubic feet. Eighty times the price per foot, $18.40, made a total price to the state of $1,472.00 for the mahogany table. The market price of the same table, someone pointed out triumphantly in a catalogue, was $40. Gilded electroliers, bronze *torchères*, marble benches and carved architectural ornament, brass hardware and stained glass were paid for by the pound. Certain of the electric fixtures had been lined with lead so that, according to one of Huston's comments to a reporter, they would be too heavy for thieves to carry away.

Governor Pennypacker, by now retired, fought the investigation and Treasurer Berry. Republicans contributed funds to support the ex-Governor, and Berry later admitted, "I was subject to extraordinary expense in exposing the Capitol steal. . . . I accepted the financial help of several Democrats."[48] The ex-Governor argued that the state had gotten something very fine in exchange for its money. What was more, the building had cost less than either the New York State Capitol or the new St. Regis Hotel in New York City. He later wrote:

> The Governor of Pennsylvania is one of the most potent rulers on earth.
> . . . In defining the power of the Governor of Pennsylvania the Constitution of the State uses the strongest word in the English language and makes him "supreme." It is the adjective applied to the Deity. . . . While it would not be discreet or wise for the Governor to exercise such a power, he may, like Richelieu . . . in case of real necessity, order not only the furnishing but the building of a Capitol . . . and it would be the duty of the Legislature answering to their oaths to appropriate the money to pay for them. . . . The work of the Investigation Commission . . . entirely failed to discover . . . that the building and equipment had been paid for without withdrawing the balance in the treasury.[49]

In mid-August the hearings came to an end. Specific opinions were published in great detail. The Governor had used poor judgment in operating the Board of Public Grounds and Buildings as he did, and the commission had been wrong in permitting him such authority, even if he was its chairman. It had been the intention of the architect, interior decorator, and the contractors to "cheat and defraud the state" through "false certificates and fraudulent invoices upon which warrants were issued."

The Attorney General was instructed to "institute such criminal and civil proceedings as may, in his judgement, be warranted by the law and the facts found by the Commission against any and all persons concerned in the fraudulent transactions . . . to the end that the money unlawfully taken from the State may be recovered and punishment meted out to all offenders."[50] The trials of Huston and Sanderson attracted the most attention. Both were convicted of criminal acts, making something of a prophet of the late Matt Quay, who had advised a friend: "Keep out of that Capitol job. Everybody in that will go to the penitentiary."[51] Only the architect lived to serve time in prison.

While Pennsylvania and Arkansas were digging out of scandals, the state of Idaho erected the first part of a Capitol to replace the territorial building E. E. Myers had built twenty years before. In the act admitting Idaho into the Union, certain federal lands had been set aside to assist in funding the Capitol project. A competition was held in 1905, shortly after the new Capitol was authorized. Only two of the twenty-one competitors are known: the Boise firm of J. E. Tourtellotte & Co., the winners, and J. H. Kent of Bell & Kent, Helena. Kent's entry was similar to his Helena design, but modernized like C. E. Bell's South Dakota Capitol. John Tourtellotte's plan was a combination of characteristic features from nearly all the current capitols, crowned by a dome that was as close to being a reproduction of the dome of the national Capitol as had been built in many years.

Tourtellotte, a native New Englander, was a serious, businesslike man in his late thirties. A migrant to Idaho in territorial days, he became a successful architect and builder. His firm still exists. The legislature appropriated $250,000 to add to the money made from the sale of the land; there would be no secret about how much money there was to spend. The drawings Tourtellotte entered in the competition were initially for the construction of the central block of what would eventually be a three-block plan. Both dome and portico would be included in the first stage. It was quite categorically of Renaissance design but by no means high style: some parts seemed too simple and others too decorative, an imbalance inherited from the capitols of the Gilded Age.

In describing the finished Capitol in 1913, Tourtellotte vaunted the symbolism of the white interiors: "Are the ideals of the people of Idaho morally white and pure?" If they were, then "the great white light of conscience must be allowed to shine and by its interior illumination make clear the path of duty and in the clarity of that vision . . . they must act and go forward with courage, to perfect the outward form. . . ."[52]

His interior, decorated chiefly with white and pale-gray scagliola columns and panels, did indeed offer a visually white light. The rotunda, open from the basement to the inner shell of the dome, was ringed with balconies, all white and each outlined in electric light bulbs set in gilt lilies. Balanced legislative chambers were extended into low-domed flanking wings in 1919, according to the original intention; before that, the temporary legislative quarters were plain and meant to be divided ultimately into halls and offices.

Towering over the flat grid of Boise, in a circle of snow-peaked mountains, the Capitol is singularly effective. The structure seems to exist for its rotunda, which is entered from the main portico on the second level. There is no Abbey or Oakley to adorn it, but among the artworks is a statue of George Washington carved locally in 1869 by a German named Charles Ostner out of a single log of yellow pine. It was his winter's project in one of the gold camps, and the appreciative legislature added a special touch: a coating of Idaho gold leaf.

Frankfort, Kentucky, is like Boise, set in a ring of mountains, though the ones overlooking the Kentucky Capitol are only hills by Idaho standards. Gideon Shryock's landmark temple tottered on the brink of demolition for forty years. It was considered too small for an even longer time; competition for a new Capitol was held as early as 1869. The Bradshaw & Vodges Co. of Louisville submitted the winning plan. The building was to be in the "Roman Corinthian order, or what is popularly known as Italian. . . . Complete arrangements will be made . . . for illuminating the dome both inside and outside."[53] The east wing, on the site of one of the old flanking office buildings, was occupied in 1871. The central section, which was to replace the Shryock temple, and the west wing beyond it were never built. Until early in the twentieth century, most official activities of state were conducted in the new wing, a large and forlorn-looking structure.

In 1904 C. C. Calhoun, a Lexington attorney, won for the state of Kentucky a suit against the Federal government for Civil War damages and various services performed in the Spanish-

Idaho Capitol, by John E. Tourtellotte, central section, 1912;
wings added, 1919

American War. The $1,000,000 settlement was more readily conceded by the Federal court when Calhoun suggested it be earmarked as a new capitol fund. A Capitol Commission was appointed by the legislature as soon as the money was in hand.

The superintendent, C. M. Fleenor of Bowling Green, Kentucky, was appointed in the spring, and after many interviews, Frank Mills Andrews of Dayton, Ohio, was appointed Capitol Architect. He was thirty-seven, a graduate in literature from Iowa State College and in architecture from Columbia University. He was in Dayton on a building job when he got the Frankfort prize. Businessmen liked him in the same way they liked Mead and Gilbert. Though he eventually became a world-famous architect of hotels, his capitol interlude included two important works—the Kentucky Capitol, begun in 1905, and Montana's two new wings, built in 1910.

Andrews was personally attracted to the sort of "international" design which interior decorators in New York were selling in the form of antique and reproduced "period rooms." One reason his later hotels were so successful was his own eye for palatial architectural effects and appropriate furnishings. To Kentucky's Commission he sold an Italian Renaissance scheme

251

which he said had been improved with certain French features in order to make it, in some sense, "international." For example, he pointed out how instead of the dome of St. Peter's, his dome was derived from the one on the Chapel of the Invalides in Paris. A bedazzled commission went a step further: They ordered a marker placed on their floor corresponding to the spot where Napoleon's sarcophagus stands under the Paris dome.

Externally, the traditional three blocks are faced with Indiana limestone and decorated with monolithic columns. Over the central portico there is an elaborately carved pediment. All these features delighted a commission which must have felt intimately involved in the planning; the amiable Andrews spent almost a year with them in Frankfort while executing the final designs.

The completed building seems to have followed Andrews's plans, with only minor changes in the interior decoration. Andrews was usually in Frankfort one week each month while he maintained his office in Dayton. After his removal to New York in 1907, he assigned more of the responsibility to Fleenor, and was in the area himself mainly while the rich New Yorkers were on their nearby horse farms in the spring, during the Kentucky Derby season. The commission was pleased with its architect, although one suspects that Fleenor provided cushions whenever the going got rough.

Certain elaborations of the design seem to have resulted from Andrews's current associations in New York. He revised the official reception room, which opened onto the principal portico, in the stage-set manner that was becoming his trademark. Fleenor later wrote:

> To the stickler of "styles" and the lover of "Francaise" the State reception room will perhaps make the strongest appeal, as it is decorated and furnished after the period of Louis XIV. It cost nearly $10,000 to fit out this chamber . . . the walls are canvassed and hand-painted with reproductions of famous French scenes about the royal city of Versailles . . . the hardwood floor is covered by a one-piece rug. . . . The large French windows are draped with costly lace and hung with damask portieres of color and shade to harmonize. . . . The chairs, benches and sofas are of richly carved Circassian walnut, upholstered with velvet. . . . The center table is of the same material . . . but richer still in carving and covered with a genuine Breche Violette marble top.[54]

So enthralled were the commissioners when Andrews assured them that the room with its reproduction *Louis quatorze* furniture was an "exact copy" of a salon of Marie Antoinette, that they advertised for proposals for a new Governor's Mansion patterned after the Petit Trianon!

The new Kentucky Capitol had little of the restraint of the Providence structure or even of those at Helena, Pierre, and Boise. Its free use of decoration was rather in the tradition of the Minnesota Capitol. This was not without a certain irony, for Cass Gilbert, whose schemes for the Montana wings won only second place, wrote a letter about the victorious Frank Andrews to a friend at the Montana Club: "STRICTLY CONFIDENTIAL . . . Andrews came . . . to New York a few years ago and has his offices in the Waldorf-Astoria where he frequents the hotel

Kentucky Capitol, by Frank Andrews, as completed in 1910

corridors. . . . He has a current reputation here so far as he is known as being a contractor's architect. . . . I am curious to know what is the inside story and of course you will let me know if it comes to your ears."[55]

But Andrews was not disdained in Kentucky. For the dedication in June of 1910, he arrived in Frankfort with his new wife, the pretty Broadway star Pauline Frederick, who wore a tailored frock with a split skirt the city never forgot. More than 2,000 out-of-town spectators attended the opening of the Capitol. While predictably the French reception room got the most attention, the grand Piranesian transverse axis was the Capitol's most triumphal feature—a gorgeous vista between the doors of the two legislative halls, across one marble stairhall, then the rotunda, and into another marble stairhall. The superb *allée* of Ionic columns executed in pale-gray scagliola, colored by the art glass overhead, was an effect rivaling the grandest American hotels of the day.

The good fortune of Kentucky's million-dollar settlement was matched in Utah in 1911 by the receipt of $798,546.00 in inheritance taxes on the estate of the railroad magnate E. H. Harriman. A legislative appropriation of $1,000,000 followed immediately. Since the abandonment

253

of the completed wing at Fillmore, Utah had used temporary quarters in Salt Lake City as its state Capitol. In 1888 a lofty site was presented to the state by Salt Lake City. Several efforts to build there had come to nothing, and the last effort to gain public support for a bond issue had been defeated. Now a new Capitol would cost Utah only about $200,000, which pleased everybody. Harriman's widow later said that the finished building "stands as a memorial to Mr. Harriman."[56]

Utah's seven-man commission was able to draw on advice from Minnesota, Rhode Island, Idaho, and California, which had recently added separate "Renaissance" annexes before its Sacramento Capitol. Olmsted Brothers, the late Frederick Law Olmsted's firm, was hired to make a topographical survey of the site and do studies for a landscape plan and even for parking facilities.

A competition was advertised. Any Utah architect who stated his intention in writing by a certain date could enter. Seven outside firms which had already made inquiries were invited to participate; five of the seven were familiar in state capitol competitions—Frank Andrews, George B. Post, Cass Gilbert, J. E. Tourtellotte, and G. Henri Desmond, the Boston architect who had rebuilt Bulfinch's Maine Statehouse. Only ten of the thirty official participants actually entered projects. Gilbert, Post, and over half the twenty-three Utah participants dropped out after protesting in vain the four-month deadline. The first two premiums were awarded to Salt Lake City firms, the next three to the outside competitors, and the last five to Salt Lake City men, including J. H. Kent, who had hurried from Montana to form a Utah partnership and present himself as a resident of Salt Lake City.

The winning design was by Richard Kletting, a German. Educated in Munich, Vienna, and Paris, he had been a resident of Salt Lake City since the mid-1880's. In comparison to the few other projects that survive, it is not hard to see why Kletting won. His plan was the simplest and the most dramatic. Wide but not deep, its dome and its continuous range of colossal Corinthian columns echoed the national Capitol. There was so little incidental decoration that the general effect was more strictly Classical than Renaissance.

Tourtellotte's project was a lanky World's Fair pavilion in marble with a tall central arch recalling Myers's. The design was accompanied by one of Tourtellotte's verbose artistic justifications, including his insistence that "all must be sweet and sanitary."[57] Another entry nearly copied Minnesota, while the third and last of the surviving projects crudely imitated the national Capitol.

Kletting's talent for organization and the efficiency of the commission got the project under way a few weeks before Christmas, 1912. A draftsman in his office recalled years later that "Mr. Kletting never tired of remodeling Salt Lake City,"[58] for he never seems to have been satisfied with any of his designs. One plan was to bind Capitol Hill to the business district and Temple Square of the Church of Jesus Christ of Latter-day Saints. Another provided for an electrically illuminated avenue beginning at the venerable Eagle Gate beside Brigham Young's Beehive House and rising through a district of fashionable California bungalows up the steep hill to the Capitol.

To that age, the Chicago Fair and the capitols that followed it left a legacy of perfection in city planning as well as in Classical design. The architect's dream of himself as the prime artist in

Kentucky State Capitol, grand transverse axis
Kentucky State Senate

an American Renaissance converged with the layman's dream of the City Beautiful. Certainly the optimism of the latter, fed by the Progressive wind of the early twentieth century, accounted for the success of the American Renaissance. The citizen had demanded reform, and reform had begun in the cities. Dishonest political machines had been cast out of hundreds of city halls, not least New York's Tammany, which had been in control for nearly a century. The spirit had spread to the county courthouses, notoriously as dirty politically as the spittoons in their hallways, then onto the state legislatures.

Flowers now bloomed not only in the yards of courthouses and city halls but on the grounds of state capitols previously worn naked by the uncontrolled traffic of man and beast. Behind iron fences graveled walks wound through shrubbery. On clipped laws stood those graven American stelae erected by the thousands during the American Renaissance by citizen committees to commemorate both men and events. The very location of these monuments in governmental settings seemed to confirm the Progressive belief that the good, and even the perfect, was obtainable through law. Inside public buildings, electric light now lit corners traditionally in shadow, and in newer buildings interior woodwork hitherto usually dark often received a coat of creamy white paint to match the marble exteriors.

Richard Kletting was not the only Westerner with new urban visions. At Denver, Mayor Robert A. Speer was transforming the muddy mountain town into a proud capital with wide avenues shaded by cherry trees. To ornament the public parks he employed leading New York sculptors and set them to producing a flock of bronze statues. Across the central park, the rising Renaissance façade of the new City and County Building glared scornfully at the Myers Capitol with its gold-leafed dome, a relic of the rambunctious boom days that Denver liked to forget. Even today the Renaissance municipal structure is more brilliantly illuminated at night than the Capitol.

Other state capitals devised improvement programs, increasingly under the direction of special commissions. Experienced professionals in the East were frequently hired to carry out City Beautiful ideas; members of Olmsted Brothers, for example, journeyed to nearly every state in the Union in answer to requests for city plans of one kind or another. American architectural schools dealt with planning idealistically but not without practical effect. Associations of New York artists offered their services nationwide. Local art also flourished at home. California artist Arthur F. Mathews executed superb historical murals for the Sacramento Capitol, and many states likewise provided opportunities for native sons and daughters. The reactions of New York architects was varied. Frank Andrews was horrified when the Montana Capitol Commission suggested hiring its native "cowboy artist," Charles Russell, to paint Capitol murals at $5,000 apiece. Russell and other hometown talent, said the architect, should be restricted to insignificant hallways—"their work would show to best advantage in smaller panels . . . and it would in fact be a kindness to them all if too much were not expected."[59]

It was an age which believed the best was always obtainable. This Progressive notion swept across party lines, leading to an almost revolutionary movement in government to improve democratic practice. Only three states failed to adopt the primary ballot system, in which the electorate took over the selection of candidates—the historic domain of political machines.

Historic American Buildings Survey
Maine Statehouse, by Charles Bulfinch, 1828–31, as rebuilt
by Henri Desmond, 1909–12

Through the so-called initiative the electorate could propose legislation, and in some states the referendum permitted the voters to reject the acts of legislature. There was new social legislation, especially in states west of the Mississippi; but after reform became law, the law was often not enforced. The demand for broader democracy was answered only nominally in the age of perfection.

New state building programs reflected the increase in governmental services. Artists from New York now traveled more than ever before to provide murals and statues for new annexes, separate legislative libraries, and even new wings on existing capitols. In the surrounding landscaped grounds, those most recurrent expressions of the City Beautiful, ever more statuary accumulated.

It was at Olympia, Washington, that the American Renaissance in state capitol building reached its climax. The reorganized Capitol Commission needed no expert testimony to tell them that the bare foundation of Ernest Flagg's project would provide for a Capitol altogether too small for the state's twentieth-century needs. Flagg, by now a highly successful architect in New York, was invited to return to Olympia in 1911 to discuss the problem with the commission. The archi-

257

Utah Capitol, by Richard Kletting, 1913–16, shortly after completion

tect reached a novel conclusion on the site. After studying the foundation and the Colonial Revival Governor's Mansion, built in 1907, he made a new proposal, based on a last-minute legislative amendment requiring the use of the old foundation: "My idea," he wrote, "is to provide for a group of buildings, the principal one would be placed upon the existing foundations. This building would afford accommodations for the legislature and the principal executive officers. . . . The other buildings of the group could be added from time to time as they were needed." He roughly sketched a large court faced by various buildings that were to be connected by "a covered way or cloister through the ground floor," enclosing the whole area with its colonnades.[60]

Flagg went back to New York, assured that his first contract was still in effect, while the commissioners and the Governor reconsidered the situation. There was no money problem. All the land of the old Federal capitol grant had now been opened up by roads; wise commissioners back in the 1890's had only thinned the timber. Now the increased value of the property, with its timber, had swelled the capitol fund to some $6,000,000.

Space was the main concern of the legislature, crowded into the old Richardsonian county courthouse for over a decade. The commission now made a formal proposal for a group plan which "permits of a much more magnificent, picturesque and artistic treatment than could be had by the erection of any single building. . . . The wonderful effects which can be obtained by groups of buildings harmoniously planned and artistically arranged has been abundantly demonstrated in recent years at our great expositions, notably those held at Chicago, Buffalo, and at Seattle."[61]

Such a collection of Classical buildings on a plateau surmounting a green hill 117 feet above sea level proved an irresistible vision. It would be a spectacular monument, with Mount Rainier in one direction, the Olympic Range in another, and lush forest between them, all mirrored in the blue water below. The City Beautiful, a concept of perfection evolved for dense urban scenes, seemed destined now to achieve its finest expression in the natural landscape of the Pacific Northwest. No architect or dreamer could have asked for a more splendid setting.

However, the Seattle members of the Washington State chapter of the A.I.A. soon began to protest Flagg's contract, and before long various professional and political pressures effected cancellation of the contract in favor of a new competition. What was more, the A.I.A. was allowed to make the rules: The labors of Cass Gilbert and his colleagues had at last come to fruition in a state capitol. Among the many restrictions and controls was one which specified that the entrants must be "of good professional standing, experienced in and capable of carrying into execution large works regardless of the question of design."[62] The competition was, for all practical purposes, confined to the big firms, and free of the danger that some clever upstart might win with an original design. Most participants were members of the A.I.A., which, although now tenfold larger than ever before, by no means included the entire body of practitioners in the United States.

From the Northwest woods numerous carpenters inquired innocently as to their chances under such rules. Their scribbled notes on cheap paper sharply contrasted to the more typical

From American Architect, *November 24, 1915*
Wilder & White's City Beautiful scheme for Olympia, Washington, 1911

inquiries on engraved letterheads with New York and Chicago postmarks. Even so, the major Eastern firms did not ultimately enter the arena. Most of the competitors were from San Francisco and Seattle, with one from St. Louis and three from New York. The winner was the firm of Wilder & White of New York. Ernest Flagg was awarded the lowest premium.

Walter R. Wilder and Harry K. White, both draftsmen for McKim, Mead & White for many years, had formed a partnership in 1909. They conducted themselves in Olympia in a sort of parody of the old McKim, Mead & White approach to clients—what might be called the "personality package." This collection of capitol buildings was to be "somewhat reminiscent of the Acropolis at Athens, and indeed the natural conditions surrounding the capitol site at Olympia are in many ways quite similar to those of the Acropolis. . . . In its mass it is apparent the Group Plan responds primarily to the necessity of so arranging a collection of small units that they may combine to give the effect of a single structure when viewed from a distance and from all directions. Hence the Legislative Building, slightly larger than the others and surmounted by a lofty dome, occupies the center of the group."[63]

The Olympia group took many years to build, and it was never finished as originally planned. Construction began at once in 1912 on the first building, the Temple of Justice, a white marble rectangle across what would be the main court from the Flagg foundation. On a portion of that foundation the sixth structure, the domed Legislative Building, was completed in 1928. But by that time the broad scope of the City Beautiful scheme had been abandoned. Even before World War I the grandiose Wilder & White design for Capitol Park was stripped of its glamour in a revision by Olmsted Brothers. The boulevards, the plazas, and the aqueducts over the Sound, the lines of poplar trees and electric torches, were lost with the Progressive dream, when once again the United States was changed by a great war.

Unknowingly, in crowning the Olympia hill with temples, Wilder & White had realized Jefferson's dream of an American Capitoline. Their real inspiration, however, was certainly not

Department of Commerce and Economic Development, State of Washington
Washington Capitol Group as it appears today

the early Classicism of Jefferson's time, but the monumental statehouse by McKim, Mead & White at Providence. In this the Washington Group is an exception, for the usual inspiration was the Capitol at St. Paul. Cass Gilbert's mighty edifice had stated American Renaissance ideals in such a way that they became compatible with the long shadow of the U.S. Capitol. Those capitols that freely followed Gilbert's freely sprouted monumental porticoes; and most of them showed a marked preference for Wren's dome on St. Paul's in London, because it resembled the one in Washington. The Providence Statehouse was simply too refined, too plain for the vaulting Progressive spirit. Those crisp blocks and columned loggias introduced at Providence by McKim, Mead & White were imitated elsewhere only after Gilbert elaborated them in the Minnesota Capitol.

His Minnesota Capitol was clearly emulated by Bell & Kent in Montana. Years later, Bell   261 followed it even more closely at Pierre in the massing of the sharply defined blocks and the detailing of the dome.

Except for its dome, the Capitol of Idaho is also a true descendant of Minnesota's, although Tourtellotte placed a pediment over the portico, and his dome, like Kletting's in Utah, is Walterized Wren. Frank Andrews and his Kentucky commissioners adopted the richness of St. Paul, revising and brightening its sky-lit stairhalls for Frankfort. The Kentucky Capitol lacks the belated Gilded Age glitter of those at Idaho and Montana; all the same, it is not so grand as Kletting's far more restrained Capitol at Salt Lake City. Surveying the Great Salt Lake and ranges of mountains that fade to pink and violet in the setting sun, the Utah Capitol combines McKim, Mead & White's simplicity with Gilbert's taste for the spectacular. Here marble staircases rise unobtrusively at the ends of mighty transverse hallways, yet the exterior portico is that of the national Capitol glorified by monolithic shafts of marble.

While Theodore C. Link in Jackson imitated the marble *tourelles* of the Providence Capitol, his luxurious decoration within is in the tradition of St. Paul, which his commissioners had visited while it was still in construction. Governor Donaghey of Arkansas thought so highly of Link's Jackson Capitol that he even tried to replace George Mann, whom he despised, with Link; Link, with no hesitation, refused. In Donaghey's determination to rid his Capitol of any trace of Mann, he ordered Cass Gilbert to replace Mann's proposed dome with an exact copy of the dome Theodore Link had built at Jackson. The resulting Capitol at Little Rock, completed at last by the time of World War I, has the transverse stairhalls and the clear articulation in three blocks of Gilbert's Capitol of Minnesota, but its simplicity is almost raw. Both Gilbert and Mann would have described the Arkansas Capitol as more Donaghey's than theirs, and Donaghey would not have disagreed. In 1937, three years after Gilbert's death, Donaghey, by then an old man, wrote a book called *Building a State Capitol*, telling in 377 pages how personally rewarding it was to sire a great public building. In a letter to the editor, the aged George Mann cackled the true story of Donaghey's dome.

The Capitol at Madison, Wisconsin, falls chronologically halfway between Providence and the white marble Olympia. But in an otherwise neat stylistic succession, it is a renegade, for notwithstanding a certain kinship to St. Paul, its shape makes it quite different. This building, by legislative act, had to conform to the cross shape of the earlier structure; as a result, like the Raleigh Capitol before, it could never totally conform to the contemporary norm. George B. Post's revised Capitol, completed in 1917, the year the United States entered World War I, justified Daniel Burnham's comment on Post's winning project: "The [Post] design shows something more than mere scholarship. . . . This general mass is impressive and beautiful."[64]

Arriving in Madison from New York, Post had studied the site firsthand and had at once changed his popular plans. He removed from the roof the *tourelles* he had copied from Providence; and in a letter to his friend, Daniel Chester French, he asked for sketches for a "sculptured figure," something really superb to crown his dome. Albert Herter was hired to paint murals for the Supreme Court wing. In the new spirit, the commission changed all scagliola to real marble, and professors at the University of Wisconsin were invited to instruct the painters—

Herter, Hugo Ballin, and Edwin H. Blashfield—in Wisconsin history.

Wisconsin Capitol, by George B. Post & Son, 1906–17

Over the lake or the green rolling farmland, Madison is announced from a great distance by the colonnaded dome. The lower parts of the Capitol, however, nestled in the town. On any one of the eight approaches into Capitol Square, the dome is subordinate to the eight colossal façades centered on those streets. Facing the four diagonal streets are immense pedimented Corinthian porticoes in white granite. Equally tall, curved porticoes with Ionic columns between the wings line up with the perpendicular avenues and lead directly into the rotunda. The pediments contain sculptured groups by Karl Bitter and Attilio Piccirilli. Clusters of heroic figures stand at the base of the dome, over the Ionic porticoes.

The interiors, when contrasted with those at St. Paul, attest to perfection's progress, but with a decided loss of showmanship. Mosaics by Kenyon Cox fill the pendentives of the rotunda high above expanses of Labradorite, Numidian, and Wisconsin Green marbles, accented by great quantities of gold leaf. Gilbert's transverse stairhalls are repeated on a larger scale in two of the four wings. Legislative chambers and committee rooms were decorated by the mural painters and by the interior decorator Elmer E. Garnsey, whose stenciled borders had been used both at St. Paul and in the *Louis quatorze* room at Providence.

High on the walls, above the click of typewriters, the jingling telephones, the glaring electric bulbs, and America's first electric voting machines, the murals in Wisconsin's Capitol recall a prewar era only dimly remembered today. In dreamy scenes, strong heroes and blue-eyed youths and maidens carry unfurling flags through a lilac haze. There is no state capitol that could be more appropriately adorned by these idyllic vignettes than this monument built by the Progressives.

Woodrow Wilson's war message had not made its full impact on either the Progressive State or the American Renaissance in 1917, when the Capitol of Wisconsin was receiving its finishing touches. Rules had to be made to keep tourists from interfering with the legislature, already in its chambers. Only the most optimistic of the Capitol's planners eleven years before would have predicted the public's joy over the new building; but then the Capitol was far more luxurious than had originally been intended. In Wisconsin, more than in any other state, the public had shared the commission's enthusiasm over the increasing grandeur of the Capitol. The New York artists were celebrities in Milwaukee and Madison; crowds gathered when their works were unveiled.

During that historic year, Daniel Chester French's heroic statue "Forward" arrived at the Madison railroad station; it took eight mules to draw it up the street to the new Capitol. Around the square several hundred people stood transfixed as a steam mechanism with ropes and pulleys transported the golden figure up to the lantern. Many years later, after two world wars and a great depression, an old man in California remembered that day "Forward" journeyed to the crown of the dome: "My father sat in front of our store watching what was going on—and when the Statue was in its proper place at [the] tip [of] the top—he hurriedly came in the store and went into our back room shop—got a big lead pencil and wrote on the wall above the shop door—the date and exact time [and] hour & minute when that statue rested in its place."[65]

An ordinary citizen had recorded the end of the American Renaissance.

VII
THE SYMBOLS
SET FREE

Oregon State Highway Department

Oregon Capitol, by Francis Keally, 1936–38

In the long history of American state capitols, not a single capitol commissioner has recorded any awareness of the architectural symbols of American democracy. Yet it was those laymen capitol builders—lawyers, businessmen, farmers, politicians—who valiantly defended the symbols. As late as 1927 an article in the *Architectural Forum* warned architects who wanted to experiment with new forms that they must "be prepared to face and to overcome more than a little opposition. The American people are very largely . . . committed to the firm belief that a state capitol must be designed . . . in Classic fashion, replete with colonnades . . . and that the entire structure must be surmounted by a dome."[1] By innocently believing this, capitol architects set up limitations upon their freedom more stringent than those imposed by even the most meddlesome laymen. Ironically, this stood unchanged in the decades from the late 1880's to World War I, a period in which American skyscraper architects and the men of the Prairie School were leading the world.

Ever since the Civil War, Americans had been captivated by the national Capitol. The promising ante-bellum innovations in state capitols were forgotten; and New York's postwar effort to reinterpret the capitol symbols was aborted by the Civil War generation's deep feeling for the mighty new dome at Washington—a dome reborn on a huge scale, just as it was passing into history. Had Walter taken his cue from the advanced designs then being executed at Nashville and Columbus, the dome would probably never have been revived, and thus would not have stood out so bodly in the story of the symbols.

In the Gilded Age, businessmen-architects had set themselves to improving and modernizing the national model. Readily accepting the arrangement of dome, rotunda, wings, and portico, together with the new giant scale, they used the Washington model as a point of departure for their imagination. Rarely were their creations merely funny parodies; in most cases they were exciting departures from the Classical norms. Their successors, those true believers of the American Renaissance, also sought to make improvements on the original. But at the same time they accepted the great Capitol in Washington, with its iron dome, as the primary source of the American capitol form: Lacking the historical facts, architects were without convictions to inspire them to devise alternatives. They applied new inventions in engineering and materials without hesitation; design lingered in a vacuum.

Painting and sculpture were more flexible, and soon became more interesting to the layman than architecture. The American fascination with its own past increased with the years; the great success of such muralists as Edwin A. Abbey and Edwin H. Blashfield was due less to their art than their illustrations of American history. The taste for Classical architecture waned, but the interest in history increased. This could be seen in the continuing spread of the Colonial Revival in residential architecture, which began in the late 1890's to develop regional forms other than the Georgian vernacular of New England.

In capitols, the Real Presence of American History was expressed in murals and statues created to edify and, as in Roman Catholic church art, to instruct the faithful in the story of its past. Art was no longer merely interior decoration. The seductive nymphs Jerome Fedeli had painted in 1898 among the clouds and roses of the dome at Topeka came to be known after World War I as the "telephone girls," offering the right numbers to the boys home from France. To please indignant Kansas mothers, officials ordered the maintenance man up his ladder with a bucket of radiator paint. Within a few years all the frivolous decorations at Topeka were replaced by patriotic murals. Some, such as John Steuart Curry's "Tragic Prelude," are masterpieces of a kind; the rest are mere historical illustration. Every capitol in the United States was similarly affected. Even today such historical artwork is being commissioned.

The restoration of old buildings—the creation of shrines—was another aspect of this American thirst for history. The old Adobe Palace at Santa Fe, facing the ancient plaza as it had done for 300 years, was restored in 1914–15. Its resulting glow of Spanish perfection, though inaccurate, established a specifically New Mexican Colonial. American history had been glorified already in Chicago; a copy of the John Hancock House of Boston had been built near the gates of the White City. Meanwhile the Surrender House from Appomattox lay dismantled and abandoned in the Chicago warehouse of a company of patriotic citizens that continued to collect old buildings.

The attitude was brought to bear on some of the old and historic capitols in several ways. In 1910 the state of Delaware ordered the restoration of Dover's combination courthouse-Capitol, built in 1788–92, for continuing use as a Capitol. Architect and commission proved less interested in a scholarly restoration than in the removal of the Second Empire mansards and decorations added in 1874. Once that was done, they made the building over into an idealized Colonial pile, apparently inspired by New England models rather than anything in Delaware or even in Pennsylvania. When legislators complained that the building was too plain, the architect, Edward L. Tilton of New York, added to one side not only a full rotunda but a great colonnade in a new revival mode called Southern Colonial. On the other hand, the abandoned Bulfinch Statehouse at Hartford, which had not been so altered, was rescued from demolition and lovingly preserved by an army of Colonial Dames and Daughters of the American Revolution, led by Senator Morgan G. Bulkeley. And at Frankfort, Kentucky, the old temple Capitol, its leaking halls filled with refuse, was turned over to the state historical society for use as a museum, and like the Hartford Statehouse, was patched and assured a limitless old age.

American historical art emerged as a major element in capitol design just as the vigor of the real American Renaissance was declining. While muralists experimented with symbols and style, architects continued to produce much the same sort of buildings, now rather predictable. The states bought increasing numbers of murals and statues; in many regions local art owned its florescence to state patronage. Not since the demand for statues of George Washington before the Civil War and of Lincoln portraits after had the states patronized artists in this way. Figural art was taking the upper hand over Classical architecture, for in affirming the belief that Renaissance Classicism was the only perfect manner of public edifice, monumental architecture became boring, a twice-told tale.

World War I turned the layman away from Renaissance Classicism in architecture just long enough to break the spell. The Capitol of Missouri and the Capitol of Oklahoma, both commissioned and erected largely before World War I, illustrate this point. At the outbreak of the war, there was high enthusiasm for those two unfinished Renaissance structures. In 1918, however, both buildings suddenly seemed cold and superfluous. Missouri attempted to rectify the problem, but Oklahoma merely stopped the project in its tracks.

Stephen Hills would hardly have recognized his old Missouri Capitol in the last hours before it burned on February 5, 1911. Wings had been added in 1887, gaudy tin decorations were affixed inside and out, and a new tonic-bottle dome poked up from a cityscape little changed since the 1830's. The citizens of Jefferson City stood in a rainstorm to watch the blazing demise of Hills's last surviving public work.

A nationwide competition was held for "rebuilding" the Capitol. The winners were two of 267

Missouri Office of Development

Missouri Capitol, Tracy & Swartwout, 1913–18, as seen from downtown Jefferson City

New York's most admired designers, Egerton Swartwout and Evarts Tracy, both of whom had worked for McKim, Mead & White for many years. Like various others, they had left when the murder of White and the death of McKim led W. R. Mead to reduce the staff of the firm. They had practiced briefly with J. Reily Gordon and later by themselves as a very successful partnership. "Those men were *real* architects," Cass Gilbert, Jr., recalled a half-century later.[2] Writing about his first visit to Jefferson City, Swartwout remembered how he had walked from the railroad station to the riverbank where the ruins, now stripped of all their additions, "were as picturesque as . . . any old castle I've ever seen . . . blackened by the fire, touched by the last rays of the setting sun . . . surrounded by beautiful elms, on a natural bluff a hundred feet or so above the river."[3]

The original Hills building, with its end to the village, had concealed its considerable size. The colonnaded dome had effectively established the Capitol's importance, but the rest of the structure had never seemed to impose on Jefferson City.

Oklahoma Capitol, by Layton & Smith, 1914–17, after
abandonment of intended dome

From 1914 until 1917 Swartwout and Tracy filled the old site with a rectangular edifice of pale-gray limestone. It looked squarely toward the town, high above the rooftops and out beyond the farthest municipal boundary into the rolling farmland. Not an inch of the new Capitol was hidden. If anything, its size was stressed, for the American Renaissance architect as perfectionist demanded center stage for his creations. Descending to the river, which now seemed only a humble creek at the Capitol's feet, there was to be a series of balustraded terraces and stairs, only a part of which was ever built.

The Capitol stands more or less as Tracy & Swartwout designed it, a classically sheathed office building, exceptionally sharp in all its lines. "It is not a copy of any building that has ever been built," wrote the scholarly Swartwout, himself an architectural critic and historian; but the concept is all too familiar.[4] In every corner of Jefferson City one meets the Capitol's sumptuous glare. Moreover, the interior spaces are so large, so full of columns, arches, and vistas wide and narrow that it is often difficult to remember the little river town outside. The projecting section behind the portico contains a grand staircase, rising between files of marble columns—a highly theatrical entrance, like an opera set for a temple or a tomb. The germ of the idea was undoubtedly the handling of the stairs in Providence; in the Missouri Capitol the more studied dramatic effect soon becomes tiresome. Originally the riverfront portico was to have duplicated the one on the south. Swartwout changed this to a semicircular colonnaded porch, a deliberate and effective echo of the earlier Hills Capitol.

At Oklahoma City, the Capitol Commission spent its first few sessions deciding whether to hire a "practical builder" for supervisor of construction, as the legislature had directed, or to reserve that post for the architect who would be selected. By January 1914 the matter still had not been resolved. An advertisement was placed in several Western newspapers inviting "any architect desiring appointment from us as official architect or who desires to prepare plans and specifications and to supervise the construction of a Capitol Building for the State of Oklahoma, shall file with us his application for the same."[5] In almost any other part of the nation, the advertisement would have started a furor among professional architects who would have demanded, as they had in Missouri, a competition according to A.I.A. specifications. But no objection was raised in Oklahoma. There were only a few applicants, although the $1,500,000 budget, raised in part through the sale of Indian land, ensured that the Capitol would be the largest building project ever undertaken in the state.

All three commissioners were considered old settlers, in a state in existence only seven years. They well remembered territorial days and the "openings" of Indian lands by the federal government. Monumental architecture was an alien subject in such ranching country, and the commission stumbled painfully in discussing it. Legally, the commissioners were forced to confer first with the state officers on the "kind and character" of a state capitol for Oklahoma; after that the three went on a brief tour to St. Paul, Little Rock, Austin, and Jackson before selecting the architectural firm of Solomon A. Layton and S. Wemyss Smith of Oklahoma City to design a proper capitol and landscaped approach.

Layton & Smith modeled their dome more or less on that of the Invalides. The rest of their design followed Tracy & Swartwout's proposals for Missouri—a wide and basically rectangular container for office floors, and the domed scheme, with front and rear projections and Corinthian colonnades *in antis*. The one on the rear is only a simulated portico with the columns engaged; that in front is a loggia enclosed at the sides to block the brisk winds from the Oklahoma plains. Additional Corinthian colonnades were recessed into the wings. Oklahoma pink granite, used on the rusticated basement story, was not available in sufficient quantity to be adopted for the entire building, so Indiana limestone was used on the rest of the exterior. White marble from Alabama, heavily veined in dark gray, is used inside in the public spaces. Layton & Smith's plan is reminiscent of Cass Gilbert's at St. Paul but, like his Capitol at Little Rock, greatly simplified.

Construction began in 1915. During the winter of the following year the money was going faster than the commissioners had expected, and they began shaving off interior finish and asking the architects to substitute cheaper materials. Some of the costly stained glass was omitted, and marble columns and mahogany woodwork were taken out of the architects' specifications. The Atcheson, Topeka & Santa Fe Railroad was pressured to give special shipping rates for the limestone. Finally, in the autumn of 1916, the decision was made to postpone building the dome until prices came down. The Oklahoma Commission staged its dedication of the colonnaded Capitol in 1917, under a brilliant summer sun. Without its dome, the building looked like a big-city American post office of the day.

After the close of World War I, the Capitol Decoration Commission of Missouri, previously powerless, was directed to do something about its cold and barren Capitol. The five-man commission, with abundant funds, set out to garnish a building in which the public had lost interest. They traveled to St. Paul and Harrisburg, and in New York began making contacts in the art world through Swartwout, whose only other contribution to the decorating was designing the sculptured flagpoles for the grounds.

Numerous artists, some native Missourians, became involved in the project. On piers at each side of the portico, Robert Aitken executed reclining nudes in bronze symbolizing the Missouri and Mississippi rivers. From A. Stirling Calder, James Earle Fraser, and Herman A.

West Virginia Capitol, by Cass Gilbert, 1930–32, nearing completion

McNeil came heroic friezes, statues, and fountains. In the vacant interior the white wall spaces were filled with murals. The finest of them, by the English artist Frank Brangwyn, are sensitively executed in a technique and coloring that make them seem to grow out of the grain in the marble. By 1928, over $1,000,000 had been spent on artwork.

The Decoration Commission had turned to history, through art, to give their Capitol popular appeal. Missourians still rejoice over the historical canvases lining the walls—pretty Indian maidens, lusty Casket Girls and brave cavaliers of France, the noble Benton, and Mark Twain of Hannibal and the Great River. Except for a passing fascination with Tracy & Swartwout's "whispering gallery" and the architectural drama of the interior spaces, the popularity of the Missouri Capitol was revived by the murals and statues. The building itself became for the public a mere storehouse for the state's art collection.

Oklahoma made no such grass-roots effort to improve its Capitol. When the war was over, it was necessary to cut construction costs further. The commission was ready enough to abandon Layton & Smith's proposed City Beautiful setting, for the boulevard and triumphal arch were to the postwar eye but ludicrous conceits, and everyone knew formal gardens and reflecting pools were unlikely to survive even the first scorching in an Oklahoma summer. New drawings were made for the dome, however, and the work was put out for bids as far away as Chicago. The state found the price too high and the dome has not been built to this day.

The requiem for American Renaissance capitols was sung at Charleston, West Virginia, in 1922, when that state commissioned a Cass Gilbert Capitol from the master himself. It had been Gilbert's own better judgment to avoid the job entirely, but his son Cass, Jr., home from the

271

army, was excited by the challenge of following in his father's footsteps. "Between my mother and me," he later said, "the old man finally agreed to go ahead. But he never did like it."[6] Completed in 1932 largely from the younger Cass Gilbert's designs and under his supervision, the West Virginia structure presented to the winding Kanawah River the familiar massing of the capitols of the American Renaissance. Two office wings to the rear were built first. With the immense main building between, they form a Capitol group on a scale appropriate to this mountain town.

West Virginians got from Cass Gilbert exactly the Capitol they wanted. It was the very last of the American Renaissance capitols, built many years after the epoch was over. For ten years the project went steadily, if not always smoothly, forward. Getting things done had always been a special feature of the Gilbert package.

Long before the West Virginia Capitol was finished, the architectural symbols of American democracy had cast off their heavy Renaissance cloak and begun to try new costumes. The first monument of the new era of capitol building sprang up on the agricultural plains of Nebraska, in the heart of Populism. But the project was conceived in a well-known New York architectural office. Dissatisfaction with the old Nebraska Capitol had become serious in 1914. Because of the war and bad crops, however, the establishment of the Capitol Commission was delayed until early in the winter of 1919. By the following June the prominent Omaha architect Thomas R. Kimball, national President of the American Institute of Architects, had been appointed adviser to the Capitol Commission, and a national competition was announced.

The terms of the competition were an artist's dream. There were no directives as to design, plan, or materials—"each competitor shall feel free to express what is in his heart, unmindful of what has been inherited in this regard, willing even that the legacies of the masters should guide and restrain rather than fetter." To that the commissioners added, in the language of the American Renaissance, their hope for "an inspiring monument worthy of the state for which it stands; a thing of beauty so conceived and fashioned as to properly record and exploit our civilization, aspirations and patriotism, past, present and future; intelligently designed, durably and conscientiously built, and of worthy materials; and all beautifully and fittingly set, surrounded, embellished and adequately furnished . . . without friction, scandal, extravagance, or waste."[7] The sponsors of the competition clearly had in mind a group as Classical as the one being built at Olympia.

Two capitols had occupied the site in Lincoln; the last of them, a crumbling limestone pile, still stood. Designed by B. H. Wilcox of Chicago in 1879, it had been built wing by wing to replace the 1868 structure, a mail-order design by another Chicago architect, James Morris. Brought to its final form in 1888, it was composed of three blocks, a portico, and a central dome. Like its predecessor, Wilcox's dome, on its tall square base, shot up prophetically towerlike from the horizontal mass below. The commission wished to save nothing except the bare site and the Daniel Chester French statue of Lincoln which an earlier group of inspired citizens had placed in the grounds.

A preliminary competition was held in 1919 for the selection of three Nebraska architects who would then participate in the national invitational competition—a plan decided upon, Kim-

272

Nebraska Capitol, Bertram Goodhue's sketch for great hall, 1920
Nebraska State Historical Society

ball explained, because "there resided in the state . . . architects of broad vision and exalted idealism."[8] Inquiries were then sent to thirty-two firms in New York, Boston, Philadelphia, Washington, San Francisco, Chicago, Minneapolis, Toledo, and St. Louis. All were large firms, but only five of them had ever been involved with capitols before. Henry Bacon, architect of the Lincoln Memorial in Washington, D.C., had represented McKim, Mead & White at Providence; both he and his former employers were invited to Nebraska. Cass Gilbert was too busy to be bothered. The sons of the late George B. Post declined, as did R. Clipston Sturgis. Of the total of ten entries, only Tracy & Swartwout and McKim, Mead & White were veteran capitol builders.

The competition was won in the summer of 1920 by Bertram G. Goodhue of New York. His tall, towered scheme stood out in contrast to the rest. Others had proposed towers, but Goodhue's was unmistakably different. A professional magazine of the day observed: "Mr. Goodhue has been bold and original. . . . What he had done is to take the American skyscraper and with unexampled boldness and courage has fitted it into a public building."[9]

The design had something of the softness of the free adobe forms of the Southwest, with the precision of Goodhue's Gothic work in stone as well. The Capitol's base was a huge two-storied square nearly 450 feet to a side, a composition of unadorned vertical and horizontal planes—as if a few large, timeworn stones had been fitted together. In the center of the square, and flanked by four open courts of equal size, a buttressed tower rose 350 feet to form a platform for a seventy-foot octagonal lantern. The lantern's sides were pierced by square-columned loggias, and its roof was a hemispherical dome under a skin of golden tiles. Transcending the building beneath it, the lantern addressed itself to the plains, as lanterns and steeples had done from above the trees surrounding colonial villages.

Goodhue's model was probably modern European—Lars Sonck's Kallio church tower of 1910 in Helsinki. To anyone familiar with contemporary architecture in Germany and Scandinavia, the Nebraska Capitol was not a totally surprising design. What was unexpected was its acceptance by an American public building commission. In this case, the commission may have approved the recommendation of the judges the more readily because Kimball kept such a close watch over events that summer; most of the commissioners had either left for family vacations or were leaving by the time the final decision was made. Kimball warned the highly excitable Goodhue about the dangers of too much publicity, urging him to remain silent until the November gubernatorial election was over. "You know the jury has selected an architect," he wrote to Goodhue, "and I want to see that this summer is devoted to getting the people of the State into the proper state of mind to give that architect a fair chance." He encouraged Goodhue to prepare the "swellest perspective in color that can be made."[10] The winning competitor would have been wise to listen: Kimball knew the commissioners well and realized that the idealistic Goodhue would have his difficulties with them. Even while relaxing at his summer house in Montecito, California, Goodhue was not a patient man when it came to his work. During July and August 1920, he sketched and improved, mailing his notes back to his New York office. That same summer he became acquainted with a Lincoln merchant and commission member, W. E. Hardy, also on vacation in California. Hardy proved to be the most meddlesome of the five commissioners, but within him and Goodhue were kindred chords: both were positive, egotistical, spoiled by a reckless will to do as they pleased. At fifty, Goodhue was the younger of the two. He had enjoyed the financial comfort of his national success as an architect of Gothic churches. He was not, however, as rich as Hardy or as experienced in business negotiations.

For the well-trained Bertram Goodhue, professional rewards had been abundant. Apprenticed to James Renwick for six years, he understandably inherited his master's affection for historical revivals in architecture. Goodhue's formal schooling was a fleeting experience at Russell's Collegiate and Commercial Institute in New Haven, Connecticut; he left prematurely because he preferred being at home in Pomfret, where his mother, an amateur painter, encouraged his artistic interests. On the wall of his New York office hung a hand-lettered sign, a faded relic of his boyhood: "Art pre-exists in Nature and Nature is reproduced in Art."[11] Goodhue remained serious about himself as an artist throughout his career. Even when his architecture was at its most daring, it always stayed within the context of a historical revival. The theme was usually Gothic, somewhat freely adapted, as seen in the numerous churches he designed with Ralph Adams Cram in the Midwest, California, and the New York area.

Goodhue was an experienced architect before he had any opportunity to travel. Not long before World War I, new Gothic commissions took him to Latin America. There he became interested in the Spanish Colonial Revival, a movement which paralleled the Colonial Revival in the United States. The new buildings of Havana and Mexico engendered an urge to seek out and record with his pencil the real colonial Spanish monuments.

He is largely responsible for the popularity of Spanish Revival in California, which soon rivaled its reign in Florida. The architect's fascination with Spanish architecture took him to the adobe country of Santa Fe and Taos, New Mexico, which were already winter meccas for the muralists. During this period in his life he turned to the Byzantine in designing from the Gothic St. Bartholomew's Church in New York, incorporating the Neo-Romanesque portal of the old church as originally designed and executed by Augustus St. Gaudens and Stanford White. The vestry of St. Bartholomew's dampened the extremes of his Byzantine enthusiasm, but recollections of this interest lingered with Goodhue four years later when he was designing his Capitol for Nebraska. He had said that it was his dream to design a building depending entirely upon form and color and texture, with no applied decoration. When he read the competition statement of the Nebraska Capitol Commission, he told a friend: "Never in any competition have I been set free as in this one."[12]

During that summer in California, Goodhue made several changes in his project, including the addition to the main tower of four carved buffalo heads as *tourelles* around the base of the lantern. He was offended when the commission rejected the changes unanimously; they preferred the design of the building as first proposed. A local insurance man, in a letter to Commissioner Hardy, expressed his opinion after going back many times to view the original rendering: "I love this new building. There is something fascinating about the whole thing. It seems to grow on one. It sounds depths in us that we never knew existed before. Everyone seems to be inspired by its presence. I hope the reality will be as great."[13] No doubt thanks to Kimball's expert propaganda through the state A.I.A., the main topic in Nebraska by Christmas 1920 was the new Capitol.

The fact that this Capitol was to be different increased its popularity. It would be the special 275

for Lee Lawrie—"the only man in my opinion that understands the relation between sculpture and architecture."[18] A small, invitational competition was held for the artwork, "a most silly proceeding," according to Goodhue.[19] But he could not decide upon a muralist. "Of course," he wrote, "it is idle to hope to find a mural painter as sympathetic as is the sculptor with what we are trying to do."[20] He asked Augustus Vincent Tack to do some sketches. "He gratified me by promising to abandon his pointilliste methods in favor of a combination of Burne Jones, Pinturrichio, and Benozzo Gozzoli."[21] The sketches for the Governor's Reception Rooms were shown in January 1924, and Goodhue wrote: "I ought not to brag, but Tack is a good man, and I am inclined to agree with him in thinking that when, and if, finished as now proposed, this room will be one of the finest in America."[22]

Phase I was nearing completion that winter. One could walk through some of the rooms, none of them so plain as the flat exterior surfaces. Just enough of the building was visible to give an idea of what its presence might ultimately mean in Lincoln. The block seemed gigantic, dwarfing by its weight the sprawling old Capitol. It also seemed too simple to some of the legislators, and Goodhue now admitted that the cost might exceed the limit of $5,000,000. A politician questioned the architect's $25,000 per year retainer, and the political pot began to boil.

Goodhue was in trouble. He began to spend more time in Lincoln. His presence there had a calming effect, because Kimball and Hardy had made him seem above controversy, and he was virtually idolized in Nebraska. Late nights on trains rushing cross-country he smoked cigarettes and sketched. Sometimes he was alone, but often Hardy met him on the way and they sat together in the club car and talked. It was Hardy who controlled the Capitol Commission, for the other commissioners respected his ability and knew that he loved the Capitol. He would live to see the last stone in place.

A long life was not Bertram Goodhue's destiny. He died of a heart attack in New York on April 23, 1924. Close friends and family agreed that the political insults he had to endure over the Capitol had contributed to his death. In June a contract was signed to continue the work with a reorganized firm, Bertram Grosvenor Goodhue Associates, consisting of F. L. S. Sayers, Hardie Phillip, and O. H. Murray. Construction was finished in 1932, at almost exactly the same time as Cass Gilbert's West Virginia Capitol.

Seen across the broad Nebraska plains, Goodhue's solitary tower had just the effect he wanted, until the local intrusion of high-rise construction in the 1960's. The sun blazes on the gold dome and on Lawrie's finial, the male figure of the Sower, which serves as a lightning rod. Climatic conditions dramatically change the pinkish surfaces of Indiana limestone sliced by incised outlines of windows and by simple projections that are accentuated in light and shadow. Most of the Capitol's base sinks into the Lincoln cityscape—monotonous rows of commercial structures along barren and windy streets that are mostly devoid of trees. The Capitol has always seemed too big for the town, but like Tracy & Swartwout in Missouri—and in the same American Renaissance spirit—Goodhue believed the city's objective ought to be growth worthy of his great monument. If the Capitol, particularly at its base, seems very heavy and crowded by the town, the contrast would be even greater had the design been Classical. Exterior decoration, restrained almost in an excess of reaction, is restricted to the four entrances, where the ends of the wings project from the central tower. Such a concentration of ornamentation drew attention away from the plain smoothness of the rest of the low exterior.

In plan the Capitol of Nebraska is a Greek cross which is set within an outer square of offices, leaving four open courts. Ceremonial spaces and the principal rooms fill the arms of the cross. The ecclesiastical aura of the interiors is the most obvious ever created in one of democracy's temples. But light from the four courts relieves that feeling of being swallowed in a huge mass, which is so oppressive at Albany. The nave-like space along the central axis is sunlit from lunettes high above the side aisles. Gustavino vaults spring from colonnades of imported green marble screening the aisles from the nave. Mosaics of the most colorful kind are sprinkled over the vaults like Indian jewelry. Executed by Hildreth M. Meiere with glazed Gustavino tiles, these mosaics were also used to line the dome at the north, or main, entrance, and the one in the rotunda. The balanced chambers form the transepts flanking the rotunda; above rises the tower of offices, built on a steel frame—despite Goodhue's objections—instead of being entirely of bearing masonry.

It was always Goodhue's intention that the building be decorated like a cathedral over a period of several years. The work went on here for forty years, generally following the original concept. H. B. Alexander, a professor of philosophy at the University of Nebraska, was engaged by Goodhue to write inscriptions for the building. The cheeks of the main steps proclaim "Honour to Citizens Who Build An House of State Where Men Might Live Well" and "Honour to Pioneers Who Broke the Sods That Men to Come Might Live." Similar inscriptions are found in all the public areas among the illustrative murals, mosaics, and friezes. The ceremonial interiors are more Byzantinesque than original. Spiced by brilliant chrome yellows, reds, blues, and greens and the abundance of gold leaf, with predominantly black and white mosaic floors, these spaces have a contrived sort of grandeur which, like that of a stage set, soon becomes tedious.

Goodhue did not consider the Nebraska Capitol a place for quiet contemplation; in nearly full-time consultation with Lee Lawrie, he designed a building which he felt was first a work of great architecture and second, of practical and functional purpose. Nebraskans, however, saw the building as a setting for a collection of historical artwork. When the idea took hold, Goodhue was so deluged with letters suggesting native symbols from Indian lore for the Capitol that he wrote: "the building might as well be a tepee and have done with it."[23]

There is no way of knowing how different the Capitol would be had Goodhue guided it through the long years to completion. Shortly before his death, the commission had been afraid he would resign because of the political assaults. Politics distressed him, and the outspokenness of which he liked to boast only complicated his troubles. Still, the Capitol was the high point of his career and, considering the man, it is unlikely that he would have left the job unfinished.

The Nebraska Capitol was universally acclaimed as a complete break with the past. It was, more accurately, a departure from academicism, while academic capitols were still rising in Olympia, Charleston, and even one modified Classical structure in the Territory of Alaska. It was by no means a rejection of the common past of the state capitols. Nebraska's Capitol had ancestors in almost every statehouse ever built, and the symbols were all present. The dome on the lantern is remarkably like Bulfinch's on the Boston Statehouse. Ohio and New York are recalled in the plan. The colonnaded hall approaching the central rotunda is a Doric Hall of sorts, but its reflection of Myers's halls in Michigan, Texas, and Colorado is even more obvious. In spite of Goodhue's belief to the contrary, a great entrance arch was first used in America on a Capitol by Myers. That there were balanced houses of the legislature in the original scheme is often forgotten today, now that Nebraska's government is unicameral. The chambers themselves both suggest the monumental though intimate Senate at Albany and the two chambers at Providence. Ohio and Tennessee offer precedents for the open form of the rotunda. If Goodhue had been presented with the problem of housing a unicameral legislature, perhaps he would have placed its chamber at the crossing, thus realizing the old vision of the rotunda as a place for holding joint sessions.

Goodhue's tower was not designed to be a state office building. Its inspiration was purely aesthetic; well aware of the symbolic interest of a vertical landmark seen across the prairie, Goodhue first proposed the tower as an ornament. Only in anticipation of the practical demands of his clients did he introduce library stacks, and the clients themselves later filled it with offices.

The cosmopolitanism of the American Renaissance capitols erected before World War I was patriotically countered in the 1920's by works of art representing American history. If not always as illustrative in Lincoln as in Jefferson City, it was very obvious in the nativism of their symbols. From the start, antiforeign sentiment paralleled the American Renaissance. In the year after the Chicago Fair, the feeling was first manifested nationally in the Immigration Restriction League. Through the twenty-three years between that act and the war, Congress had repeatedly attempted to pacify the emotional antiforeign movement with supportive acts. The quotas established after World War I on the admission of aliens were actually intended to revitalize what was known as the Nordic Protestant strain—a strain perhaps ironically reflected in the north European influence on Goodhue's Nebraska Capitol. Once again the Ku Klux Klan appeared, this time nationally. In the mid-1920's it turned its attention from the Negro to foreigners living in the United States. Millions of quiet citizens, enjoying the prosperity of the decade, endorsed the outrages of the hysterical elements. They could agree that the sweet pastoral world of their forefathers had been defiled. Nothing had seemed really the same since the war, and people looked nostalgically back to a simpler way of life. The literary approach to history of the Colonial Revivalists and the artists of the American Renaissance was replaced by a humorless kind of sub religion, with its own sacred relics. Diffused during the 1920's, that religion gave rise to what might be called the Antiques Movement, which was to have an enduring effect upon America's humblest bungalows and her most fashionable houses.

The Antiques Movement was in many respects a logical extension of the Colonial Revival's natural tendency toward greater accuracy. It was also a reaction to the recent bewildering flash flood of change. The past was to be cherished, and the heightened affection for antique furniture and old houses was only one manifestation of a broader cult. So vivid were the visions that the Arcadian past sometimes seemed close enough and real enough to be totally recaptured. Convinced of that, in the early summer of 1928, John D. Rockefeller, Jr., announced publicly that he would restore the town of Williamsburg to the way it looked on the eve of the Revolu-

tion. The very thought of resurrecting the colonial capital of Virginia was romantic and alto-

Alaska State Library
Alaska Capitol, originally Federal and Territorial Building, built by the
Office of the Supervising Architect of the United States Treasury, 1928–30

gether spellbinding. For more than four years the possibility had preoccupied the Reverend Dr. William A. R. Goodwin, Rector of Bruton Parish Church. His willing ally was the Boston architect William Graves Perry, whose pretty sketches of what the town of Patrick Henry and Thomas Jefferson *might* have looked like kindled the patriotism of the rich patron. To Perry, an architect who had come home from the Ecole des Beaux-Arts dreaming of the City Beautiful, Goodwin's ideal had not seemed foolish, but wise and noble. To protect these dreamers, the more practical Rockefeller established a corporation, of a kind more familiar on Wall Street than in such a Virginia hamlet, and the work began.

What had attracted public interest in Williamsburg since the 1880's were the few remaining eighteenth-century structures: Bruton Parish Church, the College of William and Mary, the Powder Magazine, part of the jail, and some private houses with their crumbling outbuildings—a total of a little more than eighty edifices in all. Vine-covered and sagging along streets shaded by great trees, the appeal of these modest buildings was enhanced by the knowledge that more splendid piles had once stood among them. One of the greatest of those architectural ghosts was the Capitol. The Association for the Preservation of Virginia Antiquities very reluctantly transferred the Capitol site to the Williamsburg Holding Co., but in the deed retained substantial authority over what would be constructed there. Perry, with his two partners, Thomas Mott Shaw and Andrew H. Hepburn, invited recognized authorities to join an architectural committee that was to decide the fate of the living town, now for the first time to be under one ownership.

Real American history, it soon became clear, would have to share the vanished Capitol with the Aristocratic Virginia Legend, that Victorian apology whose lamp the A.P.V.A. had tended so faithfully since two decades after Appomattox. The question immediately arose as to which Capitol would be reconstructed: the first building so magnificently conceived by Governor Nicholson, or the cruder one with the portico that was known to the founding fathers? In May 1929, following months of fierce debate, the architects included in their minutes that they agreed with the A.P.V.A. "to restore the earlier building with its semi-circular southern apses. The clearest detailed information extant applies to this earlier building. It should be the more interesting because of its unusual form. Its relationship to the axis [of] the Duke of Gloucester Street will be unsatisfactory but explainable and admissible since it was proposed and built originally before the construction of the axial thoroughfare."[24]

Francis Nicholson's Capitol was rebuilt with steel and concrete between 1931 and 1934. Two years before it was begun the Great Crash crippled Wall Street, but mercifully spared the backers of Colonial Williamsburg. By the time the Capitol received its veneer of brick, fireproof concrete shingles, and wooden trim, the New Deal had introduced a new interpretation of the Federal system that Williamsburg had played its part in creating. Perry's town which looked as though it had burst forth in its entirety from a mural by Blashfield, Abbey, or Oakley was in the years of the Depression and World War II of interest to very few. Work slowed down; the dream of a Colonial lotus land was put aside half-finished, to await a later, more prosperous time when people might again wish to see how the heroes had lived in eighteenth-century Virginia.

Elsewhere, in spite of economic stress during the Depression, public building continued in a kind of golden age, boosted by Federal aid and relief programs. The great increase in Federal authority, although no more than the hastened result of a long tendency, seemed to shrink state governments to insignificance. Indeed, the most important responsibility of the states seemed for a while to be in the administration of Federal moneys distributed for public works. Seven capitols were under construction in the years of the Great Depression, and all of them benefited in one way or another from Federal funding. Toward the last months of their capitol construction, Nebraska and West Virginia were given large grants. The new Federal and Territorial Building at Juneau, Alaska, was designed in the office of James A. Wetmore, Supervising Architect of the Treasury, and except for the parcel of hillside land purchased by the citizens of Juneau, the building was erected entirely at Federal expense. Time would see it become Alaska's state Capitol, which it remains to this day, though perhaps not for long.

Possibly it was the windfall of Federal funds that allowed Depression-period capitols to be experimental in design. The commissions, not working exclusively with state money, felt less restricted to the tried and true, though they were still determined to be practical. Accordingly, capitol design in the Depression years, with a single exception, reflected the current commercial architecture of the cities.

The new Capitol of Louisiana was one man's statement, not the work of a commission. It paraphrased Goodhue's statehouse in Nebraska, but without comparable artistic pretension or historical tradition. Governor Huey P. Long—"the Kingfish"—had established a dominant political machine in the state during the 1920's. Many of his public works programs anticipated those of the New Deal as he turned what some compared to a little Latin American republic into a personal kingdom. Unpaved roads, unbridged bayous, and the other inadequacies of a backward state were being overcome with a sudden burst of state construction, opening rural areas to the automobile. The electric light bulb, dangling from its cord in farmhouses accustomed only to kerosene lamps, could have been called the Huey Long trademark. But for all these improvements, the state legislature still met behind the stained glass windows of the old Gothic Capitol. Ceiling fans hummed over crowded committee rooms and chambers. In 1930 Long pledged to build a new Capitol. Work began on New Year's Day 1931, continuing until the Capitol was complete, precisely fifteen months later.

A prominent New Orleans firm, Weiss, Dreyfous & Seiferth, was employed by the Board of Liquidation which was nominally in charge of the new Capitol. The three partners, Leon C. Weiss, F. Julius Dreyfous, and Solis Seiferth, recognized that Long would always have his way; Seiferth said many years later: "Long's main interest was that it be built right away. . . . Huey Long seemed to know something was going to happen to him. He knew he was a hated man in the state and whatever he was going to do he had to do in a hurry."[25] As a result, the firm suffered very little interference and received substantial protection in getting the job done. Long's own personal desire for a tower capitol was pointed out by a Louisiana newspaper in 1932. The article went on to observe that even though Nebraska had already built such a capitol, Long's idea "was original."[26]

Weiss, Dreyfous & Seiferth had, of course, little trouble getting Louisiana contractors to accept the timetable, but people outside the state were not so obliging. Lee Lawrie—the artist Huey Long especially wanted—refused outright to consider doing the sculpture on such short notice. He finally agreed to carve the architrave of the main door for a handsome price. The architects also engaged Lorado Taft, the sculptor who headed the Midway Studios in Chicago. Taft complained, even in those Depression times, about getting only $50,000 for the statues that were to flank the main entrance stair, somewhat in the manner of Barnard's at Harrisburg. "It is a catastrophe," wrote Taft. "I took the order because I hoped to add to my reputation. . . . As I foresaw, the job is costing me all that I get for it. I shall make nothing on it but it has kept my young people alive."[27] Murals and painted geometric ornaments were executed by Jules Guerin, Louis Borgo, and Andrew Mackey, who moved to Baton Rouge when the building was ready for them.

Louisiana's finished Capitol, mirrored in its lake and set in a fifty-acre park, is Huey Long's monument. Seen from a distance, it has none of the special character of the Nebraska Capitol, but looks like a city office building standing in isolation, its white Alabama limestone façades reflecting the hot Louisiana sun. Its relationship to the surrounding city and the Mississippi River remains singularly successful, enhancing an urban scene that has otherwise become increasingly uninteresting. From any level of the central tower, the summer fields of sugar cane across the river once seemed to ripple in waves at the Capitol's feet, and the Capitol's whiteness is still magnificent in the fresh green that perpetually envelops the region. Yet close up, an outdated stylishness gives it the look of a luxury hotel of its era. Like some of the Beaux-Arts capitols, it is best seen as it was built—in a hurry.

Inside, there is the Art Deco faddishness in the richly colored marble panels on the walls and the floors. "We have not adhered to the classic forms," wrote the architects to Governor

283

Long, "but have expressed this modern structure in an appropriate style, using restraint in modern motives so as to achieve a crisp freshness and originality, without resulting in forms which, within the course of the next few decades, might be considered obsolete or decadent . . . there pervades the atmosphere, or feeling, of the classic, tending toward the Greek influence."[28]

The Baton Rouge Capitol was as self-consciously conceived as the most sublime Grecian temple of the early nineteenth century. Dreyfous, many years later, called the Capitol Modern Classic, a term applied to the architecture of Paul Cret, who had been his professor at the University of Pennsylvania. The best of the building is its two chambers, lofty marble rooms flooded with sunlight through side colonnades stripped of all Classical detail. Rows of desks and chairs of cross-grained mahogany and walnut, in what was then called the Moderne, do not seem quite appropriate for one of America's rowdiest legislatures. The chamber foyers seem more fitting, having the sleek, improbable Art Deco chic of a Chicago night club.

Between the two balanced chambers and their lobbies stretches a long entrance hall decorated with murals, friezes, and heavy electric lanterns. This space was probably always intended as a ceremonial way for Capitol residents, rather than a hall to welcome visitors or to express the grandeur of the state. Directly across from the entrance portals stretch a bank of elevators, as in an urban office building; but to either side of them one may proceed almost full circle to the double doors of the Governor's office. It was from this office that Long, as a United States senator during the Depression, directed a leftist campaign against the national New Deal of other Democrats; he was leaving the suite one day in 1935 when he was shot to death by an assassin in the cramped corridor outside. The bullet-riddled marble walls have been a favorite tourist attraction ever since.

Long's Capitol revealed in its design that neither legislature nor public had been involved. Weiss, Dreyfous & Seiferth built the first domeless twentieth-century state capitol. Elevator shafts rise in the central space where a tall, open rotunda might have been. The entrance foyer, called Memorial Hall, avoids the impression of being a Doric Hall by its transverse extension. At first glance, only the balanced houses and wings seem to recall any earlier capitol. Considered more subtly, however, the tower can be taken as a return of the lantern-steeple, here blown up and put to more practical use than in Nebraska, as monumental domes could never be. The day was over when domes could hope to compete with the tall commercial structures that by the 1930's dominated almost every city of any size in the United States.

Like the skyscraper at Baton Rouge, North Dakota's new Capitol has a curious ancestry in capitol history. The old domed Capitol at Bismarck which General Grant dedicated in 1883 with a prayer by Henry Villard—the railroad magnate for whom McKim, Mead & White were then building the famous New York houses—had been destroyed by fire several days after Christmas 1930. In the winter of the following year, about a month after the excavations started in Baton Rouge, the North Dakota Capitol Act was passed.

By June 1931 the Capitol Commission had been approached by several firms, including Weiss, Dreyfous & Seiferth, but the most forceful of the firms was Holabird & Root of Chicago. Colonel H. B. Hackett, their business manager, was a man of staggering persistence; he finally persuaded the commission to visit Holabird & Root's home office, where he tried to convince them of

Louisiana Capitol, Weiss, Dreyfous & Seiferth's preliminary sketch, 1931

the firm's ability. Not entirely satisfied, the commissioners visited the Baton Rouge Capitol and were pleased with what they saw; before returning to Bismarck, they visited Nebraska, and Lee Lawrie showed them around the Capitol. The commissioners noted that those "newest capitols in the United States . . . both have a center motive in place of a dome."[29]

From the outset the commission wanted a skyscraper capitol. Having been familiar with the awkward old Capitol for so long, they had little difficulty imagining the superiority of a single tower, standing in the slightly rolling meadows of the 153-acre Capitol Park. Correspondence began with forty-two architects, and sketches, photographs of previous work, and letters of testimony poured into Bismarck. The commission accepted the hiring of a North Dakota firm as the principal architect, but insisted that that firm form an association with, according to the commission, "some architectural organization of national standing and reputation . . . the construction of the Capitol of North Dakota is not merely a local enterprise."[30] This protective clause proposed by the national A.I.A. was demeaning for state architects, and it was the first time it had ever been included in a capitol program, but by no means the last. Very little inquiry established Joseph Bell DeRemer of Grand Forks and W. F. Kurke of Fargo, both prominent North Dakota architects, as the obvious men for the job. Soon after, the commission hired the Holabird & Root as associates because of ther national prestige.

John Holabird, if not the younger John Wellborn Root, was an experienced and very well known Chicago architect. Root's father had been Daniel Burnham's creative partner; William Holabird with his partner Martin Roche had begun a prolific career of skyscraper building in 1887 with the Tacoma Building, and had continued as major figures in the triumph of Chicago in modern commercial design.

Slapped together arbitrarily and by nonprofessional commissioners, the North Dakota association, called DeRemer & Kurke & Holabird & Root, was made to order for internal trouble. In its few years of existence, the association suffered investigations, newspaper slander, and continuous political assault. Before long, because of the political investigations, there were two commissions and even two cornerstones. Testimony from one of the hearings makes it clear that DeRemer & Kurke decided only minor details—and even those were usually suggested by George Kandzie, a former employee of Holabird & Root. The first designs were made as preliminary sketches of elevations and plans by the Chicago firm in their office and brought to North Dakota by Kandzie.

Construction did not go smoothly. The day laborers making a maximum of thirty cents an hour asked for more money. While the commission was considering what to do, several legislators, butting in with a battery of newsmen, pointed to impoverished migrants on the roads and reminded the protesters that many hungry men would be in line for their jobs. Armed strikes followed, culminating in the establishment of martial law in Capitol Park.

Despite all its troubles, the North Dakota Capitol was completely finished by the summer of 1934. Set starkly in its vast park, up on a ridge where the color of the earth abruptly meets the color of the sky, the building does not have the contrived look of its contemporaries in Nebraska and Louisiana. But it is unlike them in other ways as well. The light Indiana limestone

Don Engle for the North Dakota Historical Society
North Dakota Capitol, by Holabird & Root, 1932–34

walls fit precisely on a heavy base of Wisconsin black granite, the contrast echoing that of the landscape. Vertical lines somewhat like stripped-down *antae* crisply rib the full height of the walls. On the main façade are three elements: a tall tower to the right, called by the architects the Life Tower; a rectangular ceremonial entrance facing a plaza in the center; and to the left the legislative wing that presents a semicircular wall matched on the rear façade.

Memorial Hall's transverse extension was copied from Louisiana, but this hall is better illuminated by natural light from tall windows. Walls of Yellowstone Travertine, with some accents of black marble, and floors of gray marble are ornamental only in the high polish that reveals their veined surface patterns. Large expanses of glass are strengthened by bronze grilles in simple geometric designs. In the base of the tower the executive offices are paneled with walnut, mahogany, and rosewood; in the Governor's Reception Room, visitors often point out monkey faces formed by the wood grain. Beyond the long Memorial Hall, in the wing opposite the tower, balanced chambers flank a smaller hall. The chambers, like those in Mississippi, terminate in semicircular bays. Maple, American chestnut, and rosewood are used profusely for decoration, unifying the walls, desks, and galleries.

If the legislative wing were turned ninety degrees, the plan would be almost identical with that of the simplest sort of colonial courthouse capitol such as the one at Trenton. The tower was once again the tower-steeple so long absent from capitols; its location on a separate foundation was a surprising reminiscence of the tower-steeple in Philadelphia, the first democratic symbol demanded by laymen. In plan the analogy with Philadelphia's Independence Hall is very close, but at Bismarck the concept is expanded. This tower, though no less a visual climax, contains offices and elevators instead of an open well to house a bell and a staircase.

Colonial analogies seem clearer in the Delaware Capitol at Dover, but never had there been such a confusion of the architectural symbols of American democracy. In the Depression years the state of Delaware built a capitol group, or more accurately, a Capitol village. Unaware of the group in Olympia, the builders found their inspiration in restored Williamsburg. Though still mainly on paper, that restoration had by this time progressed enough to titillate the mildest Colonial Revivalist.

By 1930 state officials realized that the Deleware government could no longer function in the old Statehouse on the Green, regardless of the many efforts to save it through remodeling. So many people, including the Colonial Dames, were telling the Governor what to do that he appointed a commission of four citizen advisers. The small group, a model of smooth operation, continued for three years, first as an Advisory and later as a Capitol Commission. Members included W. W. Harrington, a vice-president of the du Pont Company, and Harry L. Cannon, president of a family-owned food canning company at Bridgeville. Neither businessman had much to say. Questions of taste were resolved by H. Rodney Sharp of Wilmington, and Delaware history was the special realm of Mabel Lloyd Ridgely.

From her house on the Green, Mrs. Ridgely had dynamically led the Colonial Dames in their historical projects for forty years. Sharp was from an old Delaware family and loved his state. After his marriage to Isabella du Pont, he spent his long life as a quiet and effective benefactor of Delaware art and higher education. Both he and Mrs. Ridgely found the look of the modern world ugly and oppressive. In the spirit of the American Renaissance, they were eager for change; only through change, after all, could one achieve perfection.

The Statehouse Advisory immediately hired as a consultant Norman Isham, the Rhode Island architect who had restored Newport's Colony House. Isham was America's first real restoration architect, an articulate champion of historical buildings; but restoration, because of limited demand, was not his main endeavor: He was also an active Colonial Revivalist and writer on historical architecture. On January 6, 1931, the advisers made their report to the Governor: "It is universally recognized that Eighteenth Century Architecture in America has a character of its own that is unsurpassed. It cannot be improved upon either from an artistic or practical standpoint." The Governor and legislature, thus informed, were urged to save the "colonial atmosphere" of the little town by the construction of a series of state buildings "properly arranged" in scale with the old structures on the Green.[31] A convincing little model, made in Isham's office, accompanied the report. Three months later the report was accepted, and the Advisory, now the State House Commission, was ordered to begin building the Legislative Hall. While Isham was retained as a consultant, E. William Martin of Wilmington was the actual architect, and Sharp and Mrs. Ridgely seem to have called the tune.

Work began just before Christmas 1931. The commission was already considering what the interiors should be like. A furnishing committee was headed by Henry Francis du Pont, who was assembling at his family estate, Winterthur, the largest private collection of the whole Antiques Movement. Du Pont approved the reproductions illustrated in the catalogs of Virginia Craftsmen, Incorporated, among the leading makers of Colonial Revival furniture. It was arbitrarily agreed that only the oldest and the most "tasteful" of the paintings owned by the state would be allowed to hang in the new Legislative Hall. This, surprisingly, began the most successful fine arts program of any American state capitol; but even under the best of plans, some

Delaware Hall of Records
Delaware Capitol group as built by E. William Martin and others, 1931–1966

things suffer: "The Crusaders," a heroic World War I memorial mural which showed the hovering ghosts of Washington, Lafayette, and Joan of Arc keeping watch over the doughboys, was hauled away on a flat-bed truck. It had been a special favorite of the legislators.

Delaware's Legislative Hall, as completed in 1933, and much later provided with new end wings, was the only state capitol ever built in the Georgian vernacular of colonial America. The commission had no desire to be exceptional; it was their inherent traditionalism that attracted them to the Capitol program in the first place. In opposition to those "cement-minded legislators" who wanted a fireproof tower-capitol, Mrs. Ridgely, backed by Sharp, contended that Delaware needed a building to confirm American traditions architecturally. They had set out to re-create an accurate specimen of the architecture of colonial days, a time that now seemed cleaner and purer against the background of the deepening Depression.

When people turn to history for validation, they are usually misled. The neat red brick surfaces trimmed in snow-white moldings were true enough to colonial models; paneling, doors, even hinges in the new Capitol were designed after examples still visible in old houses in Delaware and Pennsylvania. But the building in fact is a fraud. It is by no means plausibly colonial, and it is certainly not a traditional state capitol. In their determination to follow the capitol form, and thus to stress the importance of the Legislative Hall in the Capitol group, those in command were careful to organize the colonial elements along recognizable state capitol lines. The

289

individual architectural symbols were combined into one—but that was hardly colonial, for it had first been done at Harrisburg, over forty years after the American colonies had become states of the Union. Wallowing helplessly in history, these zealots rejected the dome for the steeple, its colonial ancestor; but they placed it directly on the roof, as if it were a capitol dome—something which had not been done since Chauncey Swan's day in Iowa City. Yet here the departure from tradition was even more extreme; for beneath the rooftop steeple was a void—a stairhall designed as a basilican saloon—which tied the colonial tower-steeple into the building's mass in a curious parody of the dome-and-rotunda theme. With the historic syndrome shattered, the Capitol of Delaware, for all its colonial pretensions—themselves radical in a capitol—rejected real tradition quite as much as other capitols of the early 1930's that were intentionally modern.

Several years later, in the Far West, the Oregon Capitol Commission also tried to capture the essence of local history. Those commissioners, however, had none of the fear of modernism that was such a negative force in Delaware. One cannot suppose the old Oregon Capitol, which burned down on the snowy night of April 25, 1935, was much lamented. Its Gilded Age façade had as yet no nostalgic Victorian appeal. Justus F. Krumbein, a Portland architect, had designed it in 1872, and it had been built soon after by convict labor. On that site had stood the first Salem Capitol, the utterly forgotten Greek-Revival block of 1853–54, with its Ionic porticoes at the sides and deep *antae* on the ends.

A special session of the Oregon legislature passed an act in 1935 authorizing a new capitol, and a nine-member commission was formed. Meetings were usually held not in Salem but in the Imperial Hotel in Portland, through the nearly three years of the Capitol's construction. A national competition was announced in March, after the newly created Federal Emergency Administration of Public Works (PWA) pledged to cover forty-five per cent of the cost. The legislature had specified that not more than $2,500,000 would be spent on the "capitol building or buildings." Strict federal rules about the competition and construction had to be maintained, and all plans and specifications were subject to the approval of the State Director of the PWA. Any architect could enter the competition, and more than 400 wrote to inquire. Many of the big firms, if they had survived at all, were existing on federally funded work, so their interest in Oregon is not surprising. The competition attracted 123 actual entries from nineteen states, with twenty-eight from New York City alone. California architects submitted twenty-one projects; and most of the twenty Oregon entries were from Portland. Some of these projects deserve passing notice, for they illustrate the two conflicting currents, the historical and the Moderne, that dominated American building in the Depression decade.

Beyond a doubt the most peculiar project was the one in which the architects had made the most effort to be traditional. A former McKim, Mead & White designer, Thomas Harlan Ellett, had, in association with a younger man, Thomas A. Fransioli, slightly modernized an academic elevation that was based upon the United States Capitol as completed by Bulfinch. This source was mainly evident in the elevational drawing, for the wings were brought forward, and the main portico screened a forecourt. But the strangest feature was the hemispherical dome; the designers had lifted it up several stories onto the top of a short but very conspicuous tower. Another less striking traditional project by Wesley Sherwood Bessell of New York recalled the old New York City Hall, but with Greek Revival detailing, complete with ranges of *antae*. There were several projects similar to the Nebraska Capitol, and at least four with the arrangement used at North Dakota. William Mooser and Charles F. Maury of San Francisco combined Nebraska, Louisiana, and North Dakota into a composition of the kind later associated with small-city airport terminals. The project of W. C. F. Gillam of Burlingame, California, was reminiscent of E. E. Myers's at Austin and Denver and of Bell & Kent's at Helena.

Most of the entries seem to have been Moderne or Modernistic, nearly interchangeable names for the mode that had been gaining momentum in America since the 1920's and the sort of architectural style principally sponsored by the federal works programs. Unadorned, geometric, and stressing verticality, the Moderne developed out of traditional forms. The entries in the Oregon competition that were published in the professional magazines either had those traditional roots or were imitations of the new skyscraper capitols. Several California entries, barren of ornament and flat of roof, suggested at least some interest in the European International Style which was making its first American appearance in Southern California in the mid-1920's.

The winner was Francis Keally of New York, in association with the experienced firm of Trowbridge & Livingston, famous builders of hotels and commercial buildings mainly on the East Coast. Keally, a former instructor at the University of Minnesota and New York University, had practiced in New York for nine years. His alliance with a large Manhattan firm was arranged only to satisfy the demands of the competition in Oregon, although in the development stage Keally had taken the advice of Goodhue Livingston and George W. Jacoby of the Trowbridge office.

Keally's scheme approached the Moderne but was not Classical; he had taken the established American state capitol pattern and stripped it to the bones. To the press he said: "The building could not very well be a skyscraper . . . it also seemed to us that a building of average height—between eight and twelve stories—would not be appropriate. Such a building might be anything —a financial or insurance building or a courthouse—but it would not be identifiable as the Capitol. We felt that it *should* be immediately recognized as a Capitol building by the average citizen." Asked what the "style" was, George W. Jacoby hesitated: "Greek refinement," he said, "and Egyptian simplicity, without the classical details of the former." Keally said, "We can't tag the style of architecture. It was built for Oregon, and was based on early Oregon history."[32]

The Moderne, usually more derivative than was realized at the time, admittedly had its foundations here in the American Greek Revival that reached Oregon in the 1840's. As a local vernacular in wood or rough stone, the Greek Revival had been well represented on the same site by the Territorial, and later state, Capitol. The smooth surfaces of the lightly veined marble of the new building are devoid of ornament except for the varied rectangular planes and vertical projections that can almost be described as *antae*.

Between the Oregon Capitol and the Greek Revival Capitol of Ohio there is a strong kinship in the round, flat-topped lantern ringed by the modified *antae* and seemingly unattached to the building below. The rotunda has the openness of the one in Columbus and is likewise flanked by transverse staircases. At Salem the features inside are again small and naked, except for the

of Depression and war had reduced much state activity to mere administration, for legislatures became all too willing to transfer their financial problems to Washington.

Revolutionary changes in the 1930's had softened some of the public's fears of federal authority. Millions of men and women had worked for the government during the war. As eyes turned to the national government, capitols in every state suffered from neglect. Except for opening days and especially controversial sessions, House and Senate galleries gathered dust. Only in the 1950's did this begin to change, when the Federal government, as the principal collector of revenue, accelerated its distribution of money to the states in the form of grants-in-aid, breathing new life into state functions. Increasing numbers of those responsibilities which had been passing from the state to the Federal government now stayed home, or were returned from Washington.

During that decade of the 1950's, and still more in the 1960's, new state building programs were undertaken once more. Initially, in almost every state, annexes were erected in the vicinity of the capitols. Amounting to no more than office buildings, their designs usually attest rather monotonously to their mundane purpose. In 1953 the state of California completed a 940-room office wing on the rear of the old Capitol. A tourist guide published at the time records that the annex had "nine types of floors—terrazzo, linoleum, asphalt, rubber and plastic tile, cork, carpeting and wood blocks, and . . . Missouri Marble." There were in the steel and marble building "30,600 rivets and 20,000 bolts. . . . The building contains 1,100 doors. . . . The telephone system requires some 6,000 lines, with a total capacity of 3,753 stations. This is approximately the number required to serve a community the size of Ukiah or Mill Valley."[33] In tragic contrast to that, the magnificent old Capitol is officially considered so menaced by earthquakes that visitors today are warned they enter at their own risk.

But once the states really began to feel their authority returning, the desire revived to proclaim the fact architecturally. Since nearly every state already had a permanent and monumental capitol, most of this new interest took the form of improvements programs. Numerous schemes initiated by local architects and contractors proposed the demolition of old capitols and the building of new ones, but all of the programs failed in their original forms. The public has so far preferred renovation to new construction.

The most familiar combination of the democratic symbols, virtually abandoned in the years between the two world wars, emerged again and triumphed at Salem. In the twenty years that passed before the next new capitol was planned, the democratic symbols themselves might well have vanished forever. But as soon as the proposed new Capitol for Arizona reached the design stage, the symbols reappeared unharmed. A new and yet unfinished historical circle was begun with a state capitol that was never built.

A need for more office space and modern conveniences such as air conditioning prompted the appointment of the Pyle Commission in Arizona in 1954. In addition to the new needs of multiple state agencies, Arizona, like every other state over the previous thirty years, was now providing private or semiprivate offices for the legislators. By the 1950's this demand was weighing heavily on all capitols. Arizona Governor Howard C. Pyle approved the recommendation of the commission for enlarging the "existing archaic, termite-ridden State Capitol," but the legislature rejected the proposal as extravagant.[34] Two years later the legislature created the State Planning and Building Commission, which announced the availability of $4,500,000 from various sources to spend on a Capitol. What was needed was a master plan. Suddenly the Capitol was of the greatest interest to architects all around the state. A group called the Associated State Capitol Architects, made up of four prominent Arizona firms, was hired by the commission.

After a survey and considerable discussion, the association presented a proposal for a three-part skyscraper scheme, masking the entire front of the old Capitol. Published in January 1957 by the association's Phoenix members—H. H. Green, Lescher & Mahoney, and Edward L. Varney Associates, and the one Tucson member, Lew Place—the scheme was approved at once by the Senate. The House, however, adjourned without making a decision, so the rushed program slowed down, and the public had time to discuss the proposed state Capitol.

Opposition soon crystallized. The association's major opponent, operating from his winter headquarters in the desert nearby, was the eighty-eight-year-old Frank Lloyd Wright. Wright, long a resident of Arizona in its most beautiful seasons, had experienced in the state's wildernesses a quality worthy of protection against the "commercial architecture" then filling the crowded cities. He denounced the Capitol design of Arizona's "provincial copycats" as "a horrible little skyscraper building with a derby hat on it and a trashbasket on each side—the House on one side and the Senate on the other."[35] Through friends in the legislature he took a public stand against the Capitol plan by offering a "humanized and beautiful" design of his own. In February 1957 he released a circular describing a shadowy desert temple called Oasis. A very familiar kind of furor blew up. It had been a long time since a state capitol had mounted into the headlines coast to coast.

The flamboyant Oasis was not to occupy the original Capitol site but the desert hills of scenic Papago Park outside Phoenix. Planned for the hot Arizona climate, it was in outline reminiscent of the ancient Indian thunderbird symbol—the Governor's office as the head, followed by the Supreme Court, then offices in the outspread wings, and the balanced chambers and public ceremonial spaces in the body and pointed tail. The rooms housing the official branches of the state government were individual hexagonal buildings; the rest of the Capitol flowed from these on a long straight axis shaded, except for the solidly roofed wings, by a giant canopy of pierced concrete. On the principle of a wooden-slatted greenhouse, the 400-foot cover broke the direct fierceness of the sun, permitting exotic plantings—an old but forgotten tradition in Arizona's Capitol. From the outside, the roof's resemblance to an Indian tepee would have amused Bertram Goodhue. It was weighted near the edges by a pair of tall steeples and crowned over the center with a lofty cupola. The democratic symbols of capitol building were conspicuously present: The central space was a vast memorial hall of history, more open and grand than Ohio's, for example, although the traditional monumental dome was dead by this time, Wright himself referred to the great concrete canopy by that name.

In the thick of controversy, Wright compared his building to the Alhambra in Spain. There was perhaps a closer Spanish parallel in the tradition that the law of the Defenders of the Faith must be administered under the branches of a tree: The Capitol canopy, Wright said, was like "a great tree, filtering sunlight over subordinate but beautiful buildings and gardens standing together beneath the canopy in harmonious relation to this hexagonal domed shelter and to each other . . . in green gardens, fountains playing, pools reflecting. Great vistas of beauty are everywhere."[36] The proposal delayed the Capitol project of the Associated Architects only so far as it created statewide and even national interest. Newspaper coverage made more of an issue out of the Capitol affair than ever really existed. The Constitution of Arizona specified that the Capitol had to be located in Phoenix, and Papago Park was outside the city limits. What was more, the Federal deed granting the park land to Arizona required that the land be returned to the United States if it was used for other than recreational purposes.

Associated State Capitol Architects built the legislative wings of the new Capitol between 1957 and 1960. Faced with Arizona tufa and Minnesota granite, the plain International Style rectangles had expanses of glass screened by pierced concrete sunbreaks. The center tower which would unite the wings into a three-part skyscraper composition was postponed indefinitely, leaving Reily Gordon's villa, standing back from the pair of side wings, as the symbolic heart of the Arizona Capitol group.

Wright's proposals passed into history. He had gained very little support among the politicians, for they had always considered the legendary seigneur of Taliesin West an impractical man. The controversy was the source of much bitterness to the architect in his last two years. But the incident seems to have had its real roots in Wright's rage over the desecration of the desert landscape by what he called "pole and wire men and political slaves-of-the-expedient."[37]

In this open land, where the ugliness of the advance of Western man was not hidden by trees and vines, there were a few people other than Wright whose search for a compatible architecture was very real. To them, the businessman was a devil in the garden, ruthlessly chopping into pieces something that belonged together as a single creation. The endless grids on the Western land maps were ominously burlesqued in the façades of the high-rise buildings now appearing in the towns. Commercial architecture had come to be a kind of visual exploitation of the once-unbounded earth. Those who looked for appropriate architecture faced new circumstances in the West. As Americans had always done, they turned to history for answers. Overlooking on principle the architectural revivals based on the white man's history, they found inspiration in the abstract emblems of the Indian. The Indian, they said, had not been a destroyer when the wilderness was his to rule.

As Wright had done a decade before, the prominent Santa Fe and Albuquerque firm of W. C. Kruger & Associates searched the Indian past for inspiration for their New Mexico Capitol design. Since the nineteenth century, Americans had been enchanted by Santa Fe's adobe buildings, presided over by the grand dowager of North American public architecture, the Adobe Palace. The town's architecture was under the strict control of local private organizations so that Santa Fe's unique charm might be preserved forever. Under this well-meaning protection the rich pastiche that had made Santa Fe so different fell victim to one of the longest and most disastrous Colonial Revival campaigns in the nation's history.

The area around the ancient plaza had already been converted by renovation and subjective restoration into its own imaginary version of early New Mexico when, in 1949, it was decided that the domed Capitol of 1895–1902 was next in line for a face-lift. Tin dome, columned portico, and other frivolous architectural details were torn away, and from the remaining core there grew a pleasant little fake Spanish village coated with pinkish-golden stucco and presided over by a tall belfry. Although several architects worked on the village, W. C. Kruger was the designer of the section with the belfry, the main element in the group.

Taken as a whole, the Capitol village was far more theatrical than the Dover group and, in its massing of smooth plastered blocks, considerably more effective. It was more or less a complete ensemble by 1953. In local jargon the buildings were in "Territorial style," meaning that the essential inspiration was in the old adobe architecture, but features from the Spanish vernacular and the American Greek Revival were superimposed. Santa Fe's best-known exponent of the New Mexico revivals was the architect John Gaw Meem. Through experience, he had learned as far back as the 1920's that his largely Anglo-American clients for revivalism felt at home with the Territorial, while they often rejected the more purely Indian or Spanish.

Few buildings have enjoyed the popularity of the Capitol group in Santa Fe. When the legislative facilities were pronounced inadequate in 1963 and a new Capitol Bill was passed, it specified that the group would not be damaged and that the new structure would be merely a legislative and executive building. The Kruger firm won over thirty competitors in an informal competition. Kruger's design was based upon the ancient sun sign of the Zia Indian Pueblo. A symbol of life, the emblem of Father Sun had endured in the folklore of the Keres-speaking people; since 1925 it had been a part of the flag of the state of New Mexico. The new Capitol was to be round, lifted up on a larger round terrace and approached by four equally spaced projecting promenades to simulate the sunrays which appear in the Zia symbol. In elevation the upper part of the proposed design, with its inward-slanting sides, somewhat resembled the lantern on the Oregon Capitol.

From every direction the commission received hot blasts of protest. The architects explained that for many reasons it was best that the new building make no attempt to relate to the existing "village" complex or to the nearby row of authentic adobe houses on East DeVargas Street. Even on the Capitol grounds, the new building was meant to seem aloof. But the historical opposition would accept nothing but a revision of the proposal along Territorial lines, and they got their way. Modification amounted to a nearly complete change of design, with the retention of some of the desirable interior arrangements.

The resulting Capitol, completed in 1966, was a strange creation. One of its five stories is sunk in the earth so the building's scale would match that of the plaza area where the Adobe Palace reposed behind its Revival façade. The sun symbol was brought up from the terraces into the plan, where it retained its round outline, with four rectangular radiating bays containing entrances. Seen merely as a bare form, the circular stuccoed mass, buttressed by powerful rectangles, is admittedly striking, on its hilltop just outside the crowded network of the old town. It was the demand for Territorial additions that turned the Capitol into a curiosity. The projecting bays are connected by simulated wooden portals, giving a bracelet effect; in addition to these, there are doorways and windows crowned with simplified pediments—all the glaring white of marble, not the painted wood of their prototypes.

Built on a budget under $5,000,000, the new Capitol at Santa Fe was nevertheless a brave step. Regardless of its tawdry exterior decorations, it is still far more of a public monument than a modern office building would have been. A central rotunda rises to a small domed skylight which is minimized externally, so that from outside the building seems to have a flat roof. The House and Senate Chambers are balanced, and the colonnaded portals can perhaps pass for porticoes refashioned in a local way. All the "capitol" features, ripped from the 1900 Capitol when the Territorial group was erected, are reshaped in the Kruger structure. The new building is a state capitol in its symbolic credentials; its faults are the result of a feeble and overscaled effort to convey the Territorial message—the addition in the wrong materials of the sort of derivative veneer so often demanded still by an insecure public craving historical sanction.

The circle of capitol design that began with Wright's Arizona proposal, and was realized in Kruger's New Mexico Capitol, was taken up in the new state of Hawaii. From the very first, the geography of those Pacific islands had a heavy influence on the new Capitol, as it does on all Hawaiian life. History and legend intertwine in the Hawaiian story, and the legends assume the authority of history. Rather than fading out in recent years, the mystical history of Hawaii has regained a living presence. Like anything that romantic, in a setting that beautiful, the legend has attracted adoring strangers since the first white outsiders at the time of the American War of Independence saw the islands looming in the mists of the sea.

A committee to locate the new Capitol was appointed just before statehood was granted in 1959; it was all but ignored when it declared that the new Capitol should be built on a commanding point at the entrance to Honolulu Harbor. The legislature specified that the Capitol must be in a historic location, near the old Iolani Palace, a site well within the city that is dominated by one of the most historic buildings in the Pacific.

The Iolani Palace was completed in 1883 from the design of Thomas J. Baker, a wandering builder who had lived in San Francisco before moving to Honolulu. The previous Palace was a Greek Revival structure of wood, with deep porches and a columned belvedere reminiscent of a Louisiana plantation cottage of the 1840's. The elected King Kalakaua, under the influence of American and British business interests, sought to create at Iolani Palace a more orthodox court life than Hawaii had ever known before. His new Palace was built with the not-improbable idea that it would one day shelter the throne of a union of the whole Pacific island world.

The architectural style was that of midcentury Europe. Mansarded, it has towers on its façades, and tiled verandas, framed in two levels of iron columns, give the impression of an American cast-iron front without windows. In its few but very large rooms—all fitted out by the Davenport Company of Boston—the King entertained an endless file of foreign ship captains, consuls, authors, adventurers, and investors who might be of benefit to Hawaii. They usually benefited themselves. The Palace was largely a ceremonial structure; the King and Queen each had small private houses on the grounds, the most delightful of these being the King's Royal Bungalow, a pink-latticed parody of a riverboat, grounded in the shade of a lush garden.

King Kalakaua's coronation took place at the Palace in the year of its completion. It was the first such coronation in Hawaiian history, and left no question about the authority of the King or the headquarters of that authority, Iolani Palace. When King Kalakaua died, he was suc-

Office of W. C. Kruger

New Mexico Capitol, by W. C. Kruger, 1965–66

ceeded by his sister Mrs. Dominis, who became Queen Liliuokalani. She was deposed in 1893, ending the ninety-eight year reign of the United Hawaiian monarchy, which had descended from the ancient kingdoms of a galaxy of island chiefs.

Under the Hawaiian Republic and as Territorial Capitol under the United States, the Palace served sixty-six years as the seat of the elected legislature. The House of Representatives sat in the former Throne Room beneath the glass electroliers installed by the King; the Senate occupied the smaller State Dining Room across the hall. After a structural renovation in 1930, the territory began putting copies of the historic Throne Room furniture in place between sessions and opening the Palace to tourists. This was something like sweeping a democratic function under a royal rug; but the visiting public—and the Hawaiians—have always been highly nostalgic about our only American king. A real restoration of the Palace began in 1969 with a $3,000,000 program under the direction of the Honolulu architect Geoffrey W. Fairfax. That began after the government at last moved to a new Capitol of its own.

As early as 1902 there were plans to enlarge the Palace to make it a better Capitol. Wings were designed in belated Second Empire style to contain legislative chambers patterned on those by Link in Mississippi. The proposal came to nothing. Except for the patching of certain parts from time to time, the Palace deteriorated. Some of its porches were walled in for secretarial offices. The enchanting Royal Bungalow saw its last service in 1917 as a military center for physical examinations before it was surrendered to the termites.

An Architect Selection Committee, headed by Robert R. Midkiff, a banker, and Representative George M. Koga, began interviewing architects from various parts of the United States. The effect of this survey was to convince the committee that the new Capitol should be built by a Hawaiian firm, but with a stinging postscript requiring that the firm be associated with a mainland organization experienced in monumental building. This was not at all well received by Honolulu architects, one of whom later said only Hawaii's "hopeless provincialism" caused the Committee to impose such a restriction on the local architects.[38] In any event, the architects set about making their associations and appeared before the commission as salesmen with elaborate packaged presentations. Belt, Lemmon & Lo, the firm finally selected, became prominent in Hawaiian architecture, particularly on the island of Oahu, soon after the close of World War II. An association was formed for purposes of the Capitol competition with the San Francisco architect John Carl Warnecke, who was then doing considerable major Federal building in the national capital.

Cyril W. Lemmon, architect in charge, took the lead in directing the project; his partners were Robert M. Belt, a civil engineer, and Donald Lo, a structural engineer. Warnecke sent Lun Chan and Morton Rader to Honolulu, and under Lemmon's direction these two designers formulated a scheme that was an instant success with the committee. Praising its "dignity and poetry without ostentation," the committee set out to convince the legislature, which was still meeting in the Palace.[39] In 1961 no funds were allotted; the second year saw only a token office budget. After the initial appropriation was finally made in 1965, the committee became, as Lemmon later said, "a tremendous mover" under the leadership of the politically powerful Koga. Construction began in 1966, and the Capitol was occupied in 1969.[40]

The architects' inspiration was not the history of Hawaii, nor its mythological symbols, but the island setting in which Hawaiian life existed. Lemmon and the designers had insisted, even before funds were set aside, that no portraits, murals, or statues would "ever" be introduced into the building. They had originally envisioned a place for "significant works of art," but soon decided that Hawaii's Capitol "must speak only through its architecture."[41] While this professional conceit was predictably honored only briefly, the architecture does tell the Capitol's meaning quite unmistakably.

Set in a great pool, the new Capitol is a simple rectangle like the nearby Palace. But there are stronger echoes of the Greek Revival Palace of 1845 that had first occupied the Iolani site, though the columns supporting the huge overhanging office floors are patterned on palm trees,

James Y. Young

Hawaii Capitol, by Belt, Lemmon & Lo, 1965–69

not any Grecian order. While the idea was not new to architecture, it was particularly effective here. These columns encircle the balanced ground-level legislative chambers which are encased in simulated volcanic rock. Emerging from the rippling surface of the pools, these mounds represent volcanoes in the sea, recalling the geological origin of the islands. Over a broad causeway and through the columns one passes only briefly under shelter, then into a galleried inner court—a tremendous saloon—open to the sky.

All the diverse trends in capitol design since Goodhue's plan at Lincoln are avoided here, while some much older features are born again. The high-rise tower, its stacks of office floors a practical necessity in the twentieth century, is reinterpreted as a series of broad stories, lifted above the balanced chambers and the inner ceremonial court to form terracelike horizontals. As at Albany a century before, the saloon has become an open court, though the central space at Honolulu is really more than a court. The architects first intended to close it with a shallow dome of pierced concrete, rather resembling a hill in contour and faintly resembling Wright's Oasis. Even when that peak of roof was omitted, the upward curving ribs intended to support it were partially retained. The opening was reduced to a square oculus framing a view of the real skies in the way the inner domes of the American Renaissance had framed frescoed ones.

The capitols of the twentieth century that came after the Classical epoch have each adapted the lantern or steeple in some way. At Honolulu the lantern element is expanded into a great rooftop bungalow house, the executive suite, which is lifted a full floor above the rest of the building on the terrace that covers the highest office floor. It is from the roof of this terminal story that the great concrete ribs thrust out over the saloon, further calling attention to its presence.

Scores of small rooms fill the secondary office floors, all with partitions that can be readily rearranged. Under the floor of the court the public hearing room recalls the early idea of having the central saloons, and later rotundas, house joint sessions and public meetings. The plan of the main floor, with its semicircular chambers so plainly articulated and the open space between, is, in a manner of speaking, the child of Governor Nicholson's Capitol at Williamsburg built more than 250 years before. There is even a suggestion of Bulfinch's Doric Hall in Boston as later repeated elsewhere in the arrangement of columns in the middle passage. By suppressing the tall vertical roof element and finding a practical application for Bulfinch's recessed attic and the traditional lantern, the architects surrendered visual preeminence to the commercial skyscrapers downtown. Hawaii's Capitol is in fact designed to be seen first from the air, not from the ground.

The vertical element which had been for a century the most dominant of the architectural symbols of American democracy had survived the reinterpretations of forty years, only to be reduced in the newest circle of state capitols to its place among the rest.

NOTES

CHAPTER I

1. Governor Francis Nicholson to the Virginia House of Burgesses, May 18, 1699, *Journals of the House of Burgesses of Virginia, 1695–1702*, p. 167.

2. "Acts of the House of Burgesses," April 1699 Session. Jefferson Papers, Library of Congress and cited in the research report on the Capitol done by the Colonial Williamsburg Foundation and in manuscript form in its archives.

3. Governor Francis Nicholson to the Board of Trade and Plantations, "memorial," March 3, 1705, Public Record Office, London.

4. Captain Francis Goelet, "Journal," *New England Historical and Genealogical Register*, 1870, p. 72.

5. *Pennsylvania Gazette*, August 6, 1741.

6. Samuel Harding Accounts, General Loan Office, Norris Collection, Historical Society of Pennsylvania.

7. *Pennsylvania Gazette*, February 5, 1747.

8. Governor William Gooch to the House of Burgesses, March 30, 1747, *Journals of the House of Burgesses of Virginia 1742–1749*, p. 236.

9. Governor William Gooch to the House of Burgesses, October 27, 1748, *ibid.*, pp. 256–57.

10. Lyon G. Tyler, ed., "The Diary of John Blair," *The William and Mary Quarterly*, vol. VII (January 1899), p. 138.

11. No dependable views of the rebuilt Capitol survive, although there was a sketch done in the 1820's at about the time the building was partially demolished. What then remained of the Capitol burned down in 1832. Most of our information about the building's eighteenth-century appearance has come from vouchers in the records of the Treasury of Virginia that are housed in the Virginia State Archives. Detailing indicated in these vouchers was related to surviving drawings of actual architectural elements known to have existed in eighteenth-century Williamsburg. We were further assisted by a sketch of the Gloucester Street façade made in the office of Perry, Shaw & Hepburn, Architects, around 1929, while final decisions on the restored Capitol's ultimate form were still being made. We presented all this material to our artist, and from them he made the conjectural restoration which appears in this book. There are various verbal descriptions of the Capitol as it was rebuilt in the mid-eighteenth century, but the best we know about is the one by Thomas Jefferson. In his *Notes on the State of Virginia*, 1781, he wrote: "The capitol is a light and airy structure, with a portico in front of two orders, the lower of which, being Doric, is tolerably just in its proportions and ornaments, save only that the intercolonations are too large. The upper is Ionic, much too small for that on which it is mounted, its ornaments not proper to the order, nor proportioned within themselves. It is crowned with a pediment, which is too high for its span. Yet, on the whole, it is the most pleasing piece of architecture we have."

12. David Ridgely, *Annals of Annapolis* (Baltimore: 1841), quoting a letter by William Eddis dated October 1769.

13. Maryland Assembly, *Acts of the November Session, 1769*, chapter 14.

14. *Maryland Gazette*, April 2, 1772.

15. Maryland House of Delegates, *Votes and Proceedings, November 1779*, p. 78.

16. Maryland House of Delegates, *Votes and Proceedings, November 1784*, p. 25.

17. Joshua Botts to "Sir," Scharf Collection, Maryland Historical Society and cited in Morris L. Radoff, *The State House at Annapolis* (Annapolis: 1972), p. 17.

18. Samuel Vaughan, Diary, June–September 1787, Library of Congress.

CHAPTER II

1. Richard Switzer, trans., *Chateaubriand's [1791] Travels in America* (Lexington: 1969), pp. 14–15.

2. P. L. Ford, The Writings of Thomas Jefferson, 1893, vol. 2, pp. 106–07.

3. William Short to Thomas Jefferson, Richmond, July 28, 1784, Jefferson Papers, Library of Congress.

4. James Buchanan and William Hay to Thomas Jefferson, Richmond, March 20, 1785, *Writings of Thomas Jefferson* (Princeton: 1953), pp. 48–49.

5. Thomas Jefferson to James Buchanan and William Hay, Paris, August 13, 1785, *ibid.*, p. 367.

6. James Buchanan and William Hay to Thomas Jefferson, Richmond, October 18, 1785, *ibid.*, p. 648.

7. Thomas Jefferson to James Buchanan and William Hay, Paris, January 26, 1786, *ibid.*, p. 221.

8. "Estimate of the Building of the Capitol According to a Plan Presented to and Approved of by the Directors, 1785," Executive Communications 1785–1789, Virginia State Archives.

9. Edmund Randolph to Thomas Jefferson, Richmond, July 12, 1786, *Writings*, p. 133.

10. William Hay to Thomas Jefferson, Richmond, May 3, 1787, *ibid.*, pp. 48–49.

11. *Hennings Statutes* [of Virginia] *1789–1792* (December 19, 1789), p. 61.

12. Thomas Jefferson to James Madison, 1789, as cited in "Letters of Jefferson Relative to the Virginia Capitol," *William and Mary Quarterly*, vol. V (April 1925), pp. 95–98.

13. Charles Bulfinch to Statehouse Committee, Boston, November 5, 1787, Massachusetts State Archives.

14. Ellen Susan Bulfinch, *The Life and Letters of Charles Bulfinch, Architect* (Boston: 1896), pp. 41–42.

15. John Chester's Travel Voucher, September 1792, Connecticut State Library, State Records Center, and cited in Newton C. Brainard, *Hartford Statehouse of 1796* (Hartford, 1964), p. 8.

16. John and Simeon Skillin, Bill for Carving, Boston, January 4, 1798, Massachusetts State Archives.

17. Ephraim Thayer, Samuel Summer, Amos and Jed Lincoln, Mr. Vose, *et al.*, various bills for furniture, furniture parts, japan wares, window shades and stoves, etc., March 1797–May 1799, Massachusetts State Archives.

18. James Douglass, various undated bills, particularly for the wainscot and "window architraves and venetian windows . . . £10." Also see Douglass's bill for November 27 and December 5, 1800, Pennsylvania State Archives.

19. Phillip Hooker, bill to the commissioners for erecting the new statehouse, April 1806, as cited in Edward W. Root, *Phillip Hooker* (New York: 1929), p. 111.

20. Committee to take into Consideration the Expediency of Building a State-House, etc., *Report* (Concord: 1814).

21. *Laws of New Hampshire*, vol. VII, p. 547.

22. Albe Cady, Memorial to the Statehouse Committee [1819], New Hampshire State Archives.

23. Asher Benjamin, bill presented to the state of New Hampshire, Boston, July 28, 1819, New Hampshire State Archives.

24. William S. Lane and Mr. Smart, bill presented to the State of Georgia, Milledgeville, November 7, 1805, Georgia State Archives; Leola Selman Beeson, "The Old State Capitol in Milledgeville and Its Cost," *The Georgia Historical Quarterly*, vol. XXXIV (September 1950), pp. 197–201.

25. William Strickland to Nicholas Biddle, Philadelphia, February 24, 1817, as cited in Agnes Addison Gilchrist, *William Strickland, Architect and Engineer, 1788–1854* (New York: 1969), p. 50; *see also* Strickland to Nathaniel B. Boillau, Harrisburg, October 1, 1816, Pennsylvania State Archives.

CHAPTER III

1. Phillips Bradley, ed., *Democracy in America*, by C.A.H.C. de Tocqueville (London: 1835), vol. II, pp. 14–15.

2. Committee Who Were Appointed to Examine the State of the Public Buildings, Report, December 25, 1818, Archibald D. Murphy Papers, North Carolina State Archives.

3. Isaac Winslow, Journal, Raleigh, 1824, Duke University Library.

4. *Journal of the Kentucky House of Representatives*, January 24, 1826, p. 356.

5. *Ibid.*

6. *The Huntsville Democrat*, July 31, 1829.

7. *Public Acts of Maine* [Maine Session Law], 1827, p. 1,128 (chapter 366, section 4); *see also* Joint Standing Committee on Public Buildings, *Report* (Augusta: February 22, 1833).

8. William King to Reuel Williams, Bath, Maine, February 5, 1828, Reuel Williams Papers, Maine Historical Society.

9. Charles Bulfinch to William King, Esq., Washington City, May 29, 1829, William King Papers, Maine Historical Society.

10. *Ibid.*

11. The Kennebec *Journal*, January 1, 1831.

12. Thomas Hamilton, *Men and Manners in America* (Philadelphia: 1833), vol. II, p. 380.

13. J. S. Buckingham, *Slave States in America* (London: 1842), vol. I, p. 538.

14. Leola Selman Beeson, "The Old Statehouse in Milledgeville and its Cost." *The Georgia Historical Quarterly*, vol. XXXIV (September 1950), pp. 197–201.

15. *The Mississippian*, February 19, 1836; *see also* Statehouse Committee, *Report* (Jackson: February 10, 1836).

16. W. N. Blane, *An Excursion Through the United States and Canada, 1822–1833* (London: 1824), p. 114.

17. *The Argus of Western America*, January 17, 1827.

18. *Ibid.*

19. *The Kentucky Gazette*, May 11, 1827; *Journal of the Kentucky House of Representatives*, November 6, 1827, December 5, 1827, and January 11, 1828; *see also The Western Luminary*, May 23, 1827.

20. *Journal of the Kentucky House of Representatives*, December 28, 1830, p. 130.

21. *Atkinson's Casket: Gems of Literature, Wit & Sentiment*, no. 12 (April 1833), p. 553.

22. *Ibid.*

23. *The Argus of Western America*, May 11, 1827; *The Kentucky Reporter*, May 19, 1827.

24. *The New Haven Register*, 1828, from a clipping in the collection of the New Haven Colony Historical Society.

25. Joint Committee to Whom is Referred the Reports of the Committee for Building the Statehouse in New Haven, Report, May 1829; Committee for Building the Statehouse, *Senate Report* (New Haven: May 1829).

26. Committee for Building the Statehouse, *Report to the General Assembly Sitting at New Haven* (New Haven: May 1828).

27. [Nathaniel Hawthorne?] "New Haven," *The American Magazine of Useful Knowledge*, vol. III (1836), p. 25.

28. From an unidentifiable newspaper, probably in Indiana, but almost certainly somewhere on the route of the National Road, clipping, 1832, Indiana State Library.

29. Ithiel Town, Articles of Agreement with the State of Indiana, 1832, Noah Noble Papers, Indiana State Library; A. J. Davis Day Book, entry for October 17, 1831, Davis Papers, Avery Library, Columbia University.

30. *The Raleigh Register and North Carolina Gazette*, June 23, 1831.

31. *Debate in the Legislature of North Carolina on a Proposal Appropriation for Rebuilding the Capitol and on the Convention Question in the Months of December and January 1831–1832* (Raleigh: 1832), p. 49.

32. *The Raleigh Register and North Carolina Gazette*, June 23, 1831.

33. Joint Select Committee, *Report* (Raleigh: December 23, 1834), pp. 3–4.

34. *The Arkansas Gazette*, May 23, July 3, July 10, July 17, July 24, and July 29, 1833.

35. *The Arkansas Gazette*, July 29, 1834.

36. G. W. Featherstonhaugh, *Excursion Through the Slave States*, vol. II (London: 1844), p. 63; *The Arkansas Gazette*, December 5, 1837, and December 9, 1837.

37. James L. Minor to E. Stabler, Esq., Jefferson City, Missouri, August 1, 1839, Western Historical Manuscripts Collection, University of Missouri.

38. *Ibid.*, October 8, 1839.

39. *Ibid.*, June 8, 1839.

40. Charles J. Latrobe, *The Rambler in North America* [in 1832 and 1833], vol. I (New York: 1835), pp. 50–51.

41. *The Burlington Free Press*, May 10, 1830.

42. Capitol Commission to Gov. Wm. A. Palmer, Montpelier, May 29, 1833, *Journals of the House of Representatives* (Montpelier: 1833), pp. 30–32.

43. *Ibid.*, p. 31.

44. [Nathaniel Hawthorne?] "Vermont Statehouse," *American Magazine of Useful Knowledge*, vol. III (1836), p. 210.

45. *The Sangamo Journal*, January 19, 1839.

46. Thomas Cole to William A. Adams, Catskill, New York, July 29, 1839, Albany Institute of History and Art.

47. William A. Adams to Thomas Cole, Columbus, Ohio, June 18, 1838, Albany Institute of History and Art.

48. State House Commissioners, *Report* (Columbus: December 28, 1839).

49. Thomas Cole to William A. Adams, New York, June 1839, Albany Institute of History and Art.

50. Thomas Cole to William A. Adams, Catskill, New York, July 29, 1839, Albany Institute of History and Art.

51. State House Commissioners, *Report* (Columbus: December 28, 1839).

52. State House Commissioners, *Report* (Columbus: 1863), p. 17.

53. Gideon Shryock to John M. Bass, Esq., Louisville, Kentucky, May 12, 1846, Tennessee State Archives.

54. Capitol Commission, *First Annual Report* (Nashville: October 10, 1845); *see also* Capitol Commission, Minutes, entry for June 16, 1844; and Robert H. White, *Messages of the Governors of Tennessee*, vol. IV (Nashville: 1962 and 1963), p. 64.

55. *Ibid.*

56. A. C. Bruce, a statement about the Capitol of Tennessee written in 1920, Kentucky Historical Society.

CHAPTER IV

1. J. E. Alexander, *Transatlantic Sketches*, vol. II (London: 1833), pp. 242–43.

2. Charles Mackay, *Life and Liberty in America* [1857–1858], vol. I (London: 1859), p. 123.

3. Mary Howett, ed., *America of the Fifties by Fredrika Bremer* [1849–1851] (New York: 1924), p. 169.

4. C. D. Arfwedson, *The United States and Canada in 1832, 1833 and 1834*, vol. I (London: 1834), p. 153.

5. *The Huntsville Democrat*, November 24, 1847.

6. *The Montgomery Advertiser and State Gazette*, September 3, 1850.

7. *Journal of the Vermont House of Representatives* (Montpelier: February 20, 1857), p. 121.

8. Thomas W. Silloway to the Committee of Citizens of Montpelier, *Journal of the Vermont House of Representatives* (Montpelier: February 18, 1857), p. 103.

9. Superintendent of Construction of the Vermont Statehouse, *Report* (Montpelier: October 15, 1857), p. 12.

10. *Ibid.*, pp. 13–14.

11. Thomas Powers, *Vermont Capitol and the Star Chamber* (Montpelier: October 1858), p. 4.

12. August Gottlieb Schoenborn, Memorandums I and II, August 1895 and January 1898 as cited in Turpin C. Bannister, "The Genealogy of the Dome of the United States Capitol," *Journal of the Society of Architectural Historians*, vol. XVII (January to June 1948), pp. 1–31.

13. *Ibid.*, p. 24.

14. W. F. Colcock to Dear Sir, Charleston, South Carolina, July 29, 1854, George Edward Walker Papers, South Caroliniana Library.

15. Commissioners of the Statehouse, Annual Report Number One, Columbia, October 1, 1857, South Carolina State Archives.

16. John R. Niernsee and George E. Walker to the Chairman and Commissioners of the State-house, Architect's Office, Columbia, December 13, 1854, South Carolina State Archives.

17. George E. Walker to Colonel E. C. White, Columbia, March 20, 1835, George E. Walker Papers, South Caroliniana Library.

18. R. Bedon to George E. Walker, Plantation, March 24, 1855, George E. Walker Papers, South Carolinian Library.

19. Commissioner's report to Brigham Young, Great Salt Lake City, Utah Territory, November 27, 1851, Utah State Archives; *see also* various vouchers for November 1851, and the accounts of the individual commissioners as presented to the territorial government for reimbursement, all in the Utah State Archives.

20. Truman O. Angell, Journal, p. 3, entry for December 1851, Church Historian's Office, Church of Jesus Christ of Latter-day Saints.

21. William Felshaw to Truman O. Angell, Fillmore, June 26, 1852, Church Historian's Office, Church of Jesus Christ of Latter-day Saints.

22. August Gottlieb Schoenborn, Memorandums I and II, p. 21.

23. *San Francisco Bulletin*, April 21, 1857.

24. *Sacramento Daily Union*, May 22, 1860.

25. Capitol Commission, Minutes and Proceedings, 1860 through 1863, entry for May 28, 1860, California State Archives.

26. *Acts of the United States Congress*, April 16, 1862.

27. John Eaton, *Grant, Lincoln and the Freedman* (New York: 1907), p. 535.

28. G. P. Cummings to Mrs. Reuben Clark, Sacramento, May 5, 1866; Capitol Commission to Mrs. Clark, payment in the amount of $100; Reuben Clark to the Capitol Commission, February 15, 1862, April 29, 1862, and May 12, 1862. California State Archives.

29. George Duffield, *The New Capitol or The Wilderness Rejoicing* (Lansing: 1878), pp. 21–22.

30. Written on the flyleaf of M. C. Weld, *Histoire Générale des Voyages Tome Dix-Huitième Depuis le Commencement du XV Siècle* (Paris: 1741). The book is now in the Louisiana Collection, Louisiana State University.

31. Earl Schenck Miers, ed., *When the World Ended: The Diary of Emma Le Conte* (New York: 1957), pp. 45–46.

32. *Chicago Daily Tribune*, May 5, 1865; *see also* Caroline R. Heath, *Four Days in May* (Springfield: 1965), and appropriate dates in *Harper's Weekly*.

CHAPTER V

1. Senate Document #59, 1864, State of New York; also see New York State Land Office, Minutes, 1864–1869, Secretary of State.

2. Board of Statehouse Commissioners, Minutes for March 26 and March 27, 1866, Kansas Historical Society; Henry J. Adams, statement at Topeka, August 21, 1938, Kansas Historical Society.

3. *Kansas State Record*, December 22, 1869.

4. Gridley J. F. Bryant, *Report to the Governor of New Hampshire* (Concord: 1864), p. 3.

5. E. E. Myers to the Secretary of State of Connecticut, Springfield, Illinois, February 10, 1872; Myers to Marshall Jewell, Springfield, February 17, 1872, Department of Legislative Research, Connecticut General Assembly.

6. George B. Post, *Description of the Plans for the New State House for the State of Connecticut* (New York: December 30, 1871), Department of Legislative Research, Connecticut General Assembly.

7. Peabody & Stearns, *Description of Drawings Presented for the Hartford State House* (Boston: 1871), Department of Legislative Research, Connecticut General Assembly.

8. T. L. Langerfeldt, Specification, Boston, March 1872, Department of Legislative Research, Connecticut General Assembly.

9. Gambrill & Richardson, *Descriptive Report and Schedule for Proposed Capitol Building of the State of Connecticut* (New York: 1872), Department of Legislative Research, Connecticut General Assembly.

10. H. H. Richardson to Marshall Jewell, New York, April 3, 1872, Department of Legislative Research, Connecticut General Assembly.

11. Richard M. Upjohn to Marshall Jewell, New York, April 4, 1872, Department of Legislative Research, Connecticut General Assembly.

12. Horace Bushnell to Marshall Jewell, Hartford, March 28, 1872, April 6, 1872, and September 14, 1872, Department of Legislative Research, Connecticut General Assembly.

13. Richard M. Hunt to Richard M. Upjohn, New York, June 30, 1872, Department of Legislative Research, Connecticut General Assembly.

14. Connecticut Capitol Commission, Minutes, August 4, 1873, Department of Legislative Research, Connecticut General Assembly.

15. Connecticut Capitol Commission to Governor John E. Ingersoll, Hartford, May 26, 1874, Commission Letterbook, Department of Legislative Research, Connecticut General Assembly.

16. Richard M. Upjohn to A. E. Burr, Esq., New York, July 18, 1874, Department of Legislative Research, Connecticut General Assembly.

17. *The Daily State Register* [Carson City], January 1, 1871; *see also* Peter Cavanaugh, Jr., to the Nevada Capitol Commission, San Francisco, May 6, 1879, Nevada State Archives.

18. *Ibid.*, and *The Carson City Appeal*, June 10, 1870, and June 12, 1870; *see also* the *Gold Hill News* [Virginia City], January 1, 1871.

19. Illinois Capitol Commission, *General Outlines and Details for Architects Who May Prepare Plans and Designs for a New State House at Springfield* (Springfield: March 24, 1867), pp. 2–4.

20. Committee to Inquire into the New Statehouse, *Report* (Springfield: 1871), p. 163.

21. "Public Buildings in Illinois: the New State House," *The American Architect and Building News*, vol. II (February 24, 1877), p. 62.

22. Iowa Capitol Commission, Minutes, October 5, 1870, Iowa State Archives.

23. Committee of Investigation, *Report* (Springfield: 1871), p. 167.

24. J. C. Cochrane to the Board of Capitol Commissioners of Iowa, Chicago, October 16, 1871, Iowa State Archives.

25. Iowa Capitol Commission, Minutes, February 23, 1872, Iowa State Archives.

26. Iowa Capitol Commission, Minutes, September 3, 1872, Iowa State Archives.

27. "Public Buildings in Illinois: the New State House," *The American Architect and Building News*, vol. II (February 24, 1877), p. 62.

28. E. E. Myers to Governor H. P. Baldwin, Springfield, April 24, 1871, Michigan State Archives.

29. E. E. Myers to Governor Baldwin, Springfield, April 16, 1871, Michigan State Archives.

30. E. E. Myers to Governor Baldwin, Springfield, May 9, 1872, Michigan State Archives.

31. *E. E. Myers & Son, Architects and Superintendents*, printed advertisement, Wyoming State Archives.

32. *People* [Indianapolis], March 30, 1878.

33. *The Madison Courier*, July 23, 1878.

34. *The Franklin Democrat*, May 30, 1880.

35. *The Indianapolis Journal*, March 19, 1880.

36. "The Texas Capitol Competition," *The American Architect and Building News*, vol. XII (September 30, 1882), p. 154.

37. *Ibid.*, p. 154.

38. Texas Capitol Commission, *Report* (Austin: 1888), p. 48.

39. N. L. Norton to the Texas Capitol Com-

Commission, Program for a Competition for a Proposed General Architecture Plan, pp. 4–9, Washington State Library.

63. Wilder & White, "Capitol Group at Olympia for the State of Washington," *The American Architect,* vol. CVIII, part 2 (November 14, 1915), pp. 337–46, 349–50.

64. Daniel H. Burnham, Design Report, Chicago, July 11, 1906, The State Historical Society of Wisconsin.

65. William A. Van Deusen to Rufus F. Wells, Hollywood, California, July 24, 1968, The State Historical Society of Wisconsin.

CHAPTER VII

1. Joseph H. Freedlander, "Designing Capitol Buildings," *The Architectural Forum,* vol. XLVI (June 1927), pp. 504–08.

2. Cass Gilbert, Jr., to William Seale, Washington, D.C., May 12, 1973, in conversation.

3. Egerton Swartwout, "The Missouri State Capitol," *The Architectural Record,* vol. LXI (February 1927), pp. 105–20.

4. Egerton Swartwout to Mrs. Earl F. Nelson, New York, April 21, 1917, Western Historical Manuscripts Collection, The University of Missouri.

5. Oklahoma Capitol Commission, Minutes, October 4, 1913, Oklahoma State Archives.

6. Cass Gilbert, Jr., to William Seale, Washington, D.C., May 12, 1974, in conversation.

7. Nebraska Capitol Commission, "Nebraska State Capitol Competition," *The American Architect,* vol. CXVIII, pt. 1 (July 21, 1920), pp. 79–80.

8. Thomas Kimball, Competition Program, Stage I, 1920, Nebraska State Historical Society.

9. "The Nebraska State Capitol," *The American Architect,* vol. CXXI (May 10, 1922), pp. 375–81.

10. Thomas P. Kimball to Bertram G. Goodhue, Omaha, July 17, 1920; Bertram G. Goodhue to W. E. Hardy, Esq., New York, September 28, 1921, Nebraska State Historical Society.

11. F. H. Cunningham, *The Capitol: Lincoln, Nebraska* (Lincoln: 1931).

12. Charles Harris Whitaker *et al.,* "The Nebraska State Capitol," *The American Architect,* vol. MXLV (October 1934), pp. 4–93.

13. Fred B. Humphrey to W. E. Hardy, Lincoln, July 7, 1920, Nebraska State Historical Society.

14. Bertram G. Goodhue to W. E. Hardy Esq., New York, May 25, 1921, Nebraska State Historical Society.

15. *Ibid.*

16. *Ibid.*

17. Austin Whittlesey, Report of the Meeting with the Capitol Commission on January 14, 1921, same date, Nebraska State Historical Society.

18. Bertram G. Goodhue to W. E. Hardy, Esq., Lincoln, June 22, 1921, Nebraska State Historical Society.

19. Bertram G. Goodhue to W. E. Hardy, Esq., New York, June 14, 1921, Nebraska State Historical Society.

20. Bertram G. Goodhue to Lee Lawrie, New York, March 13, 1924, as told by H. B. Alexander in a letter to Charles W. Bryan, Lincoln, May 20, 1924, Nebraska State Historical Society.

21. Bertram G. Goodhue to Dr. H. B. Alexander, New York, December 1, 1923, as later quoted by Dr. Alexander in a letter he wrote to Charles W. Bryan, Lincoln, May 20, 1924, Nebraska State Historical Society.

22. *Ibid.,* January 25, 1924.

23. Bertram G. Goodhue to W. E. Hardy, Esq., New York, December 6, 1920, Nebraska State Historical Society.

24. Report of the Advisory, May 1929, Archives, The Colonial Willamsburg Foundation.

25. Solis Seiferth to Arthur Scully, Jr., as written by Scully to William Seale, New Orleans, June 22, 1972; *see also* Julius Dreyfous to William Seale, New Orleans, May 3, 1972, Capitols File, Victorian Society in America.

26. *The Morning Advocate,* May 16, 1932.

27. Loredo Taft to Leon C. Weiss, Chicago, January 30, 1922, Collection of Solis Seiferth.

28. Weiss, Dreyfous & Seiferth to the Honorable Huey P. Long, New Orleans, February 17, 1930, Collection of Solis Seiferth.

29. North Dakota Capitol Commission, Report, 1935, p. 5; *see also* Minutes for July 7, 1931; Capitol Investigation Committee Minutes for January 19, 1933; and Capitol Commission, *Report* (Bismarck: 1932), North Dakota State Historical Society.

30. North Dakota Capitol Commission, Minutes, June 24 and July 7, 1931; *see also* the Committee of Investigation Minutes for January 19, 1933, North Dakota State Historical Society.

31. Statehouse Committee of Delaware, *Report* (Dover: January 26, 1931), p. 6.

32. Walter H. Thomas, "The Oregon State Capitol Commission," *Pencil Points,* vol. XVII (July 1936), p. 359.

33. *Guide to the California State Capitol* (Sacramento: May 15, 1953), pp. 2–3.

34. Pyle Commission, *Report* (Phoenix: 1954), Arizona State Archives.

35. Frank Lloyd Wright to Jeffery Ellis Aronin, taped interview, New York, December 1957, Collection of Jeffery Ellis Aronin.

36. Frank Lloyd Wright, *Oasis: Plan for Arizona State Capitol* (Phoenix: 1957).

37. *Ibid.*

38. Cyril Lemmon and Francis S. Haines to William Seale, Honolulu, February 15, 1972, in conversation.

39. Belt, Lemmon & Lo and John Carl Warnecke & Associates, *Preliminary Plans for the Capitol Building for the State of Hawaii* (Honolulu: 1961).

40. Cyril Lemmon to William Seale, Honolulu, February 15, 1972, in conversation.

41. *Ibid.*

PRINCIPAL SOURCES

ALABAMA

1. *Cahaba Capitol*, 1818–1820; demolished 1833, and the cupola placed on the Lowndesboro, Alabama African Methodist Episcopal Church, where it remains.

Alabama House of Representatives, *Journal* (Cahaba: 1820).

Bibb, William W., Notice, Coosada, Alabama, March 1, 1819, Alabama State Archives.

Brantley, William H., *Three Capitals: A Book About the First Three Capitals of Alabama* (Boston: 1947).

2. *Tuscaloosa Capitol*, 1827–1830; burned 1914, having been in use as a Female Institute for half a century.

Alabama House and Senate, *Journals* (Tuscaloosa: 1828).

The Huntsville Democrat, July 31, 1829.

The Huntsville Southern Advocate, April 30, 1830, and April 28, 1832.

Jennings, Samuel R. and J. M., Inventory of Furniture of the State Capitol, Tuscaloosa 1850, Alabama State Archives.

Kennedy, J. R., Jr., "Examples of the Greek Revival Period in Alabama," *The Brickbuilder*, vol. XIII (June–July 1904), pp. 121–24 and pp. 144–47.

Nichols, William, to the State of Alabama, May 15, 1827, Auditor's Records, Alabama State Archives.

3. *First Montgomery Capitol*, 1846–1847; burned 1849.

Capitol Commissioners to William Garrett, Montgomery, n.d., Alabama State Archives.

The Euphala Democrat, December 25, 1845.

The Greensboro Beacon, April 25, 1848.

The Huntsville Democrat, November 24, 1847.

The Mobile Daily Herald and Tribune, December 15 and 16, 1849.

Webster, Richard J., "Stephen D. Button: Italianate Stylist," unpublished M.A. thesis, University of Delaware, 1963.

The Wetumpka State Guard, December 15, 1849.

4. *Second Montgomery Capitol*, 1850–1852; expanded 1885–1886 and restored and further expanded 1903–1911, and still in use as the state Capitol.

Alabama Capitol Commission, *Report* (Montgomery: September 15, 1915).

Historic American Buildings Survey, *Report* (Washington, D.C.: 1935).

The Montgomery Advertiser and State Gazette, April 16 and 30, May 11, June 4, and September 3, 1850.

Olmsted, Frederick Law, and J. C. Olmsted to Thomas Seay, Springfield, Massachusetts, n.d., Alabama State Archives; *see also* Olmsted Brothers and State of Alabama, Contract for Landscape Work, August 21, 1928, Alabama State Archives; and Henry Hubbard to James C. Gregg, Brookline, Mass., February 12, 1943, State Planning Board Files, State of Alabama.

ALASKA

1. *Alaska State Capitol*, 1929–1931; concrete cornice removed in 1957, and the chambers gutted and rebuilt in 1969. Still in use as Capitol.

Alaskans United, *The Capitol Should Stay in Juneau* (Juneau: n.d.).

Parks, George R., *Address* (Juneau[?]: 1931).

Typescript, "The Capitol Plaza on Chicken Ridge," Juneau, n.d., Alaska State Library.

Wetmore, James, files of the Office of the Supervising Architect of the United States Treasury as they apply to the construction of the Federal and Territorial Building (now the Alaska State Capitol), Washington, D.C., Chicago, and Juneau, 1927–1932, National Archives.

ARIZONA

1. *Arizona State Capitol*, 1899–1900; first west wing added 1918–1920, second west wing added 1938–1939, and separate Senate and House wings added 1957–1960. Still in use as Capitol.

The Arizona Republican, March 14, September 11 and 15, October 29, 1890; January 13, March 4, May 22, 1899; and November 29, 1900.

Arizona Capitol Commission, Biennial Report, 1898, Department of Library and Archives of Arizona.

Capitol Site Commission, Report, 1891, Department of Library and Archives of Arizona.

Gordon, J. Riley, The Capitol of Arizona, San Antonio, Texas, n.d. (c. 1900), Department of Library and Archives of Arizona.

John Carl Warnecke & Associates, with Hart, Krabatsky and Stubbe, *Arizona State Capitol Complex* [proposal] (Phoenix and San Francisco: 1968).

Miller, Joseph, Arizona State Capitol, 1864–1919, unpublished manuscript, 1957, Department of Library and Archives of Arizona.

———, The Capitol Additions of 1918–1919, unpublished manuscript, 1957, Department of Library and Archives of Arizona.

The Phoenix Herald, February 10 and March 1, 1890; *see also* March 27, 1891.

Theodore Barry & Associates, *Capitol Complex Space Planning Study* [proposals] (Phoenix: 1968).

State Planning and Building Commission, *Report* (Phoenix: 1956).

———, *Proposed State Capitol Building* (Phoenix: 1957).

2. *The Frank Lloyd Wright Proposal*, 1957; not built.

Aronin, Jeffrey, Frank Lloyd Wright Tapes, recorded in New York variously in the late summer and autumn of 1958, Jeffrey Ellis Aronin Collection.

Associated State Capitol Architects, *Plan for the Arizona State Capitol* (Phoenix: 1957).

"Proposed State Capitol for Arizona by Frank Lloyd Wright," *Architectural Forum*, vol. CVI (April 1957), p. 108.

Spectrum, Albert B., Background Statement of Events Leading Up to the Wright Controversy, Phoenix, April 18, 1957, Department of Library and Archives of Arizona.

Wright, Frank Lloyd, *Oasis* (Scottsdale: February 23, 1957).

ARKANSAS

1. *Little Rock Capitol*, 1833–1840; remodeled and expanded 1885 and restored as a museum 1948–1950.

The Arkansas Gazette, June 26, July 3, 10, 17, 24, October 2, 1833; January 1, July 29, 1831; November 15, 29, 1836; May 23, 1837; November 21, 1838.

Commissioner of Public Buildings, *Report* (Little Rock: November 3, 1838).

Donaghey, George W., *Building a State Capitol* (Little Rock: 1937).

Ferguson, John L., *The Old Statehouse: Some Questions and Answers* (Little Rock: 1968).

Historic American Buildings Survey, *The War Memorial Building* (Little Rock and Washington, D.C.: 1936).

Kennan, Clara B., "Arkansas' Old Statehouse," *Arkansas Historical Quarterly*, vol. IX (Spring 1950), pp. 33–42.

Arkansas Senate, *Journals of the Legislative Council* (Little Rock: October 22, 1831).

———, *Journals* [including the Governor's report] *of the Legislative Council* (Little Rock: November 7, 1837).

———, *Journals* (Little Rock: September 17, 1836).

Vaughn, Myra McAlmont, "A History of the Old State House," *Arkansas Historical Association Publication*, vol. III (1911), pp. 249–55.

2. *Arkansas State Capitol*, 1899–1916; still in use as Capitol.

"Arkansas State Capitol, Little Rock, Arkansas," *The American Architect and Building News*, vol. LXXI (March 2, 1901), p. 71.

Arkansas State Planning Board, *Report on the Capitol* (Little Rock: 1937).

Blackwood, John W., *In the Matter of the Adjustment Suit with Caldwell & Drake . . . Abstract of the Record and Testimony* (Little Rock: 1915).

Day, Frank Miles, *Report* (Asticoro, Maine: September 3, 1901).

General Assembly Joint Committee on the State Capitol, Report, Little Rock, 1907, Arkansas History Commission.

Records and Testimony, State Supreme Court of Arkansas, Special Arbitration Court, December 1916, Supreme Court of Arkansas.

State Capitol Commission of Arkansas, Minutes 1899–1909, Arkansas History Commission.

State Planning Board, *Report* (Little Rock: 1937).

Treon, John A., "Politics and Concrete: The Building of the Arkansas State Capitol," *The Arkansas Historical Quarterly*, vol. XXXI (Summer 1972), pp. 99–149.

CALIFORNIA

1. *Benicia Capitol*, 1852; used as a municipal structure after its brief term as Capitol and restored as a historic site by the state in 1956.

California Department of Parks and Recreation, *Benicia Capitol: State Historic Park* (Benicia: 1956).

Vouchers and Inventories 1853–1856 pertaining to the Benicia Capitol, California State Archives.

2. *Reuben Clark Project*, 1856; never built.

Capitol Commission of California, Reports, Correspondence, Vouchers 1856–1858, California State Archives.

Clark, Reuben, plans and elevations of his project, 1854–1856, California State Archives.

The San Francisco Bulletin, April 21, 1857.

3. *California State Capitol*, 1860–1878; remodeled 1906–1908 and again in 1928, then expanded 1949–1952. In use as the Capitol.

"California's Capitol: New East Wing," *Architect and Engineer*, vol. XCIII (April 1953), pp. 25–27, 45.

California Capitol Commission, Correspondence, Reports and Vouchers 1860–1878, California State Archives.

————, Minutes and Proceedings 1863–1867; also 1868–1878, California State Archives.

————, Specifications for The New Capitol, Sacramento and San Francisco, May 19, 1862, California State Archives.

Department of Finance, *California State Capitol* (Sacramento: 1960).

Jaqueth, H. H., "Public Building Group Planned for Tree Shaded Mall," *American City*, vol. LVI (January 1941), p. 79.

Joint Committee on Public Buildings, *Report* (Sacramento: 1868).

The Sacramento Daily Union, May 22, 1860.

Statutes of California, 1856, 1861, 1872.

Vouchers and construction bids to the Capitol Commission and the Governor, San Francisco, October 27, 30, 31, and November 1, 1856, California State Archives.

COLORADO

1. *Colorado State Capitol*, 1886–1909; still in use as Capitol.

Board of Capitol Managers, Biennial *Reports* 1–6 (Denver: 1885, 1887, 1889, 1891, 1893).

————, Letterpress books, Minutes 1883–1886, vouchers and correspondence 1893–1904.

Geddus & Seerie, Estimate Books, I, II and III, Colorado State Archives.

MacMechen, Edgar C., ed., *Robert A. Speer: A City Builder* (Denver: 1919).

CONNECTICUT

1. *Hartford Statehouse*, 1793–1797; cupola added c. 1827–1829; after its abandonment as a Capitol in the 1880's the statehouse served municipal and county functions until its restoration as a museum in 1911–1921.

Benjamin, Asher, *The Architect or Practical House Carpenter* (Boston: 1841).

Brainard, Newton C., *The Hartford Statehouse of 1796* (Hartford: 1964).

Bulfinch, Susan Ellen, ed., *The Life and Letters of Charles Bulfinch, Architect* (Boston: 1896).

Historic American Buildings Survey, *Report* (Hartford and Washington, D.C.: 1936 and 1965).

Keller, George, "Letter to the Editor: Hartford," *The American Architect*, vol. LXXI (January 7, 1895).

Municipal Art Society of Hartford, *The Old Statehouse: Why It Should Be Preserved* (Hartford: 1911).

Place, Charles A., *Charles Bulfinch: Architect and Citizen* (Boston: 1925).

Statehouse Investigating Committee, *Reports* 1803–1804, Connecticut Historical Society.

Vouchers, Connecticut Comptroller's Office 1793–1801, Connecticut State Library.

2. *First New Haven Statehouse*, 1763–1765; remodeled immediately after the Revolution and again after the War of 1812; demolished in 1830 before the temple Capitol was completed.

Committee on the New Haven Statehouse, Report, June 28, 1826 and Report 1827, New Haven Colony Historical Society.

Doolittle, Amos, Map of New Haven 1824, New Haven Colony Historical Society.

3. *Second New Haven Statehouse*, 1827–1832; in use until the completion of the permanent Capitol at Hartford, when it was demolished.

Buckingham, J. S., *The Eastern and Western States of America*, vol. I (London: 1842).

Building Committee, Furnishings Report, 1829, New Haven Colony Historical Society.

"The Old New Haven Statehouse," *The American Architect and Building News*, vol. XXII (December 31, 1887), p. 316.

Town, Ithiel, Papers, New Haven Colony Historical Society.

4. *Jewett Proposals*, 1857; never built.

Jewett, F. S., oil painting on canvas, "proposed capitol, charter oak place, 1857," Connecticut Historical Society.

5. *Connecticut State Capitol*, 1873–1879; with few changes, still in use as the Capitol.

Batterson, James G., *Remonstrances* (Hartford: 1875).

Capitol Commission, vouchers, correspondence, reports, minutes, 1871–1886, Department of Legislative Research, Connecticut General Assembly.

Hersey, George L., "Replication Replicated, or Notes on American Bastardy," *Perspecta* nos. 9–10 (1965), pp. 211–48.

Jacobus, Melancthon W., "The Hartford State

Capitol," *The Connecticut Historical Society Bulletin*, vol. XXXIII (April 1968), pp. 41–72.

———, "The Soldiers and Sailors Memorial in Hartford," *The Connecticut Historical Society Bulletin*, vol. XXXIV (April 1969), pp. 33–64.

Joint Special Committee on the Dome of the Capitol, Investigation into its Safety, February and March 1879, Department of Legislative Research, Connecticut General Assembly.

"A Model State Capitol," *Harper's Monthly Magazine*, vol. LXXI (October 1885), pp. 715–34.

State Capitol Government Center Commission, *Connecticut Capitol Center* (Hartford: 1967).

Upjohn, Richard M., Elevations and Working Drawings, 1872–1878, Connecticut State Library.

———, *The State Capitol, Hartford, Connecticut* (Boston: 1886).

DELAWARE

1. *Dover Statehouse*, 1789–1796; expanded 1836, remodeled into a mansarded building 1873–1874; restored 1910, 1925, and 1973–1976.

Commissioners for Building a Courthouse and Offices in Dover, Report of December 19, 1787, Delaware State Archives.

Holcomb, Chauncey P., correspondence with Mrs. J. E. Hays, New Castle, Delaware, March 28, 1941, Georgia State Archives.

Journals of the House and Senate (Dover: 1909–1911).

Memoranda, transcripts, and various original manuscript papers relating to the Old Statehouse, Delaware State Archives.

Scharf, Thomas J., *History of Delaware* (Philadelphia: 1888).

"Statement by Mrs. Mabel Lloyd Ridgely on the restoration of the old Statehouse," Dover, Summer 1960, Delaware State Archives.

Tilton, Edward L., "Restoration and Addition: Delaware State Capitol, Dover, Delaware," *Architecture*, vol. XXI (May 15, 1910), p. 70.

2. *State Legislative Hall*, 1931–1933; wings added 1968–1969.

Buck, Governor C. Douglas, Cornerstone Address, July 3, 1933. Delaware State Archives.

Legislative Building Commission, *Report* (Dover: 1966).

Legislative Hall File, newspaper clippings, letters, and contracts, Delaware State Archives.

Martin, William E., plans, elevations, and specifications for the Legislative Hall, Delaware State Archives.

Statehouse Committee, *Report* (Dover: January 6, 1931).

FLORIDA

1. *Tallahassee Capitol*, 1825; demolished in an unfinished state in 1841.

House Journal (Tallahassee: 1839).

Kilgore, John, manuscript history of the Florida State Capitol, n.d., Florida State Archives.

Senate Journal (Tallahassee: 1839).

2. *Florida State Capitol*, 1841–1845; cupola added 1891; the building expanded 1901, 1921–1922, and still in use as Capitol.

Acts of Florida 1839–1845 (Tallahassee: 1845).

Adjutant General, *Reports* (Tallahassee: 1872, 1874, 1879, 1880, 1887–1889, and 1892).

Board of Commissioners of State Institutions, *Report, 1965–1967* (Tallahassee: 1967).

Capitol Center Planning Committee, *Report 1965–1967* (Tallahassee: 1967).

Florida Centennial Commission, *Florida Becomes a State* (Tallahassee: 1945).

The Florida Herald, October 10, 1839.

Hutchinson, Charles, to his sister, Tallahassee, September 1, 1840. Board of Trustees of the Internal Improvement Trust Fund, State of Florida.

Statutes at Large (Washington: 1839 and 1844), acts of Congress for March 3, 1839, and June 14, 1844.

GEORGIA

1. *Milledgeville Capitol*, 1805–1811; remodeled and expanded 1826–1829, burned 1941, and reconstructed 1942–1943.

Beeson, Leola Selman, "The Old State Capitol in Milledgeville and Its Cost," *The Georgia Historical Quarterly*, vol. IV (September 1950), pp. 195–202.

Committee of the Town of Milledgeville, correspondence and minutes 1804–1815, Georgia State Archives.

Hamilton Fulton Papers, Georgia State Archives.

Mitchell, Ella, *The History of Washington County* (Atlanta: 1924).

2. *Georgia State Capitol*, 1884–1889; with few changes, still in use as the Capitol.

Board of Capitol Commissioners, *First Annual Report* (Atlanta: 1884).

———, *Second Annual Report* (Atlanta: 1886).

———, *Final Annual Report* (Atlanta: 1889).

———, minutes, correspondence, vouchers, and various bills and bids, 1868–1900, Georgia State Archives.

HAWAII

1. *Iolani Palace,* 1879–1883; in use as a Royal Palace until 1893, then as a Capitol until 1969. Restored 1969–1975 as a museum.

Cliver, E. Blaine, and Geoffrey W. Fairfax, *Iolani Palace Restoration Architectural Report* (Honolulu: 1972).

"Coronation at Hawaii," *Lippincott's Magazine,* vol. XXXIII (April 1883), p. 37.

Peterson, Charles E., "The Iolani Palaces and Barracks," *Journal of the Society of Architectural Historians,* vol. XXII (May 1963), pp. 91–103.

The Commercial and Pacific Adventurer, January 3 and 17, 1880.

The Hawaiian Gazette, December 9, 1874, December 10, 1879, and March 31, 1880.

2. *Hawaii State Capitol,* 1965–1969; still in use as Capitol.

"A New State Capitol for the Newest State," *Architectural Record,* vol. CXXIX (June 1961), pp. 153–56.

Belt, Lemmon & Lo, and John Carl Warnecke & Associates, *Preliminary Plan of the Capitol Building for the State of Hawaii* (Honolulu: 1961).

Lemmon, Freeth, Haines & Farell, Drawings by the Office of Belt, Lemmon & Lo, 1965, Office of Lemmon Freeth, Haines & Farell, Honolulu, Hawaii.

Lemmon, Cyril W. to William Seale, interview, Honolulu, February 15, 1972, Victorian Society in America.

Territorial Planning Office, *Report* (Honolulu: 1959).

IDAHO

1. *Boise Territorial and State Capitol,* 1885–1886; demolished in 1912.

The Avalanche, June 13, 1885.

Idaho State Historical Society, *Reference Series: Leaflet #132, Old State Capitol* (Boise: n.d.).

Thirteenth Legislature, *Journals* (Boise: 1884).

2. *Idaho State Capitol,* 1905–1912; wings added according to original scheme, 1919–1920; the building is still the Capitol.

Capitol Commission, records, correspondence, vouchers 1905–1912, 1919, and 1920. Idaho State Historical Society.

———, First, second, third, and fourth *Biennial Reports* (Boise: 1912–1915).

Tourtellotte, J. E., *Capitol of Idaho* (Boise: 1913).

———, "Idaho State Capitol Building," *Pacific Coast Architect,* vol. VIII (1914), pp. 11–12.

ILLINOIS

1. *Illinois State Capitol,* 1837–1854; raised a full story from the ground level in 1899; demolished and reconstructed as a museum 1965–1968.

Abraham Lincoln Association, *The Illinois State Capitol 1839–1876* (Springfield: n.d.).

Bingham, Charles C., *Old Statehouse: Life and Life Anew* (Springfield: 1968).

Board of Auditors and Board of Capitol Commissioners, Journals, February 2, 1841–September 21, 1853, Illinois State Archives.

Ferry & Henderson, Architects, *Old Capitol Complex* (Springfield: 1965).

———, Capitol study records, office files, Ferry & Henderson, Springfield, Illinois.

Henderson, Earl W., "Sleuthing the mid-1800's," *Journal of the American Institute of Architects,* vol. XLVIII (November 1967), pp. 56–62.

Rague, John F., "Report" in the *Senate Journal 1838–1839* (Springfield: 1839).

Smith, C. Ray, "Restored National Monument Sparks Urban Revitalization," *Progressive Architecture* (February 1970), pp. 52–63.

2. *Illinois State Capitol,* 1869–1888; main entrance steps removed 1900. Still in use as the Capitol.

Capitol Commissioners, correspondence and minutes 1869–1871, Illinois State Archives.

Illinois General Assembly, *Information on the Illinois Statehouse in Five Parts,* 5 vols. (Springfield: 1869, 1871, 1873, 1875, and 1879).

"Public Buildings in Illinois: The New Statehouse," *The American Architect and Building News,* vol. II (February 24, 1877), pp. 61–62.

INDIANA

1. *Indianapolis Statehouse,* 1832–1835; demolished 1886.

Davis, A. J., Daybook, vol. I, New York Public Library.

———, Capitol of Indiana, manuscript description probably written in the 1880's, New York Public Library.

Schraeder, Christian, A Little History Started But Discontinued, Indiana State Library.

Town, Ithiel, copy of his contract for the Indiana Capitol, 1832, Indiana State Library.

2. *Indiana State Capitol,* 1878–1888; remodeled 1965

and still in use as the Capitol.

"Capitol Bill," *The American Architect and Building News*, vol. II (March 1877), pp. 98–100.

Indiana Historical Bureau, *The Indiana Capitol* (Indianapolis: 1938).

"The Indiana Statehouse," *The American Architect and Building News*, vol. XXXIX (February 18, 1893), pp. 79–109.

The Indianapolis Centinnel, December 31, 1877.

The Lansing (Michigan) *Republican*, June 1, 1877.

May, Edwin, *Description of the New Statehouse to Be Erected at Indianapolis*, 2 vols. (Indianapolis: 1878).

May, Edwin, and Adolph Scherrer, plans and specifications for the new statehouse 1876–1888, Indiana State Library.

Statehouse Commission, papers, correspondence, vouchers, minutes 1877–1888, Indiana State Library.

Statehouse Commission, *Report to the Governor* (Indianapolis: 1879–1881, 1884, and 1886).

IOWA

1. *Iowa City Capitol*, 1840–1842; remodeled 1921–1924 by the University of Iowa and restored as a museum 1972–1976.

House of Representatives, *Journal* (Iowa City: various times from 1841 to 1852).

Journal of the Council of the Legislative Assembly (Iowa City: 1833–1846).

Keyes, Margaret, Old Capitol materials for the Old Capitol Restoration Committee, various notes and files compiled in the course of restoration research, Old Capitol, Iowa City, Iowa.

————, "Old Capitol," *Annals of Iowa*, vol. XLII (Summer 1973), pp. 1–16.

Shambaugh, Benjamin F., "This Town," *The Palimpsest*, vol. XX (May 1939), pp. 137–76.

————, *Iowa City: A Contribution to the Early History of Iowa* (Iowa City: 1893).

————, *Executive Journal of Iowa 1838–1841* (Iowa City: 1906).

2. *Iowa State Capitol*, 1871–1887; dome revised 1879–1880. The building is still the Capitol.

Board of Capitol Commissioners, *Biennial Reports* (Des Moines: 1872, 1873–1883).

"Iowa State Capitol," *The American Architect and Building News*, vol. II (October 13, 1877), p. 325.

Piquenard & Cochrane, Specifications for the Iowa State Capitol, Illinois State Library.

KANSAS

1. *Lecompton State Capitol*, 1856; abandoned at foundation stage.

Ballou's Pictorial Magazine, July 5, 1856.

"Kansas in 1855," *Debow's Review*, vol. XIX (April 1855), p. 185.

2. *Kansas State Capitol*, 1869–1873 (east wing), 1879–1880 (west wing), 1891–1903 (central portion); entire building renovated in 1965–1969 and still in use as Capitol.

Adams, Franklin, "The Capitols of Kansas," *Kansas Historical Collection*, vol. VIII (1903–1904), pp. 331–51.

Office of the State Architect, plans and elevations c. 1871–1966.

Richmond, Robert W., "Kansas Builds a Capitol," *Kansas Historical Quarterly*, vol. XXXVIII (Autumn 1972), pp. 249–267.

State Capitol Commission, minutes, correspondence, and some vouchers and bids, 1866–1888, Kansas State Historical Society.

————, scrapbooks and notebooks and reports 1867–1909, Kansas State Historical Society.

KENTUCKY

1. *Second Frankfort Statehouse*, 1814–1816; central building burned 1824.

Collins, Lewis, *History of Kentucky* (Covington: 1878).

Hardin, Bayless E., "The Capitols of Kentucky," *The Register of the Kentucky Historical Society*, vol. XLIV (1945), pp. 2–34.

The Greenfield (Massachusetts) *Gazette*, December 30, 1824.

2. *Third Frankfort Statehouse*, 1828–1830; by the later nineteenth century one flanker had burned and the other was removed. The wing of a proposed new Capitol was built adjacent to the old statehouse, but that project was abandoned. The government moved out in 1909; the building became a museum and was restored 1973–1976.

Andrews, Alfred, "Gideon Shryock—Kentucky Architect and the Greek Revival Architecture in Kentucky," *The Filson Club Quarterly*, vol. X (April 1944), pp. 67–77.

The Argus of Western America, January 17–31, 1827.

Federal Writer's Project, *Old Capitol and Frankfort Guide* (Frankfort: 1939).

Field, Elizabeth Shryock, "Gideon Shryock, His Life and Work," *The Register of the Kentucky*

Historical Society, vol. II (April 1952), pp. 111–29.

Haggard, John, "The Architecture of Gideon Shryock," M.A. Thesis, University of Virginia, 1971.

House of Representatives, *Journals* (Frankfort: 1827, 1828, 1829, and 1830).

Lancaster, Clay, "Gideon Shryock and John McMurtry," *Art Quarterly*, vol. LVI (August 1943), pp. 257–75.

Old State Capitol, files of William Barrow Floyd, Curator, Old State Capitol Restoration, Frankfort.

Shryock, Gideon, "The Kentucky Statehouse," *Atkinson's Casket: Gems of Literature, Wit and Sentiment*, vol. III (1833), pp. 553–54.

3. *Kentucky State Capitol*, 1905–1909; still in use as the Capitol.

Board of State Capitol Commissioners, *Financial Report* (Frankfort: January 1, 1910).

———, *Report of the Retiring Board as Presented to the Superintendent of Construction* (Frankfort: December 1907).

Fleenor, C. M., *Kentucky's New State Capitol and Its Construction* (Frankfort: 1910).

Gilbert, Cass, correspondence with G. H. Carsley, New York, June 7, 1909, Minnesota Historical Society.

Project Engineer's daybook 1905–1909, University of Kentucky Library.

"The New Capitol," *Register of the Kentucky State Historical Society*, vol. VI (September 1908), pp. 6–14.

LOUISIANA

1. *Contrôle de la Marine*, 1760; wings added probably in the 1780's; the building burned in 1828.

Inventory of Buildings Belonging to the French Government in New Orleans, July 25, 1767, National Archives of France.

Repair Bill, n.d. (1789–1794) and construction account, Casa del Governador, Nueva Orleans, Archives of the Indies.

Wilson, Samuel, ed., *Benjamin Latrobe's Impressions of New Orleans* (New York: 1951).

2. *Second New Orleans Statehouse*, 1815; occupied by the government 1834 and demolished 1850.

Nichols, William, various legal documents, May 1828 through November 1836, Acts of Notary William Christy, New Orleans Notarial Archives.

"Specifications of work to be done on Government Houses . . . on Canal Street, according to the plans made by Mr. Wm Nichols," June 25, 1835,

Acts of W. Y. Lewis, New Orleans Notarial Archives.

Zimple, Charles F., map of the city of New Orleans with cartouche showing the statehouse, 1834, Library of Congress.

3. *First Baton Rouge Capitol*, 1847–1849; burned 1862, reconstructed 1882 and restored as a museum 1970–1972.

Afleck, Thomas, papers 1858–1859, Louisiana State University Library.

Dakin, James, diary 1847–1850, Louisiana State University Library.

Quitman, Annie Rosalie, diary 1854, Louisiana State University Library.

Scully, Arthur, Jr., *James Dakin, Architect* (Baton Rouge: 1973).

4. *Louisiana State Capitol*, 1931–1932; virtually unchanged except for the reconstruction of the Senate in 1972 after the chamber's total destruction by dynamite. Still in use as the Capitol.

The Baton Rouge Morning Advocate, May 16, 1972.

Dreyfus, Julius to William Seale, New Orleans, May 3 and 29, 1972, The Victorian Society in America.

J. Fair Hardin papers, Louisiana State University Library.

Scully, Arthur, Jr., interview with Solis Seiferth, New Orleans, June 22, 1972, Victorian Society in America.

Seiferth, Solis, papers of Weiss, Dreyfous & Seiferth, New Orleans, Collection of Solis Seiferth.

Weiss, Dreyfous & Seiferth, "Louisiana State Capitol, Baton Rouge," *Architectural Forum*, vol. XXXLV (December 1932), pp. 519–34.

MAINE

1. *First Maine Statehouse*, 1828–1831; remodeled 1852, wing added to rear 1890–1891. Structure demolished 1909, except for the Bulfinch portico, and rebuilt much larger.

Bulfinch, Charles, drawings for the Maine Statehouse, 103 sheets, Washington and Boston, April 15, 1829, through April 17, 1830, Maine State Library.

Commissioners of public buildings, accounts, 1829–1832. Maine State Library.

McLanathan, Richard B. K., "Bulfinch and the Maine Statehouse," Ph.D. Thesis, Harvard University, 1951.

———, "Bulfinch's Drawings for the Maine Statehouse," *Journal of the Society of Architectural*

Historians, vol. XIV (May 1955), pp. 12–17.

Reuel Williams Papers, Maine Historical Society.

Superintendent of Building, continuing property inventories 1828–1873, Public Buildings Office, state of Maine.

William King Papers, Maine Historical Society.

2. *Maine State Capitol*, 1909–1910; remains in use as the Capitol.

Capitol Planning Commission, *Report* (Augusta: 1909).

Commission on the Enlargement of the Statehouse, *Report* (Augusta: 1911).

Federal Writer's Project, *Maine Capitol* (Augusta: 1939).

Governor's schedule of warrants, 1909–1915, Maine State Library.

MARYLAND

1. *Maryland Statehouse*, 1771–1779; steeple-dome added 1785–1787, octagonal rear bay demolished and replaced by great octagonal annex 1858, portions of the interior gutted and remodeled 1876–1878. Colonial Revival library annex added 1886, large porticoed annex replaced those earlier ones in 1902–1905. Various restorations undertaken in 1886, 1894, and 1902–1905. General renovation and free restoration of entire building 1937–1940, and again in 1947 and 1949. Still in use as the Capitol.

Anderson, Joseph Horatio (attributed), plans of the Maryland Statehouse, c. 1771–1779, The Johns Hopkins University Library.

Clark, Joseph, and Thomas Dance, carpenter's and plasterer's bills to the state of Maryland, 1792, Maryland Hall of Records.

Burne, Rosamond Randall, "Two Anonymous Annapolis Architects: Joseph Horatio Anderson and Robert Key," *Maryland Historical Magazine*, vol. XXV (March 1909), pp. 186–95.

Decouncey, Thomas, "The Old Senate Chamber," *Maryland Historical Magazine*, vol. XXV (December 1930), pp. 365–84.

"Description of the Statehouse at Annapolis, Maryland," *The Columbian Magazine* (February 7, 1789), pp. 81–84.

Executive papers, 1785 through 1791, Maryland Hall of Records.

Intendents' Letterbook #12, February 24, 1785, Maryland Hall of Records.

Proceedings of the Governor and Council (Annapolis: 1788–1791).

Radoff, Morris L., *The Statehouse at Annapolis* (Annapolis: 1972).

Ridgely, David, *Annals of Annapolis* (Baltimore: 1841).

State of Maryland, auditor's records, 1792, Maryland Hall of Records.

The Maryland Gazette, June 27, 1782, and December 25, 1783.

"The Maryland Statehouse," *The American Architect and Building News*, vol. II (June 16, 1877), p. 191.

Treasurer of the Western Shore, ledgers C, D, E, and F, Annapolis 1785–1789, Maryland Hall of Records.

Wallace, Charles, and Joshua Johnson, receipts and correspondence, Independents' Letterbook #1 and #2, 1771 through 1778, London and Annapolis, Maryland Hall of Records.

Wilson, J. Appleton, "Restoration of the Old Senate Chamber," *Maryland Historical Magazine*, vol. XXII (March 1927), pp. 54–62.

MASSACHUSETTS

1. *1712 Statehouse*, 1712–1714; partially burned 1747 and restored 1747–1750. Remodeled variously during the nineteenth century and restored in 1881. Now a museum known as the Old Statehouse.

Benton, Josiah, *The Story of the Old Boston Town House 1658–1711* (Boston: 1908).

Boston National Historic Sites Commission, *Study of the Old Statehouse*, House Document #107, United States Congress.

City Council of Boston, *Rededication of the Old State House* (Boston: 1887).

Read, Charles F., "The Old Statehouse and Its Predecessor the First Town House," *Bostonian Society Proceedings*, vols. XXVI–XXX (1908).

Whitehill, Walter M., *Boston: A Topographical History* (Boston: 1968).

2. *Massachusetts Statehouse*, 1795–1798; expanded 1831, and again in 1853–1855. Those additions were destroyed in 1886–1887; a new wing was begun at once and finished in 1895, at which time refurbishing began on the "Bulfinch Front." Side wings added 1913–1919.

Boston Evening Transcript, November 27, 1826.

Bostonian Society, Statehouse file, Bostonian Society, Old Statehouse.

Bowditch, Ernest W., *Landscape Proposals* (Boston: 1899).

Bryant, G. J. F., *Drawings of Additions and*

Proposed Additions to the Massachusetts Statehouse (Boston: 1867).

————, proposed additions and schemes for modifications, 1853–1854, Massachusetts State Archives.

Bulfinch, Charles, correspondence to "Gentlemen," Boston, November 5, 1787, Massachusetts State Archives.

Burrill, Ellen Mudge, research papers on the Boston Statehouse, Massachusetts State Library.

Centennial of the Bulfinch Statehouse, *Exercises Before the Legislature* (Boston: 1898).

Commission to Consider Remodeling the Statehouse, *Report* (Boston: 1887).

Commission to Enlarge the Statehouse, records and two volumes of minutes 1853–1855, Massachusetts State Archives.

Committee on the Statehouse, *Extension of the Statehouse of Massachusetts* (Boston: 1907).

Governor's Council of Massachusetts, records and warrants 1795–1832, Massachusetts State Archives.

Fay, Clement K., *Save the Statehouse* (Boston: 1889).

Hearings on the Preservation of the Bulfinch Front, 1888, Massachusetts State Library.

Hitchings, Sinclair H., and Catherine H. Farlow, *A New Guide to the Massachusetts Statehouse* (Boston: 1964).

Kirker, Harold and James, *Bulfinch's Boston 1787–1817* (New York: 1964).

Kirker, Harold, "Bulfinch's Design for the Massachusetts Statehouse," *Old Time New England* (Fall 1964), pp. 43–45.

"Massachusetts Statehouse," *The American Architect and Building News*, vol. XLVIII (June 29, 1895), p. 48.

Massachusetts Statehouse Commission, *Reports* (Boston: 1889 through 1902).

Mitchell, George, "Details of the Original Senate Chamber Massachusetts State Capitol Building," *Architecture*, vol. XXXII (December 1925), p. 22.

Pickens, Buford, "Wyatt's Pantheon, the State House in Boston and a New View of Bulfinch," *Journal of the Society of Architectural Historians*, vol. XXIX (May 1970), pp. 124–43.

Robbins, Edward H., various warrants, May 11, 1795, through November 27, 1802, Collection of William B. Osgood.

Roe, Alfred S., *The Old Representatives Hall 1798–1895* (Boston: 1895).

Rogers Isaiah, drawings for additions to the Massachusetts Statehouse, 1831, Massachusetts State Archives.

Sampson, Alden, and Arthur Rotch, "State House Reconstruction," reprinted from the *Boston Evening Transcript* 1898, broadside, Massachusetts State Library.

State House Agents, accounts and disbursements 1795–1799, Massachusetts State Archives.

State House Commission, *Report* (Boston: 1913).

Towle & Foster, *Proposed Additions* (Boston: 1853).

MICHIGAN

1. *Michigan State Capitol*, 1871–1878; major subdivision of existing office spaces 1970–1973. Otherwise unchanged, it is still in use as the Capitol.

Board of State Building Commissioners, correspondence, and some vouchers and bids 1871–1878, Michigan State Archives.

————, *Documents Relating to the Erection of the New Capitol of Michigan* (Lansing: 1871–1872, 1874, and 1877–1879).

Butler, Alexander R., "The New Capitol of Michigan 1871–1879," *Michigan History*, vol. XXXVIII (1954), pp. 273–84.

Crosby, Jack T., *The State Capitol of Michigan* (Lansing: 1968).

Duffield, George, *The New Capitol or The Wilderness Rejoicing* (Lansing: 1878).

Koellner, Martha Ann Kuepper, "Elijah Myers, Architect," M.A. Thesis, Western Illinois University, 1972.

"Michigan State Capitol Development," *Weekly Bulletin of the Michigan Society of Architects*, vol. XXI (February 25, 1947), p. 4.

Myers, Elijah E., plans and elevations for the Michigan Capitol 1871, Michigan State Archives.

Straham, Simon, various reports from the interior decorators 1874–1878, Michigan State Archives.

Stross, Allen, *The Michigan State Capitol* (Lansing: 1969).

Tenison, O. A., scrapbooks and newspaper clippings 1871–1890, State Library Services, Michigan Department of Education.

MINNESOTA

1. *Minnesota State Capitol*, 1851–1853; expanded 1872 and between 1876 and 1881, when it burned.

Commissioners of Public Buildings, specifications, abstracts of proposals, correspondence, bids 1851–1853, Minnesota State Archives.

Office of the Territorial Governor, letters received by Governor Alexander Ramsey 1850–1853, Minnesota State Archives.

2. *Temporary Capitol*, 1881–1905; demolished 1938.

Dean, William B., "A History of the Capitol Buildings of Minnesota With Some Account of the Struggles for Their Location," *Minnesota Historical Society Collections*, vol. XII (December 1908), pp. 1–42.

3. *Minnesota State Capitol*, 1896–1905; preserved by law 1967–1971 and still in use as the Capitol.

Board of State Capitol Commissioners, correspondence, vouchers, minutes 1893–1907, contracts 1896–1905, and scrapbooks 1903–1907, Minnesota State Archives.

Capitol Improvements Committee, *Report* (St. Paul: 1961).

Cass Gilbert Papers 1881–1884, Minnesota Historical Society.

———, 1897–1934, New-York Historical Society.

———, 1886–1934, Library of Congress.

———, watercolors and photographs, 1878–1934, Smithsonian Institution.

Channing Seabury Papers 1893–1897, Minnesota Historical Society.

Cox Kenyon, "The New State Capitol in Minnesota," *Architectural Record*, vol. XVIII (August 1905), pp. 94–113.

Fridley, Russell W., "Minnesota State Capitol," unpublished manuscript, Minnesota Historical Society.

Forster, Benjamin, *Guide to the Capitol of Minnesota* (St. Paul: 1905).

Gilbert, Cass, plans and elevations and various studies for the Minnesota Capitol 1895–1903, Minnesota Historical Society.

Gilbert, J. F., *Cass Gilbert: Reminiscences and Addresses* (New York: 1935).

Minnesota Department of Administration, *The Minnesota Capitol, Official Guide and History* (St. Paul: 1963).

"Minnesota State Capitol," *The Western Architect* vol. IV (October 1905), pp. 3–32.

"Mural and Sculptural Decoration of the St. Paul Capitol," *International Studio*, vol. XXVI (October 1905), pp. 81–94.

Nichols, A. R., "State Center for Minnesota: A Proper Setting for the Minnesota State Capitol," *State Government*, vol. XIX (January 1946), pp. 14–16.

Pattison, J. W., "Blashfield's Mural Decorations in the Capitol of Minnesota," *International Studio*, vol. XXIV (February 1905), pp. 87–91.

Robinson, Charles Mulford, "Ambition of Three Cities," *Architectural Record*, vol. XXI (May 1907), pp. 337–46.

Sturgis, Russell, "Minnesota State Capitol, Cass Gilbert, Architect," *Architectural Record*, vol. XIX (January 1906), pp. 31–36.

MISSISSIPPI

1. *First Jackson Capitol*, 1833–1839; restored 1959–1961 and presently a museum.

Board of Capitol Commissioners, "Report," *House Journal* (Jackson: 1840).

Committee to Investigate the Statehouse, "Report," *House Journal* (Jackson: 1836).

Committee On Public Buildings, Report February 12, 1840, Mississippi Department of Archives and History.

Laist, Theodore, "Two Early Mississippi Valley State Capitols," *The Western Architect*, vol. XXXV (May 1926), pp. 53–59.

McCain, William D., *The Story of Jackson*, vol. I (Jackson: 1953).

The Mississippian, November 28, 1834.

Notary Records of New Orleans, Acts of William Christy, May 11, 1834.

Rowland, Mrs. Dunbar, *The History of Mississippi's Old Capitol and the Movement for Its Preservation* (Natchez: 1916).

Taylor, J. R., "Capitol Buildings of Mississippi," *Official and Statistical Register of the State of Mississippi* (Nashville: 1904).

2. *Mississippi State Capitol*, 1901–1903; in a nearly perfect state of interior preservation and still in use as the Capitol.

"Design for Proposed State Capitol, Jackson, Mississippi," *The American Architect and Building News*, vol. LXII (October 1, 1898), p. 7.

The Jackson Evening News, June 3, 1903.

Link, Theodore C., correspondence with the state officials of Mississippi. Mississippi Department of Archives and History.

The Memphis Morning News, August 22, 1903.

Mississippi Statehouse Committee, Report, 1902. Mississippi Department of Archives and History.

Proceedings Connected with Laying the Cornerstone of Mississippi's New Statehouse, June 3, 1903 (Jackson: 1903).

State of Mississippi, Official Guide to the Mississippi State Capitol. Mississippi Department of Archives and History.

MISSOURI

1. *First State Capitol*, 1822; burned 1837.

"Capitols That Have Been," *Manual of Missouri* (Jefferson City: 1914), pp. 15–17.

Viles, Jonas, "Missouri Capitols and Capitals," *Missouri Historical Review*, vol. XIII (1918–1919), pp. 232–50.

2. *Second Missouri Capitol*, 1838–1840; burned 1911.

Boggs, Governor Liburn, correspondence, 1837, Western Historical Manuscripts Collection, University of Missouri.

Capitol Commission, receipts and vouchers 1837–1841, Western Historical Manuscripts Collection, University of Missouri.

F. Earl Nelson Papers 1917–1936, Western Historical Manuscripts Collection, University of Missouri.

Hardin, Governor Charles H., correspondence, October through December 1876, Western Historical Manuscripts Collection, University of Missouri.

James L. Miner Papers, 1839, Western Historical Manuscripts Collection, University of Missouri.

Meyer, Herman J., *Universorium* (New York: 1851).

Reynolds, Governor Thomas, correspondence 1841–1842, Western Historical Manuscripts Collection, University of Missouri.

3. *Missouri State Capitol*, 1913–1918; still in use as the Capitol.

"A State Capitol Building Competition," *The American Architect and Building News*, vol. CI, plate 2 (May 1, 1912), pp. 207–08.

Missouri State Capitol Decoration Commission, contracts and correspondence, 1913–1914, Missouri State Archives.

Pickard, John, *Report of the Capitol Decoration Commission, 1917–1928* (Jefferson City: 1928).

Roach, Cornelius, *Official Manual of the State of Missouri, 1913–1914* (Columbia: 1914).

State Capitol Committee Board, *Final Report 1912–1921 and 1922* (Jefferson City: 1923).

———, *Report* (Jefferson City: December 31, 1912).

Swartwout, Egerton, "A Description of the Plans Submitted by Tracy & Swartwout, Architects, in the Missouri State Capitol Competition," *The American Architect and Building News*, vol. CII, plate 2 (October 23, 1912), pp. 147–50.

———, "The Missouri State Capitol," *Architectural Record*, vol. CXI (February 1927), pp. 105–26.

MONTANA

1. *Montana State Capitol*, 1898–1902; wings added 1910–1912; entire structure remodeled 1964 and still in use as Capitol.

Cass Gilbert Papers, Minnesota Historical Society.

Davis, Seymour, *Report of the Expert* (Helena: 1896).

Montana Capitol Commission, correspondence, minutes, vouchers, and bids 1896–1912, Montana Historical Society.

———, *Rules and Regulations* (Helena: 1896).

———, *Reports* (Helena: 1896–1904 and 1909–1912).

NEBRASKA

1. *Omaha Capitol*, 1857–1859; demolished 1870.

Berry, Myrtle D., *Nebraska: Territory and State* (Lincoln: 1968).

Photographs collection, Nebraska State Historical Society.

2. *Lincoln Capitol*, 1868; west wing added 1879–1881, east wing added 1882, central wing razed and replaced 1888, and entire building demolished 1926–1932.

Capitol Commission, correspondence, records, minutes 1879–1888, Nebraska State Historical Society.

3. *Nebraska State Capitol*, 1922–1932; Senate chamber abandoned 1935 when Nebraska instituted a unicameral legislature. The building, carefully preserved, remains the Capitol.

Capitol Commission, records, minutes, vouchers, bids, correspondence, and reports, Nebraska State Historical Society.

Cunningham, Francis Harry, *The Capitol, Lincoln, Nebraska* (Lincoln: 1931).

Goodhue Associates Papers 1924–1933, Nebraska State Historical Society.

Goodhue, Bertram G., correspondence with the Capitol Commission and with Kimball 1920–1924, Nebraska State Historical Society.

———, plans, elevations, and studies for the Nebraska Capitol, 1920, Nebraska State Historical Society.

Lee, Anne, "Hildreth Meiere Mural Painter," *Architectural Record*, vol. LXII (August 1927), pp. 103–12.

"Lee Lawrie's Sculpture for the Nebraska Capitol," *American Magazine of Art,* vol. XIX (January 1928), pp. 13–16.

Lee Lawrie Papers 1919–1938, Library of Congress.

"Mural Decorations by Augustus Vincent Tack, Nebraska State Capitol," *American Magazine of Art,* vol. XIX (January 1928), pp. 5–12.

"Nebraska State Capitol Competition: Designs Submitted by John Russell Pope, McKim, Mead & White and H. Van Buren Magonigle," *The Architectural Review,* vol. XI (March 1920), pp. 49–50 and 73–80.

"Nebraska State Capitol," *The American Architect,* vol. CXLV (October 1934), pp. 17–22.

Walker, C. H., "Wing Design in the Nebraska State Capitol Competition," *The Architectural Review,* vol. XI (June 1920), pp. 81–82, 86.

NEVADA

1. Nevada State Capitol, 1869–1871; octagon library added to rear in 1909, wings added to ends 1910–1914, separate legislative building occupied 1969. Capitol restored 1969–1970 and still used as Capitol.

The Carson City Daily Appeal, February 20 and March 2, 1909.

Gale, Frederick C., *The History of the Capitol Building and Governor's Mansion* (Carson City: 1968).

The Gold-Hill News, January 1, 1871.

Gosling, Joseph, plans and elevations, in part original and in part tracings, for the Nevada State Capitol 1869–1871, Nevada State Archives.

Kavanaugh, Peter, Jr., correspondence with the Capitol Commission, Carson City and San Francisco, May and June 1869, Nevada State Archives.

Koontz, John, *Political History of Nevada* (Carson City: 1965).

The Nevada State Journal, December 13, 1866, February 23, 1869, April 2, 1870, and January 1, 1871.

Statutes of the State of Nevada (Carson City: 1869, 1871, 1873, 1875, and 1912).

NEW HAMPSHIRE

1. *New Hampshire Statehouse,* 1816–1820; expanded and remodeled 1864–1866, remodeled again 1909–1910 and still in use as Capitol.

Anderson, Leon, *The Statehouse 1819–1967* (Concord: 1969).

Bryant, Gridley J. F., "A Complete Catalogue of My Plans, Drawings, Specifications and Photographs, Boston 1890," New Hampshire Historical Society.

————, *Enlargement of the State Capitol* (Concord: 1864).

Committee of Citizens, *Enlargement of the Capitol* (Concord: 1863).

Dedication of the Remodeled Statehouse (Concord: 1911).

Gale, Benjamin F., *Memorial of the City of Concord in Reference to the Resolution as to the Enlargement of the Statehouse* (Concord: 1864).

Laws of New Hampshire (Concord: June 24, 1814, June 22, 1816, and June 22, 1820).

New Hampshire Governor and Council, *Proposed Improvements* (Concord: 1905).

New Hampshire Senate, *The Statehouse of New Hampshire: Old and New* (Concord: 1943).

Statehouse Commission, *Reports* (Concord: 1915 through 1819).

————, vouchers and correspondence 1816–1822, New Hampshire Records and Archive Center.

NEW JERSEY

1. *New Jersey Statehouse,* 1789–1792; expanded 1845–1848 and remodeled 1871–1872, then partially burnt down 1885. Restored and greatly elaborated 1886–1887. Still in use as the Capitol.

Bush, Bernard, "Historical Views of the New Jersey Statehouse," *Proceedings of the New Jersey State Historical Society,* vol. LXXX (July 1962), pp. 3–17.

Cohan, Zara, "A Comprehensive History of the Statehouse of New Jersey and Recommendations for Its Continuation as a Historic Site," M.A. Thesis, Newark State College 1969.

Federal Writer's Project, Chronology of Appropriations for Building from 1794–1903, New Jersey State Archives.

New Jersey Legislature, Votes of the Assembly 1791–1792, New Jersey State Archives.

New Jersey State Architect's Office, Capitol plans and elevations file 1886–1969, Architect's Office, Trenton.

Notman, John, drawings for remodeling and expanding the New Jersey Statehouse 1845–1846, The New Jersey Historical Society.

Statehouse Commission, minutes 1898–1944, New Jersey State Archives.

Statehouse File, random correspondence, minutes, and vouchers, New Jersey State Archives.

NEW MEXICO

1. *Adobe Palace*, 1610–1611; as adobe must be in a constant state of being refreshed and patched, the changes in the old Palace have been, and are, continuous. The movement for its preservation began c. 1882; the building was rather creatively restored in 1914–1917, and in 1974 began serious archaeological digs beneath its ancient floors. Now the Museum of New Mexico.

Anderson, Clinton P., *The Adobe Palace* (Washington, D.C.: 1948).

Blume, Lansing B., "New Mexico Under Mexican Administration," *Old Santa Fe*, vols. I and II (July 1913–April 1915), pp. 24–40, 7–28.

A History of Public Buildings Under the Control of the Treasury Department (Washington, D.C.: 1901).

"New Mexico Architecture," *Art and Archaeology*, vol. VII (January 1918), pp. 37–49.

Nusbaum, Jesse L., correspondence relative to the restoration of the portal, to Edgar L. Hewett, Santa Fe, May 13, 1915, State of New Mexico Records Center.

———, cost estimates on restoration 1914–1915, State of New Mexico Records Center.

———, notarized description before Anna M. Leeson about what he did to restore the Palace, Santa Fe, January 7, 1916, Museum of New Mexico.

———, provisional plan for the repair of the east end of the Palace, 1913, State of New Mexico Records Center.

Records of the Territorial Building and United States Depository (Adobe Palace), 1848–1884, National Archives.

Shishkin, J. L., *The Palace of the Governors* (Santa Fe: n.d. [guidebook of the Museum of New Mexico]).

2. *Territorial and State Capitol*, 1853–1889; the work was abandoned soon after it began and was not taken up again until 1885 and 1888. The building burned down in 1892 and a new one replaced it 1895–1902. This replacement was in turn totally refashioned into a hacienda-type Capitol group in 1952–1955 and remains a part of the Capitol complex at Santa Fe.

Capitol Rebuilding Commission, Records 1895–1900, State of New Mexico Records Center.

The Daily New Mexican, May 13, 1892.

Records of the Santa Fe, New Mexico Courthouse 1856–1885, National Archives.

Ritch, William G., *The History, Resources and Attractions of New Mexico* (Boston: 1885).

Ross, Edmund G., Governor's Papers 1885–1889, State of New Mexico Records Center.

Writer's Project Files, materials on the Capitol, 1935, State of New Mexico Records Center.

3. *New Mexico State Capitol*, 1965–1966; still in use as the Capitol.

Capitol Buildings Improvements Commission, news releases 1965–1966.

The New Mexican, December 8, 1966.

(NOTE: All Capitol Commission records for this building were closed and under restriction at the time this book was written. They are in the State of New Mexico Records Center.)

NEW YORK

1. *Old City Hall, Manhattan*, 1704; remodeled 1763, completely renovated in the Classical style 1788–1789 and demolished in 1815.

Torres, Louis, "A Construction History of the City Hall on Wall Street, 1699–1788," unpublished monograph 1962, Collection of the National Park Service.

———, "Federal Hall Revisited," *Journal of the Society of Architectural Historians*, vol. XXIX (December 1970), pp. 327–38.

2. *New York City Hall*, 1802–1812; still in use.

Benjamin Henry Latrobe Papers, competition drawings for the New York City Hall competition 1802, Library of Congress.

Ezra Weeks Papers, competition elevation for the New York City Hall competition 1802, Metropolitan Museum of Art.

John McComb Papers, 1802–1812, New-York Historical Society.

Stillman, Damie, "New York City Hall: Completion and Execution," *Journal of the Society of Architectural Historians*, vol. XXIII (October 1964), pp. 129–42.

3. *Albany Capitol*, 1804–1809; demolished 1883.

Commissioners for Erecting the New Statehouse, vouchers 1806–1808, State Comptroller's Office, Albany.

Gleason's Pictorial Drawing-Room Companion, March 27, 1852.

Root, Edward W., *Philip Hooker: A Contribution to the Study of the Renaissance in America* (New York: 1929).

4. *New York State Capitol*, 1867–1897; never finished in some of its richest interior detailing. Library burned in 1911 and was rebuilt by the close of 1912. Ceiling of the House chamber was lowered in the

1880's. With many abuses, this amazingly magnificent pile is still in use as Capitol.

"The Art of Spoiling Public Buildings," *Eclectic Engineering Magazine*, vol. VI (1886), p. 66.

American Institute of Architects, *Proceedings: the Annual Convention* [1867–1875] (New York: 1867–1876).

Chronological History of the New State Capitol (Albany: 1879).

Dickson, Walter, correspondence to Governor Reuben Fenton in *Capitol Proposal* (Albany: 1866).

Fuller, Thomas, specifications for the New York State Capitol at Albany, 1869, New York State Library.

Hollingsworth, Emma, *Capitol Guide & Catalog* (New York: 1910).

Land Commission of New York, minutes 1864–1878, State of New York, Department of General Services.

Langsam, Walter E., "The New York Capitol, 1863–1876," M.A. Thesis, Yale University, 1968.

———, notes and manuscripts on and about the New York State Capitol 1864–1897, Collection of Walter E. Langsam.

Mather, Frederick G., "The Old Capitol at Albany," *Harper's Weekly*, vol. XXVII (September 15, 1883), pp. 587–88.

McKee, Harley J., "Building for the State of New York 1790–1890," *Empire State Architect*, vol. XVI (January and February, March, April, May and June, July and August, September and October, November and December 1956) and vol. XVII (January and February, March and April, May and June, July and August, and September and October 1957).

"New State Capitol Building at Albany New York," *Architect*, vol. III (1870), p. 8.

New State Capitol Commission, *Annual Reports* (Albany: 1872, 1875, 1878, 1879, 1881, and 1882).

"The New York State Capitol," *The American Architect and Building News*, vol. I (April 15, 1876), p. 125.

New York State Capitol Commission, minutes, 2 vols., 1834–1875, New York State Library.

———, *Report for February 14, 1896 through December 18, 1881* (Albany: 1897).

Office of the Commissioner of the New Capitol, *Report of Work on the New Capitol During the Year 1884* (Albany: 1885).

Perry, Isaac, clippings in Perry's scrapbook 1883–1899, New York State Library.

Phelps, Henry P., *History and Description of the Capitol at Albany* (Albany: 1897).

"Report on the New York State Capitol," *The American Architect and Building News*, vol. I (March 11, 1876), pp. 82–83.

"Report on the New York State Capitol," *The American Architect and Building News*, vol. I (April 8, 1876), pp. 114–15.

Roseberry, Cecil R., Capitol notes collection, New York State Library.

Sherwood, M. E. W., "The Palace of the People," *Popular Monthly*, vol. XIII (April 1882), pp. 408–14.

State of New York in Assembly April 10, 1869, the memorial of O. B. Latham in reference to the proposed plan for the new capitol and other matters (Albany: 1869).

State of New York: Remonstrances of Certain Citizens of . . . New York Against the Charges (Albany: December 1876).

State of New York in Senate: The Remonstrance of Thomas Fuller and Others, Architects, Against Proposed Changes in the Plans for the New Capitol (Albany: April 3, 1876).

Supervising Commissioners of the Capitol, *Report* (Albany: 1896).

NORTH CAROLINA

1. *Tryon's Palace, New Bern*, 1767–1770; burned by vagrants in 1798 and conjecturally restored 1952–1959 as a museum.

Hawks, John, contract, plan, and elevation for the "Governor's House," Newbern, 1767, British Public Records Office.

———, project and drawings for the "governor's house to be built at Newbern, North Carolina," 1766, New York Historical Society.

2. *First Raleigh Statehouse*, 1792–1794; remodeled 1818–1821 and burned 1831.

Elliott, Cecil D., "The North Carolina State Capitol," *The Southern Architect*, vol. III (May 1958), pp. 19–22.

The Raleigh Register and North Carolina Gazette, October 19, 1821.

The Spirit of the Age, January 11, 1854.

Treasurer's and Comptroller's Papers 1793–1808 and 1831–1840, North Carolina State Archives.

3. *North Carolina State Capitol*, 1833–1840; left virtually unchanged. In 1960 the two houses of legislature moved to a Legislative Building several blocks away. In 1972–1976 the Capitol was restored and it still serves as Capitol.

Capitol Commissioners, *Reports* (Raleigh:

325

1836, November 26, 1838, November 1840, and December 10, 1840).

Davis, A. J., correspondence, diary, and drawings relative to the North Carolina Capitol and Ithiel Town's and his involvement, New York Public Library.

———, drawings relative to the North Carolina Capitol, Avery Library, Columbia University.

———, drawings relative to the North Carolina Capitol, Metropolitan Museum of Art.

Elliott, Cecil D., "The North Carolina State Capitol," part II, *The Southern Architect*, vol. III (June 1958), pp. 8–12.

Joint Select Committee, *Report* (Raleigh: December 23, 1834).

Legislature of North Carolina (House of Commons), *Debate on a Proposed Appropriation for Rebuilding the Capitol* (Raleigh: 1832).

Sanders, John L., "The North Carolina Statehouse and Capitol, 1792–1972," Chapel Hill, 1973, unpublished manuscript, Collection of John L. Sanders.

State Capitol Planning Commission, *Report* (Raleigh: 1965).

NORTH DAKOTA

1. *Territorial and State Capitol*, 1883–1884; expanded 1894 and 1903, then burned down in 1930.

The Bismarck Tribune, July 13, August 3, 17, 24, and September 7, 1883.

Libby, Orin, "The Arikara Narrative," *North Dakota Historical Collection*, vol. VI (September 1940), p. 10.

North Dakota Capitol Commission, *Report* (Bismarck: 1905).

Vyzralek, Frank, "North Dakota's First Capitol Building, 1883–1930," *Plains Talk* (Spring 1970), pp. 5–7.

2. *North Dakota State Capitol*, 1932–1934; little changed and remains the Capitol.

Board of State Capitol Commissioners, *Report* (Bismarck: 1935).

———, minutes, vouchers, correspondence, bills, and bids 1931–1935, North Dakota State Archives.

Capitol Investigation Committee, correspondence and testimony, January to July 1933, North Dakota State Archives.

Holabird & Root, "North Dakota's New Capitol: A Reply," *American Magazine of Art*, vol. XXVII (June 1934), p. 349.

Melhouse, James C., "Construction of the New North Dakota Capitol," *Plains Talk* (Summer 1970), pp. 1–6.

Morand, Dexter, "Edificio gubernamental de Dakota del Norte: Architects Bell de Remer and Burke, Associate Architects Holabird & Root," *Nuestra Arquitectura*, vol. III (April 1937), pp. 125–33.

OHIO

1. *Ohio State Capitol*, 1838–1860; considerable renovation in the rotunda in 1967, but the building remains otherwise rather unchanged and is still in use as Capitol.

A. J. Davis Papers 1838–1841, New York Public Library.

Cole, Thomas, correspondence with William Adams 1838–1844, Albany Institute of History and Art.

Cummings, Abbott Lowell, "The Ohio State Capitol Competitions," *Journal of the Society of Architectural Historians*, vol. XII (May 1953), pp. 15–18.

———, "Ohio's Capitols at Columbus, 1810–1861," Special Report for the Ohio Legislature, 1948, Ohio Historical Society.

"The New Statehouse at Columbus," *The Builder*, vol. X (October 16, 1852), pp. 658–59.

"Ohio Statehouse," *Illustrated London News*, vol. XVII (November 2, 1850), pp. 343–44.

Statehouse Commission, *Competition Details* (Columbus: April 10, 1838).

———, *Reply to the Report of the Legislative Joint Council Investigating Public Buildings* (Columbus and Cincinnati: 1857).

———, *Reports* (Columbus: 1838, 1839, 1847, 1854, 1860, and 1861).

OKLAHOMA

1. *Oklahoma State Capitol*, 1914–1917; dome never executed, but except for various offices the building is rather as it was when finished at the time of World War I. It is still the Capitol, now surrounded by a field of oil "pumpers."

State Capitol Commission, minutes, correspondence, vouchers, photographs, and clippings 1913–1924, Oklahoma State Archives.

OREGON

1. *First Salem Capitol*, 1853–1855; burned unfinished 1855 presumably by arsonists.

Barnum, E. M., and A. W. Ferguson, Report to the Legislative Assembly of the Territory of Oregon on the Building of the New Statehouse, January 26, 1855, and December 22, 1853, Oregon State Library.

Joint Committee to Whom Was Referred the Claims Against the Commissioners for the Erection of the Statehouse, January 24, 1856, Oregon State Library.

Rector, William H., and Charles Bennett, Contract with John P. Gaines, March 8, 1853, and Articles of Agreement between Rector and the Governor March 8, 1853, Oregon State Library.

2. *Second Salem Capitol*, 1873–1876; burned 1935.

Capitol Planning Commission, *Development of the State Capitol Area* (Salem: 1876, 1889, 1890, 1893, 1894, and 1900).

Legislature of Oregon, "Description of the State Capitol and Grounds," in *Messages and Documents* (Salem: 1899).

The Oregon Statesman, March 30 and August 21, 1852.

3. *Oregon State Capitol*, 1936–1938; unchanged and still in use as the Capitol.

"Competition for the Oregon State Capitol, Salem," *Architect and Engineer*, vol. CXXVI (July 1936), pp. 13–30.

"Competition for the Oregon State Capitol, Salem," *American Architect and Architecture*, vol. CXLIX (January 1937), pp. 27–34.

"Competition for the Oregon State Capitol, Salem," *Pencil Points*, vol. XVII (June 1936), pp. 352–74.

"Competition for the Oregon State Capitol, Salem," June 1936; The Winning Design Trowbridge & Livingston and Francis Keally, Associated Architects," *Architectural Forum*, vol. LXV (July 1936), pp. 2–10.

Keally, Francis, to William Seale, Salem, Oregon, February 5, 1972, Victorian Society in America.

Morin, Roi L., "The Oregon Competition—in Retrospect: Minutes of the Jury Show Unusual Deliberations," *Architect and Engineer*, vol. CXXVII (April 1937), pp. 11–21, 43.

"Program for Open Competition for Oregon State Capitol," *Architect and Engineer*, vol. CXXIV (March 1936), pp. 45–52.

State Capitol Reconstruction Commission, *Report of the State Capitol Reconstruction Committee to the Governor and the Oregon Legislature* (Salem: January 1939).

———, *Program of the Conditions to Govern a Competition for Selection of an Architect for the Oregon Capitol Building* (Salem: 1936).

———, vouchers, minutes, and correspondence 1935–1938, Oregon State Library.

PENNSYLVANIA

1. *Pennsylvania Statehouse* (Independence Hall), 1739–1748; steeple added 1750–1753 and demolished 1781–1782, then reconstructed in a modified form in 1828. The building has undergone countless renovations over the years. In 1961 the National Park Service began a long and very sensitive restoration project on the building; the central structure resembles as closely as possible its appearance in 1776.

Belisle, D. W., *History of Independence Hall from the Earliest Period to the Present Time* (Philadelphia: 1859).

"Early Architects for Independence Hall," *Journal of the Society of Architectural Historians*, vol. XI (October 1952), pp. 23–26.

General Loan Office Records 1750–1768, Historical Society of Pennsylvania.

Hamilton, Andrew, papers relative to the Pennsylvania Statehouse, 1732, Historical Society of Pennsylvania.

National Park Service, *Historic Structures Report Part I, On Independence Hall* (Philadelphia: 1959).

———, *Historic Structures Report, Part II* (Philadelphia: April 1962).

Nelson, Lee H., *Historic Structure Report: Architectural Data Section On Old City Hall* (Philadelphia: 1970).

Provincial Council of Pennsylvania, *Colonial Records and Minutes*, vols. I–V (Harrisburg and Philadelphia: 1851 and 1852).

Riley, Edward M., "The History of the Independence Hall Group," *Transactions of the American Philosophical Society*, vol. XLIII (March 1953), pp. 7–42.

2. *Harrisburg Capitol*, 1810–1821; great rear wing added 1854–1856, but otherwise no major changes until the central building was gutted by fire in 1897, and the flanking offices were demolished to make way for the new building early in the twentieth century.

Cummings, H. M., "Stephen Hills and the Building of Pennsylvania's First Capitol," *Pennsylvania History*, vol. XX (October 1953), pp. 417–37.

Department of the Auditor-General, Internal Improvements Records, Public Buildings and Grounds 1810–1822, Pennsylvania State Archives.

Hills, Thomas, and William Sanford, *The Hills*

Family in America (New York: 1904).

Historic American Buildings Survey, conjectural drawings of the old Harrisburg Capitol, 1936, Library of Congress.

3. *Pennsylvania State Capitol*, 1898–1902 and 1903–1907; in a perfect state of preservation and still used as the Capitol.

"Arrests in Pennsylvania Capitol's Fraud Cases," *Outlook*, vol. LXXXVII (September 28, 1907), pp. 146–47.

Board of State Capitol Commissioners, *Programme of a Competition for the Selection of an Architect for the New State Capitol* (Harrisburg: 1897).

Board of Public Building, *Report 1905–1907* (Harrisburg: 1909).

Caffin, C. H., "New Capitol of Pennsylvania," *World's Work*, vol. XIII (November 1906), pp. 8,195–210.

Capitol Investigation Committee, Executive Session 1907, Pennsylvania State Archives.

Carson, Hampton L., *Report On the Capitol Investigation* (Harrisburg: 1907).

Commonwealth Cases, vols. I, II, III, and V (Harrisburg: 1909–1910), Superior Court of Pennsylvania.

"Harrisburg Frauds," *Independent Magazine*, vol. LXX (January 26, 1911), pp. 209–10.

The New York Sun, December 20 and 21, 1911.

"Pennsylvania's Costly Capitol," *Outlook*, vol. LXXXV (April 13, 1907), pp. 830–31.

"Pennsylvania's State Capitol Competition," *The Architectural Review*, vol. IV (1896), p. 42.

Pennypacker, Samuel Whitaker, *The Desecration and Profanation of the Pennsylvania State Capitol* (Philadelphia: 1911).

"Report on the Capitol Investigation," *Outlook*, vol. LXXXVI (August 31, 1907), pp. 934–35.

Seaber, Louis, "Pennsylvania's Palace of Graft," *Independent Magazine*, vol. LXII (May 30, 1907), pp. 1,235–241.

RHODE ISLAND

1. *Newport Colony House*, 1739; various work done on the second floor in 1784; the building underwent many changes before its restoration in 1917. Presently a museum, with some restoration done 1973–1974.

Downing, Antoinette F., and Vincent J. Scully, *The Architectural Heritage of Newport, Rhode Island* (New York: 1952).

Green, John F., *The Building of the Old Colony House at Newport* (Newport: 1941).

Isham, Norman M., "Colony House at Newport, Rhode Island," *Old Time New England*, vol. VIII (December 1917), pp. 3–20.

MacDonald, William, "The Old State House at Newport," *Newport Historical Society Bulletin, Number 11* (1914).

Terry, Roderick, "The History of the Building of the Old Colony House, Newport," *Newport Historical Society Bulletin Number 20* (October 1927).

2. *Rhode Island Statehouse*, 1895–1906; little changed and still used as Capitol.

Capitol Commission, minutes, vouchers, and some correspondence 1893–1904, Archives of the Rhode Island Department of State.

"Competitive Design for the Rhode Island Statehouse, Providence, Rhode Island," *The Architectural Review*, vol. III (September 1898), plate 7.

"Competitive Design for the Rhode Island Statehouse, Providence, Rhode Island," *The American Architect and Building News*, vol. XXXV (February 13, 1892), p. 110.

McKim, Mead & White, plans, elevations, and working drawings of the Rhode Island Statehouse 1892–1906, New-York Historical Society.

Rhode Island Statehouse Clippings File, Rhode Island Historical Society.

Statehouse Commission, *Report* (Providence: 1892).

State of Rhode Island, *The Rhode Island Statehouse: A Guide* (Providence: n.d.).

SOUTH CAROLINA

1. *First Columbia Statehouse*, 1788–1792; various little alterations especially c. 1844. Moved to a temporary foundation 1853 and burned during the Civil War, 1865.

Commissioners of Columbia, accounts 1788–1794, South Carolina State Archives.

Public Buildings Records, 1800–1887, South Carolina State Archives.

Public Improvements Records, 1800–1830, South Carolina State Archives.

Records of the Keeper of the Statehouse, 1808–1847, South Carolina State Archives.

Statehouse Commission, *Reports* (Columbia: 1854–1862, 1866, 1868, 1886, 1889, and 1900–1909).

2. *South Carolina Statehouse*, 1853–1868; the building was never finished in the original towered form but underwent several cheap completions particu-

larly in 1886 and was refashioned 1902–1907 into an adequate sort of a capitol form, but one far different from the original scheme. Still in use as the Capitol.

Fant, Christie Zimmerman, *The Statehouse of South Carolina* (Columbia: 1970).

Milburn, Franklin Pierce, *Designs From the Work of Frank P. Milburn, Architect, South Carolina* (Columbia 1901 and 1903).

New Statehouse Commission, records, minutes, vouchers, bids, correspondence 1853–1857, 1854–1863, 1865–1877, and 1885–1909, South Carolina State Archives.

Salley, Alexander S., *The Statehouses of South Carolina 1751–1936* (Columbia: 1936).

Wodehouse, Lawrence, "Frank Pierce Milburn, A Major Southern Architect," *The North Carolina Historical Review*, vol. L (July 1973), pp. 289–303.

Walker, George Edward, correspondence, bills, and other material relating to the statehouse 1854–1858, South Caroliniana Library.

SOUTH DAKOTA

1. *South Dakota State Capitol*, 1907–1910; wing added 1931, whole building remodeled in 1964–1965 and still in use as the Capitol.

Canady, Dayton W., *State Capitol of South Dakota* (Pierre: 1972).

Capitol Building Commission, minutes, correspondence, vouchers 1905–1920, South Dakota State Historical Society.

"The South Dakota Capitol Building, Pierre, South Dakota, C. E. Bell Architect," *Western Architect*, vol. XVII (April 1911), pp. 42–43.

Wheelock, Ralph W., "Bismark's Hospitality," *South Dakota Historical Collections*, vol. V (1910), pp. 163–65.

———, "The New Capitol," *South Dakota Historical Collections*, vol. V (1910), pp. 179–245.

TENNESSEE

1. *Tennessee State Capitol*, 1845–1860; remodeled and enlarged 1956–1960.

"An Inheritance Preserved: The Restoration and Repair of Tennessee's State Capitol," *State Government*, vol. XXXII (Summer 1959), pp. 3–8.

Capitol Commission, minutes, correspondence, and bids, 1844–1861, Tennessee State Library and Archives.

Capitol Construction Records, bids, bonds, furnishings bills, and wage ledgers 1846–1860, Tennessee State Library and Archives.

Dekle, Clayton B., "The Tennessee State Cap-

itol," *Tennessee Historical Quarterly*, vol. XXV (Fall 1966), pp. 3–78.

Gilchrist, Agnes, *William Strickland: Architect and Engineer 1788–1854* (New York: 1969).

Historic American Buildings Survey, Report on the Tennessee Capitol, 1951 and 1971, Library of Congress.

Samuel Morgan Papers 1828–1900, Tennessee State Library and Archives.

TEXAS

1. *Capitol of the Texas Republic at Houston City*, 1837; government moved west in 1840, and the building was demolished in the early 1870's after years of use as a hotel.

Photograph, c. 1860, University of Texas Archives.

Ward, Thomas William, agreement with Augustus Chapman Allen, New Orleans, February 18, 1837, Acts of William Christy, Notarial Archives of New Orleans.

2. *Texas State Capitol*, 1853–1856; burned 1881.

Brown, Frank, The Annals of Travis County and Austin, Texas 1840–1880, Travis County Collection, Austin Public Library.

Capitol Commission, Capitol papers, contracts, reports on investigations 1852–1874, Texas State Archives.

Terrell, Alexander W., "The City of Austin from 1839–1865," *Southwestern Historical Quarterly*, vol. XIV (October 1910), pp. 113–14.

Texas Siftings, November 12, 1881.

Voight, F., report on the condition and furnishings and grounds of the state capitol, Houston 1874, Texas State Archives.

3. *Temporary State Capitol*, 1881–1882; burned 1899.

Bandy, Phillip A., and Gary L. Moore, Frank A. Weir, John E. Keller, R. Whitley Jarvis, Catherine H. Yates, K. Joan Jeeks, *Temporary Capitol of Texas, 1883–1888* (Austin: 1972).

Roberts, O. M., "The Capitals of Texas," *Texas Historical Association Quarterly*, vol. II (1898), p. 117.

Ruffini, F. E., plans and elevations for the temporary Capitol 1881–1882, Texas State Archives.

4. *Texas State Capitol*, 1882–1888; renovated variously and partially restored in 1969. In a nearly perfect state of preservation and still the Capitol.

The Austin Daily Statesman, April 30, 1881.

Board of Capitol Commissioners, minutes, correspondence, contracts, letterpress books, vouchers, and clippings 1881–1890, Texas State Archives.

Capitol Building Commissioners, *Reports* (Austin: 1883–1888).

Greer, Joubert Lee, "The Building of the Texas State Capitol 1882–1888," M.A. Thesis, University of Texas, 1932.

Myers, Elijah E., plans, elevations, and working drawings 1881–1886, Texas State Capitol, Texas State Archives.

Rotch, Melvin M., "The Dome of the Texas State Capitol," lecture Texas A & M College, March 10, 1972, notes from the Rotch Collection.

UNITED STATES CAPITOL

1. *The Capitol of the United States*, 1793–1867; expanded and changed many times since then. At the time of this writing all that remained to be seen externally of the original Capitol was Bulfinch's west portico of the 1820's, and it was in danger of being demolished. Walter's historic dome remains the same.

Architect of the United States Capitol, manuscripts collection, historical files, and original drawings 1851–1973.

Bannister, Turpin C., "The Genealogy of the Dome of the United States Capitol," *Journal of the Society of Architectural Historians*, vol. XVII (January–June 1948), pp. 1–30.

Brown, Glenn, *History of the United States Capitol*, 2 vols. (Washington, D.C.: 1900 and 1903).

Frank Leslie's Illustrated Newspaper, January 19, 1861.

Hamlin, Talbot, *Benjamin Henry Latrobe* (New York: 1955).

Skramstad, Harold K., "The Engineer as Architect in Washington: The Contribution of Montgomery Meigs," *Records of the Columbia Historical Society*, vol. LXV (1969–1970), pp. 266–83.

The National Intelligencer, December 18, November 27, 1862, and February 24, 1863.

The Washington Evening Star, September 18, 1893.

Walter, Thomas U., "The Dome of the U.S. Capitol," *Architectural Review and Builders Journal*, vol. II (March 1869), pp. 343–45.

UTAH

1. *Territorial Capitol Project*, 1851–1855; abandoned after the completion of one wing and used for various purposes until restored in 1928 as a museum.

Angell, Truman O., journals 1851–1856, Archives of the Church of Jesus Christ of Latter-day Saints.

———, plans, details, and perspective watercolor of the Fillmore Capitol, Archives of the Church of Jesus Christ of Latter-day Saints.

Ashton, Wendell J., *There Is the Kingdom* (Salt Lake City: 1945).

Historic American Buildings Survey, Report 1967, Library of Congress.

"Manuscript History of Millard's Stake," n.d., Archives of the Church of Jesus Christ of Latter-day Saints.

Noyce, Gladys, "Utah's First Statehouse," Salt Lake City, May 18, 1973, Archives of the Church of Jesus Christ of Latter-day Saints.

Payne, Richard W., "A History of Utah's Territorial Capitol Building at Fillmore 1857–1869," M.S. Thesis, Brigham Young University, 1971.

Seat of Government Committee, accounts 1851 for the trip to Fillmore, Utah State Archives.

Young, Brigham, "Statehouse Hall Was Dedicated to the Lord," Great Salt Lake City, December 11, 1855, Archives of the Church of Jesus Christ of Latter-day Saints.

2. *Utah State Capitol*, 1913–1916; unchanged and still in use as the Capitol.

Kletting, Richard K. A., plans, elevations, working drawings of the Utah State Capitol 1913–1916, Utah State Archives.

Capitol Building Commission, minutes, correspondence, vouchers, bills, bids and competition papers (no drawings) 1911–1917, Utah State Archives.

Tourtellotte, John E., *et al.*, competition drawings 1912, The University of Utah Library.

VERMONT

1. *Second Montpelier Statehouse*, 1833–1836; burned 1857.

The Ladies Literary Repository, September 25, 1841.

Silloway, Thomas W., "Report of the Committee of Citizens of Montpelier," in *Journal of the House of Representatives* (Montpelier: February 18, 1857).

Statehouse Committee, correspondence, vouchers, and the plans, elevations, and specifications of Ammi B. Young, Vermont Historical Society.

Wodehouse, Lawrence, "Ammi Young's Architecture in Northern New England," *Proceedings of* the *Vermont Historical Society* (Spring 1968), pp. 53–60.

2. *Vermont Statehouse*, 1857–1859; survives in a remarkable state of preservation and still in use as the Capitol.

Ames, Winslow, "The Vermont Statehouse," *Journal of the Society of Architectural Historians*, vol. XXIII (December 1964), pp. 193–99.

Avery, W. W., and H. B. Davis, *A Description of the State Houses of Vermont* (Montpelier: 1859).

House of Representatives, *Memorial of Thomas W. Silloway* (Montpelier: 1858).

Minority in the Joint Committee on Claims, *Report* (Montpelier, 1861).

Nye, Mary Greene, *Vermont Statehouse* (Montpelier: 1931).

Powers, Thomas E., *Vermont's Star Chamber* (Montpelier: 1858).

Silloway, Thomas W., *A Statement of Facts Concerning the Management of Affairs Connected with the Rebuilding of the Capitol at Montpelier, Vermont* (Burlington: 1857).

———, plans, elevations, and specifications for the Vermont Statehouse, Vermont Historical Society.

Superintendent of Construction of the Statehouse, *Report* (Montpelier: October 15, 1857).

Testimony and Defense of the Superintendent of Construction of the Vermont Capitol (Montpelier: October 1858).

VIRGINIA

1. *Nicholson's Capitol at Williamsburg*, 1699–1703; burned 1747 and conjecturally reconstructed in 1931–1934 for museum purposes.

Architectural Advisory Committee, minutes 1928–1932, Colonial Williamsburg, Archives of the Colonial Williamsburg Foundation.

Capitol Research File, Archives of the Colonial Williamsburg Foundation.

Goodwin, Rev. W. A. N., and the Association for the Preservation of Virginia Antiquities, correspondence with the architects Perry, Shaw & Hepburn and the various consultants of the Williamsburg Restoration 1928–1932, Archives of the Colonial Williamsburg Foundation.

Governor's Council, *Journals*, 1699–1703 (Richmond: 1925).

House of Burgesses of Virginia, *Journals*, 1695–1702 and 1703–1712 (Richmond 1905).

———, journals, 1662–1702, Library of Congress.

Whiffen, Marcus, *The Public Buildings of Williamsburg* (Williamsburg: 1958).

2. *Second Williamsburg Capitol*, 1751–1752; partially demolished in the 1820's and burned in 1832. For most of its career after its public life it was a school, and toward the last bore little resemblance to the Capitol known during the Revolutionary era.

Archaeological Report 1929–1930, Archives of the Colonial Williamsburg Foundation.

Harwood, Humphrey, ledger 1779, Archives of the Colonial Williamsburg Foundation.

Kimball, Fiske, "Jefferson and the Public Buildings of Virginia," *The Huntington Library Quarterly*, vol. XII (February 1949), pp. 115–21.

House of Burgesses, *Journals, 1742–1749* (Richmond: 1905–1915).

Latrobe, Benjamin H., *Journal* (New York: 1905).

The Pennsylvania Gazette, February 5, 1747.

Powell, Benjamin, repair bills for the Capitol, Williamsburg, September 28, 1777, through May 4, 1778, Virginia State Archives.

Shelley, F., ed., "The Journal of Ebenezer Hazard in Virginia 1777," *The Virginia Magazine of History and Biography*, vol. LXII (October 1954), pp. 407–09.

3. *Virginia State Capitol*, 1785–1798; remained much the same through the nineteenth century except for repairs after the collapse of one of the upper floors in 1870. Gutted in 1909 and reconstructed rather freely as part of a sweeping Beaux-Arts expansion program.

Executive Communications 1785–1789, Virginia State Archives.

Improvements to the Capitol Building, Report of the Committee to the Government and the General Assembly of Virginia, Senate Document #12 (Richmond: 1911).

Jefferson, Thomas, projects, plans, elevations of the Virginia State Capitol 1779–1787, Massachusetts Historical Society.

Kimball, Fiske, "Jefferson and the Public Buildings of Virginia, Part 2, 1779–1780," *The Huntington Library Quarterly*, vol. XIII (May 1949), pp. 303–10.

———, *Thomas Jefferson and the First Monument of the Classical Revival in America* (Harrisburg and Washington, D.C.: 1915).

"Letters to Jefferson Relative to the Virginia Capitol," *The William and Mary Quarterly*, vol. V (April 1925), pp. 95–98.

Measured and colored pencil drawings of the

Capitol and Executive Mansion made May 19, 1815, delineator unknown, Virginia State Archives.

McRae, Sherwin, *Virginia State Capitol* (Richmond: 1871).

Public Square Papers, 1787–1800, compiled by the State Library of Virginia, Virginia State Library.

WASHINGTON

1. *Flagg Capitol*, 1893–1895; project abandoned at the foundation stage; portions of the foundation were used in the much larger foundation of present Legislative Hall.

Flagg, Ernest, correspondence with M. E. Hay, Governor, New York, January 18, 1911, Washington State Archives.

State Capitol Committee, minutes and correspondence 1893–1901, Washington State Archives.

———, *Reports* (Olympia: 1895, 1897, 1899, and 1903–1905).

2. *Washington State Capitol Group*, 1912–1926; while the Legislative Hall is the main interest here, this group includes many buildings. The principal Classical group contains the Temple of Justice (1912–1921), the Administration Building (1921), the Insurance Building (1920) and Legislative Hall, sometimes called the Legislative Building (1923–1926). The magnificent landscape scheme was abandoned in 1917.

Capitol Commission, *Argument in Favor of Adopting a Group Plan for the Construction of the Capitol Buildings* (Olympia: 1910).

"Competitive Design for the State House at Olympia, Washington," *The American Architect and Building News*, vol. XLVII (February 23, 1895), p. 87.

"Extracts from the Competition Program, Washington State Capitol, Olympia, Description of Site, etc.," *The American Architect and Building News*, vol. C, plate 1 (September 13, 1911), pp. 106, 108.

Permanent State Capitol Committee, correspondence, clippings, 1922–1936, Washington State Archives.

Savidge, Clark V., *A Brief Outline of the History of Washington's State Capitol Group* (Olympia: 1927).

State Capitol Committee, minutes and correspondence 1909–1921, Washington State Archives.

"Washington's Capitol and Its Native Stone," *The Architect and Engineer of California*, vol. LII (February 1918), pp. 94–95.

Wilder & White, General Specifications of the

Temple of Justice, Washington and New York, 1912, Washington State Archives.

———, plans, elevations, and drawings for the Legislative Hall, 1912–1927, Washington State Archives.

———, sketches for the Capitol Group 1912–1917 (photo copies in part), Washington State Archives.

WEST VIRGINIA

1. *West Virginia State Capitol*, 1930–1932; construction of east wing 1925–1927 and the west wing 1924–1925. The central part was built 1930–1932 and is still in use as the Capitol.

Capitol Commission, correspondence, vouchers, bids, bills, contracts, photographs 1922–1934, West Virginia State Library.

Gilbert, Cass, correspondence regarding the West Virginia Capitol, Minnesota Historical Society.

———, correspondence regarding the West Virginia Capitol, Library of Congress.

———, construction photos taken for the Gilbert firm, West Virginia State Library.

Gilbert, Cass, Jr., to William Seale, Washington, D.C., May 12, 1973, Victorian Society in America.

WISCONSIN

1. *Madison Capitol*, 1857–1861; dome completed 1866–1869. Whole structure partially ruined by fire 1904; remaining north wing demolished in 1913 to make way for the new Capitol.

Capitol Improvements Commission, minutes, correspondence, and letterbooks 1903–1906, The State Historical Society of Wisconsin.

Executive Department Papers 1851–1899, The State Historical Society of Wisconsin.

Gilbert, Cass, letters to Channing Seabury and to Governor La Follette relative to the burned Capitol, Minnesota Historical Society.

Kutzbock, A., correspondence and account book, 1864, The State Historical Society of Wisconsin.

[Mikkelsen, Michael A.], "The Wisconsin State Capitol," *The Architectural Review*, vol. XII (September 1905), p. 177.

2. *Wisconsin State Capitol*, 1906–1917; restored and renovated 1965, and in a perfect state of preservation. Still in use as the Capitol.

Mikkelsen, Michael A., "The New Wisconsin

State Capitol," *Architectural Record,* vol. XLII (September 1917), pp. 194–233.

Post, George B. & Sons, plans, elevations, perspectives of the Wisconsin Capitol 1906–1917. The State Historical Society of Wisconsin.

Wisconsin Capitol Commission, minutes, correspondence, proposals and vouchers 1906–1917. The State Historical Society of Wisconsin.

WYOMING

1. *Wyoming State Capitol,* 1886–1888; east wing added 1888–1890, and further east and west projections were added 1915–1916. In a fair state of preservation, with its dramatic setting wholly intact, it is still the Capitol.

Board of Capitol Commissioners, minutes, correspondence, letterpress books, bids, inventories, contracts 1885–1888, 1888–1916, and 1934–1939, Wyoming State Archives.

The Cheyenne Leader, May 18 and 19, 1886.

Gibbs, David W., plans, elevations, specifications, Wyoming State Archives.

"The Wyoming Capitol," *Wyoming Historical Notes,* vol. I (1897), pp. 113–15.

INDEX

Italic numbers refer to illustrations.